6 GROUP BOMBER COMMAND

An Operational Record

6 GROUP BOMBER COMMAND

An Operational Record

Chris Ward

Pen & Sword
AVIATION

First published in Great Britain in 2009 by
Pen & Sword Aviation
an imprint of
Pen & Sword Books Ltd
47 Church Street
Barnsley
South Yorkshire
S70 2AS

Copyright © Chris Ward 2009

ISBN 978 1 84884 155 0

A CIP catalogue record for this book is
available from the British Library

Typeset in Times by
Phoenix Typesetting, Auldgirth, Dumfriesshire

Printed and bound in England by
CPI UK

Pen & Sword Books Ltd incorporates the Imprints of Pen & Sword Aviation,
Pen & Sword Maritime, Pen & Sword Military, Wharncliffe Local History,
Pen & Sword Select, Pen & Sword Military Classics and Leo Cooper.

For a complete list of Pen & Sword titles please contact
PEN & SWORD BOOKS LIMITED
47 Church Street, Barnsley, South Yorkshire, S70 2AS, England
E-mail: enquiries@pen-and-sword.co.uk
Website: www.pen-and-sword.co.uk

Acknowledgements

Most of the figures used in the statistics section of this work, have been drawn from *The Bomber Command War Diaries* by Martin Middlebrook and Chris Everitt, and I am indebted to Martin Middlebrook for allowing me to use them.

A special mention is due to Chris Salter, now retired, and a founder of Midland Counties Publications, without whose generous assistance and encouragement at the outset, I would not have been able to compile a complete list of all operational aircraft on charge with Bomber Command squadrons during the war period, a list, incidentally, that comprises some 28,000 entries.

I am greatly indebted to Danny Bouchard in Canada for sourcing and processing the photographs, and for obtaining the permission of Library and Archives Canada to reproduce them in this publication. Danny is a serving police officer in Quebec, the holder of the Medal of Bravery, and is also a professional genealogist.

Contents

General Notes

This profile is a reference work on the activities of the Group and the squadrons serving with it in an operational capacity at some time during the Second World War. Bomber Command operated exclusively from stations in the UK, and used overseas bases purely for shuttle operations, or as advanced staging posts for specific purposes. For this reason, periods spent on detachment, or permanent postings to overseas Commands do not fall within the scope of this work.

This work is not intended to serve as a comprehensive history of the Group or squadrons, but to provide as much information as possible in the space available in a non-anecdotal form. The brief history narrative is basically an account of Bomber Command's war, with the Group's involvement interwoven into it. The publications listed in Section 5 are not only recommended reading, but represent some of the best available sources of information for serious students of the subject. The operational record is based almost entirely on the figures provided in *The Bomber Command War Diaries* by Martin Middlebrook and Chris Everitt, and I am indebted to Martin Middlebrook for allowing me to use them.

An aircraft is included in aircraft history section if; a) it spent time on squadron charge, no matter how briefly, and irrespectively of whether or not it operated and b) the type was used operationally by the squadron. Where a squadron has a Conversion Flight involving a type with which it is intending to re-equip, but then does not, as in the case of 101 and 460 Squadrons, these have been included, on the basis that they sometimes found themselves on operations. Information is restricted in most cases to where from and where to, unless it completed its service with the squadron, in which case, some detail of its demise appears. Aircraft that failed to return have the date and target recorded. Where no information follows the serial number of a type still in use when the squadron departed Bomber Command, or at war's end, it can be assumed that the aircraft was still on squadron strength. However, where there is a blank space following the serial number of a type that has been withdrawn from service with Bomber Command, it signifies that I don't know its ultimate fate. An absence of information does not imply that the aircraft flew no operations during its time with the squadron.

Finally, information has been drawn from a variety of sources, ranging from Records Branch to individuals with squadron connections, and I am grateful for their contributions. There will inevitably be errors and omissions when dealing with a subject as vast as Bomber Command, and I am happy to be corrected and/or updated by readers.

CHAPTER ONE

A Narrative History

The Seeds are Sown

On the 31st of October 1939, negotiations began between representatives of the British and Canadian governments on the subject of the British Commonwealth Air Training Plan (BCATP). Both sides approached the talks with entirely different perceptions and goals, and this would lead to protracted discussions and acrimonious relations over the following three years. The 'Canadianisation' of Royal Canadian Air Force personnel serving with the Royal Air Force was enshrined in Article XV of the BCATP agreement, which was signed on the 7th of January 1941, and originally called for the formation of twenty-five RCAF squadrons overseas. These were to be financed by Canada's contribution to the Plan, still known to this day in the UK as the Empire Air Training Scheme, which was agreed at $350 million. From the outset the talks were dogged by the questions of control of the RCAF contingent and finance, and the Canadian negotiators found themselves being constantly out-manoeuvred by their British counterparts. Canada envisaged an independent air force operating alongside the RAF, much as the American 8th Air Force would from 1942. Britain, however, saw Canada as a source of manpower, and intended to integrate Canadian personnel into existing RAF Squadrons, or at least, to place the RCAF squadrons within RAF Groups. Canada expressed itself unwilling to finance RCAF personnel over whom it had no control, and after much wrangling, a compromise was eventually reached, which would allow all RCAF squadrons to operate from stations within close proximity to one another, and under the same RAF Group. All such units were to be numbered in the 400–450 series. Once sufficient squadrons had been formed, a RCAF Group would come into existence. By the time that negotiations had reached this stage, it was already 1942, and only four RCAF squadrons had thus far been formed, all in 1941. In the event, outside influences caused the programme to be cut back, allowing for just seven new squadrons in 1942, making a total of eleven. However, the number was considered acceptable to constitute an effective Group, and this compromise became a cherished dream in itself, achieving realisation on the 1st of January 1943. Ultimately, this was the best that Canada could wrest from the deal, having been backed into a corner by its own negotiators, and thus the RAF acquired the manpower and the control, while Canada footed the bill.

On the day of its formation 6 Group comprised eight squadrons operating either Halifaxes or Wellingtons. 408 Squadron was stationed at Leeming under its long-standing commanding officer, W/C 'Tiny' Ferris, and had only recently converted from Hampdens to the Rolls-Royce Merlin-powered Halifax Mks II and V. 419 and 420 Squadrons were at Middleton St George under W/Cs Fleming and Bradshaw respectively, the former having also recently traded in its Wellingtons for Halifaxes, while the latter owned a mixture of Wellington IIIs and Xs. 424 Squadron and its Wellington Mk IIIs and Xs resided at Topcliffe under W/C Carscallen, while the Wellington-equipped 425 and 426 Squadrons occupied Dishforth under the leadership respectively of W/Cs St Pierre and Blanchard. The two remaining Wellington squadrons were 427 at Croft with W/C Burnside at the helm, and 428 under W/C Earle at Dalton.

The founder member squadrons of 6 Group arrived at this historic moment by means of different routes. 408 Squadron was the senior founder member, having come into existence on the 24th of June 1941, following in the wake of 405 Squadron's formation just two months earlier. 408 Squadron began life in 5 Group, which dictated that it would fly twin-engine Handley Page Hampdens. The Hampden had given excellent service since being introduced early in 1939, but it was now becoming obsolete, and was in the process of being replaced by the new Avro Manchester, another twin-engine type whose performance in the hands of 207 and 97 Squadrons was giving cause for concern and was a source of much frustration. The failure of the Manchester would turn out to be a blessing, as it forced Avro's designers to turn the basically excellent airframe into a four-engine bomber powered by Rolls-Royce Merlins. The Lancaster would transform Bomber Command, but at the time of 408 Squadron's birth the Manchester still had a year of service ahead of it, and most 5 Group squadrons would have to cope with the inadequacies of its Rolls-Royce Vulture engines. 408 Squadron was declared operational in mid August 1941, and during the ensuing twelve months carried out 191 operations and 1,234 sorties, including a single one by a Manchester. Posted to 4 Group in mid September 1942, 408 Squadron took on Halifaxes, but conducted no operations before being posted to 6 Group.

419 Squadron became the first from Canada to enter 3 Group after its formation on paper on the 15th of December 1941. It existed physically when taking up residence at Mildenhall on the 21st under the command of W/C John 'Moose' Fulton, a Canadian with seven years' RAF service, and a tour of operations behind him. Another Canadian, S/L Turner, was appointed as A Flight commander, and B Flight came under the command of a British officer, S/L Reid, both men also having extensive operational experience. The squadron's progress to operational status was hampered somewhat by an initial lack of aircraft, and it was not until the 2nd of January 1942 that the first Wellington Ic, X9748, arrived to be taken on charge. On the night of the 11/12th 419 Squadron launched its first sorties in anger, when W/C Fulton and P/O Cottier and their crews operated against Brest. The night of the 28/29th of July became a tragic night for 419 Squadron when W/C Fulton failed to return from Hamburg. A message was received from X3488 suggesting that it had been attacked by a night fighter, wounding some of the crew, and it is presumed to have crashed into the North Sea. It was a bitter blow to the squadron, and shortly afterwards, as a token of the high esteem in which W/C Fulton was held, his nickname Moose was added to the squadron title, and its permanent place confirmed when His Majesty the King authorised the squadron's official crest in June 1944. His replacement, W/C Walsh, was undertaking his second operation with the squadron on the night of the 2/3rd, when under two hundred aircraft delivered a telling blow on Karlsruhe. For the second time in five weeks, 419 Squadron was forced to post missing its commanding officer, and it was later learned that W/C Walsh had been killed with his entire crew when a night fighter accounted for X3711 over Belgium. W/C Fleming arrived as his replacement, and he was still at the helm when the squadron was posted to Middleton St George in November 1942. By this time the squadron had been stood down in preparation for conversion to the Halifax Mk II. There would be no further operations for the squadron during what remained of 1942, and it was declared operational on the day 6 Group became a reality on New Year's day 1943.

420 Squadron had been formed in 5 Group at Waddington on the 19th of December 1941 under the command of W/C Bradshaw. Although many of that Group's squadrons had converted to the ill-fated Avro Manchester by this time, and 44 Squadron was about to begin the process of working up to operational status as the first Lancaster unit in the Command, 420 Squadron was to begin its operational career on the trusty, if obsolete, Hampden. The squadron's formation came during what was almost certainly the Command's lowest point of the entire war. Back on the 18th of August 1941 civil servant, Mr D M Butt, completed his analysis of recent Bomber Command operations, and its disclosures were to send shock waves reverberating around the Cabinet Room and the Air Ministry. Having studied more than four thousand photographs taken during a

hundred night raids in June and July, he concluded that only a tiny fraction of bombs were falling within miles of their intended targets. This swept away at a stroke any notion that the Command had in any way reduced Germany's capacity to wage war thus far, and demonstrated the claims of the crews to be wildly optimistic. 420 Squadron went to war for the first time on the night of the 21/22nd of January 1942 when contributing five of twelve Hampdens for an attack by a total of thirty-eight aircraft on Emden. Three Hampdens and one Whitley failed to return, among them AT130, the aircraft captained by 420 Squadron's B Flight commander, S/L Wood. It was brought down by flak over Holland, but the entire crew survived to fall into enemy hands. 420 Squadron left 5 Group for 4 Group on the 6th of August and took up residence at Skipton-on-Swale. It would take some time to fully re-equip with Wellington IIIs, but the first one, BJ644, arrived immediately, to be followed on the 11th by X3808 and X3809. Three more were taken on charge on the 19th, X3814, Z1724 and BJ717, while X3963 arrived on the 27th and BJ966 on the 28th. The remainder were received in September, chronologically X3800, BK235, BJ915, BK295, BK296, BK297, BJ917 and BK331, but it would be the following month before the squadron was declared operational. The Snowy Owls moved to their current home at Middleton St George on the 14th of October.

425 Squadron was assigned to 4 Group on its formation at Dishforth under W/C St Pierre on the 25th of June 1942, but it would take until early October for the squadron to work up to operational readiness on its Wellingtons. It was on the night of the 5/6th that the squadron contributed eight aircraft to a force of over 250 targeting Aachen in bad weather conditions. As a result the attack was only modestly effective, and some of the bombs fell well outside of the target, in fact some seventeen miles away on the Dutch town of Lutterade. (This was not appreciated at Bomber Command HQ, which would select a power station in the town for the first Mosquito Oboe bombing operation in December, believing it to be free of bomb craters, and, therefore, suitable for use as a calibration check on the device's margin of error.) 424 Squadron was one of two Canadian units to come into existence on the 15th of October 1942. It was formed at Topcliffe under the command of W/C Carscallen, and was destined to begin life on Wellingtons, although it carried out no operations with the type before the transfer took place to 6 Group. BJ658 was the first example to be taken on 424 Squadron charge six days after formation, and twelve more were added by the 8th of November. This allowed the process of working up to operational status to begin in earnest, and no aircraft or crews were lost during the training period. 426 Squadron received its first four Wellingtons, BJ888, DF617, DF619 and DF620, on the 23rd of October and began the process of working up to operational status under the watchful eye of W/C Blanchard, although it would be the New Year before the squadron went to war.

427 Squadron was formed on the 7th of November 1942, on the same day that 428 and 429 Squadrons came into existence as the eighth, ninth and tenth Canadian units in Bomber Command after 405, 408, 419, 420, 425, 424 and 426 Squadrons. Most began life in 4 Group, and with the exception of 427 Squadron, those formed late in 1942 would not gain operational status until after their transfer to 6 Group on its formation on New Year's Day 1943. 427 Squadron's first home was at Croft, and its nucleus was provided by ten crews from 419 Squadron, who remained on the station, while their colleagues moved to the Heavy Conversion Unit at Topcliffe and ultimately Middleton St George to take on Halifaxes. Three more crews were added from elsewhere, and sixteen Wellington IIIs were made available on the 9th, so that training could begin under the experienced eye of the commanding officer, W/C Burnside. The first home for W/C Earle's 428 Squadron was in 4 Group at Dalton, where it took on Wellingtons, the first two, X3545 and X3546, arriving from 466 RAAF Squadron on the 26th of November. Eleven more aircraft had been taken on charge by the 8th of December, allowing working up to operational status to get underway.

Shortly before 427, 428 and 429 Squadrons' formation a new phase of the bomber offensive had begun, as Harris was forced to switch his attention upon Italian targets in support of Operation *Torch*, the Allied landings in North Africa. The campaign, which would occupy most of the remainder of 1942, opened with a 5 Group attack on Genoa on the 22/23rd, with 3 and 4 Groups following up twenty-four hours later, although actually bombing the coastal town of Savona in error. Later on the 24th 5 Group raided Milan to good effect in daylight, to be followed by elements of 1 and 3 Groups after dark, and this effectively ended the month's operations. The campaign continued with four raids on Genoa during the first half of November and four on Turin in the second half. There were only two major operations against German cities during the month, the first of which was Hamburg on the 9/10th. This was not outstandingly successful, and neither was an operation against Stuttgart on the 22/23rd, when the Pathfinders failed to identify the city centre, and most of the bombs fell in the suburbs destroying fewer than a hundred houses. By this time 427 Squadron had suffered its first training accident, when BK276 lost engine power as it took off on a night circuit training exercise on the 15th, struck trees and came to earth in a field about half a mile from the airfield. Sgt Southwood and his crew emerged unscathed from the written-off Wellington, but their adventures were far from over.

The Lions were declared operational on the 1st of December, remarkably soon after formation, and now had eighteen Wellingtons on charge. Two crews took theirs to Middleton St George on the 4th to take on mines for the squadron's maiden operation, but poor weather conditions forced it to be called off. December had begun for the Command with a failure at

Frankfurt on the 2/3rd, and another one at Mannheim on the 6/7th, these preceding the final three raids on Italy, which were all directed at Turin between the 8/9th and the 11/12th. 427 Squadron eventually opened its account on the night of the 14/15th, when three of the former 419 Squadron crews, those of Sgts Gagnon, Higgins and Fellner, took off from Middleton St George in Z1626, BK364 and Z1676 respectively as part of a mining operation around the Frisians. Only the first mentioned found his pinpoint and delivered his mines, while the others had to bring their vegetables home. Sadly, and by coincidence, all three of these pilots would be taken from the squadron in June 1943, two fatally on the same night, and the other as a seriously wounded PoW. The most significant operation in December was that carried out by six Mosquitos of 109 Squadron against the power station at Lutterade in Holland on the 20/21st as an Oboe calibration test, to check the device's margin of error. Led by W/C Hal Bufton, three aircraft bombed successfully, while the other three suffered failure of their Oboe equipment, and joined in the main force attack on Duisburg instead. It proved impossible to identify the fall of the Oboe-aimed bombs because of the craters left by stray bombs intended for Aachen a few months earlier. Further calibration tests would be flown over the succeeding weeks, however, and the device would be ready in time for the forthcoming Ruhr offensive. Returning crews assessed the Duisburg operation as successful, but another by elements of 1, 5 and 8 Groups against Münich on the following night missed the target almost completely.

It had been a year of highs and lows for the Command, with a number of spectacular successes punctuated by many failures. There had, though, been a marked improvement on the performance of the previous year as Harris's tactics evolved, while the advent of the Pathfinders and the development of electronic bombing aids promised much for the future. As far as the Canadians were concerned, there were now sufficient operational RCAF squadrons to constitute a Group, and the official formation of 6 Group would be the first act of the coming year. As the clock ticked towards midnight on New Year's Eve, Canada's government prepared for a moment of significance. They awaited not so much the New Year, but that which came with it, the birth of 6 Group RAF Bomber Command, a shining symbol of the burgeoning status of the independent Canada. There were many non-British squadrons in Bomber Command, but this was the first foreign organisation to muscle in with its own Group, and while in public there was harmony between the two high commands, in private it was a different matter. Harris was strongly opposed to the formation of a Canadian Group. He valued Canadian airmen, and welcomed their presence in the war, although he found it difficult to come to terms with their lax attitude in matters of RAF etiquette and discipline. He wanted to distribute them throughout the existing RAF Groups, but Whitehall wanted otherwise, and Whitehall won. Harris also had an intense dislike for Air Marshal Edwards, the Commander-in-Chief of Canada's overseas Air Force, and for the man who would initially be Air-Officer-Commanding 6 Group, AVM Brookes. Both were British born, and neither, as far as Harris was concerned, was worthy of holding a position of authority, particularly anywhere near his Bomber Command. A Headquarters was established in the baronial Allerton Hall, on the two thousand acre estate of Allerton Park, the ancestral home of Lord Mowbray, four miles east of Knaresborough. Its dark, somewhat angular and forbidding aspect soon saw it renamed Castle Dismal by the Canadians.

1943

As the year turned not all RCAF squadrons in Bomber Command were immediately posted to 6 Group. It began life with eight operational squadrons, all based on former 4 Group stations in Yorkshire and County Durham, while a few other units remained in 4 Group for the time being. The founder units were 408 and 419 Squadrons, each equipped with Halifaxes, and 420, 424, 425, 426, 427 and 428 Squadrons, which were soldiering on with the trusty Wellington. The Canadian government was demanding Lancasters, and the type would eventually become dominant in the Group, but that would be by war's end. In the meantime, most of the existing Wellington units, and those awaiting posting in or still to form, would eventually find themselves operating the unpopular Halifax. For the purpose of this account we will detail 427 Squadron's experiences as a Wellington unit, 419's as a Halifax unit and 408 Squadron as an operator of the Lancaster II. There was no fanfare to herald the operational debut of the new Group, in fact, it was a damp squib, as the appalling weather conditions forced the cancellation of the intended maiden operation on New Year's night. It was not until the 2/3rd that half a dozen 427 Squadron Wellingtons disappeared into the murk at the end of the runway at Croft on the Group's first operation to lay mines off the Frisians. Another squadron should have contributed six more to the occasion, but was dissuaded by the conditions from taking part. W/C Burnside and two other crews returned early with technical difficulties, but P/O Bennett and Sgts Johnson and Chambers completed their assigned tasks, thereby bringing 6 Group into the war. The last mentioned returned home with a large hole in his starboard wing courtesy of flak.

Inhospitable weather was to characterise January, and there would be no major activity during the first half of the month. The first aircraft to be written off under 6 Group was 427 Squadron's BJ604, which overshot the runway at Middleton St George at the end of a transit flight, and ended up on a railway line, where it was demolished by a train. Sgt Harwood and his crew had walked away from the scene by this time, but were not destined to survive their tour. The Group next went to war on the evening of the 9th, when putting up twenty-five Wellingtons and thirteen Halifaxes for mining duties off the Frisians. The Wellingtons were provided by 420, 425 and 427 Squadrons, and four of them failed to locate the drop point, while two others returned early with technical problems. This first foray for the Geese of 408 Squadron and the Moosemen of 419 Squadron in Halifaxes resulted in the first of many lost examples of the type over the next two years. The latter's W7857 went into the sea, and took with it to their deaths the crew of Sgt Barker, and these were also the first casualties sustained by 6 Group. F/O Porter and crew almost joined them in the abysmal weather conditions, but somehow avoided the fire from three flak ships at point blank range, and narrowly missed hitting the surface of the sea. Sadly for the pilot, he would not survive to complete his tour, and his crew would spend the last two years of the war as guests of the *Reich*. A recent resurgence in U-Boat activity continued to take a heavy toll of Allied shipping in the Atlantic, and confirmation of this came with a new Air Ministry directive on the 14th, which authorised the area bombing of those French ports providing bases and support facilities for U-Boots. A target list was drawn up headed by Lorient, and that night 122 aircraft took off for the first of eight attacks against it over the ensuing month. This was 6 Group's first bombing operation for which 426 Squadron provided seven of the sixteen Wellingtons in what was at best only a modestly effective raid. W/C Blanchard led the Thunderbirds into action, and his Wellington, Z1599, was involved in an inconclusive combat with a JU88 before returning safely to Stanton Harcourt. The squadron's BK165 failed to make it back, and was lost without trace with the crew of P/O Milne. 408 Squadron also took part, and its five Halifaxes returned without incident. Meanwhile, 425 Squadron sent six crews mining, and these also came home safely.

Bomber Command's year had actually begun with a series of small-scale operations as part of the Oboe trials programme. Seven raids on Essen and one on Duisburg involving 109 Squadron Mosquitos and Lancasters from 1 and 5 Groups were mounted during the first two weeks of January alone. On the 8th the Pathfinder Force was granted Group status as 8 Group, and the stations under its occupation were transferred over from 3 Group. Lorient was raided for the second time on the 15/16th, this time with a contribution from all 6 Group squadrons with the exception of 428 Squadron. More than eight hundred buildings were destroyed in an effective operation, but 427 Squadron's BK364 failed to return to Croft with the crew of A Flight commander, S/L Williams, and it was later learned that the Wellington had crashed in the target area with no survivors. Two disappointing attacks were mounted against Berlin by predominantly Lancaster forces on the 16/17th and 17/18th, and the only matters of significance arising out of the former was the complete destruction of the Deutschlandhalle, the largest covered arena in Europe, and the loss of a single Lancaster. The latter raid produced no useful damage, but cost twenty-two aircraft. The Group was out in force on the 21/22nd, when sending fifteen Halifaxes and twenty-five Wellingtons back to the Frisians for another mining operation. 420 and 427 Squadrons each posted missing a crew, and no trace was ever found of BJ966 and X3873 or the crews of F/S Gergly and F/L Shead respectively. A daring daylight raid on Essen by six Wellingtons from 420 and 425 Squadrons passed without casualty, although a number of aircraft unsurprisingly sustained flak damage. The Group's two Halifax squadrons contributed to a further attack on Lorient on the 23/24th, while fifty Wellingtons took part on the 26/27th. As a result 424 Squadron posted missing the crew of F/S McHarg in BJ714, which crashed on French soil killing the pilot and two others. Twenty-two Halifaxes and forty Wellingtons headed back to Lorient on the night of the 29/30th, and encountered icing conditions in the target area. 408 Squadron's HR662 failed to return with the crew of F/O Roux, after crashing in France, and there were no survivors. Thus they became the first to fail to return from operations on behalf of 408 Squadron as both a Halifax and a 6 Group unit. 420 Squadron lost two Wellingtons, DF626 to a crash near Exeter during the outward flight, with the loss of W/O Sanderson and three of his crew, while DF615 was lost without trace with the crew of P/O Stanton.

419 Squadron participated in just three bombing operations during January, all against Lorient, and the only aircraft casualty arising from them involved DT623, which returned on the 29/30th to a wheels-up landing without damage to the crew. The pilot on this occasion was F/L Alec Cranswick, a slightly built Englishman, whose exploits until his untimely death in action in July 1944, would typify the very best in those who went to war in bombers. Having served his first tour with 214 Squadron in 1940, he volunteered for a posting to the Middle East theatre to avoid being rested, where he completed seventeen operations with 148 Squadron, before moving on to West Africa as a ferry pilot. After recovering from a serious bout of malaria, he returned to operational duties with 148 Squadron out of Kabrit, and was eventually sent back home in early 1942 with a total of sixty-one operations to his credit. Much of the year was lost through recurring ill-health, but in December, he was declared fully fit for flying duties, and was posted to 1659 HCU for Halifax conversion. By the end of the year, he and his blue Alsatian, Kluva, had joined 419 Squadron for what would be a brief stay, and on the 1st of February, after adding five more operations to his personal tally, he was posted as a trainee Pathfinder to 35 Squadron. He remained at 35 Squadron until rested in October, but lived for the day when he could return, and his frequent requests bore fruit in April 1944, when he was posted back to 35 Squadron.

The Command lost one of its finest sons when S/L Cranswick's Lancaster was shot down over Villeneuve-St-George on the 4/5th of July, officially his 104th sortie, although his biographer credits him with substantially more.

In between the last two-mentioned operations against Lorient the first Oboe ground marking ahead of the heavy Pathfinder aircraft was attempted on the 27/28th. This led to an effective raid on Düsseldorf, in which over 450 houses were destroyed, along with a number of industrial and public buildings. A daylight raid was mounted on the 30th by eleven Wellingtons from 424, 425, 426 and 427 Squadrons against Oldenburg, near Bremen. 426 Squadron's Z1689 was lost without trace with the crew of F/L Lowe, and 427 Squadron's BK389 similarly disappeared with the crew of P/O Bennett. As Harris sought the most effective method of target marking, the first H2s (a blind bombing radar device) attack of the war was mounted against Hamburg on the 30/31st. It was not an entirely successful debut for the device, but with time and practice it would emerge as a useful addition to the Command's armoury of electronic aids, particularly for use against targets beyond the range of Oboe.

A combination of path-finding techniques was employed against Cologne on the 2/3rd of February with disappointing results, on a night when 6 Group contented itself with thirteen mining sorties by Halifaxes. The weather spared Hamburg from a telling blow on the following night, by forcing many crews to return early, and providing difficult conditions for the Pathfinder markers. 408 and 419 Squadrons provided twenty-five Halifaxes between them, and both squadron commanders were among the early returns. Each also lost an aircraft, 419 Squadron posting missing the crew of F/S Mackenzie, who was killed with three others when DT630 was shot down by a night fighter over Holland. The campaign against Lorient continued on the 4/5th, the night on which 428 Squadron finally opened its account against Hitler after sitting on the sidelines since the start of the year. It was an all-incendiary attack without Pathfinders, and successfully created areas of fire. One 428 Squadron Wellington returned early, and the remainder came home without major incident. 427 Squadron opened its month's account on this night, and suffered another loss. BJ668 was brought down by flak in the target area, and P/O Parsons died with all but one of his crew, while the survivor was taken into captivity. The Group's two Halifax units, meanwhile, contributed to a damaging raid on Turin by a mixed force numbering some 180 aircraft, and all returned without major incident. On the night of the 6/7th six 6 Group squadrons committed twenty-eight Wellingtons to mining sorties along the occupied coast, from which one each from 424 and 425 Squadrons failed to return. Then it was Lorient again on the 7/8th, for which 6 Group provided eighteen Halifaxes and forty-nine Wellingtons. The two-wave assault by over three hundred aircraft was highly accurate, and cost 6 Group one 408

Squadron Halifax. Wilhelmshaven was subjected to its most destructive raid to date on the 11/12th, when complete cloud cover forced the Pathfinders to employ parachute flares as sky markers. This was the least reliable of all techniques, but, despite the difficulties, the marking was accurate and the bombing concentrated. One bomb load hit a naval ammunition dump, and the resulting explosion devastated an estimated 120 acres, and caused extensive damage in the dockyard and town. 6 Group did not take part in this operation, but sent a force of twenty-four Wellingtons from 420, 424 and 425 Squadrons to mine the waters around the Frisians and Brest.

On the following night twelve Wellingtons from 426 and 427 Squadrons were dispatched to mine the waters around the Frisians again. The Lions' BJ778 was damaged by flak and almost made it home, but crashed in Yorkshire killing Sgt Adlam and his crew. The penultimate attack on Lorient was delivered on the 13/14th, when 6 Group's contribution to the overall force of 460 aircraft amounted to twenty-three Halifaxes and sixty-nine Wellingtons, of which just one 420 Squadron crew failed to return. The following night was devoted to Cologne and Milan, and it was to the former that 6 Group sent twenty Halifaxes and twenty-seven Wellingtons. The operation enjoyed only modest success and cost 426 Squadron its commanding officer, W/C Blanchard, when X3420 was shot down by a night fighter over Holland, killing all on board. The other operation by Lancasters of 1, 5 and 8 Groups was more effective, and created fires visible from a hundred miles away. S/L Crooks was promoted from his flight commander post for what would prove to be a six-month tenure as commanding officer of 426 Squadron.

Lorient was pounded for the final time on the 16/17th of February, and was left a deserted ruin after eight raids in which almost seventeen hundred aircraft had dropped four thousand tons of bombs. 6 Group's contribution was twenty-four Halifaxes and some fifty Wellingtons, of which nine of the latter were put up by 427 Squadron. It seems that Z1676 was hit by flak in the target area, which destroyed the compass, and Sgt Holloway and his crew became lost on the way home, eventually arriving over Waterford in Eire. The pilot carried out a crash-landing, in which one member of the crew sustained a head injury, and the crew then set fire to the Wellington. The five crewmen were taken into custody, and began a period of comfortable internment, which, for all but the injured man, who was quickly repatriated, lasted until 1944. The Group sent fifteen Halifaxes and fifteen Wellingtons back to the Frisians for mining duties on the 18/19th, as a result of which, the 419 Squadron crew of F/S Levasseur went missing without trace in DT639. Also taking place on this night was the first of three follow-up raids on Wilhelmshaven. Four 6 Group Halifaxes contributed to a disappointing attack, which saw most of the bombing find open country. The following night brought the same destination and an even more ineffective result from a larger force that included twenty-five Halifaxes and around sixty Wellingtons from 6 Group, of which one 426 Squadron aircraft failed to return. W/C Earle relinquished command of 428 Squadron on the 20th, and W/C Smith became his successor. A further raid on Wilhelmshaven by 6 and 8 Groups on the 24/25th again failed to make an impact. The Group put up twenty-six Halifaxes and sixty-six Wellingtons, and all returned safely to home airspace, where a 424 Squadron Wellington crashed on landing killing a number of the crew. The unfavourable conditions over Nuremberg on the 25/26th helped to push the bombing onto its northern fringes and beyond into open country, but this was a night when most of 6 Group stayed at home and just a few of its Halifaxes and Wellingtons went mining around the Frisians. The Group was in action on the following night in numbers when contributing twenty-six Halifaxes and sixty-four Wellingtons to an attack on Cologne, where the south-western districts sustained moderate damage in return for the loss of ten bombers. 427 Squadron's BJ886 was shot down by a night fighter over Holland, and there were no survivors from the crew of Sgt Harwood. Meanwhile, BK268 was on its way home with an engine on fire, and having reached the East Midlands, an attempt was made to land on the 5 Group airfield at Woolfox Lodge in Rutland. Sadly, the station was out of commission having new runways laid, and the Wellington crashed, killing Sgt Taylor and all but one of his crew. The Group devoted the night of the 27/28th to mining around the Frisians, and 419 Squadron's Sgt Gray was forced to ditch DT615 after it was severely damaged by flak. Twenty-two hours later, the cold and tired crew was safely picked up and returned to duty. On the last night of the month St Nazaire became the second of the French ports to be attacked under the latest directive. This was a successful operation by over four hundred aircraft including eighty from 6 Group, which caused heavy damage in the port area, and left an estimated 60% of the town's built-up area in ruins. It was another bad night for 427 Squadron, however, which lost BK343 to a crash in the sea, and Sgt Hartney perished with four of his crew, while the lone survivor was picked up by the enemy. Sgt Southwood and his crew found themselves lost over the Irish Sea on the way home, and abandoned a fuel-starved X3563 over County Roscommon in Eire to begin a short period of internment.

Earlier in the day, 405 Squadron concluded its five-month detachment to Coastal Command, and began the process of moving back to Topcliffe to join 6 Group for what would prove to be a brief period of service. During the course of its maritime adventure, the squadron carried out 349 sorties, and filled an important gap, while Coastal Command formed and trained its own Halifax squadrons. The squadron's commanding officer during most of the period away from Bomber Command and for the duration of the forthcoming 6 Group service was W/C Clayton, another of the long serving Canadian officers in the RAF. Pitt Clayton had undertaken his first tour with 83 Squadron on Hampdens in 1940/41, and served alongside Guy Gibson of Dambuster fame. On page 105 of his book, *Enemy Coast Ahead*, Gibson makes reference to Clayton force-landing on a beach in the middle of a minefield. However, this incident is exactly the same as one experienced by F/L Barker on the 15/16th of October 1940, which is documented, while Clayton's is not. The passage of time has shown a number of inaccuracies in the book, and I believe this to be one example. On leaving 83 Squadron, Clayton became a founder member and flight commander with the second RCAF unit to form in Bomber Command, 408 (Goose) Squadron. This came into existence in 5 Group on the 24th of June 1941, two months after 405 Squadron's formation, and began Hampden operations in August. On the 26th of March 1942 Clayton was promoted to Wing Commander and was given command of the squadron, but was himself posted out three weeks later.

The first Canadian unit to be formed in Bomber Command, 405 Squadron had come into existence on the 4 Group station at Driffield on the 23rd of April 1941 under the temporary command, on paper at least, of S/L Tomlinson DFC. It operated the Merlin-powered Mk II Wellington, and would, in fact, be only the second squadron in Bomber Command to be entirely equipped with the variant. The first was 104 Squadron, with which 405 Squadron shared Driffield during its brief residency. A few examples of the type had by this time found their way into radial-powered Wellington squadrons, where their superior lifting power enabled them to carry a 4,000 lb 'Cookie' bomb into battle. On the 20th of May W/C Gilchrist was posted in from 35 Squadron at Linton-on-Ouse, where he had been a flight commander, and was installed as 405 Squadron's first official commanding officer. 35 Squadron had been given the responsibility of introducing the new Halifax into operational service, and the then S/L Gilchrist, a Canadian serving in the RAF, had taken part in the type's very first operation, against Le Havre on the 10/11th of March. On return to England, his Halifax, a type still shrouded in secrecy, was intercepted by a RAF night fighter, and shot down to crash on the Surrey/Hampshire border. Only Gilchrist and one other were able to parachute to safety, and this was an experience he would have to repeat with 405 Squadron. Over the succeeding three weeks he oversaw the training of the crews as they worked up to operational status, but even when this was achieved, the squadron's initial contribution to the offensive would be modest. It took time to build up a strong Canadian presence, and in the meantime, the squadron was a polyglot of nationalities, just like any other in the Command. The legendary Johnny Fauquier commanded the squadron for five months to early August, overseeing in the process the conversion to the Halifax in April. Operations on behalf of 4 Group continued until late October, when the transfer to Coastal Command occurred. An entry in the

405 Squadron Operations Record Book dated the 16th of February 1943, just two weeks before its posting to 6 Group, reads:

> Information has been received from British Columbia House, London, England, to the effect that 405 RCAF Squadron has been officially adopted by the city of Vancouver. A cable received from the Honorary Secretary of the Vancouver Women's Canadian Club explained that the city would be delighted to provide for the squadron's needs, and request details concerning what the adoption might truly mean. It is certain that the squadron personnel will receive generous consideration by this organisation, and that every thought and care will be shown towards the welfare of the personnel. To celebrate this adoption, 10,000 cigarettes have been received from B.C. House, London for distribution amongst personnel, which will undoubtedly be the forerunner of a very happy association between this squadron and the Club.

From this point on, the squadron would go to war proudly bearing the title of 405 (Vancouver) Squadron.

March would bring with it the first major campaign of the year against Germany, and the first offensive of the war for which Bomber Command was truly prepared and adequately equipped. Most of the front line squadrons were now operating genuine heavy bombers, although Wellingtons would continue to feature prominently until well into the second half of the year. The magnificent pioneering work on Oboe carried out by 109 Squadron had born fruit, and whilst the device was not yet problem free, it was ready to be used against the Ruhr. Tactics had been honed to the point where only actual operational experience could bring about fine-tuning, and enough target marking techniques were to hand to cope with most contingencies. This said, bombing was by no means yet a precise art, and would remain something of a lottery for a long time to come, particularly at the more distant targets. The Ruhr offensive would begin on the night of the 5/6th, but in the meantime, major operations were mounted against Berlin and Hamburg. Both lay well beyond the range of Oboe, and H2s would provide the reference point for the Pathfinder crews. Three hundred aircraft took off for the Capital on the night of the 1/2nd, including a contingent of twenty-one Halifaxes from 6 Group, and the shortcomings of H2s became apparent over the target. Confronted by the massive urban sprawl of any large city, it was extremely difficult for the H2s operators to interpret what they were seeing on their screens, and to pick out the specific area designated as the aiming point. On this night the main weight of bombs fell into the south-western districts, but the attack in general was scattered over a hundred square miles. Despite this, it was the most effective raid on Berlin of the war to date, in which almost nine hundred buildings were destroyed, and many factories sustained serious damage. On the debit side, over 5% of the attacking force failed to return, and 419 Squadron posted missing the crew of P/O Herriott, who all died when DT641 disappeared into the North Sea, while 408 Squadron also lost one Halifax to a night fighter. Three 427 Squadron Wellingtons were among a small 6 Group force sent mining around the Frisians on the following night, and the worrying rate of attrition for the Lions continued. X3390 crashed in the target area, and there were no survivors from the crew of Sgt Lymburner.

The marking at Hamburg on the 3/4th was mostly again miles from the planned aiming point, and the small town of Wedel received most of the bomb loads from the attacking force of around four hundred aircraft, which included eighteen Halifaxes and more than fifty Wellingtons from 6 Group. The Hamburg civil defence had to deal with a hundred fires before going to the assistance of Wedel, where the harbour area was hardest hit. This time a 425 Squadron Wimpy represented the Group's solitary loss, while 419 Squadron's P/O Dickson's gunners claimed a BF110 and a JU88 destroyed, the pilot and rear gunner, P/O Wagner, each being awarded the DFC. Twenty-one Mk X Wellingtons had arrived on 427 Squadron charge at the start of March, and S/L Earthrowl took one of them on the Hamburg trip and returned safely.

As feverish activity on the bomber stations signalled preparations for the opening of the Ruhr campaign on the 5th, 405 Squadron was moving out of Topcliffe and installing itself at Leeming. It would not be ready to operate for almost another week, but would only miss the opening round of the offensive that night. Some 442 aircraft took off for Essen, but an unusually high number of early returns and the bombing of alternative targets reduced the numbers actually bombing the city to 362. The three-wave attack was opened by Oboe Mosquitos, which marked the city centre with great accuracy, paving the way for the all Halifax first wave, Wellingtons and Stirlings in the second, and the Lancasters bringing up the rear. Oboe nullified the industrial haze, which had always protected the city in the past, and the operation was a resounding success. Over three thousand houses were destroyed, and the mighty Krupp complex received hits to fifty-three of its buildings. Losses were relatively light at fourteen aircraft, and it was a highly satisfactory start to what would be a five-month long offensive. 6 Group put up twenty Halifaxes for this momentous occasion, of which 419 Squadron contributed half, led by S/L Clarke. The other crew captains were F/L Sills in DT617, F/O Porter in DT616, F/Ss Bell and Goddard in BB283 and DT689 respectively, and Sgts Bakewell, Heintz, Jackson, McSorley and Maddock in DT646, DT634, DT672, DT798 and W7817. DT646 was damaged by flak over the target, and was finally dispatched by a night fighter over Holland, but Sgt Bakewell and all but one of his crew survived the encounter, and one of them ultimately evaded capture. Of more than fifty Wellingtons taking part, 420 and 426 Squadrons each lost one, while 427 Squadron's F/S Vandekerckhove almost became another casualty statistic after Z1572 developed an engine fire on the way home. The Wellington eventually shed the propeller over the sea before a safe landing was carried out at Catfoss.

Round two of the campaign would not be launched for another week, and in the meantime Harris turned his attention upon southern Germany, sending forces against Nuremberg, Münich and Stuttgart on the 8/9th, 9/10th and 11/12th respectively. Wellingtons were not involved in any of these operations, but the Group contributed nineteen Halifaxes for Nuremberg, which delivered their bomb loads over the target at between 17,000 and 18,000 feet. The bombing was spread along the line of approach in an example of the creep-back phenomenon, which was an almost ever-present feature of large raids, but even so, six hundred buildings were destroyed, and a number of important war industry factories were damaged. While this operation was in progress 6 Group Wellingtons revisited the shipping lanes around the Frisians. At Münich a strong wind pushed the emphasis of the raid into the western half of the city, where almost three hundred buildings were reduced to rubble, and 2,800 others were damaged to some extent. 6 Group again provided a contingent of nineteen Halifaxes, while 425 and 426 Squadrons sent some crews mining in northern waters around the Kattegat and Heligoland for the loss of one Thunderbird. The Stuttgart operation was not a success, for which the first recorded examples of dummy target indicators were partly to blame. The main force arrived late at this notoriously difficult to locate target, and a modest 118 buildings were destroyed in the south-western suburbs. 405 Squadron was declared operational in time to return to the fray for this operation, and it enabled the Group to put up a record thirty-five Halifaxes. It was to be a sobering re-introduction to the bombing war for the Vancouverites, from whence came four of the six missing Halifaxes in an overall casualty figure of eleven aircraft from a total force of 314 aircraft. Because of the time spent with Coastal Command away from bombing operations, many 405 Squadron crews were carrying second pilots gaining experience, and three of the missing aircraft contained eight-man crews. The deputy A Flight commander, F/L Shockley, died with his crew, when W7803 was shot down over France. BB212 was outbound over Germany and approaching the target when the end came at the hands of a night fighter, but F/S Chretien and all but his rear gunner managed to save themselves to fall into enemy hands. DT745 was also over France when it was caught by a night fighter and shot down, but this time the whole crew of P/O Rea escaped by parachute, the flight engineer and rear gunner ultimately evading capture. Finally, BB250 became another night fighter victim while on the way home over France, and although the flight engineer and a gunner were killed, P/O Dennison and four of his crew retained their freedom, leaving only the rear gunner to fester in a PoW camp. In a rather inadequate recompense for these losses, Sgt Daggett's American rear gunner shot down a BF109, and had the satisfaction of seeing the glow as it impacted the ground. 419 Squadron's S/L Clark claimed the destruction of a Messerschmitt 210 as the Moosemen came through unscathed, but 408 Squadron posted one crew missing.

The Ruhr offensive resumed on the following night, the 12/13th, with a return to Essen by over four hundred aircraft including twenty-three 6 Group Halifaxes and a contribution from all of the Wellington units. Eleven 427 Squadron aircraft took part, including another of the Mk Xs, HE653, in the hands of F/O Ganderton, who would be commanding the squadron in less than eighteen months time. Although the bombing on this night was generally less accurate that that of a week earlier, the Krupp complex sustained 30% more damage, and around five hundred houses were destroyed in central and north-western districts. As BK164 approached the target in the hands of the commanding officer, W/C Burnside, a burst of flak killed the navigator, W/O Heather, and seriously injured the wireless operator, Sgt Keen, severing his right foot. W/C Burnside continued with his bombing run, and during the two-hour return journey Sgt Keen attempted to repair the damaged radio, and also fill in for the navigator. A landing was made at the 3 Group airfield at Stradishall, and W/C Burnside later received a Bar to his DFC, Sgt Keen the much coveted CGM, the first to be awarded to an RCAF man, and the bomb-aimer, P/O Hayhurst, was awarded the DFC for continuing at his post after being drenched in glycol from the de-icing tank. 420, 424 and 425 Squadrons each lost one aircraft, but the Halifaxes all returned home. 427 Squadron now began a thirteen-night break as generally minor operations held sway, and almost immediately lost its first Mk X Wellington to a training accident on the 14th. HE278 lost engine power as it lifted off in the hands of Sgt 'Indian' Schmitt, a German born Canadian, and the undercarriage collapsed as it came back down. The Wellington was written off, but the crew emerged unscathed to fight another day. It was at around this time, that the squadron was informed of MGM film studio's interest in adopting the squadron, and this would become a reality in May.

The second raid on St Nazaire took place on the 22/23rd, when 283 crews reported a concentrated attack on the port area. 6 Group set a new record when launching thirty-eight Halifaxes, and all returned safely. After another three-night lull, 455 aircraft set out for Duisburg, 6 Group dispatching more than a hundred aircraft for the first time, including a contingent of twelve Mk X Wellingtons from 427 Squadron. 6 Group's three Halifax units contributed thirty aircraft, but their effort was largely in vain, as problems afflicting the Pathfinder Oboe element forced five of its Mosquitos to return early, and a sixth was lost. The subsequent sparse marking in cloudy conditions led to scattered bombing, and the city escaped with superficial damage. A 426 Squadron Wellington went down in the North Sea on the way home, and was the only failure to return. One note of concern for 6 Group on this night was a 10% rate of early returns, and this, together with a higher than average loss rate over a considerable period, would characterise the opening phase of its operational career. In time this would change, and by war's end, 6 Group would achieve an impressive record of efficiency and reliability, but in the meantime, crews saw little prospect of surviving a tour of thirty operations. A disappointing raid on Berlin on the 27/28th cost the Group two of its thirty-one participating Halifaxes, one of which was a 408 Squadron aircraft. The other was 419 Squadron's DT634, which was hit by flak while outbound over northern Germany. P/O Porter elected to continue on to the target, where the bomb load was delivered, but the Halifax was picked up by a night fighter near Hamburg on the way home, and all but the pilot escaped with their lives to become PoWs. The night of the 28/29th brought another accurate assault on St Nazaire, in which the Group's Halifax units played a relatively minor part, putting up just fifteen aircraft between them. The sole 6 Group casualty was 419 Squadron's BB283, which crashed in France with no survivors from the crew of Sgt Beckett. 428 Squadron's W/C Smith reported witnessing the incident, describing an aircraft crashing in flames at 22.45 hours after being coned in searchlights. All of the Group's Wellington units participated, and the fourteen 427 Squadron aircraft landed safely, although only seven at Croft as the remainder were diverted. Twenty-two 6 Group Halifaxes joined over three hundred other four-engine bombers in a trip to Berlin on the 29/30th. 408 Squadron posted missing two crews from this ineffective operation carried out in poor weather conditions, when the bulk of the bombing found open country south-east of the Capital. 419 Squadron's casualty resulted from an early return due to the icing conditions, when JB860 crashed during the attempt to land. Happily, P/O Ainsworth and his crew were able to walk away unscathed. While this operation was in progress 149 Wellingtons carried out a diversionary raid on Bochum in the Ruhr. The attack failed on a moonless and cloudy night, and 8% of the force fell to the defences. It was an expensive night for 6 Group, as 420 and 428 Squadrons each posted missing two crews, and 426 Squadron one. 427 Squadron contributed eleven Wellingtons, and it too had one fail to return in the form of HE744, which was lost without trace with the crew of Sgt McFadden.

April would be the least rewarding month of the Ruhr offensive, largely because of the number of operations directed at targets outside of the region, and beyond the range of Oboe. 6 Group welcomed a new arrival on the 1st in the form of 429 (Bison) Squadron, which, as already mentioned, had been formed in 4 Group on the 7th of November 1942, the same day that 427 and 428 Squadrons came into existence. 429's station of East Moor also transferred to 6 Group control at the same time. The squadron's first four Wellingtons, BJ798, BJ799, BJ908 and DF625 had arrived on the 24th of November, and a total of twenty-six aircraft were on strength by the 10th of December. This allowed working up to operational status to proceed apace under W/C Owen. The squadron actually eased itself gently into operational mode with a sea search by six aircraft on the 21st of January and all returned safely to East Moor, although without having sighted any downed crews. The Bisons' first offensive operation took place that night, when they contributed aircraft to a force sent to the Frisians for a mining operation. BK432 was shot down by flak over the Waddenzee, and F/O Johnson and his crew were all killed.

The new month began for 6 Group with two small-scale contributions to an attack on St Nazaire and the final operation against Lorient under the January directive. Harris was delighted when three days later the Command was released from further responsibility from this distraction. The month began in promising fashion for the Command generally, with another successful tilt at Essen on the 3/4th, when, in clear conditions, over six hundred buildings were destroyed in central and western districts. This was the first occasion on which two hundred Lancasters were launched, and they shared in a 6% loss rate. The Halifaxes were hardest hit, however, and 6 Group figured prominently in the twelve examples of the type failing to return. 405 and 408 Squadrons each posted missing two crews, and a further Goose was written off in a crash on return, although without crew casualties. For the fourth raid in succession 419 Squadron registered a casualty, this one involving the loss to a night fighter over Holland of DT617, and there were no survivors from the crew of P/O Boyd. 427 Squadron was not called into action on this night, but contributed seventeen of more than a hundred 6 Group Wellingtons and twenty-three Halifaxes on the following night, when Harris dispatched 577 aircraft, the largest non-1,000 force to date, to Kiel. Sadly, the massive effort was not rewarded with success, as heavy cloud, strong winds and decoy fire sites conspired to nullify the Pathfinder attempts to mark the target accurately, and only eleven buildings were destroyed by the few bombs finding the mark. 405 Squadron lost one aircraft, as did 408 Squadron along with a flight commander, S/L Gilmore, and one 428 Squadron Wellington also failed to return. 427 Squadron's Sgt Ash and crew took off late on the 6th for a night training exercise, but HE743 swung on take-off and came to grief in an orchard on the edge of the airfield. The pilot and one of his crew died in the crash, and the other crew members sustained burns when the wreck exploded. Meanwhile, ten Halifaxes from 405 and 408 Squadrons joined aircraft from other Groups to mine the sea lanes around La Rochelle and Brest, and one from 405 Squadron failed to return.

424 Squadron moved to Leeming on the 8th, and would remain there until the 2nd of May, before moving to a transit station to prepare for duties overseas. Almost four hundred aircraft were sent back to Duisburg

in difficult weather conditions that night, when 27% of the 6 Group participants returned early. Cloud over the target reduced the attack to a
shambles, and at least fifteen other Ruhr towns reported bombs falling on
and around them. 419 Squadron's BB327 failed to return home, and it was
later discovered to have crashed in the Ruhr with just one survivor from
the crew of Sgt Morris. 427 Squadron sent ten aircraft, and all returned
safely, but 420, 425 and 428 Squadrons each had the sad task of posting
missing a crew. A follow-up raid by Lancasters twenty-four hours later was
equally unrewarding as Duisburg's charmed life continued. Frankfurt had
also proved a difficult target to hit effectively, and a raid by five hundred
aircraft on the 10/11th went the way of the others. 6 Group contributed
twenty-four Halifaxes and over eighty Wellingtons, and 426 and 429
Squadrons each had one of the latter fail to return, while 420 and 424
Squadron sustained casualties in crashes at home. 427 Squadron welcomed
back all ten of its crews on this night, although one landed heavily at West
Malling with flak damage. It was later learned that a few bombs had fallen
in the suburbs, but this was a poor return for the effort of mounting such
a large-scale operation and the loss of twenty-one aircraft. Later on the
11th W/C Bradshaw's long tenure as the first commanding officer of 420
Squadron came to an end, and he was replaced by W/C McIntosh, who was
promoted from flight commander and would himself enjoy a long spell at
the helm. That night a 425 Squadron Wellington was lost while mining off
Texel.

Stuttgart was the target for over four hundred aircraft on the night of
the 14/15th, when 6 Group managed a total of thirty Halifaxes and more
than eighty Wellingtons. The Pathfinders claimed to have marked the
centre of the city, but the main weight of bombs was concentrated in
the north-east along the line of approach. The creep-back phenomenon
could work for or against the success of an attack, and on this night it was
for. The bombing spread across one industrial suburb and two of a more
residential nature, and almost four hundred buildings were destroyed. The
route to and from Stuttgart required a long flight across France, and enemy
night fighters were waiting on the return leg to catch the unwary and tired
crews. Two 408 Squadron Halifaxes fell victim to them, but only two of the
fifteen crewmen involved lost their lives. 420 Squadron also posted missing
two crews including that of flight commander S/L Taylor, who was one of
two evaders from his aircraft. 425 Squadron likewise had two empty dispersals next morning, while 428 Squadron had one. The ten participants from
427 Squadron managed to avoid contact with the night fighters, and all
returned safely, nine of them landing at Coltishall. This operation was the
last for 405 Squadron before its posting to 8 Group on the 19th as the sole
Canadian Pathfinder unit. The 16/17th proved to be a night of heavy
operational activity, when Harris sent over three hundred Lancasters
and Halifaxes to distant Pilsen in Czechoslovakia to bomb the Skoda arma-

ments works, and a diversionary force of predominantly Stirlings and Wellingtons to Mannheim. 6 Group put up twenty-seven Halifaxes for the main event and around ninety Wellingtons for Mannheim. Confusion over the Pathfinder route markers led to a complete failure at Pilsen, from which thirty-six aircraft, eighteen of each type, failed to return. It turned into an awful night for 408 Squadron when four of its aircraft didn't make it back, and there was not a single survivor from among the twenty-nine crewmen involved. The Mannheim force also lost eighteen aircraft, among them HE547 from 427 Squadron, in which Sgt Tomyn lost his life, while his crew fell into enemy hands. HE745 suffered engine trouble on the way home, and crashed while trying to land at Twinwood Farm airfield in Bedfordshire, although fortunately without serious injury to Sgt Chambers and his crew. It was from this airfield that the legendary American band leader Glenn Miller took off in December 1944 never to be seen again. Other squadrons to post missing a crew from this operation were 420, 425, 426 and 429. The total of fifty-four missing aircraft from the two operations represented the Command's highest loss in a single night to date. On the 17th W/C Carscallen relinquished command of 424 Squadron, and was succeeded by the newly promoted W/C Roy, who was posted in from 425 Squadron, where he had served as a flight commander.

During a nine-night break for the Lions the port of Stettin, located right at the eastern end of Germany's Baltic coast, hosted a successful attack by three hundred four-engine heavies on the 20/21st. It was perhaps the only urban target in Germany never to escape lightly at the hands of the Command. On this night it suffered the destruction of thirteen industrial premises and 380 houses in an area of devastation in its central districts estimated at a hundred acres. It was arguably the most effective operation to a non-Ruhr target, beyond the range of Oboe, during the entire period. Twenty-one 6 Group Halifaxes took part, and 419 Squadron's JB912 was the only one to fail to return after falling victim to a night fighter over northern Germany. P/O Jackson and all but one of the eight men on board survived as PoWs. 405 (Vancouver) Squadron, made its Pathfinder debut at Duisburg on the 26/27th, its crews acting as supporters, and carrying only bombs to 'beef-up' the Pathfinder presence. In time they would graduate to the role of backers-up, in which they would maintain the aiming point with fresh target indicators throughout the course of the raid. Experienced crews became illuminators, blind markers and ultimately visual markers, if they were able to survive and reach the required standard. The force of 561 aircraft taking off between midnight and 01.00 hours included a contingent of seventeen 6 Group Halifaxes and over sixty Wellingtons, eleven of them from 427 Squadron. At the target the Oboe ground marking appeared to progress according to plan, crews returning at dawn reporting fires visible from a hundred miles away, and a pall of smoke hanging over the city. However, photographic reconnaissance later revealed the main weight of the attack to have fallen across the north-eastern districts, where three hundred buildings were destroyed. There were no losses among the 427 Squadron crews, but HE771, which had been borrowed by a 420 Squadron crew, crashed near Darlington on return, killing the pilot. The Snowy Owls also lost another aircraft to a night fighter. 429 Squadron posted missing two crews, including that of flight commander S/L Cairns, and 428 Squadron was another to record a missing crew. The 426 Squadron commanding officer, W/C Crooks, struggled home with a badly damaged HE867 after an encounter with a night fighter, and he and his crew took to their parachutes once safely over England. Three Lion crews joined in a record mining operation between the Bay of Biscay and the Frisians on the following night, which involved 160 aircraft including nineteen Halifaxes and fifteen Wellingtons from 6 Group. The record was exceeded on the following night, when 207 aircraft sowed vegetables in northern waters. In contrast to the loss of just one aircraft from the former operation, twenty-two were missing from the latter, most of them falling to the light flak which was so lethal to low flying aircraft. 419 Squadron's JB923 was absent from its dispersal in the morning, and the fate of it and the crew of Sgt Smallwood remains unknown. Two 428 Squadron Wellingtons also failed to make it home, and neither produced a survivor. Four 427 Squadron aircraft took part on this night to complete the Lion's operational career on Wellingtons, and, indeed, its war service from Croft. The last night of the month brought the fourth raid of the campaign against Essen, for which three hundred aircraft were prepared. As the target was expected to be cloud-covered, Oboe Mosquitos were to drop sky markers for the following main force crews. It was impossible to assess the results of the bombing during the operation, and Harris had to wait for reconnaissance photographs. These showed fresh damage right across the city, with further hits on the Krupp works, but no point of concentration, and many other Ruhr towns again found themselves under the bombs. Twenty 6 Group Halifaxes took part, and all returned.

432 Squadron was the twelfth Canadian unit to join Bomber Command, and this it did as part of 6 Group on the 1st of May 1943 on its formation at Skipton-on-Swale. On the following day S/L McKay and five crews arrived on posting from 427 Squadron's B Flight to form the nucleus, along with eleven Wellingtons, which were also transferred over. W/C Kerby was appointed as the squadron's first commanding officer, and under his leadership the crews would soon achieve operational status. Before joining Bomber Command W/C Kerby had served two tours with Fighter Command. Two days later the rest of 427 Squadron began moving to Leeming, which it would ultimately share with 429 Squadron, and where eighteen Mk V Halifaxes awaited the crews, who would spend the month working up to operational status. May was to see a return to winning ways with a number of spectacular successes. Bombing operations began at

Dortmund on the night of the 4/5th, for which a new record non-1,000 force of 596 aircraft took off in the late evening. Among them were thirty-two 6 Group Halifaxes accompanied by Wellingtons from 426, 428 and 429 Squadrons. It was the first large-scale raid of the war on this city, and it opened in promising fashion with accurate Pathfinder marking. Some of the Pathfinder backers-up allowed their markers to fall short as the attack progressed, and a decoy fire site also drew off a proportion of the effort. Despite this, at least half of the bomb loads fell within three miles of the aiming point, inflicting extensive damage in central and northern districts. More than twelve hundred buildings were classed as totally destroyed, while two thousand others were seriously damaged, and the death toll of around seven hundred, which included many prisoners of war, was the highest yet at a German urban target. It was not a one-sided affair, however, as the defenders fought back fiercely to claim thirty-one bombers. Six of these were from 6 Group, at least three of which fell victim to night fighters. 419 Squadron posted missing two crews, the first in what would prove to be a very expensive month for the Moose men. DT794 crashed into the centre of the target city, probably as a result of the intense flak defence, and the entire crew of F/O Elliott died, while W7817 was brought down by a night fighter over Holland, F/O Vaillancourt surviving with five others of his crew to be taken into captivity. 408 and 428 Squadrons were the others to post missing two crews each. For the following week minor operations held sway, allowing the Pathfinder and main force squadrons to concentrate on training.

It was not until the night of the 12/13th of May that the next major raid was mounted, and this was the fourth attempt of the Ruhr offensive to deliver a telling blow on Duisburg, Germany's largest inland port. A total of 572 aircraft took off, among them nineteen 6 Group Halifaxes and over forty Wellingtons, and for once, everything proceeded according to plan, beginning with accurate Pathfinder marking, which was exploited by the main force as it followed up with concentrated bombing of the city's central districts and the port area. Almost sixteen hundred buildings were reduced to rubble, a number of important war industry factories were hit, and sixty thousand tons of shipping was either sunk or damaged in the port. The value of the region to the German war effort always guaranteed a hot reception for the crews, however, and in the black humour of the day the Ruhr would come to be known as 'Happy Valley'. A record loss for the campaign to date was sustained on this night of thirty-four aircraft. Of these eight belonged to 6 Group, and 419 Squadron was once more one of the afflicted units. JB719 fell victim to flak when leaving the target area, and the pilot, W/O McMillan, was killed. His crew all managed to abandon the stricken Halifax to fall into enemy hands, but one of them later died from his injuries. JB861 was shot down by a night fighter over Holland, and sadly, none survived from the crew of F/S Palmer. Six Canadian Wellingtons were also missing, two each from 426, 428 and 429 Squadrons, and only one of the Thunderbirds produced survivors, one of whom ultimately evaded capture.

On the following night over four hundred aircraft from all but 5 Group raided Bochum to moderately good effect, and despite decoy markers drawing off some of the effort, almost four hundred buildings were destroyed in return for the loss of twenty-four bombers. 6 Group put up twenty-six Halifaxes and around forty Wellingtons from three squadrons, and six failed to return. The trend for losing two aircraft per raid continued for 419 Squadron on this night, when DT672 crashed in Germany with no survivors from the crew of Sgt Adams, and JD113 was caught by a night fighter over Holland on the way home, and Sgt Buckwell and three of his crew were killed. 408 Squadron posted missing flight commander S/L Campbell and his crew, and the other casualties came from 426 and 429 Squadrons.

A nine-day lull in main force operations followed, and it was during this period, on the 16th May, that 420, 424 and 425 Squadrons prepared for a tour of duty overseas by dispatching their ground crews to Tunisia by sea. The ferrying of aircraft would begin on the 5th of June, and by the 23rd all would be installed at Kairouan to begin operations three days later as 331 Wing. Also during this break in main force activities 617 Squadron entered bomber folklore with its epic attack on the dams on the 16/17th, a raid in which many Canadians played their part magnificently. Also on this night 6 Group's remaining Wellington squadrons contributed to mining operations around the Frisians. A similar operation on the night of the 21/22nd cost 428 Squadron two Wellingtons, from which just one man survived.

Refreshed and replenished, the Pathfinder and main force crews returned to the fray with another record non-1,000 raid against Dortmund on the 23/24th. A massive number of 826 aircraft included twenty-eight Halifaxes from 6 Group and over fifty Wellingtons, among the latter fifteen from 432 Squadron undertaking its maiden operation. Although three Leasiders returned early, the remaining twelve all came home without major incident. The huge force delivered a stunning blow on this important industrial city, leaving central northern and eastern districts devastated by accurate bombing, and two thousand buildings, mostly houses, in ruins. Industrial premises also took a pounding, and a large steel works was put out of action. Bomber losses continued to climb, and this night saw a new record high for the campaign of thirty-eight, almost half of them Halifaxes.

419 Squadron's JB862 seemed to be ill-fated from the start, and experienced engine problems while outbound. Eventually, and before the target was reached, a combination of flak and a night fighter finished off the Halifax over Germany, and Sgt Green was killed with all but one of his crew. BB384 ran out of fuel on final approach, and crash-landed about two

miles from the airfield without injury to F/O Weedon and his crew. 408 and 426 Squadrons were the other 6 Group units to post missing one crew each. Although still a 4 Group unit, 431 Squadron had been operating in concert with its 6 Group Wellington cousins, and would be posted over to the Canadian Group in mid July.

It is worth relating the experiences of one of its crews on this night. HE198 was coned twice by searchlights, and F/L Hall put the Wellington into a steep dive on each occasion in a vain attempt to escape. It required the assistance of Sgt Sloan, the bomb-aimer, to pull out of the second dive, and sometime during the incident the aircraft sustained a flak hit. In the belief that a fire had broken out the pilot gave the order to bale out, although some members of the crew failed to hear it. F/L Hall and the rear gunner departed, and it was only then that Sgt Sloan discovered he and two others were alone. He took over the controls, and with the assistance of his crew mates returned to England to pull off a perfect landing at Cranwell. He was awarded the coveted CGM, and the wireless operator and navigator the DFC and DFM respectively. The two latter joined the crew of W/C Coverdale, while Sgt Sloan took a pilot's course, and returned to operations with 158 Squadron in January 1945, ultimately to survive the war.

Over seven hundred aircraft attacked Düsseldorf on the night of the 25/26th, and failed to find the mark in a major operation for the first time during the month. Two layers of cloud prevented the Pathfinders from identifying the aiming point, and decoy markers and fire sites may have attracted a large number of bomb loads. The result was a widely scattered raid, which destroyed no more than a hundred buildings, and the death toll among the crews far exceeded that on the ground. 408 Squadron contributed all nine of the 6 Group Halifaxes on duty, and they returned home safely, but 426 and 428 Squadrons each lost a Wellington.

The fifth raid of the campaign on Essen took place on the 27/28th, and involved a little over five hundred aircraft. 6 Group put up twenty-three Halifaxes and a contingent from the four Wellington units. The target was cloud-covered, and the use of sky-marking led to scattered bombing across central and northern districts. Almost five hundred buildings were never the less destroyed for the loss of twenty-three aircraft. 408 Squadron again lost an aircraft, while 428 Squadron lost two, one of them to a ditching on return from which all but the rear gunner were rescued.

The final operation of the month was mounted on the 29/30th against the town of Barmen, which, with its twin Elberfeld, forms Wuppertal on the southern side of the Ruhr Valley. On the order of battle for the first time as a Halifax unit was 427 Squadron, and this enabled 6 Group to put up thirty-eight Halifaxes along with a contribution from each of the Wellington units. Over seven hundred aircraft set off on that Saturday night either side of 23.00 hours, and delivered one of the two most devastating attacks of the entire offensive. Concentration was always the key to success, and both the Pathfinder marking and main force bombing satisfied this criterion. The narrow streets in the old centre soon became engulfed in a fire, which ran out of control, and would ultimately account for 80% of the town's built-up area. Fire and blast destroyed four thousand houses, five of the six largest factories and scores of other industrial premises. Almost nineteen hundred other buildings, mostly houses, were left seriously damaged, and the death toll was eventually set at 3,400 people. Some of the shocked and homeless residents of Barmen might have been cheered by the news, that thirty-three aircraft carrying around 250 of their tormentors would not be returning to England that night, but it would have been scant consolation.

427 Squadron had two early returns and two other aircraft come back with minor flak damage, but there were no casualties or absentees. Four other 6 Group squadrons were not so fortunate, however, and lost a total of seven aircraft. 419 Squadron's JB793 was on the way home when it succumbed to a night fighter over Belgium, and three men escaped with their lives from the crew of Sgt Winegarden. JB805 met a similar fate, also over Belgium, and the crew of Sgt Johnson all died in its wreckage. Two 428 Squadron Wellingtons were among the missing, but it was later learned that one crew had survived intact to fall into enemy hands. 432 Squadron had one Wellington fail to return, and another struck high ground near Richmond on the way home killing the pilot and his 'second Dickey'. The other 6 Group casualty was a 429 Squadron Wellington, which was lost without trace.

On the 31st 2 Group carried out its final operations as part of Bomber Command. Since the outbreak of war it had carried the fight to the enemy predominantly by daylight, and in generally outdated and outclassed aircraft. Only with the advent of the Boston, Mitchell and, most crucially, the Mosquito, had its crews been blessed with equipment up to the task. The raw 'courage by daylight' displayed by its crews in the finest traditions of the Service, particularly during 1940 and 1941, remains unsurpassed. 2 Group no longer fitted comfortably into an organisation committed to transporting the maximum tonnage of bombs to Germany by night, and on the 1st of June it became the nucleus of the 2nd Tactical Air Force, with which its outstanding tradition would continue. W/C Owen concluded his tour as commanding officer of 429 Squadron at the end of May, and was replaced by W/C Savard, who was posted in on promotion from 425 Squadron on the 1st of June. This was the same day on which 428 Squadron moved to Middleton St George, which it would share with 419 Squadron for the remainder of the war, and prepared to take on Halifaxes. That night 428 and 432 Squadrons laid mines in the waters around the island of Texel, and 426 and 429 Squadrons followed suit two nights later, before, like the Command's other heavy units, settling down to enjoy nine nights away from the action.

At around 23.00 hours on the 11th of June over 780 aircraft set off for Düsseldorf, while seventy-two 8 Group crews took part in a massed H2s trial at Münster. An errant Oboe marker fourteen miles from the main target inevitably caused some bomb loads to be wasted in open country, but the bulk of the effort fell into the city's central districts, where around forty square kilometres were severely affected by fire. Over fourteen hundred separate large fires were recorded, dozens of factories suffered a complete or partial loss of production, and eight ships were either sunk or damaged in the inland port. In human terms almost thirteen hundred people lost their lives, while a further 140,000 were bombed out of their homes. The death toll among the bomber crews was also high, as the losses equalled the campaign's highest to date of thirty-eight. 6 Group put up a record fifty-one Halifaxes along with a contingent of Wellingtons, and seven Canucks failed to return. 429 Squadron was the hardest-hit, losing three Wellingtons to night fighters, and the soon-to-be 6 Group 431 Squadron also lost two. A 428 Squadron Wellington crashed on take-off killing all but the pilot, Sgt Lachman, who had been the pilot involved in the earlier-mentioned ditching on return from Essen two weeks before. This proved to be 428 Squadron's final Wellington operation as it was already in the process of converting to the Halifax. 427 Squadron's DK192 was hit by flak and landed at Oulton, where it was nudged by a 431 Squadron Wellington and damaged, but later repaired. None of the crew of F/O Colquhoun was injured in the incident.

On the following night Oboe enabled the centre of a cloud-covered Bochum to be accurately bombed, and this resulted in an estimated 130 acres of destruction. 6 Group supplied thirty-eight Halifaxes in an overall force of five hundred aircraft, the crews of twenty-four of which paid the price for this success. Each of the Group's Halifax units posted missing one crew, and it would later emerge that a total of fifteen men had survived and were PoWs. 427 Squadron's DK183 contained the crew of P/O Fellner, and had lost its starboard-inner engine during the outward flight. Although Bochum was visible in the distance, control problems made it necessary to bomb an alternative target and turn for home. The bombs were dropped on a built-up area, and as the Halifax headed westwards it began to lose height. Shortly afterwards, at 02.13 hours local time, as it was crossing the Dutch coast, it was attacked by a night fighter flown by Major Leuchs from Leeuwarden, the night fighter airfield in Holland known by the *Luftwaffe* as *Wespennest*, or Wasp's Nest. The Halifax caught fire, and the ailerons stopped responding to the pilot's commands. The navigator believed they were still over land, and on hearing this, the mid-upper gunner decided to bale out. Sadly, the navigator was in error, and he drowned. As the rear gunner was trapped in his turret, the pilot opted for a crash-landing on Texel, and ordered the remainder of the crew to their crash positions. The aircraft slid on its belly for a few hundred metres, eventually ending up in a cornfield. The forward section of the aircraft, including the cockpit, broke away from the main fuselage, and the wireless operator was killed. The navigator was seriously injured and died shortly afterwards. The rear gunner managed to extricate himself from his turret, but was unable to walk, and he was attended to by the flight engineer, Sgt Imms, the only Englishman in the crew, and the bomb-aimer. At around 04.00 hours local time German soldiers arrived on the scene, and those airmen able to stand did so with their hands up. Inexplicably, one of the first soldiers to arrive shot Sgt Imms in the abdomen from close range. Imms did not die immediately, but knew he had received a fatal wound, and was at a loss to understand why he had been shot. All of the injured were taken to hospital in Amsterdam, and before he passed away, Imms asked the rear gunner to visit his parents when he got home after the war. The pilot sustained severe head and leg injuries, and he, the bomb-aimer and the rear gunner spent the rest of the war in captivity. An all-Lancaster heavy force pounded Oberhausen on the 14/15th at a cost of seventeen of their number, and this amounted to a hefty 8.4% of those dispatched.

In between the last two described operations 434 (Bluenose) Squadron was formed in 6 Group. Its first home was at Tholthorpe, where it became the first Canadian squadron to form on four-engine heavy bombers, the Halifax, the others having been equipped initially with Wellingtons. The name Bluenose derived from the nickname given by Canadians to Nova Scotians, and the Rotary Club of Halifax adopted the squadron. W/C Harris was installed as commanding officer on the 15th of June. He was a Canadian with a fine record of service behind him, and had commanded 88 Squadron in 2 Group from November 1941 to June 1942. There he had overseen the introduction of the Boston as a replacement for the Blenheim.

427 Squadron would have six nights off after Bochum, and during this period, on the 16th, DK140 crashed on landing in the hands of F/S Johnson and his crew during training, but although the Halifax was a write-off, the crew emerged unscathed. 1, 5 and 8 Groups delivered a moderately useful attack on Cologne that night. On the 18th 426 Squadron completed its move out of Dishforth and took up residence at Linton-on-Ouse, where it became the first Canadian unit to receive the Lancaster, not the Merlin-powered Mk I and III, but the Hercules-powered Mk II, of which around two hundred were built. 408 Squadron also arrived on the station and would become the second RCAF unit to take on the Lancaster. Working up to operational readiness would occupy the next two months, while around them the bomber offensive against the Ruhr continued. It was the turn of the Lancasters to stay at home on the 19/20th while Halifaxes and Stirlings of 3, 4, 6 and 8 Groups attempted the precision bombing of the Schneider armaments works at Le Creusot in France. This had been the scene of an epic daylight raid by 5 Group in the previous October, when only moderate success had been achieved against the factory buildings.

A second target, the nearby transformer station at Montchanin, had been targeted then by a small formation led by W/C Guy Gibson, who was commanding 106 Squadron at the time, but it escaped virtually intact. In 1943 main force crews were not used to bombing small targets, however, and found great difficulty in identifying their aiming points. The result was that only 20% of the bombs hit the factory at Le Creusot, while the crews of the second force misidentified the transformer station, and it again remained intact. 6 Group's contribution was forty-two Halifaxes from its four operators of the type as 428 Squadron had now returned to the fray. 427 Squadron's W/C Burnside's Halifax was hit by flak, and the mid-upper gunner was slightly wounded, but they returned safely. The Group's only failure to return was from 408 Squadron.

A hectic round of four operations in five nights began at Krefeld on the 21/22nd, when over seven hundred aircraft were dispatched, including forty-four Halifaxes from 6 Group along with a contingent of Wellingtons. The Pathfinder marking was flawless, and most of the 619 main force crews delivered a total of 2,300 tons of bombs with great accuracy and concentration within three miles of the aiming point. The central districts became a raging inferno, which consumed 47% of the city's built-up area, and more than five and a half thousand houses were destroyed. A thousand people were killed on the ground, but the attackers also suffered heavy losses at the hands of night fighters, which found their prey easily in the moonlight. Forty-four aircraft were shot down, a new record for the campaign, and six of them were from 35 Squadron, one of only two Pathfinder units equipped with Halifaxes. Two 6 Group squadrons experienced a particularly torrid time, 408 losing three Halifaxes and 429 four Wellingtons. 428 Squadron sustained its first Halifax casualties in an aircraft borrowed from 419 Squadron, and 431 Squadron lost its commanding officer, W/C Coverdale.

427 Squadron came through without major incident, and prepared for the following night's effort, which saw 557 aircraft set off for Mülheim. It developed into another outstandingly accurate attack, which left devastation in central and northern districts, and in the eastern districts of the neighbouring town of Oberhausen. Over eleven hundred houses were destroyed, a further twelve thousand were damaged to some extent, and scores of industrial and public buildings were also hit, disrupting war production and city administration. A total of 64% of Mülheim's built-up area was estimated as destroyed, but the Command again paid a heavy price for its success, the losses amounting on this night to thirty-five. Just twenty-five 6 Group Halifaxes took part from 408, 419 and 427 Squadrons, as 428 Squadron sent a handful to lay mines off the Frisians in company with a few from 419 Squadron. It turned into a massively bad night for 427 Squadron after four of its aircraft failed to return. DK139 crashed near Duisburg without survivors from the crew of P/O Cadmus, and DK191 went down over Holland with the crew of F/O Reid, again with total loss

of life. DK141 and DK225 fell to night fighters also over Holland, and in each case just one man survived from the crews of Sgt Hamilton and F/L Webster respectively. It was a sombre occasion also for 429 Squadron after two more of its Wellingtons failed to return. HZ312 was carrying W/C Savard and his crew, and all perished, although the circumstances are unclear. The squadron sent four aircraft on a sea search later on the 23rd, but nothing was sighted.

Two nights after Mülheim and a month after the destruction of Wuppertal's Barmen, over six hundred aircraft turned their attention upon its twin, Elberfeld. Among them were thirty-seven Halifaxes from 6 Group and a contingent of Wellingtons. Despite a modest creep-back the majority of the main force crews exploited the accurate Pathfinder marking, and their bombs destroyed three thousand houses and 171 industrial premises. Thousands of other buildings were severely damaged, and the death toll reached eighteen hundred people. When the smoke had cleared, photo-graphic reconnaissance revealed that at least 90% of the town had been reduced to rubble. On the debit side the Command lost another thirty-four aircraft and crews, and 427 Squadron was again represented. DK135 crashed in Holland, killing F/O Somers and four of his crew, while the two survivors joined their two colleagues from the previous night's disaster as guests of the *Reich*. 419 Squadron posted missing two crews including that of a flight commander, and 428 Squadron lost another crew in a Halifax borrowed from 419 Squadron. Of three Wellingtons failing to make it home two belonged to 432 Squadron. The Command's run of successes came to an end at the oil town of Gelsenkirchen on the 25/26th, when, in an echo of the past, bombs were sprayed liberally around the Ruhr. It had always been among the most elusive of targets, and on this occasion malfunctioning Oboe equipment contributed largely to the failure, which cost another thirty aircraft. 427 Squadron's contribution got off to an inauspicious start, when DK144 crashed during the take-off run after developing a swing, but W/C Burnside and his crew walked away. The squadron's ill luck continued through the night with the failure to return of DK180 and DK190, both of which fell victim to night fighters over Holland. P/O Gagnon and his crew all baled out of the former successfully, but the pilot landed in a canal and drowned, and the others were taken prisoner. Sadly, F/S Higgins and his crew all perished in the wreckage of the latter. There were no operations over the succeeding two nights, as Harris prepared for a three raid series against Cologne spanning the turn of the month. A force of 608 aircraft took off for the Rhineland Capital late on the 28th, and despite cloud cover over the target, the failure of Oboe equipment in five out of the twelve Mosquitos and the use of sky-marking, which was late in starting, Cologne was subjected to its most destructive assault of the war. The degree of devastation far exceeded that inflicted by the Thousand Force a year earlier, and, in fact, almost twice as many buildings were completely destroyed. The death toll of over 4,300 people was a thousand more than the previous highest, recorded at Barmen a month before. 427 Squadron's EB148 was severely damaged by a night fighter during the outward flight, and F/L Ganderton, a future Lions commanding officer, turned back immediately after jettisoning the bombs. Once over England they abandoned the Halifax to its fate, and it crashed in Cambridgeshire, while the crew landed safely with a couple of minor injuries between them. The only 6 Group failure to return was a Halifax belonging to 419 Squadron. Earlier in the day W/C Piddington had been installed as the new commanding officer of 429 Squadron, but like his predecessor, his tenure would be brief.

The Group dispatched a few Halifax and Wellington 'gardening' sorties on the night of the 2/3rd of July, and then prepared for the second Cologne raid, which involved 650 aircraft on the following night. This attack was aimed at that part of the city situated on the east bank of the Rhine, and it was again stunningly successful, reducing a further 2,200 houses to ruins, along with twenty industrial premises. Thirty aircraft were lost, to add to the twenty-five missing from the earlier raid, but this time 427 Squadron was not represented among them. 408 Squadron lost two Halifaxes and 419 Squadron one, while 432 Squadron had two Wellingtons fail to return and two others crash at home through lack of fuel and poor weather conditions. 429 Squadron was also represented among the missing after LN296 was shot down by a night fighter over Belgium, and F/L Brinton was killed with his crew. The series against Cologne concluded at the hands of an all-Lancaster force, and therefore without a 6 Group contribution, on the 8/9th, again with great success, and this attack reduced over 2,300 houses and nineteen industrial premises to rubble. Later, when the city authorities were able to assess the results of these three raids, they documented more than 11,000 buildings destroyed, 5,500 people killed, and 350,000 others bombed out of their homes. The mini campaign had cost the Command sixty-two aircraft and crews, at an average of almost twenty-one per operation, which, in the light of recent experiences, was relatively modest.

Another disappointing operation was played out at Gelsenkirchen on the 9/10th July, for which 6 Group put up forty-one Halifaxes. Faulty instruments caused a 408 Squadron aircraft to crash on take-off without injury to the crew, and two others failed to return. 428 Squadron also registered a missing Halifax, and that was the one captained by flight commander S/L Bowden. Although two more operations to the region would take place in the final week of the month, this effectively brought the Ruhr offensive to an end. Harris could look back upon the past five months with a genuine sense of achievement, and take particular satisfaction from the performance of Oboe. Much of Germany's industrial heartland now lay in ruins, and it must have been clear to the civilian population that this was only the start. There was so much slack in the German industrial capacity, however, that production could still increase dramatically over the next twelve months. That apart, the disruption had been massive, and would be further exacerbated by the dispersal of industry to safer regions of the *Reich*. Losses to the Command of aircraft and crews had been grievously high, but the factories and flying training schools were more than keeping pace with the rate of attrition, and even allowed for an expansion in many squadrons by the addition of a third flight. Buoyed up by his success, Harris sought an opportunity to deliver a knockout blow against one of Germany's premier cities, to send shock waves to rock the foundations of Nazi morale. Having been spared by the weather from hosting the first thousand-bomber raid at Cologne's expense, Hamburg now presented itself as the ideal objective for the aptly named Operation *Gomorrah*.

In the meantime, an all-Lancaster force raided Turin on the 12/13th of July, and then Halifaxes, Wellingtons and Stirlings formed the main force for an attack on Aachen on the following night. Both were highly successful operations, the latter particularly so, resulting as it did in the destruction of almost three thousand buildings. 6 Group contributed forty-eight Halifaxes and twenty-one Wellingtons, and 428 Squadron was the hardest-hit with three of the former failing to return. The only positive note was the survival of twelve crew members, a number of whom managed to evade capture. 427 Squadron's DK142 did not make it back to Leeming, and news eventually filtered through, that Sgt Sobkowicz and his crew were in enemy hands. 408, 419 and 432 Squadrons were the other 6 Group units to post missing a crew. On the 15/16th of July an all-Halifax force was sent to Montbeliard in south-eastern France to attack the Peugeot motor works. Sadly, the target indicators were not accurately placed, and most of the bombs fell into the town of Sochaux, of which Montbeliard was a suburb. This was an ever-present danger, despite a relatively low bombing altitude, and in the pre-invasion campaign from March to June 1944 such 'friendly fire' incidents would be frequently re-enacted. 6 Group was excluded from this operation and remained on the ground. Earlier on the day of the 15th 431 Squadron arrived at Tholthorpe having been posted in from 4 Group as 6 Group's latest recruit. It had been formed on the 11th of November 1942 as the eleventh Canadian unit in Bomber Command, and took up residence at Burn, where W/C Coverdale was installed as commanding officer on the 1st of December. The squadron was equipped with Wellington Mk Xs, but it would be a full three months before the Iroquois took them into battle for the first time. Their maiden operation was launched on the night of the 2/3rd of March 1943, when a handful of Wellingtons were dispatched to join forces with others of the type from 6 Group to mine the waters around the Frisians. From then on it became standard practice to operate in concert with 6 Group. W/C Coverdale remained at the helm until failing to return from Krefeld on the night of the 21/22nd of June. W/C Bill Newson was installed as the new commanding officer four days later, having previously served as a flight commander with 408 Squadron, and he saw the squadron through its final operations on the trusty Wellington and the transfer to 6 Group. Now he would oversee the squadron's conversion to the Halifax, which would not be complete until October.

There now followed a lull in main force operations as preparations continued for the forthcoming assault on Hamburg. Many factors had to be considered when mounting a series of operations, not least of which was the reason behind it. The morale of Germany's civilian population had been a documented War Cabinet priority since July 1941. To achieve maximum effect throughout the *Reich*, rather than simply locally, the objective required political status beyond the norm. Berlin, as the Capital, clearly satisfied that requirement, but Harris was not quite ready to take on such a massive undertaking at this juncture. As Germany's Second City, Hamburg was next in line, particularly as Cologne, its third great city, had only recently been devastated. There were, however, other considerations of a more operational nature, which pointed to Hamburg as the ideal choice. Firstly, it was a major industrial city, and was particularly important to Germany for its ship and U-Boat construction. Secondly, it could be approached from the sea without the need for the bomber stream to traverse great tracts of hostile territory. It was also close enough to the bomber stations to allow a large force to get in and out in the few hours of darkness afforded by mid summer. Thirdly, situated as it was beyond the range of Oboe, which had proved so decisive at the Ruhr, it boasted the wide River Elbe through its centre to provide a strong H2s signature for the navigators high above. The final week of July had become the traditional time to attack Hamburg, and so it was now, and as the crews prepared for the first operation on the afternoon of the 24th, a new device was being loaded into their aircraft. Window had actually been devised a year earlier, but its use had been vetoed in case the enemy copied it for use against Britain. Ironically, the German scientists had already developed their own version known as Düppel, which had also been withheld for the same reason. It consisted of aluminium-backed strips of paper packed in bundles, which, when released into the air stream, floated slowly to earth in giant clouds. This swamped the enemy radar system with false returns, making it impossible for night fighter, searchlight and flak crews to identify and lock on to a genuine target. Windowing would begin at a predetermined point over the North Sea on the way in, and continue throughout the raid until a second point was reached on the way out.

A force of 791 aircraft stood ready for take-off in the late evening of the 24th, among them forty-seven Halifaxes and twenty-one Wellingtons from 6 Group. The outward flight was relatively uneventful as the bombers made little or no contact with enemy night fighters. A number of aircraft were shot down during this stage of the operation, but each was off course, and outside of the protection of the bomber stream. The efficacy of Window was immediately apparent to the crews on their arrival in the Hamburg defence zone, where the usually efficient co-ordination between the search-lights and flak batteries was absent. The defence was accordingly random and sporadic, thus giving the Pathfinder crews a rare, almost unhindered run at the aiming point. The markers were a little scattered, but most fell close enough to the city centre to provide a strong reference point for the main force crews, and over the next fifty minutes, almost 2,300 tons of bombs were delivered. The bombing began near the aiming point, but a pronounced creep-back developed, which cut a swathe of destruction from the city centre along the line of approach across the north-western districts, and out into open country, where a proportion of the effort was wasted. Never the less, it was a highly destructive attack, in which fifteen hundred people lost their lives, and this was the highest death toll at a target beyond the range of Oboe. An added bonus for the Command was the loss of a very modest twelve aircraft, for which much of the credit belonged to Window, and 6 Group came through unscathed. At a stroke the device had rendered the entire enemy defensive system impotent for the time being. An advan-tage was rarely held for long, though, before a counter-measure was found, and this would eventually see the balance swing back in the enemy's favour. Harris decided to switch his attention to Essen on the following night to take advantage of the body blow dealt to the enemy's defences by Window. Forty-seven Halifaxes and seventeen Wellingtons from 6 Group completed a force of seven hundred aircraft, and the result was another highly accu-rate and concentrated assault on this city. The Krupp complex sustained its heaviest damage of the war, and over 2,800 houses and apartment blocks were destroyed. 419 and 429 Squadrons each posted missing one crew, while 432 Squadron's S/L Sinton ditched his Wellington off Cromer, from where he and his crew were picked up safely.

After a night's rest 787 aircraft took off to return to Hamburg for round two of Operation *Gomorrah*. 6 Group managed to put up a record sixty Halifaxes along with eighteen Wellingtons, and what followed their arrival over the city was unprecedented, unforeseeable and the result of a lethal combination of circumstances. A period of unusually hot and dry weather had left tinderbox conditions in parts of the city, and the initial spark to ignite the situation came with the Pathfinder markers. These fell two miles to the east of the planned city centre aiming point, but with unaccustomed concentration into the densely populated working class residential districts of Hamm, Hammerbrook and Borgfeld. The main force crews followed up with uncharacteristic accuracy and scarcely any creep-back, and delivered most of their 2,300 tons of bombs into this relatively compact area. The individual fires joined together to form one giant conflagration, which sucked in oxygen from surrounding areas at hurricane velocity to feed its voracious appetite. Such was the ferocity of this meteorological phenomenon, that trees were uprooted and flung bodily into the flames, along with debris and people, and the temperatures at its seat exceeded one thousand degrees Celsius. The inferno only began to subside once all the combustible material had been consumed, and by this time, there was no one left within the firestorm area to rescue. It would actually be weeks before many of the burned-out buildings had cooled sufficiently to allow access to basements, where some of the more gruesome finds would be made, and an accurate assessment of casualties could begin. At least forty thousand people died on this one night alone, and on the following morning the first of an eventual 1.2 million inhabitants began to file out of the tortured city. Among the seventeen missing aircraft was JA114 from 429 Squadron, in which W/C Piddington was undertaking his third sortie since assuming command of the Bisons a month earlier. The Wellington fell victim to a night fighter over Germany during the outward flight, and W/C Piddington and two of his crew lost their lives, while two others were taken into captivity. This would prove to be the squadron's final loss of a Wellington. 408 Squadron also posted missing the eight man crew of F/L Stovel.

Another night's rest preceded the third Hamburg raid, for which a force of 777 aircraft took off, including fifty-nine Halifaxes and twenty-three Wellingtons from 6 Group. Early returns had reduced the numbers to 707 by the time the target was reached, but these carried another 2,300 tons of bombs to deliver onto the city centre. The Pathfinders were again two miles east of the aiming point with their markers, which fell a little to the south of the firestorm area. The main force approached the markers on a north-south heading, and a creep-back developed as some crews bombed the first markers or fires they encountered. This took the bombing across the firestorm devastation of two nights earlier, before it fell onto other residential districts beyond, where a new area of fire was created, although of lesser proportions. The city's fire service was already exhausted, while access to the freshly afflicted districts was denied by rubble-strewn and cratered streets, and there was little to be done other than to allow the fires to burn themselves out. The defences were beginning to recover from the shock of Window, however, and as they did so the bomber losses began to rise. Twenty-eight aircraft failed to return on this night, and for the second operation in a row 6 Group had to post missing one of its commanding officers. 432 Squadron's LN294 was shot down by a night fighter over Germany, as the result of which W/C Kerby died with three of his crew, while the sole survivor fell into enemy hands. The other 6 Group casualty was a 428 Squadron Halifax, which fell to a night fighter killing seven of the eight occupants. Later on the 30th of July S/L McKay was promoted and appointed as the new commanding officer of 432 Squadron. W/C Patterson became the new commanding officer of 429 Squadron also on the 30th, having previously served as a flight commander with 419 Squadron. That night a relatively modest force of under three hundred

Halifaxes, Stirlings and Lancasters, in roughly equal numbers, devastated the previously unbombed Ruhr town of Remscheid, destroying over three thousand houses, laying waste to 83% of its built-up area and killing eleven hundred inhabitants. Of the thirty-three 6 Group Halifaxes committed to the operation two failed to return, one from 408 Squadron and EB242 from 427 Squadron, in which, it was later learned, F/S Westerberg was the sole fatality, and his crew were now in enemy hands. It was this operation that brought down the final curtain on the Ruhr offensive.

Operation *Gomorrah* was concluded on the night of the 2/3rd of August, when 740 aircraft, including fifty-four Halifaxes and nineteen Wellingtons from 6 Group, departed their stations and headed into violent electrical storms on the route to northern Germany. This persuaded many crews, among them ten from 427 Squadron, to abandon their sorties, and either jettison their bombs over the sea or drop them on alternative targets. Some crews pressed on to Hamburg, but the bombing was scattered in the absence of target indicators, and little further damage was inflicted upon the city. Four 6 Group aircraft failed to return, two from 428 Squadron containing eight-man crews, none of whom survived, a 419 Squadron Halifax and a 432 Squadron Wellington, the last-mentioned also involving total loss of life. This proved to be 408 Squadron's final outing on Halifaxes before its conversion to Lancaster IIs. 427 Squadron took part in all four of the Hamburg raids suffering no losses from fifty-five sorties, and also negotiated that against Essen without major incident. Its only other loss during this period came on the 29th of July, when DK242 crash-landed at Leeming at the end of a training flight in the hands of Sgt Welch and crew, who walked away unhurt. As far as 6 Group as a whole was concerned, it committed 225 Halifaxes and eighty-seven Wellingtons to Operation *Gomorrah*, of which 250 bombed the target. For its efforts the Group registered five missing Halifaxes and three Wellingtons, and a casualty figure of forty-three dead and eleven in captivity. On the night of the 3/4th of August 429 Squadron carried out its final Wellington operation, when mining the sea lanes around St Nazaire and Lorient. Thereafter the Bisons were stood down pending a move to Leeming, where the squadron would convert to Halifaxes.

There were no further operations during the first week of August, but something of future significance for Canadian squadrons took place in their homeland on the 6th. This was the day selected for the naming ceremony of the very first Canadian-built Lancaster, KB700. The occasion was turned into a massive media event with live coverage on the radio, and a commentary provided by the actor Lorne Greene. The minister for munitions and supply declared the Lancaster the 'greatest weapon of destruction that Canada had produced during the war.' The name, *Ruhr Express*, was bestowed upon the aircraft by Mrs C G Power, wife of the minister for National Defence for Air, and the impression was given by the general hype, that it would immediately take off for England and war against tyranny. *Ruhr Express* did, indeed, take off, with S/L Reg Lane at the controls, he having returned to Canada at the completion of his second tour of operations and term as flight commander with 35 Squadron. Far from flying to England, however, KB700 was barely able to fly anywhere. She was short of vital instruments and equipment, but in a country seeking to demonstrate its industrial prowess, and in view of the publicity, a postponement of the show was unthinkable. Lane flew the Lancaster to Dorval, Quebec, where the outfitting was completed, and he would indeed, in time, fly KB700 to England.

The second week of August began with the first of a series of raids on the major cities of Italy, which was now teetering on the brink of capitulation. Bomber Command's involvement was designed to help nudge it over, and elements of 1, 5 and 8 Groups began the process on the night of the 7/8th with attacks on Genoa, Milan and Turin. On the 9/10th over 450 crews took off for a raid on Mannheim on the east bank of the Rhine in southern Germany. 6 Group put up thirty-nine Halifaxes from 419, 427 and 428 Squadrons, and they exploited a solid marking effort to contribute to a highly effective attack, which destroyed thirteen hundred buildings, and caused loss of production at forty-two factories for the modest loss of nine aircraft. Three 427 Squadron crews returned early, and then EB257 was attacked by FW190s, one of which the crew of F/S Biggs claimed as destroyed. The Halifax's starboard wing caught fire, and the flight engineer cut a hole in the fuselage to successfully attack the flames with fire extinguishers. The elevators had also been damaged, and the control yoke had to be lashed in a forward position to enable the aircraft to maintain an even keel. Once over Hampshire the eight-man crew took to their parachutes and all landed safely. The only 6 Group failure to return was a 419 Squadron aircraft from which there were no survivors. Twenty-four hours later it was the turn of Nuremberg to suffer its most effective raid to date at the hands of around six hundred aircraft including forty-one 6 Group Halifaxes, all of which returned home. Considerable damage resulted in central and southern districts, where preserved medieval houses were destroyed, and a large area of fire developed.

The Italian campaign continued on the 12/13th, when 1, 4, 5 and 6 Groups provided the main force at Milan, while 3 Group did likewise at Turin, and returning crews claimed heavy and concentrated attacks. 434 Squadron launched its operational career on this night, and all of its aircraft returned, although four landed away from base because of a shortage of fuel. 427 Squadron also had five of its crews land away for the same reason, while F/S Countess pushed on to North Africa and returned later. 6 Group did lose one aircraft on this night, a 432 Squadron Wellington sent mining off Brest. 429 Squadron completed its move to Leeming on the 13th, where it would share the facilities with 427 Squadron.

It was around this time that the first Mk II Lancaster arrived at Leeming for 408 Squadron's conversion from the Halifax, something that would be appreciated by the crews, who had not been overly happy with the former equipment. Milan was hit again on the 14/15th and 15/16th, and the campaign concluded at Turin on the 16/17th. This was a 3 and 8 Group show, but despite the enthusiastic claims at debriefing it was an inconclusive raid. The weather on return forced many 3 Group crews to divert to other airfields, and a goodly number would not regain their stations until quite late on the 17th, too late to take part in one of the most important operations of the war that night.

Since the start of hostilities, intelligence had been filtering through concerning German research into rocket weapons. Through the interception and decoding of signals traffic the centre for such activity was found to be at Peenemünde, an isolated location on the island of Usedom on Germany's Baltic coast. Regular reconnaissance flights helped to build up a picture of the activity there, and through listening in on signals, the brilliant scientist Dr R V Jones was able to monitor the V-1 trials being conducted over the Baltic, and gather much useful information on the weapon's range and accuracy. Churchill's chief scientific adviser, Professor Lindemann, or Lord Cherwell as he became, steadfastly refused to give credence to rockets as weapons, and even when confronted with a photograph of a V-2 on a trailer at Peenemünde, taken by a PRU Mosquito as recently as June, he stubbornly remained unmoved. It required the urgings of Dr Jones and Duncan Sandys to persuade Churchill of the need to act, and it was finally agreed that an operation should be mounted at the first available opportunity. This arose on the night of the 17/18th of August, for which a detailed plan was meticulously prepared.

The Peenemünde research and development establishment consisted of three main areas, the housing complex where the scientists and workers lived, the assembly buildings, and the experimental site. Because of this the operation was to take place in three waves, each wave assigned to a specific aiming point, beginning with the housing estate, and the Pathfinders were charged with the heavy responsibility of shifting the point of aim accordingly. 3 and 4 Groups were to go in first, followed by 1 Group, while 5 and 6 Groups would bring up the rear at the experimental site. The entire operation was to be controlled by VHF by a Master of Ceremonies, or Master Bomber, in the manner pioneered by Gibson at the Dams, and the officer selected was G/C Searby of 83 Squadron, who had been Gibson's successor as commanding officer of 106 Squadron. Two deputy Master Bombers were appointed to assist Searby, and to take over if he was lost or forced to return early. W/C Fauquier was the first deputy, and he would be flying 405 Squadron's first Lancaster sortie. W/C John White, a highly experience Pathfinder and flight commander with 156 Squadron, was the second deputy, sadly, a man with only three months to live. All three

Master Bombers and their crews would be required to remain in the target area throughout the raid within range of the defences, directing the marking and bombing, and exhorting the crews to press home their attacks. G/C Leonard Slee, commanding officer of 139 Squadron and formerly of 5 Group's 49 Squadron, was to lead a spoof raid on Berlin with eight Mosquitos an hour before zero hour at Peenemünde. The intention was to draw off the enemy night fighters, and provide the heavy crews with a clear run at the target, where the bombing would be conducted from medium to low level.

A total of 597 aircraft answered the call for a maximum effort, the numbers somewhat depleted by the unavailability, as already mentioned, of a proportion of the Stirling brigade. At Linton-on-Ouse 426 Squadron's crews prepared for their operational debut on Lancasters, and nine of the type stood bombed up and fuelled, one of them awaiting W/C Crooks and his crew. The Group's main contribution was fifty-four Halifaxes provided by 419, 427, 428 and 434 Squadrons. Most aircraft got away between 21.00 and 22.00 hours, and set course in clear conditions for southern Denmark. The initial marking of the housing estate went awry, when the first markers fell onto the forced workers' camp at Trassenheide, more than a mile beyond the intended aiming point. This inevitably attracted a proportion of the 3 and 4 Group element, and about a third of them delivered their bombs here, inflicting heavy casualties upon the friendly foreign nationals trapped inside their wooden barracks. W/C White, the second deputy Master Bomber, used his reserve markers at this stage to help pull the bombing back on track. Once rectified, this phase of the operation proceeded according to plan, and a number of important members of the establishment's technical staff were killed. The 1 Group attack on the assembly sheds was hampered by a strong crosswind, and such was the layout of the establishment, that bombs either found the mark, or fell harlessly among dunes or into the sea. Ultimately, this area too sustained severe damage, leaving just the experimental site for 5 and 6 Groups. It was at this point, that the night fighters arrived belatedly from Berlin, and proceeded to take a heavy toll of aircraft both in the skies over Peenemünde, and on the route home towards Denmark. The 5 Group crews were authorised to adopt their 'time and distance' method of bombing if the target became obscured by smoke, and some did so, although this was perhaps the least effective part of the operation. W/C White had used his target indicators at a critical time during the operation, but W/C Fauquier retained his, and delivered his bombs in the final minute of the raid. During his time in the target area he made seventeen passes, and exhorted the crews to press home their attacks. Forty aircraft failed to return home, and twenty-nine of these were 5 and 6 Group aircraft from the final wave. 427 Squadron dispatched twelve Halifaxes, eleven of which bombed the target. DK227 was attacked four times by a BF109, which Sgt Schmitt's gunner shot down on what proved to be its final pass. The Halifax sustained damage to its port rudder and wing, but crash-landed safely at Mildenhall with no crew casualties. Less fortunate were Sgt Brady and four of his crew, who were killed when DK243 was brought down over Germany, and the two survivors became PoWs. 426 Squadron's DS681 was brought down, presumably by a night fighter, as it tracked west-wards with the Baltic coastline in sight on the starboard flank. W/C Crooks died with five of his crew, and only the bomb-aimer was able to escape with his life to become a PoW. DS674 was lost without trace with the crew of F/L Shuttleworth, and presumably lies on the sea bed somewhere near the north German coast. 419, 428 and 434 Squadrons each posted missing three crews in what became a tragic night for the Canucks. 419 Squadron's JD163 provided a fix that put it just thirty minutes from base, but it never arrived and was lost without trace. In total 6 Group registered sixty-six men killed and nineteen survivors as PoWs. The operation was sufficiently successful to set back the development programme of the V-2 by a number of weeks, and the testing was ultimately moved eastwards into Poland.

The vulnerability of Peenemünde to air attack caused a major rethink by the German authorities, and it was decided to move the production of secret weapons underground. Almost immediately, construction of an underground factory began at Nordhausen, and once completed, it would be manned by forced workers. W/C Bill Swetman was appointed as the new commanding officer of 426 Squadron later on the 18th. He had recently joined the Thunderbirds to begin his second tour as a flight commander. Unlike his predecessor, who was an Englishman from Peterborough, Swetman was Canadian, and had begun his operational career as a Sergeant pilot flying Wellingtons with 405 Squadron in 1941.

Harris had long believed that Berlin, as the seat and symbol of Nazi power, held the ultimate key to victory. He maintained the belief that bombing alone could win the war, and if this could be achieved, it would remove the need for the kind of protracted and bloody land campaigns that he had personally witnessed during the Great War. At the time it was a perfectly reasonable theory, and Harris was the first commander in history in a position to put it to the test. It is only in the light of recent conflicts, that we know with absolute certainty of the necessity to physically occupy the enemy's territory, in order to gain complete submission. Before embarking on the first phase of what would be the longest and most bitterly fought campaign of the war, Harris sent 460 aircraft to Leverkusen in the Ruhr, where the IG Farben factory was the aiming point. 6 Group's contri-bution amounted to fifty-five Halifaxes and eight Mk II Lancasters. Problems with Oboe led to a scattered and ineffective raid, which afflicted many neighbouring towns. The only 6 Group casualty was a 434 Squadron Halifax, which was lost with its eight-man crew.

The campaign against Berlin began on the night of the 23/24th, and nothing before or after would come closer to breaking the Command's spirit. 6 Group contributed fifty-nine Halifaxes and eight Lancasters to the 727 aircraft taking off for the Capital in mid evening, and on arrival the Pathfinders were confronted by the usual difficulties of trying to identify the city centre from the jumble of images on their H2s screens. In the event, they marked the southern outskirts of the city, and some of the main force crews approached from the south-west instead of a more southerly direction, thereby depositing many bomb loads onto outlying communities and open country. This would be a feature of the entire campaign, but at least on this night, considerable damage was inflicted on the southern districts, where 2,600 buildings were destroyed or seriously damaged, and this represented the best result yet at the 'Big City'. On the debit side the loss of fifty-six aircraft was a new record. In a desperate measure to counter the effects of Window the *Luftwaffe* had begun to employ single-engine day fighters over the target, using the light from burning cities and searchlights to pick out the bombers. This 'Wild Boar' system would eventually be combined with a running commentary for the standard night fighters, known as 'Tame Boar', to produce a highly effective and lethal defence for the German homeland and its occupied territories. 426 Squadron's DS676 failed to return after being shot down by a night fighter over Germany, and F/L Shaw died with the other seven men on board. How the two 427 Squadron Halifaxes came to grief is uncertain, but DK184 crashed in Germany and EB243 in Holland with the crews of F/O Baum and Sgt Cornelius respectively. The flight engineer from the former was the only survivor, and he was taken prisoner. 428 and 434 Squadrons also lost one aircraft each, but the Bluenose pilot, flight commander S/L McLernon, managed to evade capture to return to England, and in time would become the commanding officer of 408 Squadron.

A four-night break from operations allowed a little respite before the next major outing for the heavy squadrons, which was to Nuremberg on the 27/28th. 6 Group put up fifty-five Halifaxes and eleven Lancasters for what turned out to be an unsuccessful operation, despite accurate early marking by the Pathfinders. A creep-back developed, which could not be corrected because of communications difficulties and problems with H2s sets among the 8 Group contingent. As a result most of the bombing hit open country, although there was a scattering across the south-eastern and eastern suburbs. Thirty-three aircraft failed to return, and once more 428 and 434 Squadrons registered a loss each. Earlier in the day 408 Squadron completed its move from Leeming into Linton-on-Ouse. 427 Squadron's Oxford communications aircraft crashed in Yorkshire during a ferry flight on the 29th, and Sgt Henry and three ground crew were killed. The twin towns of Mönchengladbach and Rheydt provided a much less distant objective for over six hundred aircraft on the 30th/31st, and it was the first heavy assault on these frontier towns. 6 Group managed to put up fifty-one Halifaxes, eleven Lancasters and fourteen Wellingtons from 432 Squadron. It required the Pathfinders to shift the aiming point from one to the other during the course of the attack, and this was done without a hitch, enabling more than 2,300 buildings to be destroyed. 427 Squadron's LK629 failed to return to Leeming having crashed in Belgium, and there were no survivors from the crew of F/S Buxton. W/C Burnside's Halifax was attacked five times by an enemy night fighter, but no damage resulted. A 432 Squadron Wellington was lost with all of its crew, and 434 Squadron's run of ill luck continued with the failure to return of another Halifax with an eight-man crew.

It was back to the Capital for a force of over six hundred aircraft twenty-four hours later, with take-off around 20.00 hours. Forty-eight Halifaxes and eleven Lancasters represented 6 Group's effort, but the presence of some cloud in the target area combined with H2s equipment failures to prevent accurate marking. This caused the target indicators to fall well to the south of the intended city centre aiming point. An extensive creep-back extending some thirty miles back along the line of approach further reduced the effectiveness of the bombing, and the result was a disappointing attack, which destroyed less than a hundred buildings, while a ferocious defence claimed forty-seven aircraft. 427 Squadron had to post missing the crew of P/O Vanderkerckhove when EB251 failed to return, and the pilot died with five of his crew, while the two survivors became PoWs. It was a bad night for 419 Squadron with three empty dispersals to contemplate next morning, while 428 Squadron posted missing two crews. Five of the eleven Lancasters waved off by 426 Squadron returned early for various reasons, and another failed to return altogether. DS677 crashed in Germany, and there were no survivors from the crew of F/O McKay.

6 Group opened its September account with mining sorties by Halifaxes, Lancasters and Wellingtons around the Frisians on the 2/3rd, for which 426 Squadron provided two aircraft, and then detailed three for the following night. This was for the operation that would conclude the current phase of the Berlin offensive. An all-Lancaster force totalling more than three hundred aircraft took off in mid evening, timed to arrive over the Capital after 23.00 hours. Four Pathfinder Mosquitos dropped spoof flares some distance from the route to attract night fighters as the force approached the city from the north-east. The Pathfinders again mostly undershot the aiming point, and the main force crews inevitably did likewise, but some of the bombing did hit residential districts and the industrial suburb of Siemensstadt, where a number of war industry factories suffered a serious loss of production. In the absence of Stirlings and Halifaxes, which generally suffered higher percentage casualties, twenty Lancasters were shot down, and this represented almost 7% of those dispatched. Apart from an inconclusive attack on one of its aircraft by a JU88, the Thunderbirds all returned without major incident. Harris called a halt to the campaign at

this point, possibly in response to the loss of 125 aircraft in just three operations.

W/C Burnside concluded his period in command of 427 Squadron on the 5th of September, but would return to the operational scene at the start of October 1944 as the commanding officer of 3 Group's 195 Squadron, remaining in post until the end of the bombing war. W/C Turnbull was installed as the new commanding officer. With Berlin off the menu there were still plenty of other industrial cities in Germany to keep the crews busy, and on the 5/6th it was the turn of Mannheim and Ludwigshafen, facing each other from the east and west banks of the Rhine respectively. Their location provided a perfect opportunity to use creep-back to good advantage, by approaching from the west, and marking the eastern half of Mannheim. 6 Group's contribution to an overall force of six hundred aircraft was forty-nine Halifaxes and six Lancasters. A highly successful attack ensued, which proceeded exactly according to plan, and resulted in massive damage in both of the target cities. A thousand houses were destroyed in Ludwigshafen alone, and the important I G Farben chemicals factory, which was engaged in synthetic oil production, was severely damaged. Bomber losses were again high, however, and reached thirty-four on this night. 427 Squadron's steady rate of attrition continued on this night with the loss of Sgt Fletcher and his crew, who all died when LK636 crashed in Germany. 419 Squadron posted missing two crews with just one survivor from among the fourteen crew members. It was sometime during the early part of the month that S/L Lane ferried KB700 to England with the assistance of a ferry pilot. Lane had volunteered for a third tour of operations, despite having already completed fifty-one sorties up to returning to Canada in July, and he would be joining 405 Squadron in October. A raid of moderate size against München on the 6/7th was rendered inconclusive by cloud, most crews having to bomb on estimated positions after a timed run from a lake south-west of the city. Thirty-eight 6 Group Halifaxes participated along with five Lancasters, of which five of the former failed to return. 427 Squadron's DK255 crashed in France with the crew of F/O Pery-Knox-Gore, who all died in the wreckage, and LK628 fell to a night fighter over Germany, killing P/O Biggs and four of his crew, while the three survivors became PoWs. 428 and 434 Squadrons each posted missing one crew, the Ghosts blessed with six survivors, but the Bluenoses none.

What became a controversial operation took place on the 8/9th of September, and 432 Squadron was the only 6 Group unit to take part. Operation *Starkey* had been devised to mislead the enemy into believing that an invasion was imminent, and it involved all of the armed services. Harris was not amused at being ordered to participate in what he described as play-acting, and when the time came, he gave it less than his full commitment. *Starkey* began in mid August with highly visible troop movements, and the assembly of glider fleets and landing craft, which any self-respecting enemy reconnaissance crew could not fail to notice. Attacks on heavy gun emplacements on the French coast were to have begun in the final week of August, but poor weather conditions continued into September, and it was not until the night of the 8/9th that operations could take place. By this time the Air Ministry had revised its demands on Harris, and in the interests of keeping civilian casualties at an acceptable level, reduced the commitment of heavy bombers. The targets for this night were two coastal batteries, code-named *Religion* and *Andante*, situated respectively north and south of the small resort town of Le Portel near Boulogne. Phase I, against the northern site, involved Oboe Mosquitos and Pathfinder Halifaxes marking for fifty-seven Stirlings and sixty-one Wellingtons from 91 and 93 Training Groups. The Phase II force was of similar size and make-up, except for twelve Wellingtons from 432 Squadron and 92 Group representing the Training Groups. Sadly, the operation was a failure, and neither battery was damaged, while Le Portel itself suffered grievously, and around five hundred of its inhabitants lost their lives.

There were no further operations for the main force crews until the night of the 15/16th of September, when 369 crews from 3, 4, 6 and 8 Groups were briefed for an attack on the Dunlop Rubber factory at Montluçon in central France. This operation signalled the return to action of 429 Squadron, this time as a Halifax unit, having completed its working-up period without any serious mishaps. Its presence enabled the Group to put up a record sixty-three Halifaxes while the Lancasters and Wellingtons stayed at home. W/C 'Dixie' Dean of 35 Squadron controlled the operation as Master Bomber, and he presided over an accurate attack, which left every building in the factory complex damaged. One of the two missing Halifaxes was LK913, which contained the crew of 428 Squadron's commanding officer, W/C Smith. They had been hit by falling incendiaries over the target, and had been forced to crash-land in France, where W/C Smith and three of his crew were captured as four others managed to evade. 427 Squadron's DK253 crashed in Middlesex on the way home, and Sgt Chibanoff and his crew all perished. The Ghosts welcomed a new commanding officer on the following day in the form of W/C Bill Suggitt, who was promoted from flight commander. On the following night a similar force tried to repeat the success at the important railway yards at Modane on the main route into Italy with a contribution from 6 Group of fifty-six Halifaxes. The location of the target in a steep valley thwarted the crews' best endeavours, however, and the operation failed. At least on this occasion there were no empty dispersals to concentrate the minds at 427 Squadron, but the Lions had lost nine crews over the past four weeks, and that represented half of its strength. 419 Squadron posted missing one crew, but later learned that all eight men had survived, four of them ultimately to evade capture. 432 Squadron began to move out of Skipton-on-Swale mid month and was fully installed at east Moor by the 19th.

A series of four operations against Hanover began on the night of the 22/23rd of September. They would be spread over a four-week period, and it would prove to be a tough campaign. Over seven hundred aircraft took part in this first raid, including a record contingent of sixty-nine 6 Group Halifaxes along with six Lancasters and fourteen Wellingtons. Despite clear skies over the target the operation failed because of a stronger-than-forecast wind, which drove the markers and bombing towards the south-eastern corner of the city. A diversionary raid by a small force of Pathfinder Lancasters and Mosquitos on Oldenburg near Bremen involved the dropping of much Window and many flares, and this possibly reduced the losses from the main raid. Even so, twenty-six aircraft were lost, including two from 428 Squadron, one from 434 Squadron and two 432 Squadron Wellingtons. The Leasiders' Sgt Tierney and his crew all survived the loss of LN547 to fall into enemy hands, but Sgt Barlow and one of his crew lost their lives in LN554. This Wellington was hit by flak over the target and its fuel tanks were holed. It finally ran out of fuel over the North Sea some sixty miles off Flamborough Head, and had to be ditched. Three members of the crew managed to gain the sanctuary of the dinghy and awaited rescue. Later on the 23rd four 432 Squadron crews set off to carry out a sea search, and it was F/O Mercier and crew who spotted the dinghy. They circled the spot to guide a rescue launch, and the three men were picked up.

On the following night Mannheim hosted its second heavy assault of the month, this one aimed at its northern districts, which had escaped relatively lightly two and a half weeks earlier. Another heavy blow was delivered by a force containing fifty-eight 6 Group Halifaxes and five Lancasters, and it left over nine hundred houses, twenty industrial premises and a number of public buildings in ruins. Sadly, a small 8 Group diversionary raid on Darmstadt could not prevent the loss of thirty-two aircraft, but the Lions came through unscathed for the second operation in a row. Not so 419 and 428 Squadrons, which posted missing another two crews each, with just three survivors from one of the Ghost aircraft. 426 Squadron continued to operate in modest numbers, and one of its participants almost became a casualty statistic. DS714 was attacked twice by JU88s, and sustained heavy damage to flying and control surfaces, airframe, hydraulics and instruments, and both gunners were wounded. The crew of F/L McCaig claimed one of its assailants as destroyed and then nursed their crippled Lancaster home to a crash-landing at Thorney Island on the south coast. The Thunderbirds were now given another two weeks off the order of battle, and would miss a busy period of operations, beginning with the second of the series against Hanover. Before that, on the 25th 433 Squadron became the last Canadian bomber squadron to be formed overseas. Based at

Skipton-on-Swale the squadron's nucleus consisted of five crews who had reputedly been removed from other squadrons because of some kind of disciplinary problems. Initially, as the squadron began what would be an unusually protracted working up period, it stooged around in borrowed Wellingtons, until finally getting its hands on Halifaxes, the first of which, HX268, would not be taken on charge until the 3rd of November. The next Hanover raid was undertaken by 678 aircraft on the 27/28th, for which 6 Group put up a record seventy-three Halifaxes along with nine Leaside Wellingtons. The bombing was well concentrated, but inaccurately fore-cast winds caused it to be concentrated five miles north of the city centre, where it was wasted on outlying communities and open country. The disappointment was compounded by the loss of thirty-eight aircraft, plus another from a diversionary raid on Brunswick. 427 Squadron's rate of early returns was beginning to look suspect after another three occurred on this night, but its remaining participants all came home safely. It was another very bad night for 434 Squadron, whose casualty record since beginning operations just six weeks earlier was already alarming, and was now even made worse by the failure to return of three more aircraft.

428 Squadron's problems began early, when severe icing conditions forced P/O Kogan and his crew to turn back early with a failed engine, and after baling his crew out over Lincolnshire the pilot carried out a crash-landing at Ludford Magna. Much later, at around 01.00 hours, a badly damaged DK270 arrived over Suffolk in the hands of Sgt Wilson. Unusually for a 6 Group crew, the pilot and five others were RAF, while only the mid-upper gunner wore the uniform of the RCAF. The Halifax had been coned in searchlights over the target and then hit by flak, which knocked out the port outer engine. The bombs were jettisoned, and Sgt Wilson turned for home with the firm intention of making it back to Middleton St George. Another salvo of flak at the Dutch coast hit the port inner engine, although it continued to provide some power, and a general difficulty to control the aircraft suggested some damage to the flying surfaces. The US base at Framlingham responded to the wireless operator's emergency call, and the crew could pick out the landing lights in the distance. During the course of a difficult approach the port-inner engine cut, and the Halifax tipped over onto its port side, clipped trees and crashed short of the runway. Four of the crew died in the wreckage, while the pilot sustained severe injuries including a smashed pelvis. The rear gunner was also injured, but the mid-upper gunner emerged almost without a blemish and went to find help. In the conditions it took an hour for the American emergency services to arrive on the scene, but the injured were tended and recovered from their ordeal. In a sense, that was the good news. The bad news was that three other 428 Squadron crews would not be coming home at all. JB968 crashed in Germany killing the crew of F/O Sherback, EB215 was a shattered wreck in a Dutch field containing the remains of Sgt

Farmer and all but one of his crew after they were brought down by flak, and LK915 fell to a night fighter over Germany with just F/O Whalley and one of his crew surviving as PoWs. The other 6 Group casualty from this night's operation was a 432 Squadron Wellington, from which two of the six-man crew survived as PoWs. An effective attack on Bochum by over three hundred aircraft on the 29/30th ended the month, and 427 Squadron had now negotiated five operations, four of them over Germany, without losing a crew. However, in the space of eleven minutes German night fighter ace Hptm E Prinz zur Lippe Weissenfeld shot down two 434 Squadron Halifaxes over Holland to add to the Bluenoses' already extreme woes, and a 419 Squadron aircraft was lost without trace.

There was a hectic start to October for the Lancaster squadrons, which were involved in six major operations during the first eight nights. The month's account opened at Hagen in the Ruhr on the 1/2nd, an outstandingly accurate attack based on Oboe sky-marking, and forty-six industrial concerns were completely destroyed. On the following night over three hundred buildings were destroyed in München in a partially effective raid. It was on this night that 6 Group's 431 Squadron dispatched its maiden sorties on Halifaxes, when contributing to a mining operation in northern waters. Halifaxes and Stirlings joined the Lancaster brigade at Kassel on the 3/4th, when 6 Group managed a new record of seventy-five Halifaxes from its now six squadrons, as 431 carried out its first bombing operation. The Pathfinder blind markers overshot the aiming point, and this pushed the main weight of the attack into the city's western suburbs and beyond. Two aircraft factories were hit, however, and one suburb became a sea of flame. A 419 Squadron Halifax was attacked by a German intruder over Lincolnshire, and despite serious damage made it back to base where a successful crash-landing was carried out. 427 Squadron's LK637 was raked from stem to stern by cannon fire from a ME210 night fighter at the Dutch coast outbound, and the rear gunner and wireless operator were killed. The aircraft caught fire, but a violent corkscrew and descent extinguished the flames, and the bomb load was jettisoned into the North Sea. After the undercarriage was pumped down F/L Laird performed a safe landing, and the badly wounded flight engineer was able to receive much needed medical attention. 428 Squadron's bad run continued with the failure to return of two more aircraft, 431 Squadron posted missing its first Halifax crew, and 434 Squadron added another to its long list of missing crews.

Frankfurt suffered its first really destructive raid on the 4/5th at the hands of almost four hundred aircraft, of which fifty-four were 6 Group Halifaxes. The eastern half of the city and the inland docks sustained extensive damage, and an area of fire raged out of control, claiming many public and commercial buildings near the city centre. Six of the Group's aircraft failed to return, beginning with two from 419 Squadron, while 427 Squadron's LK920 was brought down to crash in Luxembourg without survivors from the crew of W/O Champion. There was another empty dispersal at 428 Squadron, and 429 Squadron registered its first casualty since converting to Halifaxes and returning to operations three weeks earlier. Finally, there was the inevitable aircraft and crew from 434 Squadron. A two-night break preceded an all-Lancaster attack on Stuttgart on the 7/8th, for which 1 Group's 101 Squadron operated its night fighter communications jamming ABC Lancasters for the first time in numbers. It was also 408 Squadron's maiden operation on Lancaster Mk IIs, and with 426 Squadron returning to the fray after two weeks off it enabled 6 Group to put up a total of twenty-eight of the type. 408 Squadron's DS724 did not reach Germany, in fact it was still over Yorkshire when technical problems persuaded F/S Harvey and his crew to take to their parachutes just nine minutes after take-off. One of the crew sustained injuries, but less fortunate was a civilian on the ground who was killed. The operation was moderately effective, and the loss of a very modest four aircraft suggested a successful debut for the radio counter-measures element. Sadly for 426 Squadron, one of the missing aircraft was its own DS689, which crashed in France, killing F/S Summers and five of his crew, while the two survivors evaded capture. From this point on a number of 101 Squadron Lancasters would be included in every major operation, even after the formation of 100 Group, which would be dedicated to the role from November.

W/C Fleming's long period in command of 419 Squadron came to an end on the 8th of October, and the A Flight commander, S/L McMurdy, was promoted to the position as his replacement. That night he presided over his first operation as commanding officer, although he did not accompany the squadron element to Hanover. This was the third of the series against the city, and for once everything proceeded according to plan. A force of five hundred aircraft included one hundred from 6 Group made up of seventy Halifaxes, sixteen Lancasters and fourteen Wellingtons. A devastating attack ensued, in which most of the bombs fell within two miles of the city centre aiming point, destroying almost four thousand buildings, while thirty thousand others were damaged to some extent, and twelve hundred people lost their lives. This proved to be the final bombing operation by Wellingtons under Bomber Command, and the honour fell to 6 Group's 432 Squadron and the Poles of 1 Group's 300 Squadron. Sadly, this Wellington bombing swansong resulted in the final loss of a 432 Squadron crew on the type. LN451 failed to return, and F/S Baker and his crew were all killed. Sgt Slegg and crew had a close shave when their Wellington was hit by a falling bomb, while F/S Dennis was attacked by three night fighters without sustaining damage. F/O Fisher and his crew claimed a JU88 as destroyed. All of 427 Squadron's participants landed away from base and returned to Leeming later in the day. Absent was LK900 and the crew of Sgt Kelly, who had crashed in Germany without survivors. 429 Squadron posted missing its second Halifax crew on this night, while 431 Squadron lost two, one without trace and the other to a mid-air explosion after a flak hit. 434 Squadron still couldn't keep a clean sheet, and had another of its own dispatched by a night fighter.

The final Hanover raid took place on the 18/19th of October after a nine-night break for the heavy squadrons, and was an all-Lancaster affair for which 6 Group provided twenty-six aircraft. It became another failure when cloud prevented the Pathfinders from accurately pinpointing their position, and most of the bombs found open country at a cost of eighteen Lancasters. A 408 Squadron crew borrowed a Lancaster from neighbours 426 Squadron for the occasion, and ditched it three miles out into the North Sea after running out of fuel. Two nights later another all-Lancaster force of 350 aircraft took off for the first major raid on Leipzig in eastern Germany. The weather conditions were appalling, and the results were inconclusive, but all twenty-seven 6 Group participants came home safely. On the 22/23rd, and for the second time during the month, a force of over five hundred aircraft set out for Kassel in central Germany. Among them were eighty-five Halifaxes and twenty-two Lancasters from 6 Group, its best effort yet. The raid began with a degree of overshooting by the H2s blind markers, but the visual markers were able to correct the error, and deliver their target indicators onto the city centre aiming point. The main force bombing was highly accurate and concentrated, and the hapless city and its inhabitants became engulfed in a firestorm. Its intensity was less than that experienced at Hamburg in July, but was never the less devastating in its effects, and more than 4,300 apartment blocks were reduced to rubble or shells. Almost 6,500 others sustained damage to some extent, and thus 63% of the city's entire living accommodation was rendered uninhabitable in just one night. The death toll almost certainly exceeded six thousand people, and bodies were still being recovered from the ruins many months later. The defenders fought back to claim forty-three bombers, and almost a third of them belonged to 6 Group. The only missing Canadian Lancaster was from 408 Squadron, while the other twelve casualties were Halifaxes. W/C McMurdy led the 419 Squadron element for the first time, and he died with four of his crew, when JD382 was shot down over Germany by a combined effort from three night fighters working in unison. 427 Squadron lost four aircraft, although the first to go down did so close to home. DK182 was one of five from the squadron to turn back early, and crashed in Yorkshire, killing W/O Welch and his crew. DK234 and LK633 both crashed on German soil with total loss of life among the crew of F/S Minter in the former, and four survivors from the crew of P/O Harrison in the latter, although the pilot and two others were killed. Finally, LK959 crashed in Holland, and F/L Weston and his seven crew mates lost their lives. 429 Squadron posted missing two crews, 431 Squadron one and 434 Squadron a catastrophic four. While the main force was active over

Hanover 432 Squadron carried out its final sorties on Wellingtons, when sending seven to lay mines off Den Helder. This concluded the month's operations, which had again seen a number of 6 Group squadrons badly mauled.

Hercules-powered Mk II Lancasters arrived at East Moor at around this time, and the 432 Squadron crews began the process of converting. W/C Pleasance was appointed as the new commanding officer of 419 Squadron on the 25th of October. On the 26th, W/C Ferris was posted from 408 Squadron after completing a fourteen month long tour, during which he had overseen the squadron's conversion from Hampdens to Halifaxes, and Halifaxes to Lancasters. He was replaced on the 28th by W/C Mair, who had previously served as a flight commander and whose period of tenure would be brought to a premature conclusion. 428 Squadron would begin the new month with a new commanding officer in the form of W/C French. W/C Suggitt was posted to 617 Squadron on the 30th to assume the role of flight commander, reverting to the rank of Squadron Leader to do so. Sadly, his Lancaster would strike high ground a few minutes after departing Ford for Woodhall Spa in poor weather conditions on the morning of the 13th of February 1944. Seven occupants died at the scene, including F/S Pulford, who had been Gibson's flight engineer on the Dams raid, and S/L Lloyd the 617 Squadron Intelligence Officer. Bill Suggitt alone survived the crash, but succumbed to his injuries two days later without regaining consciousness.

November was to bring a new intensity for the Command as Harris turned his gaze once more upon Berlin. However, the first half of the month would be less frenetic than the start of October, and only one major operation was mounted against a target in Germany. Düsseldorf provided the main fare on the 3/4th, for which almost six hundred aircraft took off, 115 of them from 6 Group in the form of twenty-five Lancasters and ninety Halifaxes. Central and southern districts of the Ruhr city suffered extensive damage, and the defenders brought down eighteen bombers. 426 Squadron posted missing the crew of F/O Ditzler, who all died when DS713 crashed in Germany, and 408 Squadron also had one Lancaster fail to return. 429 and 434 Squadrons each registered the loss of a Halifax, but perhaps the most tragic incident concerned 428 Squadron's LK954, which made it back to home airspace despite the effects of battle damage, but crashed in Lincolnshire killing F/O Eaton and his seven-man crew. Earlier in the day Harris had sent a memo to Churchill, in which he asserted that, 'we can wreck Berlin from end to end if the USAAF will come in on it. It will cost between us 400–500 aircraft. It will cost Germany the war.' The Americans, of course, were committed to victory by land invasion, and there was never the slightest chance of enlisting their support for an all-out air assault on Germany's Capital. Undaunted as always, Harris would go it alone, and put preparations in hand for the campaign's resumption later in the month. On the 6th the three former 6 Group Wellington squadrons, 420, 424 and 425 returned to Bomber Command after their tour of duty in Tunisia, and they all began converting to Halifaxes, although it would be mid February before they attained operational status. The Snowy Owls became residents of Dalton, while 424 moved into Skipton-on-Swale and Dishforth hosted 425, and while two of the tenancies would be of a temporary nature, the Tigers now had somewhere to call home until their return to Canada at the end of September 1945. W/C Roy had relinquished command of the squadron at the end of its operational activity overseas in early October, and his replacement would not be appointed until mid December. There was a new commanding officer also at the helm of 425 Squadron, W/C Richer having succeeded W/C St Pierre on the 1st of October.

433 Squadron appointed its first commanding officer on the 9th in the form of W/C Sinton, who had previously served as a flight commander with 432 Squadron. There were plenty of Canadians in the RAF, but W/C Sinton was something of an oddity, in being a Briton in the RCAF. He commanded a predominantly Canadian outfit, but as in all squadrons, there was a healthy mixture of nationalities, and complete RAF crews could now be found in most Canadian squadrons. There can have been no tougher time to be contemplating entry into the bomber war than the winter of 1943/44, and it would be a testing time indeed for those many crews embarking on their first tour of operations. Under W/C Sinton's command 433 Squadron continued with its training programme, and doubled its complement of Halifaxes on the 10th, when HX272 arrived. 433 Squadron was, in fact, the second squadron in Bomber Command to equip with the new improved Hercules-powered Mk III version of the type, just nine days after 466 Squadron Royal Australian Air Force received its first batch, and by the end of the month twenty would be on charge. During the lull in operations over Germany over three hundred Lancasters of 5 and 8 Groups attempted to rectify September's failure at the Modane railway yards in southern France. The operation took place on the night of the 10/11th, and enough of the bombing was sufficiently accurate to cause serious damage. On the following night an attempt to further disrupt the railway link with Italy failed, when a Halifax main force from 4 and 6 Groups missed the marshalling yards at Cannes, but at least there were no 6 Group casualties. 432 Squadron launched its first four Lancaster II sorties on the 18th when called upon to carry out a sea search.

Harris rejoined the long and rocky road to Berlin later on that night of the 18/19th, for which over four hundred Pathfinder and main force Lancasters were detailed, among them twenty-nine Mk IIs from 408 and 426 Squadrons. A further four hundred Halifax, Stirling and Lancaster crews drawn from 3, 4, 6 and 8 Groups were briefed to carry out a diversionary raid on the twin cities of Mannheim and Ludwigshafen in an attempt to split the defences, or at least to confuse the enemy night fighter controller. 6 Group managed to put up ninety-four Halifaxes with a contribution from each of its six squadrons. Six 6 Group Lancasters returned early for a variety of reasons, but those reaching Berlin found it to be completely cloud-covered, and it was impossible to assess the results of the raid. It had, in fact, been only modestly effective, lacking any concentration, and only four of the 173 buildings completely destroyed were industrial. A fairly modest nine Lancasters failed to return, possibly because of the diversion, and there were no casualties among the 6 Group contingent. It was a different story for the Canadian Halifax squadrons, however, which contributed to a scattered but moderately effective attack on the two southern cities, from which a further twenty-three aircraft were missing. A third of the casualties were from 6 Group, amounting to eight aircraft. Among these was LK976 of 427 Squadron, which crashed in the English Channel, and took with it the crew of F/O Kennedy. 419 Squadron posted missing two crews, as did 431 and 434 Squadrons, and 429 Squadron one. A Halifax and Stirling attack on Leverkusen on the 19/20th scattered bombs all around the region, and only one bomb found its way into the target city. 6 Group provided sixty-six aircraft for this operation, which cost 434 Squadron a further two aircraft and crews, while 428 Squadron posted missing one crew and had another bale out over England after both port engines cut as a result of flak damage. The Halifax crashed into a cemetery at Canterbury, and all but one of the crew survived their experience.

Round two of the Berlin offensive came on the 22/23rd, when 764 aircraft took off for the Capital, among them twenty-seven Lancasters and eighty-three Halifaxes from 6 Group. Also aloft on its maiden operation was 405 Squadron's KB700, the *Ruhr Express*, on its maiden operation. Not only was it carrying the crew of F/S Floren, who hailed from Weyburn, Saskatchewan, but also a reporter and a photographer to record the first bombing operation by a Canadian-built Lancaster. Sadly, engine problems began to develop during the outward flight, and although some bombs were jettisoned, height could not be maintained, and the sortie was abandoned some sixty miles short of Berlin. The remaining crews were again denied a sight of the massive urban sprawl below, as 10/10ths cloud continued to lie across the northern half of Germany. They were only able to speculate about the accuracy of the attack at debriefing, although the consensus was that the marking and bombing had found the mark. What they did not know, was that they had inflicted upon Berlin its most devastating assault of the war, which left three thousand houses in ruins along with twenty-three industrial premises in an area stretching from the city centre westwards. A number of firestorm areas were reported, and a pall of smoke rose over the city to a height of more than eighteen thousand feet. Around two thousand Berliners lost their lives, while a further 170,000 were

PayPal

Packing Slip

Send To: paul hamill

Address: 11 redwald close
kirkby, Merseyside
L334EH
United Kingdom

Email: paulphamill@aol.com

Send From: Gerry Porter

Address: Inglenook Cottage
146 Beanacre
Melksham, Wiltshire
SN127PU
United Kingdom

Email: ga.porter@btinternet.com

Transaction ID: 8RB88480EH8766032

Auction ID effes101

Auction ID non-solum-nobis

Description	Options	Qty	Price
6 Group Bomber Command: An Operational Record by Chris Ward (Hardback, 2009) #3317903Z7593		1	£11.50 GBP

Postage & Packaging: £0.00 GBP
Delivery Insurance: £0.00 GBP
Total: £11.50 GBP
This is not a bill.

Thank you for shopping with PayPal – the safer way to pay online. It was a pleasure doing business with you.

rendered homeless in return for bomber casualties amounting to twenty-six aircraft. The Group's Lancaster squadrons avoided casualties if not entirely escaping battle damage, but there was the usual catalogue of missing aircraft from the Halifax operators. 419 and 428 Squadrons each posted missing one crew, and as had come to be expected, 434 Squadron was hardest hit with two failures to return.

A policy decision made at High Wycombe following this operation would impact on most of the Halifax squadrons of 4 and 6 Groups for the next three months. The Stirlings of 3 Group had been demonstrating a vulnerability to the enemy defences for some time, and had always produced a poor rate of serviceability. When these facts were placed alongside the type's inadequate bomb load and its lack of potential for further development in comparison with the Lancaster and Halifax, it became clear that its future had to be redefined. Fifty Stirlings had taken off for Berlin on the 22nd, and almost half had turned back early, while five, or 10% of those dispatched had been lost. Harris could not justify the risk to crews, and immediately withdrew the type from operations over Germany. This was a blow to 3 Group, which had always been in the vanguard of the Command's operations, but new roles would be found for the Stirling in bombing operations over the occupied countries, SOE operations, and it would become the primary means of mining the enemy's shipping routes. Statistics had revealed that when Lancasters, Halifaxes and Stirlings operated together, the lower-flying Stirlings were at most risk. When Lancasters and Halifaxes alone were involved, it was the Halifax that tended to sustain disproportionately higher casualties. Now, in the absence of the Stirling, the MK II and V Halifaxes could look forward to a torrid time at the hands of the *Luftwaffe*'s night fighter fraternity.

On the following night Harris sent an all-Lancaster main force back to Berlin, and guided by the glow of fires still burning beneath the clouds the crews were able to deliver another devastating blow, which destroyed over two thousand more houses, and a handful of industrial premises. The death toll on the ground was around fifteen hundred people, while twenty Lancasters failed to return. Just one of these was from among the nineteen dispatched by 6 Group, and the unlucky squadron was 408. The posting missing of crews was a sad but routine affair, and a necessary adjunct of warfare. Within hours of a crew's loss all personal belongings would have been removed from billets, and telegrams sent to relatives, these to be followed by a letter from the commanding officer. He would describe the missing son or husband as a popular member of the squadron who would be missed, and offer the crumb of comfort that he may be safe in enemy hands. There was nothing more to be done. 432 Squadron continued to ease itself gently back into the war by flying sea-search sorties on the day after each major operation. The night of the 25/26th brought an operation to Frankfurt by a 4 and 6 Group Halifax main force, for which 6 Group put up eighty-eight aircraft. It turned into a scattered attack on the cloud-covered target, and a modest amount of housing damage was achieved. There must have been celebrations at Tholthorpe when all of the 434 Squadron participants returned home, but it was a different matter at Leeming, where the return of three Bison aircraft was awaited in vain. 431 Squadron also posted missing two crews and 428 Squadron one.

After three nights on the ground the Lancaster squadrons were made ready for the fourth trip to Berlin since the campaign's resumption. Over four hundred aircraft were detailed, including thirty-nine from 6 Group, among them a contingent from 432 Squadron on its maiden offensive operation with the type. They set a course over northern France accompanied by a Halifax diversionary force containing fifty-six 6 Group aircraft, which peeled off for Stuttgart when Frankfurt was reached. The skies over Berlin were clear as the Lancasters approached from the south, but the Pathfinders overshot the city centre, and marked an area well to the north-west. Fortunately for the outcome of the raid, industrial districts lay below, and thirty-eight war industry factories were completely destroyed. The bomber stream became scattered as it withdrew from the target area, and night fighters were able to pick up individual Lancasters during the return flight. Twenty-eight failed to return home, while a further fourteen were written off in crashes in England. 408 Squadron's W/C Mair and his crew disappeared without trace in DS723, which presumably went into the sea, and he was the second 408 Squadron commanding officer to be killed in action. Another 408 Squadron aircraft returned with battle damage and crash-landed safely in Lincolnshire. 426 Squadron had three crews return early, and then DS679 disappeared without trace, taking with it the crew of flight commander S/L Hughes. Six Halifaxes failed to return from Stuttgart, among them one each from 419 and 428 Squadrons. 429 Squadron had its dramas, with one aircraft ditching off Thorney Island after twice overshooting, while a second Bison crash-landed, but there were no crew casualties. For the second operation running 434 Squadron welcomed all of its aircraft home. 408 Squadron's new commanding officer was W/C Jacobs, who had served as a flight commander with 420 Squadron, and whose first tour had been on Hampdens. Sadly, just like his predecessor, he would eventually be lost while leading his men from the front.

December began as November had ended, with an all-Lancaster main force rejoining the hazardous road to Berlin on the night of the 2/3rd. The 440-strong heavy contingent included thirty-six from 6 Group, and was supported by eighteen Pathfinder Mosquitos to lay route markers. Wrongly forecast winds led to a scattering of the bomber stream during the outward flight, and made it difficult for the Pathfinders to pinpoint the planned aiming point. As a result the marking spread over the southern half of the city, and much of the bombing hit the suburbs or fell into open country, although some useful damage was inflicted on industrial areas in western and eastern districts. It was a bad night for the Command, the forty missing aircraft making it the worst against Berlin since the opening two raids of the offensive back in August. 426 Squadron had three aircraft return early, another one failed to return altogether and F/S Coulombe landed on three engines at Snetterton Heath after a set-to with a JU88 had left both aircraft damaged. The missing crew was that of P/O Shaw, who all died when DS770 crashed in Germany. 431 Squadron registered its first missing Lancaster and crew, and had another with battle damage over-shoot and crash into a field on landing, but happily without crew casualties.

On the following night over five hundred Lancasters and Halifaxes took off for Leipzig, with a contribution from 6 Group of nineteen Lancasters and seventy-eight Halifaxes. The target was a city last attacked ineffectively in foul weather conditions back in October. On this night the force headed directly for Berlin to mislead the night fighter controller, and then, as it turned towards Leipzig, a Mosquito feint continued on to Berlin to maintain the deception. The ploy had the desired effect, and the main operation was relatively unmolested by night fighters. Accurate marking and bombing led to the most destructive attack of the war on this eastern city, in which housing and industry suffered alike. Had the bomber stream not strayed into the Frankfurt defence zone on the way home the losses would have been light, but in the event, twenty-four aircraft failed to return. The steady attrition rate continued for 426 Squadron with the failure to return of DS733, which went down in Germany killing F/S Sturley and three of his crew, while the three survivors were taken into captivity. It was an eventful night for 427 Squadron's P/O Cozens and crew, who lost their starboard-inner engine during the outward flight. They turned for home, only for the port outer to fail, and then the starboard-outer began to give problems as well. The pilot ordered his crew to bale out as soon as the coast was crossed, and shortly afterwards the starboard-outer picked up again, so P/O Cozens headed for Woodbridge. Finally the recalcitrant engine gave up altogether, leaving just one on which to carry out a crash-landing in a field on approach to Woodbridge. P/O Cozens walked away from the wreck, and his crew all landed safely. After a loss-free start to its Halifax operations 429 Squadron was beginning to feel the pain of regular missing aircraft, and there were two more from this operation. It was worse for 431 Squadron, which had four empty dispersals as testimony to its misfortunes, and one of its flight commanders was among the missing. 434 Squadron didn't escape entirely, but its loss involved an aircraft rather than a crew, who were rescued from the English Channel after lack of fuel forced them to ditch.

There were no major operations thereafter until mid month, and it was left to the Mosquitos of 8 Group's Light Night Striking Force to maintain the pressure on Germany by nightly raiding one or more targets in the

Ruhr. 431 Squadron completed its move from Tholthorpe to Croft on the 10th, when A Flight commander S/L Higgins led the crews away after lunch, performing the traditional low pass across the airfield as a farewell gesture. 434 Squadron followed the Iroquois in to Croft next day, and not to be outdone W/C Harris also led a 'beat-up' of the control tower at Tholthorpe as they departed on their way north. The two units would now share Croft until the end of hostilities. The accommodation at Tholthorpe would not remain unoccupied for long, however, as 425 and 420 Squadrons began to move out of Dalton also on the 10th and 11th respectively to take up permanent joint residence there. Here both units would take on Halifax III aircraft and spend the next two months working up to operational status, which, once achieved, would see them generally operating together. They were to be the only two 6 Group squadrons not to conduct operations on Lancasters at any time during the war.

Operations resumed on the night of the 16/17th, when Berlin was selected as the objective for an all-Lancaster heavy force numbering over 480 aircraft, including forty from 6 Group. The enemy night fighter controller was becoming accustomed to the direct route across Holland adopted by the bombers, and was able to start infiltrating his aircraft into the stream at the Dutch coast. Combats took place all the way to the target area, and the majority of the twenty-five losses occurred during the outward flight. Complete cloud cover over Berlin necessitated the use of sky-marking, but much of the bombing still fell within the city, although without achieving any significant degree of concentration. The bombers returned via a northerly route over Denmark, and thereby avoided a further confrontation with the enemy, but many crews, particularly those from 1, 6 and 8 Groups, still faced their sternest test of the night. By the time they arrived in home airspace their stations were shrouded in a blanket of impenetrable low cloud, and few, if any, had sufficient reserves of fuel to divert to other areas. The minutes between midnight and 02.00 hours witnessed the frantic search by exhausted crews for somewhere to land, and many aircraft came to grief as they stumbled around in the murk. Some flew into the ground, while others collided with obstacles or other aircraft. A few crews opted to take to their parachutes as their fuel ran out, and they were generally the fortunate ones. Twenty-nine Lancasters were lost in these cruellest of circumstances, and around 150 airmen lost their lives when so close to home and safety. It was a bad night for 6 Group, which lost aircraft to the enemy defences and the conditions at home. One 408 Squadron aircraft was lost without trace and a second flew into high ground at home killing all but the two gunners. 426 Squadron's DS846 probably met its end at the hands of a night fighter during the outward flight, and only one man from the crew of P/O Archibold survived as a PoW. Badly damaged and low on fuel, DS762 was turned towards Sweden by P/O Davies, and once he was sure they were over neutral territory, he ordered his crew to bale out. One of the gunners had sustained a fractured leg before leaving the Lancaster, but he, like his crewmates, landed safely, and ultimately all enjoyed the legendary hospitality of their hosts for the statutory period before being repatriated. DS779 crashed near Wetherby at 23.31 hours, while DS837 came down north of York some fourteen minutes later, and the only survivors were the two gunners from the crew of F/S Stewart in the former and one from the crew of S/L Kneale in the latter. 432 Squadron posted missing one crew with an American pilot, but a second crew successfully abandoned their fuel-starved chariot near Thornaby and all eight men landed safely.

The Command remained on the ground for the following three nights, during which period W/C Martin was appointed to the command of 424 Squadron on the 18th. He would oversee the conversion to Halifaxes and the working up to operational status, and would himself need to gain operational experience on the type before leading his squadron into battle. This process would prove to have fatal consequences for him. It was not uncommon for squadrons to lose crews during the training period before becoming operational, and 433 Squadron sustained its first casualties in this way. Shortly before noon on the 19th, F/S Humphreys began his take-off run in HX245 with four members of his crew on board. Within seconds of becoming airborne, and while still within the confines of the airfield, it rolled onto its back and crashed onto a parked Halifax, HX277, in which a number of ground crew were working. All five aircrew were killed, along with one of the fitters, but remarkably, three others emerged alive from the parked aircraft, one of them completely uninjured.

In the late afternoon of the 20th almost 650 Lancasters and Halifaxes took off for Frankfurt, accompanied by a small force of 1 and 8 Group Lancasters and Mosquitos bound for Mannheim as a diversion. 6 Group's contribution to the main event was thirty-three Lancasters and eighty-three Halifaxes. The enemy night fighter controller was again able to plot the bomber stream's progress, and many combats took place before the target was reached. Unexpected cloud hampered the Pathfinders' attempts to mark, and decoy fires and markers on the ground lured some of the bombing away from the city. The creep-back from this fell within Frankfurt, however, and over four hundred houses were destroyed, while almost two thousand other buildings in the city and neighbouring towns sustained serious damage. It was a bad night for the bombers, though, and forty-one failed to return home, twenty-seven of them Halifaxes, representing a 10.5% loss rate for the type. 408 Squadron sustained the loss of two Lancasters, as did 426 Squadron, and the respective fate of the Thunderbird crews starkly demonstrated the contrasting fortunes of war. P/O Stuart and the other occupants of LL630 all lost their lives, while P/O Griffin and his crew all survived, albeit in enemy hands, after abandoning DS716. The lottery of war played out the same for the occupants of 427

Squadron's LK627 and LK644. F/O Lacerte and his crew all survived as PoWs from the former, but F/O Grieve and his crew all perished after the latter crashed in Germany. F/O Weldon and crew almost became another loss statistic after two engines failed, but they landed safely. 428 Squadron lost two Halifaxes in which thirteen men died and two survived as captives. 434 Squadron's good recent run came to an end on this night when two of its aircraft failed to return, but again one crew survived intact while another perished to a man. Three nights later over 360 Lancasters provided the majority of the effort for yet another assault on Berlin, when a Mosquito feint at Leipzig was partially successful in delaying the arrival of the night fighters. Technical problems with their H2s equipment prevented the Pathfinders from taking advantage, and the marking was scattered. Most of the bombing fell into the south-eastern corner of the city, where almost three hundred buildings were destroyed, while sixteen Lancasters failed to return home.

The last but one wartime Christmas came and went in relative peace, but business as usual resumed on the 29/30th, when a force of seven hundred aircraft was made ready for the final operation of the year to Berlin. It was also to be the first of three trips to the Capital in the space of five nights spanning the turn of the year, a concentration of effort bearing down most heavily on the Lancaster crews. Taking off either side of 17.00 hours the bombers, including thirty-nine Lancasters and ninety Halifaxes from 6 Group, took a different route on this night, passing south of the Ruhr and approaching Leipzig before swinging towards Berlin. Mosquito diversions over the Ruhr, Magdeburg and Leipzig helped to keep the night fighter controller guessing, and few night fighters made it to the target area. Again the main weight of bombs fell into the southern and south-eastern districts, while some was wasted beyond the eastern city limits. Almost four hundred buildings were destroyed in return for the loss of twenty aircraft. 408 Squadron posted missing one crew, who all lost their lives, and 419 Squadron also posted missing one crew, who all survived. 427 Squadron sustained no losses on this night, but W/C Turnbull's crew was among four to return early. 429 and 431 Squadrons sustained the Group's other casualties, the former posting one crew missing and the latter two. Finally, 434 Squadron ended the year on a positive note with the return of all of its aircraft, but, sadly, one flight engineer was killed by flak during the outward flight.

It had been a tough year all round, but generally speaking, a successful one, during which Bomber Command had developed into a weapon of awesome power. When this might was directed accurately, it could reduce cities to ruins. Standing in its way, however, were two powerful enemies, the weather and the *Luftwaffe* night fighter force, and during the first quarter of 1944, they would combine to test the bomber crews to the absolute limit. As the old year slipped away, 433 Squadron was declared ready for operations with a complement of twenty Halifaxes, forty-nine officers and 473 airmen. Some squadron members had already tasted battle conditions in the Halifax by flying as spare bods in 427 Squadron aircraft, and this would stand them in good stead for what lay ahead. They would carry the name Porcupine into battle, the squadron having been adopted by the Porcupine district of northern Ontario, and the badge and motto, authorised by King George VI after the war, would reflect this.

1944

As the New Year dawned the toll of repeated operations to Berlin, eight since the resumption of the campaign, began to tell on the crews, particularly those of the Lancaster squadrons. They had been involved in every one, while the Halifaxes had been used sparingly, and the Stirlings, after a period of sustained heavy losses, had been withdrawn from operations over Germany altogether following the highly successful raid on the Capital on the 22/23rd of November. The effect of the campaign was also being felt by the inhabitants of Berlin, who had witnessed the destruction of 25% of their city's living accommodation, and seen evidence of the mounting death toll. There is little doubt, that they and the crews of Bomber Command shared a common wish for the New Year, that Berlin would cease to be the main focus of attention. In any event, Harris's belief that he could break the spirit of a people who were Berliners first and Germans second was ill founded. They were a hardy breed, and just like their counterparts in London during the blitz of 1940, they bore their trials with fortitude and humour, and got on with the business of daily life as best they could. The bombing served only to strengthen their resolve to withstand whatever Bomber Command could throw at them, and they joined together in a common bond of unity. During this, their 'winter of discontent', they paraded banners through the shattered streets proclaiming, 'you may break our walls but not our hearts'. They took solace in the words of the most popular song of the day, *Nach jedem Dezember kommt immer ein Mai*, After every December comes always a May, a sentiment that hinted at a change of fortunes with the onset of spring. As events were to prove, this was precisely how long both beleaguered camps would have to wait before their wishes were fulfilled.

Before New Year's Day was done, the first Lancasters were taking off, and by the time that the 2nd of January was an hour old over four hundred of them were heading for the Capital via an almost direct route over Holland. Not all reached their objective, twenty-nine turning back for a variety of reasons, while around sixteen others fell victim to night fighters and flak. Thirty-one 6 Group Mk IIs got away without incident and only one turned back early. The remainder found the city covered by cloud, and the sky-marking soon deteriorated in the face of a strong wind. The bombing was spread over seventeen miles from wooded country in the south-west to districts in the east, but nowhere was significant damage inflicted. The failure was compounded by the loss of twenty-eight aircraft, a goodly number of them carrying highly experienced Pathfinder crews, while 6 Group enjoyed a rare night of good fortune and welcomed all of its crews home to safe landings.

Many of the crews who collapsed wearily into bed at breakfast time on the 2nd found themselves back in the briefing room later in the day, incredulous and angry at the prospect of a back-to-back trip to the 'Big City', and the third in five nights. No diversionary measures were planned for this operation, and the route was again straight in over Holland, with a dogleg south-east of Bremen to bring the bomber stream to a position north-west of Berlin for the final approach. This was of little concern to four crews under briefing at Skipton-on-Swale, as 433 Squadron prepared for its operational baptism, a mining operation around the Frisians. This was the accepted way of introducing a new squadron to the rigours of operations, and indeed, freshman crews would normally expect to undertake a 'gardening' sortie or two before venturing over Germany.

Shortly after 20.30 hours, four Halifaxes took off and headed for the target area, although one of them was soon back in the circuit, forced to return early with technical problems. The others pressed on to complete the squadron's first operation and all returned safely home as the main event was getting under way. Some 362 Lancasters took off for Berlin along with nine Halifaxes and a dozen Mosquitos, but the strain and weakening morale manifested itself as crew after crew turned back with problems of some kind. The force was depleted by sixty aircraft in this way, and while 'boomerangs' were a fact of life for very genuine reasons, some of those aborting their sorties on this night would almost certainly have pressed on under different circumstances. Four 6 Group crews turned back out of the twenty-eight that had taken off. The enemy night fighters failed to make contact with the bomber stream until Berlin was reached, but there they took a heavy toll. Bombs were again scattered over all parts of the city, and damage was only marginally greater than twenty-four hours earlier, amounting to around eighty houses destroyed. The cost of this failure was twenty-seven Lancasters, ten of them Pathfinders, 156 Squadron alone losing five to add to the four it had posted missing on the previous night, and in less than two weeks time it would lose five more raiding Brunswick. Such losses were beginning to bleed the Pathfinders dry of quality crews, and sideways postings between the squadrons became common to maintain a leavening of experience. One 408 Squadron Lancaster failed to return, and 426 Squadron's DS760 also went down. P/O Griffiths and five of his crew died in the wreckage, while the two survivors became PoWs. LL634 was attacked three times by an FW190 and once by a JU88, but F/S Jarman and his crew came home none the worse for the experience.

432 Squadron also posted missing the crew of F/L Allen, who were all killed. F/L Allen had been flying as a second pilot two weeks earlier, when he and the other occupants had been compelled to bale out over Yorkshire on return from Berlin. Another Leaside Lancaster, DS792, sustained severe damage when it was attacked by a BF110, and lost 13,000 feet in a dive. The gunners shot their assailant down, and P/O McIntosh skilfully brought the crippled Lancaster down to a safe landing at Woodbridge. After an inspection of the damage the pilot was awarded a DFC for managing to bring home what amounted to little more than a collection of scrap metal. DS788 was also holed by a night fighter, but survived the encounter, and P/O Spink carried out a safe landing at Coleby Grange.

The surviving crews had two nights off before the next briefing was called on the afternoon of the 5th. The target was Stettin, at the eastern end of Germany's Baltic coast, for which 350 Pathfinder and main force Lancasters were accompanied by ten Pathfinder Halifaxes from 35 Squadron. The three 6 Group squadrons managed to put up thirty-five aircraft, of which two returned early. It was another very late take-off, and as the bomber stream headed for the Baltic, a Mosquito diversion at Berlin played its part in keeping the main operation largely free of night fighters. Over five hundred houses were completely destroyed, along with twenty industrial premises, while almost twelve hundred other buildings were seriously damaged, and eight ships were sunk in the port. On the debit side sixteen aircraft failed to return home, but none of the missing was from 6 Group, although one Thunderbird had an engine damaged by debris from an exploding aircraft. There now followed a welcome eight-night break from operations, which allowed the hard-pressed squadrons an opportunity to recover from the four long-range trips in the space of eight nights.

When the crews gathered for briefings on the 14th, there must have been a sense of relief as the curtains were drawn back from the wall maps, revealing that Brunswick and not Berlin was the target for the night. Situated about fifty miles beyond Hanover, the city that had proved to be a difficult and costly nut to crack in a four raid series during the autumn, Brunswick had not hosted a major operation before. A total of 498 aircraft, all but two of them Lancasters, took off either side of 17.00 hours, and headed for a landfall at the German coast near Bremen. 6 Group managed to put up a creditable forty-six Lancasters in a clear indication that the break had been effective. The bomber stream was met by a strong force of enemy night fighters as it swept across the coast, and the enemy was able to remain in contact all the way to the target and back as far as the Dutch coast. They scored steadily throughout, and by the time the survivors reached home airspace after a dismally disappointing raid, which had mostly afflicted outlying communities, thirty-eight of their number had been brought down. The Pathfinders had again sustained heavy casualties, this time amounting to eleven aircraft. 6 Group did not escape unscathed on this occasion, 408 and 432 Squadrons each posting missing two crews.

Another five-night lull prepared the crews for the next operation, a maximum effort to Berlin on the 20/21st, for which 769 aircraft took off. After three weeks away from the operational scene, apart from a very small number of mining sorties, the Halifax brigade returned to action on this night. 427 Squadron had begun conversion onto the new Mk III Halifax, but would continue to operate Mk Vs for the time being. The inclusion of a 433 Squadron element on its first bombing operation enabled the Group to put up a record contribution of 146 aircraft, made up of forty-seven Lancasters and ninety-nine Halifaxes. The bomber stream crossed the German coast at the narrow neck of land south of the Danish border and opposite Kiel, where a small Mosquito feint failed to impress the night fighter controller. Almost immediately night fighters made contact and began their deadly work, as the bomber stream pressed on for a north-west-erly approach to the target. Berlin was completely cloud covered, and it was impossible to make an assessment of the raid from the air. In fact, most of the bombs had fallen in an eight-mile swathe from north to south across the city's hitherto less severely damaged eastern districts, and there was much damage to housing, industry and railway installations. It was another night of heavy losses, however, and twenty-two of the missing thirty-five aircraft were Halifaxes. 419 Squadron posted missing two crews, but it was later established that one of them had survived intact and that only two had lost their lives from the other. 427 Squadron's F/O Cozens was making his third attempt to land LL191 at Coltishall, when he clipped a house, power lines and trees before crashing, killing one member of the crew outright. The wreckage caught fire, and a local farmer and his wife risked their lives to pull three of the injured men clear, while two of the crew managed to extricate themselves and were unhurt. Sadly all three of those rescued succumbed to their injuries, two within hours and the third on the 23rd, and P/O Cozens was among the dead. The farmer received the BEM for his actions. The squadron waited in vain for the return of EB246 and the crew of P/O Cook, who had all died in a crash in Germany. 428 Squadron reported one missing crew, but they were all alive and six of them would ultimately evade capture. 429 Squadron also had one missing aircraft, but it was a bad start to the year's operations for 434 Squadron, which, in an echo of past fortunes, had three empty dispersals to contemplate on the morning after. There would not even be the consolation of knowing the crewmen were safe, as only five of the twenty-one men involved escaped with their lives. The Group's Lancaster squadrons fared better with just the Thunderbirds registering the loss of LL628, which crashed in Germany killing F/L McCaig and his crew.

Like the recently raided Brunswick, Magdeburg had never been attacked in numbers before, and on the night the 21/22nd it would face the remains of a force of 648 aircraft that had departed their stations either side of 20.00 hours. 6 Group's contribution amounted to forty-five Lancasters and sixty-nine Halifaxes. The enemy night fighter controller plotted the progress of the bomber stream across the North Sea, and had to distinguish between the main raid and a small 5 and 8 Group diversion to Berlin. The first contact was made before the German coast was reached, and a running battle ensued from there to the target, which was reached ahead of time by some aircraft through stronger than forecast winds. Anxious to get away from the target area as quickly as possible, some crews bombed before the Pathfinder markers went down, and the resulting fires combined with decoy markers to draw off a proportion of the main force attack. The Pathfinders were not able to recover the situation, and the bombing lacked accuracy and concentration, falling predominantly outside of the city.

A massive fifty-seven aircraft failed to return, the majority of them victims of night fighters, and this represented a new record casualty figure. The Halifax squadrons once more sustained the heavier losses, amounting to thirty-five aircraft, and two of these were from 419 Squadron. 427 Squadron's LK923 was attacked and badly damaged by a night fighter on the way out, but continued on to the target despite losing fuel. Shortly after bombing the Halifax's fuel-starved engines began to fail and four of the crew baled out. F/S Toal and two others were killed in the ensuing crash. LL139 fell victim to a night fighter shortly after delivering its bomb load, and exploded in the air, throwing the bomb-aimer clear. S/L Arnot and the other six men on board were killed, including W/C Martin, the commanding officer of 424 Squadron, who was on attachment to gain operational experience. This was the first all-commissioned crew to be lost in 1944. When LL169 was hacked down by a night fighter in the target area, F/O Dickinson and his crew were able to take to their parachutes, and they all became PoWs. Finally, on this black night for the Lions, LL176 crashed in Germany, killing F/S Weir and all but one of his crew. It could have been even worse for the squadron, but two crews made it back to a landing at Wratting Common against the odds. F/S Coathup's EB248 had been attacked by a BF109, which left shell holes in both starboard engines, and then flak damaged the tailplane and fuselage. F/S Clibbery's LK735 ran into a BF110, which left it with damage to the fuselage, hydraulics and oxygen systems, instrument panel and both inner propellers. The Clibbery crew would survive a similar experience some months hence before going on to complete their tour, while the Coathup crew would be less fortunate. The other 6 Group Halifax casualties came from 428, 431 and 434 Squadrons with one aircraft each, and 433 Squadron registering its first two missing crews. Three Lancasters failed to return, one Goose and two Leasiders.

424 Squadron suffered its first Halifax casualty as the result of a training accident on the afternoon of the 22nd. The failure of an engine forced F/O

Cotnam to return to base, but he overshot the approach, and LW444 ended up in the River Swale trapping one member of the crew, who lost his life. The squadrons were given a five-night rest to lick their wounds after Magdeburg, before the next round of operations began. This was to be a three-raid assault on the Capital in the unprecedented space of just four nights. An all-Lancaster heavy force of 515 aircraft took off either side of 18.00 hours on the 27th, and flew a south-easterly course across northern Holland and into Germany, before turning north-east to a point west of Berlin. Elaborate diversionary operations pinned down a proportion of the night fighter force, and activity around the bomber stream was less intense than of late. The city was cloud covered, and a strong tail wind drove the markers across the city along the line of approach. Bombs fell in many parts of Berlin, although more in the southern half, but dozens of outlying communities were also afflicted. The operation was moderately successful, if expensive, with thirty-three Lancasters falling victim to the defences, most of them to night fighters arriving on the scene as the raid was in progress. It was a bad night for 6 Group, which had dispatched a very creditable forty-nine Lancasters and lost eight of them. 408 Squadron posted missing three eight-man crews, including that of a flight commander, and there was just one survivor between them. It was an even more disastrous night for 426 Squadron, which had four empty dispersals to contemplate on the following morning. F/L Shaw and all but one of his crew died in the wreckage of DS686 in Germany, and LL688 was lost without trace with the eight-man crew of P/O Countess. DS775 became a night fighter victim over Germany, and just two men survived as PoWs from the crew of F/L Martens. LL721 was also attacked and damaged by a night fighter over the target, eventually coming down in Germany, and F/L Wilson survived with two others to be taken prisoner. Finally, 432 Squadron registered a single missing crew, not one member of which survived. Earlier in the day W/C Blane had been appointed as 424 Squadron's new commanding officer.

Many of the crews who had survived the Berlin run found themselves back at briefing on the same day to learn that they were to go there again that very night. The inclusion of Halifaxes, among them ninety from 6 Group, added to thirty-three Lancasters, allowed a force of 677 aircraft to take off around midnight on the 28/29th, and they were routed over Denmark to approach the target from the north-west. Mosquitos bombed Berlin earlier in the evening, in the hope that this would persuade the night fighter controller that the main force was heading elsewhere. Other extensive diversionary operations were mounted, and although the outward flight was relatively free of night fighter encounters, a hot reception awaited the bombers over the target. Single and twin engine fighters accounted for twenty-seven aircraft here, but despite this, the marking and bombing was accurate and concentrated, and much damage was caused within the southern half of the city. Around 180,000 people were rendered homeless on this night, and many public and administrative buildings were damaged in south-central districts. The bomber casualties had reached forty-six by the time the survivors landed, and Croft was missing eight Halifaxes. Five of them were from 434 Squadron, and this made it the worst disaster yet for the Bluenose unit. LK649 crashed in Germany killing F/S Stanley and his crew, LK740 was brought down by flak over Germany with total loss of life among the crew of flight commander S/L Linnell, LK916 was lost without trace with the crew of P/O Devaney, and a night fighter shot down LL134 in the target area with fatal consequences for the eight-man crew of flight commander S/L Hockey. In addition to these EB256 came back on three engines, having lost the use of its port-outer just before the target was reached. The bombs were released from a lower altitude than that used by the rest of the main force, and by the time the Yorkshire coast was reached on the way home the fuel state had become critical. The starboard-inner quit as a result, and P/O Flewelling ordered his crew to bale out. All did so, but sadly, the rear gunner's parachute failed to deploy and he was killed. The loss of both flight commanders was a bitter blow to the squadron, and two more would be lost as a result of the next two operations, although these would not take place until mid February. The other Croft absentees were from 431 Squadron, one of which had run out of fuel over the Channel, forcing the crew to take to their parachutes. Three of the crew perished, but four were rescued by the Royal Navy after twenty minutes in the water. A fourth Iroquois crew wrote off their Halifax in a crash on landing at Dishforth. 429 Squadron had two aircraft fail to return, 419 Squadron one, while three 427 Squadron Halifaxes returned early, but the remainder all made it home without major incident. A 433 Squadron Halifax was badly shot up, but made it to home airspace, where its lack of controllability persuaded the crew to abandon it to its fate. Sadly, the rear gunner's parachute became snagged on the tailplane, and he went down with the aircraft. There were no casualties among the 6 Group Lancasters.

After a night's rest 534 aircraft set out again for the Capital, arriving over the city shortly after 20.00 hours. It was a predominantly Lancaster force, but eighty-two of the new and much improved Hercules powered Mk III Halifaxes also took part, including ten from 433 Squadron, along with thirty-seven MK II Lancasters. The night fighters failed to meet the bomber stream over the North Sea, and only made contact deep inside German airspace. From then until well into the return flight south of Brunswick and Hanover, they took a heavy toll of bombers, eventually achieving a score of thirty-three, all but one of them Lancasters. The single missing Halifax belonged to 433 Squadron. On the credit side, Berlin suffered a bruising raid, in which large areas of the centre and south-western quarter were engulfed in flames, and at least a thousand people lost their lives. 432 Squadron operated without loss on what proved to be its final operation on Lancasters. Mk III Halifaxes arrived on station at the start of February, and the process of converting began. As the Mk II Lancaster had essentially the same engines as the new Halifax, some remained on charge until a full complement of the latter was to hand. There were to be no operations for the first two weeks of February, as the moon period and inhospitable weather kept most squadrons on the ground. The series of raids on Berlin at the end of January had undoubtedly hurt the city grievously, while not achieving the level of destruction of the November raids, but nowhere were there signs of imminent collapse. Berlin was no Hamburg with densely populated, confined housing areas and narrow streets in its old centre. It was a modern city of concrete and steel with wide thoroughfares and open spaces to act as natural firebreaks. Each new swathe of destruction created more firebreaks and applied the law of diminishing returns. Ultimately, Berlin was just too big, too incombustible and too far, and this at a time when the *Luftwaffe* was a much more efficient and lethal adversary than in pre-Window times. As events were to prove, this was the last concerted effort of the campaign, and although two further large-scale operations would take place, they would be in isolation and six weeks apart.

As it happened, the first of these would be the very next operation to confront the crews after their two-week stand-down. In the meantime 427 Squadron lost its first Mk III Halifax to a training accident on the 1st of February, when LV828's port-outer engine failed, and the propeller eventually broke away to smash into the port-inner with such force, that it tore it from its mounting. The pilot, F/O Matherly, an American from Florida, remained at the controls while his crew baled out, but he was killed in the ensuing crash in Northamptonshire. During this period civilian contractors descended upon Croft to carry out modifications to the tailplanes of Merlin powered Halifaxes. It was discovered that rudder lock was causing quite a number of pilots to fatally lose control of their aircraft, and the original triangular fin and rudder arrangement was being replaced by the square one standard to the Mk III variant to improve stability. W/C Harris was posted from 434 Squadron to Dalton on the 6th to take over the 6 Group Battle School, and W/C Bartlett was installed as his successor on promotion and posting from 428 Squadron. On the 7th 427 Squadron's LK758 fell out of a steep turn and crashed on the edge of the airfield, killing F/S Nicol and the other five occupants. There was an early briefing on every main force and Pathfinder station on the 15th, as preparations were put in hand for what would be the penultimate raid of the war by RAF heavy bombers on Berlin. It was to be a mighty effort, involving the largest non-1,000 force to date of 891 aircraft, and it would be the first time that over five hundred Lancasters and three hundred Halifaxes had operated to a single target. Among them would be a contingent from 420 and 424 Squadrons on their maiden operation since rejoining the Command back in November on their return from Tunisia. Together with the extensive diversionary operations, which included Mosquito attacks on enemy night fighter airfields in Holland, mining in Kiel Bay and a small 8 Group Lancaster raid on Frankfurt-an-Oder to the east of Berlin, more than a thousand aircraft were to be in action.

The main operation began with a few departures before 17.00 hours, but the vast bulk of the giant armada got away between 17.00 and 18.00 hours, swinging north over Denmark, before setting an almost southerly course to the target. The night fighter controller observed the progress of the bomber stream, but held his response back until it crossed Denmark's Baltic coast a little north of Flensburg. The now familiar running battle ensued all the way to the target, and around twenty aircraft in the rear half of the stream were brought down. Consequently, Berlin was spared these bomb loads, and those of the seventy-five early returns. Even so, almost eight hundred aircraft remained, and they carried in their bomb bays a record 2,640 tons of bombs. Much of this was deposited squarely into the central and south-western districts of the city, causing almost twelve hundred medium and large fires and destroying a thousand houses and hundreds of temporary wooden barracks. Many important war industry factories were also hit, but as happened on all of the Berlin operations, scores of outlying communities found themselves in the firing line, and many bombs were wasted in this way. The bombers withdrew to the south and headed for northern Holland, making their way to the North Sea via the Ijsselmeer, but forty-three aircraft would not be coming home. 6 Group came through with surprisingly modest casualties in comparison with recent experiences, and registered just four failures to return. 427 Squadron negotiated this, its first operation on Mk III Halifaxes, without loss, but 424 Squadron was less fortunate, and lost HX311 to a crash near Berlin, in which flight commander S/L Reilander and the other seven men on board lost their lives. This cosmopolitan crew consisted of two men of the RCAF, four from the RAF and two from the RAAF. One 429 Squadron aircraft was missing, along with one from 434 Squadron carrying a flight commander, and 426 Squadron's DS794 went to the bottom of the Ijsselmeer, taking with it the crew of F/S Pattle. Returning in poor visibility a 420 Squadron Halifax crashed on its fourth overshoot, and two members of the crew lost their lives. On the following day five 432 Squadron Halifaxes carried out their first sorties in a sea search for downed crews from the night before.

The survivors were allowed three nights off before the next operation, which was to Leipzig on the 19/20th. This was the night on which 425 Squadron launched its new operational career on Halifaxes. It was to be a late take-off, either side of midnight for the force of more than eight hundred aircraft, which included thirty-one Lancasters and ninety-eight Halifaxes from 6 Group. Extensive diversionary operations were again laid on, but the enemy night fighter controller was not deceived, and reserved most of his strength to meet the main raid as it crossed the Dutch coast. The two forces remained in contact all the way into eastern Germany, where some aircraft arrived early through stronger than forecast winds. They were forced to orbit in the target area until the Pathfinder markers went down, and around twenty of them fell victim to the local flak batteries, while four others were lost through collisions. The attack was inconclusive in the face of complete cloud cover and sky marking, but what was not in question was the scale of the mauling inflicted on the Command. When all of the returning aircraft had been accounted for, there was a massive short-fall of seventy-eight, by far the heaviest casualty rate to date. The Halifax loss rate was over 13% of those dispatched, and Harris immediately with-drew the Mk II and V variants from future operations over Germany. Eighteen 6 Group aircraft failed to return, thirteen of them Halifaxes. 419 Squadron posted missing two crews, while 427 Squadron had four aircraft return early, and LV829 crashed in Germany with no survivors from the eight-man crew of P/O Olsvik. 428 Squadron had one missing Halifax, 429 and 434 Squadrons three each, 431 Squadron two and 433 Squadron one. Hardest hit of all was 408 Squadron with four missing Lancasters, while 426 Squadron lost one crew, that of F/S McKenzie, all members of which were killed when DS776 was shot down by a night fighter over Holland.

Despite the horrendous losses and the withdrawal of the older Halifaxes, almost six hundred aircraft were made ready on the following night for the first of three heavy raids over a three-week period on Stuttgart. 6 Group put up a dramatically reduced contribution of twenty-five Lancasters and forty Halifaxes as only 420, 424, 425, 427 and 433 Squadrons operated Mk IIIs. Departure was shortly before midnight, and within minutes of taking off 427 Squadron's LV836 crashed in Yorkshire, killing F/O Laut and his crew. For once, the night fighter controller was deceived by the diver-sionary measures, thus leaving the bomber stream largely unmolested during its time over enemy territory. Despite cloud cover and scattered bombing much damage was caused in the city's central districts, and also to areas in the north-west and north-east. A modest nine aircraft failed to return, including a single 425 Squadron Halifax.

A new tactic was introduced for the next two operations in an attempt to reduce the prohibitive losses of recent weeks. It was decided to split the bomber force into two distinct waves, separating them by two hours in the hope that the enemy night fighters would be caught on the ground refuelling and re-arming as the second wave passed through. The system was tried first during an operation to the ball bearing town of Schweinfurt on the night of the 24/25th, the first wave of 392 aircraft taking off between 18.00 and 19.00 hours, and the second wave of 342 aircraft departing their stations between 20.00 and 21.00 hours. 6 Group put up thirty-five Lancasters in the second wave and fifty-two Halifaxes in the first. Both phases of the attack suffered from undershooting, and the operation was a failure in that respect. However, the second wave lost 50% fewer aircraft than the first in an overall casualty figure of thirty-three, and this suggested some merit to the system. Two 408 Squadron Lancaster were lost, and the three missing Halifaxes came from 420 and 433 Squadrons. 427 Squadron had three aircraft return early, but the remainder came through unscathed and prepared for action on the following night, when the experiment was to continue at Augsburg, the beautiful and historic city in southern Germany. It had been the scene of the epic daylight raid by 44 and 97 Squadron Lancasters in April 1942, for which the since killed-in-action W/C Nettleton had been awarded the Victoria Cross. Nineteen 6 Group Lancasters and forty-four Halifaxes took off in the second wave either side of 21.30 hours, among them a contingent from 432 Squadron on its maiden offensive operation with the type. It was Augsburg's misfortune to be the victim of one of those relatively rare occasions, when all facets of the operational plan came together in perfect harmony. The unusually concentrated marking and bombing, with scarcely any creep-back, devastated the old centre of the city, obliterating for ever centuries of cultural history. Over 2,900 houses were destroyed, five thousand others were damaged to some extent, and up to ninety thousand people were rendered homeless. During the second phase of the attack some of the bombing did eventually spread into the industrial areas in the north and east, and damage was caused to at least one war industry factory. Twenty-one aircraft failed to return, among them two 408 Squadron Lancasters, from which one crew survived intact and two of its members evaded capture. 420 and 425 Squadrons each posted missing one crew, and 427 Squadron one. LK759 exploded after being attacked by a night fighter over Germany, and only the wireless operator from F/L Milton's crew was blown clear to survive as a PoW. 432 Squadron began its bombing career on Halifaxes with the loss of one aircraft. While these recent operations had been in progress, the Group's older Halifaxes had conducted mining operations, and one each from 429 and 431 Squadrons failed to return on this night.

The dawning of March brought the final month of the long and increasingly bitter winter campaign. Thereafter would come a new offensive to prepare the way for the invasion of Fortress Europe. Matters, though, were already well in hand in this regard, and the first salvoes of Bomber Command's contribution, the Transportation Plan, would be fired before the new month was a week old. In the meantime, the second raid of the series on Stuttgart was mounted on the 1st/2nd by a force of 557 aircraft, made up predominantly of Lancasters, with 129 Mk III Halifaxes in support, of which thirty were provided by 420, 425 and 432 Squadrons. Dense cloud on the route to the target prevented night fighters from making contact with the bomber stream, but also hampered the Pathfinders in their marking. No assessment of the raid by the crews was possible, but it had been a successful attack, which left further extensive damage in central, western and northern districts where housing was the main victim, although a number of important war industry factories were also hit. The operation was concluded for the remarkably low loss of just four aircraft, none of which was from 6 Group. W/C Patterson relinquished command of 429 Squadron on the 2nd, and it would be a considerable time before his successor was appointed. Most of the main force Lancaster squadrons remained on the ground for the next two weeks, and it was during this period that Halifaxes of 4 and 6 Groups, particularly the restricted Mk II and Vs, took the main role in opening the Transportation Plan. This called for the systematic dismantling by bombing of the French and Belgian railway networks ahead of the invasion, to prevent their use by the Germans to bring forces to the front. Before this, though, sixty-three of the Group's Mk II and V Halifaxes joined others from 4 Group to attack an aircraft factory at Meulan-les-Meureaux in France, and no aircraft were lost. A number of mining operations involved small numbers from the Group on the next two nights and then it was time to begin the interdiction campaign. Halifaxes opened the proceedings at Trappes marshalling yards on the 6/7th, after the marking had been carried out by Oboe Mosquitos. The eleven 6 Group Halifax units put up 119 aircraft between them without loss to contribute to a successful operation, which left track, rolling stock and installations severely damaged. Similar success was gained at Le Mans railway yards on the following night, when 6 Group provided twenty-four Lancasters and 116 Halifaxes for an overall force of three hundred aircraft, again without loss. During this period 429 Squadron had been converting to Mk III Halifaxes, and would shortly be taking them to war. It lost its first example to a training accident on the 10/11th, however, when LW685 developed engine trouble, and was ditched off the east coast of Scotland by F/S Puskas without crew casualties. A second attack by 4 and 6 Groups on the Le Mans yards took place on the 13/14th with 109 aircraft of 6 Group in attendance, all of which returned safely. This time fifteen locomotives and eight hundred wagons were destroyed, while collateral damage resulted to two nearby factories. 427 Squadron also took part in this operation, and sustained no casualties.

The Command returned to the fray in numbers on the 15/16th, when 863 aircraft, the second largest non-1,000 force to date, took off to return to Stuttgart. The force included twenty-nine Lancasters and 101 Mk III Halifaxes of 6 Group. The route, which took the bomber stream along the length of France almost to the Swiss border, delayed the inevitable contact with night fighters, but they caught up shortly before the target was reached, and began to take a heavy toll. Strong winds played a part in a disappointing marking performance, and although some bombs hit central districts, the majority fell short and into open country. Thirty-seven aircraft were missing from the operation, and 408 Squadron was represented by two, from which no crew member survived. It was two also for the other Lancaster operator, the Thunderbirds, whose DS771 crashed in Germany killing the entire crew of F/S Simard, while engine failure forced the crew of W/O McIlwaine to abandon DS829, but at least they survived to fall into enemy hands. 420 Squadron posted missing one crew and 427 Squadron two. LW559 was shot down by a night fighter on approach to the target, but F/O Milton and his crew all escaped with their lives to become PoWs. LW558 was also brought down over Germany, and only one man survived from the crew of F/O Steeves. 429 Squadron marked its debut on Mk III Halifaxes with the loss of one of them, but four of the crew survived and three of these evaded capture. While this operation was in progress the Group's operators of the older Halifaxes contributed fifty-four aircraft to an attack on railway yards at Amiens, and returned without loss. Sadly, a 500-pounder fell out of a 431 Squadron aircraft on landing, and both gunners were killed in the ensuing explosion. The same 6 Group units sent fifty aircraft back to Amiens on the following night, and again all came home.

Another massive force of 846 aircraft set out during the early evening of the 18th of March for the first of two raids in four nights on Frankfurt. Among them were twenty-five Lancasters and ninety-four Halifaxes from 6 Group. Part of the enemy night fighter response was drawn to the north to face a mining diversion, but the remainder made contact with the bomber stream as it bore down on the target. Accurate Pathfinder marking preceded a concentrated attack, which fell mainly into central, western and eastern districts, destroying or seriously damaging over six thousand buildings. Although housing accounted for most of this total, industrial, commercial and public buildings also figured prominently. The loss of twenty-two aircraft was a relatively modest price to pay for the scale of the success, and four of these were from 6 Group. One 424 Squadron Halifax was abandoned after being hit by flak, and the crew were all taken prisoner. 427 Squadron again had two empty dispersals next morning, one belonging to HX279, which crashed in France killing five of the crew, while the pilot, Sgt Miller, and one other fell into enemy hands. The other used to be occupied by LW551, which was a night fighter victim, and F/O Cooper lost his life, possibly by remaining at the controls while his crew baled out to join their squadron colleagues in captivity. On return most 427 Squadron crews landed at Bury St Edmunds because of poor weather conditions at base. The other 6 Group casualty belonged to 433 Squadron, and it was carrying the Skipton-on-Swale station commander, G/C Larry Wray, who was acting as second pilot. He survived with five others to become a PoW, but the pilot and one of the gunners lost their lives. Meanwhile, thirty-nine older Halifaxes went mining off Heligoland, and a 434 Squadron aircraft crashed on return killing all eight men on board.

Four nights later over eight hundred aircraft again took off for Frankfurt, of which twenty-seven Lancasters and seventy-three Halifaxes were from 6 Group. They contributed to an attack that was even more devastating than the one a few nights earlier. Although all parts of the built-up area were afflicted, the western districts received the greatest concentration of bombs. Half of the city was left without water, gas and electricity for an extended period, and the old Frankfurt, which had developed from the Middle Ages, was obliterated. Despite the failure of the bulk of the night fighter force to make contact, thirty-three aircraft failed to return, and one must assume that the flak batteries enjoyed a successful night. Four of the Group's Lancasters failed to return, two from each of the operators. The two missing Thunderbirds were DS741 and LL647, the former lost without trace with the crew of F/L Bow, and the latter was shot down by a night fighter during the outward flight, killing F/S Wright and four others, and delivering the two survivors into captivity. Of the Group's three missing Halifaxes, one belonged to 425 Squadron and the other two to 432 Squadron. A diversionary mining operation to Kiel Bay involving a contingent of seventy-four 6 Group Halifaxes resulted in a 419 Squadron aircraft ditching in the North Sea after both port engines caught fire. Happily, the crew was picked up by a trawler after three hours adrift, and as the Halifax, JD468, refused to sink, it had to be persuaded by gunfire to slip beneath the surface. The following night was devoted to a 3, 4 and 6 Group attack on railway yards at Laon, and all fifty-one 6 Group participants returned safely.

The time had arrived for Harris to launch the final assault of the campaign on Berlin. It would be the nineteenth since he began back in August, and the sixteenth since the resumption in November. For some 5 and 8 Group squadrons, which had participated in the diversion to Berlin on the night of the Magdeburg raid, it would be the seventeenth since then. It would also be the final raid of the war by RAF heavy bombers on the Capital, which would then be left to the Mosquitos of 8 Group's Light Night Striking Force to harass right up to the moment that Russian troops arrived in the suburbs. A total of 811 crews took part on this momentous occasion, including a contingent of twenty-three Lancasters and ninety Halifaxes from 6 Group. The aircraft departed their respective stations either side of 19.00 hours on the 24th, and took a wide swing over Denmark before crossing Germany's Baltic coast. The main feature of the outward flight was a wind of unprecedented strength from the north, which scattered the bomber stream and drove aircraft continually south of their intended track. The windfinder system, whereby selected crews assessed the wind strength and direction to transmit to Group HQs for re-broadcast, was unable to cope with the situation. The loss of cohesion denied the attack any meaningful chance of concentration, and as so frequently happened at Berlin, many bomb loads were wasted on over a hundred outlying communities. Sufficient housing was destroyed to leave twenty thousand people homeless, but industry escaped reasonably lightly. There had been little night fighter activity before the target was reached, but fourteen bombers were shot down by fighters in the Berlin defence zone. The bomber stream became even more dispersed on the return flight, and instead of passing south of Hanover and north of the Ruhr, many aircraft were driven by the wind into the Leipzig area and over the Ruhr itself. This provided the predicted flak batteries with their biggest bag of the war, and an estimated two-thirds of the seventy-two missing bombers were credited to them. 420 and 424 Squadrons each lost an aircraft, but the Snowy Owls' crew survived intact, while five of the Tigers' enjoyed a similar fate. In contrast, both missing 425 Squadron aircraft involved total loss of life. 427 Squadron registered three missing crews on this unhappy night for the Command, and there would be little good news concerning their fate. LK752 fell to a night fighter over Germany, killing four of the crew, while pilot W/O Magdalinski and two others survived in enemy hands. LW574 and LW577 were on their way home over Germany when the end came, the former, in which W/O Yaworski and four of his crew perished, as a result of flak. F/S Dowdell and four of his crew died in the latter, while the two survivors from each became PoWs. 429 Squadron also posted missing three crews with a total of eleven survivors between them, all of which were captured. Finally, one 432 aircraft failed to return along with two from 433 Squadron.

It had been an exhausting campaign against Berlin for all concerned, but some squadrons had suffered disproportionately heavy casualties. 6 Group participated in eighteen of the nineteen main operations to the Capital between August 1943 and March 1944, dispatching 688 Halifax sorties and 532 by Lancaster IIs. Fifty-five Halifaxes failed to return, a loss rate of 8.0%, and twenty-five Lancasters were lost at a rate of 4.7%. In total 437 men were killed, 127 became PoWs, nine evaded and nine were interned. 408 and 432 Squadrons shared the lowest loss rate at 3.9%, but this is deceptive as the Leasiders participated in substantially fewer operations and, therefore, dispatched fewer sorties. A better comparison for 408 Squadron is 426, which operated the same type and participated in the same number of Berlin raids, but suffered a loss rate of 6.2%. The worst loss rate of 15.6% belonged to 434 Squadron, which participated in seven operations to Berlin and lost twelve Halifaxes.

The railway campaign continued at Aulnoye on the 25/26th, but the Pathfinders were unable to mark accurately and most of the bombing fell wide of the mark. 6 Group took part with nine Lancasters and sixty-three Halifaxes, all of which came through unscathed. The Berlin offensive may now have been over, but the winter campaign still had a week to run, and two further major operations for the crews to negotiate. Essen provided the target for a force of seven hundred aircraft on the 26/27th, for which 6 Group contributed twenty-one Lancasters and eighty-four Halifaxes. The sudden switch to the Ruhr probably caught the defenders by surprise, and as it was within range of Oboe, the decisive factor in the Ruhr offensive a year earlier, the city wilted under another highly effective attack, which destroyed over seventeen hundred houses, and seriously damaged almost fifty industrial buildings. A modest nine aircraft failed to return, among them 426 Squadron's DS789, which blew up over Bottrop after being hit by flak, killing the crew of P/O Olsson. Forty-nine 6 Group Halifaxes joined others of the type from 4 Group to attack the railway yards at Vaires near Paris in excellent bombing conditions on the 29/30th, and blew up two ammunition trains in the process, reportedly killing over twelve hundred German soldiers. One 419 Squadron aircraft failed to return and was lost without trace. The final operation of the winter offensive was to be against Nuremberg, a city, which thus far, had escaped the worst ravages of a Bomber Command assault. At briefings on the 30th crews were given a forecast of protective cloud at cruising altitude, but later, a 1409 Met Flight Mosquito crew reported that this was unlikely to materialise. Despite the warning the operation was given the green light, allowing 795 aircraft to take off in the late evening, among them twenty-five Lancasters and ninety-three Halifaxes from 6 Group, and head towards the greatest disaster to afflict the Command during the entire war. A conference earlier in the day involving the Group commanders had decided upon a 5 Group inspired route, which would take the bomber stream in a long, straight leg from a point over Belgium to about fifty miles north of the target, from where the final run-in would commence. AVM Bennett, the brilliant Pathfinder AOC, was utterly and violently opposed to the plan and predicted a disaster, but he was overruled.

It was not long before the crews began to note some unusual and alarming features in the conditions, which included uncharacteristically bright moonlight, combined with crystal clear visibility. This enabled them to observe the other aircraft in the stream, something to which they were rarely accustomed. The forecast cloud did, indeed, fail to appear, but formed instead beneath the bomber stream as a white backdrop, silhouetting the aircraft like flies on a tablecloth. If this were not enough, condensation trails began to form in the cold, clear air, further advertising the bombers' presence. The final insult was the reappearance of the jetstream winds, which had so adversely affected the Berlin raid a week earlier. On this night they blew from the south, breaking the cohesion of the bomber stream, and driving aircraft well to the north of their intended track. Again, the windfinders were unable to cope with the speed of the wind, and modified their findings before transmitting them back to HQ. Here the figures were disbelieved, and were again modified before being sent back to the aircraft. The result was, that many crews, through either failing to detect the effects of the wind, or refusing to believe the evidence, wandered up to fifty miles north of track, and consequently, turned towards Nuremberg from a false position. Perhaps of greater significance, was the fact that the disputed route passed close to two night fighter-holding beacons, and this, together with the conditions, handed the bomber force on a plate to the waiting enemy. The carnage began over Charlerois in Belgium, and continued all the way to the target, the burning wreckage on the ground of RAF bombers sign-posting the way. An early victim was 427 Squadron's LV898, which was the sixth to fall, and did so over Germany, killing the second-tour eight-man crew of S/L Bissett. Eighty-three aircraft were lost during the outward flight and around the target area, and among these was another 427 Squadron Halifax, LW618, in which F/O McPhee and his crew were killed. The last but one casualty of the outward flight was 426 Squadron's DS840, which was brought down by a night fighter within sight of the target, killing F/L Cracknell and his crew. Earlier, the squadron's DS852 had been the sixty-fourth to be hacked down, and two men had died in the wreckage, while W/O Douglass and four others survived as PoWs. These massive losses on the way to the target together with the fifty-two early returns dramatically reduced the numbers available to attack the city. Other absentees from the target were around 120 crews, most of which had probably been unaware of their true position when turning towards Nuremberg. At the appointed time they found them-selves over a built-up area, and on seeing a number of target indicators, they took this to be the target. It was, in fact, Schweinfurt, some fifty miles to the north-west, and it was only on their return, that the majority discov-ered their error. In the event, Schweinfurt escaped lightly, as did Nuremberg, but the surviving aircraft did at least face a considerably reduced level of opposition on the way home. Sadly, it was not an enemy aircraft that caused the loss of a third 427 Squadron Halifax as it made its way westward across Luxembourg. LV923 collided with a 622 Squadron Lancaster and both plunged to the ground. S/L Laird and five of his crew were killed outright along with the Lancaster crew, but one man survived for three weeks in captivity before succumbing to his injuries, and another evaded capture. When all the accounting had been done, an unbelievable ninety-five aircraft were found to be missing, while others were written off in crashes at home, or with battle damage too severe to repair. The other 6 Group casualties were one 408 Squadron Lancaster, two 424 Squadron Halifaxes (one the mount of a flight commander), one 425 Squadron Halifax, two from 429 Squadron (one of which ditched in the North Sea, with all but the pilot rescued), two from 432 Squadron and one from 433 Squadron. During the course of the month, Canadian-built Mk X Lancasters had been arriving on 419 Squadron charge, and conversion training went on alongside the operations in Halifaxes.

That which now faced the crews was in marked contrast to what had been endured over the winter. The frequent deep penetration forays into Germany on dark, often dirty nights were to be replaced by mostly shorter-range hops to France and Belgium in improving weather conditions. An added bonus was that these targets, unlike Berlin, Frankfurt, Nuremberg, Schweinfurt, Augsburg, Leipzig and Stuttgart, would fall within the range of Oboe. The main fly in the ointment as far as the crews were concerned was a dictate from on high, which decreed that most such operations were worthy of counting as just one third of a sortie towards the completion of a tour. Until this flawed and ridiculous policy was rescinded, mutterings of discontent pervaded the bomber stations. The view from the top, that operations against French and Belgian targets would be a 'piece of cake' would not be borne out, and they would require of the crews a greater commitment to accuracy, to avoid as far as possible friendly civilian casualties. Now that the entire Command was available to concentrate on the Transportation Plan, it would proceed apace, and despite the prohibitive losses of the winter, the bomber force was in remarkably fine fettle to face its new challenge. Harris was now in the enviable position of being able to achieve that which had eluded his predecessor, namely to attack multiple targets simultaneously with forces large enough to make an impact. He could assign targets to individual Groups, to Groups in tandem, or to the Command as a whole, as dictated by operational requirements, and whilst pre-invasion considerations dominated, Harris was never going to entirely shelve his favoured policy of city-busting.

April began for the Command with minor operations, and the 6 Group account was opened on the night of the 1/2nd by twenty-two Halifaxes from 419 and 434 Squadrons gardening around the Frisians. There was also a change in leadership for three 6 Group squadrons during the first week. 425 Squadron bade farewell to W/C Richer on the 3rd and welcomed W/C McLernon as his successor, who, it will be remembered, had evaded capture after being shot down during the Berlin operation of the 23/24th of August 1943 while serving as a flight commander with 434 Squadron. 426 Squadron parted company with W/C Swetman on the 4th, and he was succeeded by W/C Hamber, who had previously served as a flight commander with 419 Squadron. W/C Dan McIntosh departed 420 Squadron on the 7th after his year at the helm, and W/C McKenna was appointed in his place. The new offensive did not get under way in earnest until the night of the 9/10th, when two operations were mounted against railway targets in France. A total of 239 aircraft from 3, 4, 6 and 8 Groups, including fifty-three Halifaxes from 419, 428, 431 and 434 Squadrons, attacked the Lille-Delivrance goods station to excellent effect, destroying in the process over two thousand items of rolling stock, and extensively damaging track and buildings. The success of the operation was marred only by the heavy casualties among French civilians in adjacent residential districts. Around five thousand houses were destroyed or damaged, and 456 people were killed. It was a fact of life that bombing, until the advent of laser guidance, was indiscriminate and required saturation to cope with precision targets like railway yards in built-up areas. The night's other operation at the Villeneuve-St-Georges railway yards in Paris, conducted by elements from all the Groups including a contingent of nine Lancasters and a hundred Mk III Halifaxes from 6 Group, also resulted in civilian deaths, although on a much smaller scale. It was while forming up over Yorkshire before embarking on the outward flight that 427 Squadron's LV960 collided with LW437 of 424 Squadron and sustained slight damage. Unfortunately, the Halifax became difficult to control, and was ultimately abandoned by F/S Stevens and his crew, who all landed safely.

On the following night four railway yards were targeted in France and one in Belgium, and the Group's Lancaster brigade accompanied others of the type from 3 Group to attend to those at Laon. All eleven of the Group's Halifax units contributed to the 122 aircraft assigned to Ghent, where severe damage was inflicted upon the Merelbeke-Melle railway yards, but almost six hundred buildings were destroyed in adjacent districts and 428 Belgians were killed. 427 Squadron's LV883 was hit by flak at the coast, which caused damage to an engine and forced an early return. W/C Burgess, who was on attachment from 433 Squadron prior to taking command of 426 Squadron, ordered the crew to bale out over East Anglia, and all came safely to earth. On the 11/12th Harris sent over 350 Lancasters and Mosquitos from 1, 3, 5 and 8 Groups across the German frontier to attack Aachen. It was the town's worst night of the war, and it was left with massive damage to buildings and communications, while over fifteen hundred of its people were killed. Linton-on-Ouse was stood down for this night, and along with most main force units 408 and 426 Squadrons would enjoy a week away from operations. During this lull the Thunderbirds took delivery of Halifax Mk III aircraft to replace their Lancasters, but bombing operations would continue exclusively on Lancasters until the start of May.

On the 14th of April Bomber Command officially became subject to the dictates of SHAEF for the pre and post-invasion campaigns. It would remain thus shackled until the Allied armies were sweeping towards the German frontier at the end of the summer. Also on this day 431 Squadron completed its re-equipment with Mk III Halifaxes, and could reclaim its place on the order of battle for operations over Germany. After the welcome rest for the Command, operations resumed on the night of the 18/19th, when four railway yards were attacked. 6 Group's contingent of twenty-five Lancasters and 112 Halifaxes concentrated on those at Noisy-le-Sec, where damage to the yards, locomotive sheds and workshops was extensive, and it would be long after the war before repairs were completed. Delayed action bombs made the area unsafe for a further week, but a through line was established within days. It was another tragedy for the local population, however, and over 460 French civilians lost their lives as 750 houses were destroyed. It was an eventful night for 427 Squadron with two crews reporting collisions and another failing to return. The absent crew was that of W/O Coathup, who were all killed when LV789 crashed in France. The collision involving Sgt Ellwood's aircraft occurred with another Halifax over the target, and it cost six feet of the starboard wing. 432 Squadron lost one aircraft, and 433 Squadron two, and there were just two survivors from among the twenty-two crewmen involved. 419 Squadron also posted missing one crew from a mining sortie on this night. On the night of the 20/21st, twenty-two 6 Group Lancasters joined others of the type to raid Cologne to devastating effect. At the same time 154 Halifaxes from 6 Group took part in an attack on the railway yards at Lens. Bombing was accurate, and the engine sheds and carriage repair shops in particular sustained heavy damage. One 420 Squadron aircraft failed to return, and a 428 Squadron Halifax crash-landed at Attlebridge after being attacked homebound by a night fighter and catching fire. The pilot ordered the crew to abandon ship, and three complied before the fire was extinguished and control of the aircraft regained. Another 428 Squadron aircraft was one of five Ghosts to conduct mining sorties off le Havre also on this night. An engine fire spread quickly to the wing, and the pilot, a flight commander, ordered his crew to bale out. This all but one did successfully, but one man's chute failed to open. The pilot, S/L McGugan, was unable to save himself and went down with the Halifax. On the 22/23rd almost six hundred aircraft, among them twenty-three Lancasters and 114 Halifaxes from 6 Group, took part in an area raid on Düsseldorf, which left extensive damage mostly in northern districts. Night fighters infiltrated the bomber stream, and twenty-nine bombers were shot down, eight of them 6 Group Halifaxes. Hardest hit with three failures to return was 433 Squadron. 429 Squadron lost two aircraft, and there were single losses to 424, 425 and 431 Squadrons. A simultaneous attack on railway yards at Laon resulted in the failure to return of a 419 Squadron Halifax, which was shot down by a night fighter. The American pilot and three of his crew evaded capture, while two others survived as PoWs. On the following night a 428 Squadron Halifax went down during a mining operation in the west Baltic region after being shot up by a night fighter. The pilot turned towards Sweden, but it became necessary to abandon the aircraft, and all but the pilot survived to ultimately evade capture.

Karlsruhe was the main force target for an old-fashioned area attack on the 24/25th, while 5 Group, now referred to in 8 Group circles somewhat disparagingly as the 'Independent Air Force', went to Münich. Over six hundred aircraft were involved in the main operation, including twenty-one Lancasters and 116 Halifaxes from 6 Group, on a night when cloud over the target and strong winds helped to push the marking and bombing away from the city centre and over open country, and only the northern districts sustained serious damage. Nineteen aircraft were missing, and among them were one from 420 Squadron, and two from 424 Squadron, each of which produced two survivors. There were initially fourteen survivors from the two 425 Squadron Halifaxes to be lost, but one of five evaders, W/O Dube, was caught and murdered on the 8th of August. The 427 Squadron casualty was not the result of enemy action, but rather LV968's controls icing up during the outward flight over Germany, which made it necessary for the crew to abandon ship. P/O Purvis and four of his crew fell into enemy hands, while two others went down with the aircraft. The night of the 26/27th was one of heavy activity involving three major operations at widely dispersed targets. Almost five hundred aircraft attacked Essen to good effect, while the older 6 Group Halifaxes joined others from 4 Group and 8 Group Mosquitos to continue the railway campaign with a successful assault on the yards at Villeneuve-St-Georges. 5 Group was again operating independently, and on this occasion failing to make an impression on Schweinfurt. Twenty-four Lancasters and ninety-four Halifaxes from 6 Group were present at the first mentioned, and all but one 408 Squadron Lancaster returned safely home.

The following night saw 6 Group involved in three operations, one of them a 1, 3 and 6 Group raid on the highly industrialised town of Friedrichshafen deep in southern Germany, which had been identified as a centre of tank engine and gearbox production. 408 and 426 Squadrons put up nineteen Lancasters between them, and all returned home. Meanwhile, 419 Squadron's association with the Halifax II came to an end at Montzen in Belgium, in an operation that also brought its final casualty in the type and its first sorties on Lancasters. Forty-seven 6 Group Halifaxes and eight standard Lancasters joined ninety other aircraft from 4 and 8 Groups in an attempt to dismantle the railway yards. The bombing was scattered and only half of the target was damaged. The second wave suffered heavily at the hands of night fighters, and 419 Squadron's JN954 was despatched by one of them over Holland. P/O McIvor and his crew thereby had the sad honour of being the last Moose crew to be killed in a Merlin-powered Halifax. Having operated the unpopular Mk II Halifaxes for so long, a misplaced air of confidence probably accompanied the arrival of Lancasters, and although as a type it was immeasurably superior, a spate of losses during May would dispel any such feelings. 431 Squadron was badly mauled and four empty dispersals were grim testimony to an unhappy night. 432 Squadron also sustained heavy casualties with three failures to return, and 434 Squadron lost two. The night's third operation took place against a similar target at Aulnoye, for which seven of the Group's squadrons contributed ninety Halifaxes without loss. The month ended for 6 Group with it acting as the main force for a raid on the railway yards at Somain on the night of the 30th of April. Some 114 Halifaxes took part, and although much of the early bombing fell into open country after some inaccurate marking, later arrivals caused some damage for the loss of just one 420 Squadron aircraft.

On the 1st of May Croft and Middleton St George were designated 64 Base. Having been installed as the new commanding officer of 429

Squadron also on the 1st of May, W/C Avant would have time during a coming lull in main force operations to settle into his new job. He had previously served as a flight commander with 426 Squadron. The new month began with six small to medium-scale raids on the 1/2nd against railway installations and factories in France and Belgium. A 6 Group main force of twenty-six Lancasters and eighty-nine Halifaxes delivered a highly accurate attack on the marshalling yards at St Ghislain, from which the 426 Squadron element returned intact for the last time as a Lancaster II unit. 419 Squadron's KB711 was not so lucky, and became the first Mk X Lancaster to be lost on operations when it was shot down by a night fighter. The pilot, P/O McNary, was killed along with one other member of the crew, while the six survivors fell into enemy hands. A 429 Squadron Halifax exploded during a combat with another night fighter, and the pilot, who was wearing his parachute, was thrown into space to become the sole survivor. Mining operations occupied small numbers from 6 Group for the next six nights as mostly minor operations were carried out by the Command. One exception was the operation by 1 and 5 Groups against a panzer training camp and motor transport depot at Mailly-le-Camp on the 3rd/4th. The raid was ultimately successful, but communications difficulties in the target area between the marker leader, Master Bomber and the main force element led to a delay in the opening of the attack, and night fighters took advantage of the situation to score heavily. Forty-two Lancasters failed to return, and controversy abounds to this day concerning who was to blame. It was at this time that coastal batteries were added to the growing list of targets to be attacked in preparation for the invasion. It was important to maintain the enemy belief that the main landings would take place in the Calais area, and consequently, almost every attack on a heavy gun position up to the eve of the landings took place over the Pas-de-Calais. It was not even necessary to hit them, although this was always the intention, as long as the impression was given, that they were important pre-invasion targets. On the 7th KB716 of 419 Squadron crashlanded with a burst tyre after a training flight while in the hands of 1st Lt Hartshorn of the USAAF, but he and his crew walked away unhurt.

A coastal battery at St Valery-en-Caux was the target for fifty-six 6 Group Halifaxes on the night of the 7/8th of May, and this was 426 Squadron's maiden bombing operation on Halifax IIIs. On the 8/9th a 6 Group element of thirteen Lancasters and fifty-nine Halifaxes was assigned to the railway yards at Haine-St-Pierre, where half of the yards and the locomotive sheds sustained serious damage. 425 Squadron posted missing one crew, and 426 Squadron suffered its first Halifax casualty in the form of MZ598. Both crews were captained by members of the USAAF, and both lost their lives. There were two missing Halifaxes each also from 431 and 432 Squadrons, both falling to the guns of night fighters, and both producing two evaders and two PoWs. W/C McLeish became the new commanding officer of 428 Squadron on the 9th, having previously served the squadron as a flight commander. That night twenty Lancasters and eighty-eight Halifaxes took part in a second attack on the coastal battery at St Valery-en-Caux and another at Calais, and all returned safely. On the 10th W/C Newson's tour as commanding officer of 431 Squadron came to an end, and he was posted to a non-flying job. In six months time, after promotion to Group Captain, he would return to the sharp end and assume command of 405 Squadron, remaining in post until the end of hostilities. His replacement at 431 Squadron was W/C 'Hank' Dow, who was posted in from his flight commander role with 434 Squadron on the 14th. It was back to railway targets at five locations on the 10/11th, when twenty-four Lancasters and ninety-four Halifaxes from 6 Group were assigned to the yards at Ghent. Sadly, the bombing here killed almost fifty Belgian civilians, but there were no losses among the attacking force. 419 Squadron's KB704 overshot the landing on return, but P/O Holmes and his crew survived the crash to fight another day. 427 Squadron's W/O Clibbery brought LV986 back to Woodbridge to be declared damaged beyond repair after an encounter with a night fighter. 424 Squadron, meanwhile, sent eleven Halifaxes mining off Brest and Heligoland, and lost one to a night fighter without survivors.

Twenty-four hours later a 6 Group main force of twenty-six Lancasters and eighty Halifaxes bombed railway yards at Boulogne-sur-Mer, and here too the attack was not entirely accurate, and almost 130 French civilians died. 427 Squadron's LW114 collided with NA500 of 432 Squadron over France, and both Halifaxes crashed to earth without survivors from the fifteen men on board. The Leaside aircraft was captained by flight commander S/L Barrett. The Croft squadrons were back in action on this night without loss, before the Bluenoses were stood down for two weeks to undergo conversion to the eagerly anticipated Halifax III. The 12/13th brought a raid on the railway yards at Louvain, which was being hit for the second night running. 6 Group sent ninety-six Halifaxes along with twelve Lancasters from 419 Squadron, and unlike the previous night's 3 and 8 Group assault, this one was highly effective, although heavy casualties were caused in adjacent residential districts. The attackers didn't get off lightly either, 419 Squadron losing two Lancasters and 431 Squadron one Halifax. The Moose casualties were P/O Smith and crew, who were all killed when KB710 was shot down by a night fighter over Belgium, and P/O Edwards and his crew, who likewise lost their lives when KB713 also crashed onto Belgian soil while outbound. It was a bad night for the Thunderbirds as well, who posted missing two crews. When LK883 crashed in Belgium F/O Black was taken prisoner and three others evaded a similar fate, but four members of the crew were killed. LW682 was yet another night fighter victim also over Belgium, and there were no survivors from the eight-man crew of P/O Bentz. Another training accident involving a 419 Squadron aircraft had tragic consequences for F/O McMaster and his crew, who were all killed when KB701 crashed in Yorkshire in the early hours of the 16th.

When heavy operations resumed on the 19/20th of May after a week of relative inactivity, most of the effort was directed at railway yards, although two coastal batteries and a radar station were also attacked. Fifteen Lancasters and forty-two Halifaxes from 408, 420, 425 and 426 Squadrons attended to coastal guns at Merville-Franceville in hazy conditions, and bombing was scattered. Meanwhile, fifty-eight other Halifaxes from the Group tried their luck at a similar target at Le Clipon, where results were also inconclusive. A year and one week after the last major assault on Duisburg Bomber Command returned to the Ruhr city on the 21/22nd. Over five hundred Lancasters from 1, 3, 5 and 8 Groups were accompanied by twenty-two Mosquitos, and despite cloud cover, Oboe allowed an accurate attack to be delivered. Some 350 buildings were completely destroyed, and many hundreds of others sustained serious damage. The Ruhr, however, remained fiercely protected, and in an echo of the past twenty-nine Lancasters failed to return. On the 22/23rd Dortmund hosted its first heavy raid since the Ruhr campaign, and sustained heavy damage at the hands of 1, 3, 6 and 8 Groups. The Canadian contribution amounted to twenty-seven Lancasters from 408 and 419 Squadrons, and three of these failed to return. The two 408 Squadron aircraft, DS759 and LL723, both fell to night fighters without survivors. The latter contained the nine man crew of the commanding officer, W/C Jacobs, and he became the third 408 Squadron commanding officer to be killed in action. It was a particularly sad loss, as he was just two operations short of completing his second tour. The blow to the squadron was compounded by the fact that the squadron navigation and gunnery leaders had flown with him on this night. 419 Squadron posted missing the eight man crew of P/O Patterson in KB717, and it was later learned that all had died when it was shot down by a night fighter over Germany. While this operation was in progress 112 Halifaxes from 6 Group attacked railway yards at Le Mans, and lost three of their number, one each from 425, 429 and 432 Squadrons with just one survivor between them. It was an eventful operation for 426 Squadron's P/O Mann and his crew, who had just delivered their bombs over the aiming point when another Halifax hit them from below. The port-inner engine caught fire, and although that was soon extinguished the propeller had fallen off, and the port outer airscrew was bent. The port rudder and elevator were sliced through by a propeller from the other aircraft, the bomb doors were torn off, the mid-under turret was damaged, a .303 gun was wedged through the floor, and the starboard-outer cowling was missing. Despite this catalogue of damage the Halifax landed safely without crew casualties. A 420 Squadron crew reported being involved in a collision over the target, and damage to their Halifax's topside suggests it might have been the offender.

The new commanding officer at 408 Squadron was W/C McLernon, who arrived on the 24th of May from 425 Squadron, where he had been the commanding officer for less than two months. He presided over his first operation that night, when two railway yards at Aachen, Aachen-west and Rothe Erde in the east, were targeted by over four hundred Lancasters and Halifaxes, including thirty of the former and sixty of the latter from 6 Group. Both targets were hit, but as the operation was over Germany, the attack soon developed into an area assault. As a consequence, much damage was inflicted upon the town and villages adjacent to the railway installations. 419 Squadron's KB706 was caught by a night fighter over Holland on the way home, and W/O Robson and five of his crew died in the crash, while the other member succumbed to his injuries on the following day. 427 Squadron's F/L Stephen and crew survived an encounter with a night fighter, and landed safely at Woodbridge despite severe damage to their aircraft. 424 Squadron was missing one crew, but 429 Squadron was hardest hit among 6 Group, losing two Halifaxes to flak and a third to a night fighter. 434 Squadron had not operated since Boulogne, and returned to the fray on this night for its debut on Mk III Halifaxes to attack a coastal battery at Trouville. 425 Squadron appointed a new commanding officer in the form of W/C Lecomte, who had previously served the unit as a flight commander. Over eleven hundred sorties were launched by the Command on the 27/28th, the largest force attending to the military camp at Bourg-Leopold, which had escaped serious damage during an abandoned 5 Group assault two weeks earlier. 6 Group contributed thirty-two Lancasters and 117 Halifaxes for what was described as an accurate attack, but a number of Canadian units paid a price. 420 Squadron lost an eight-man crew captained by a flight commander, S/L Beall, and one of the Tigers went missing. Another collision involving a 427 Squadron aircraft claimed the lives of P/O Devereaux and his crew, after their LV831 made fatal contact with MZ295 of 429 Squadron over Belgium, and both aircraft plunged to the ground. LW365 fell victim to a night fighter also over Belgium, and there were no survivors from the crew of P/O Scobie. The night's final casualty came from 432 Squadron. W/C McKay relinquished command of 432 Squadron on the 30th, and was succeeded by W/C MacDonald, who was promoted to the position from his role as a flight commander with 431 Squadron. 433 Squadron bade a fond farewell to the popular W/C Sinton on the 30th at the conclusion of his tour. He was posted away from the operational scene, and was succeeded on the 31st by W/C Lewington. On the last night of the month over two hundred aircraft from all but 5 Group carried out a two-wave attack on the railway yards at Trappes. The operation was successful, as was a 6 Group effort involving thirty-one Lancasters and 109 Halifaxes against a coastal transmitting station at Le Fevre. All crews returned to comment on the violence of the thunderstorms en route.

The first week of June was dominated by preparations for the impending invasion, and was characterised by unsettled weather. Some 6 Group squadrons joined the action on the night of the 2/3rd in an operation against a gun battery at Neufchatel. Fourteen Lancasters and fifty-six Halifaxes from 408, 420, 425, 426 and 432 Squadrons attacked the target from between six and eight thousand feet, and a number of crews reported night fighter activity. It was the turn of 419, 427, 429, 431 and 434 Squadrons to provide fourteen Lancasters and fifty-five Halifaxes on the 4/5th to hit a coastal battery in the Pas de Calais, and this they did without loss. Every 6 Group squadron took to the air on D-Day Eve, the 5/6th, when over a thousand Bomber Command aircraft were aloft to attack ten coastal batteries ahead of the invasion force. It was a record night from the Canadians' eleven Halifax and two Lancaster squadrons, which put up 192 and thirty-two respectively. More than five thousand tons of bombs were delivered onto the aiming points, a new record for a single night, and most of the effort was aimed at Oboe sky markers in the face of complete cloud cover. The 6 Group force was assigned to the coastal guns at Longues, Houlgate and Merville-Franceville, and bombing took place from between 9,000 and 12,000 feet. There was no direct reference to the invasion at briefings, but crews were ordered to observe strict flight levels, and were prohibited from jettisoning bombs over the sea. Aircraft were taking off throughout the night, and some of those returning in dawn's early light were rewarded with a sight of the giant invasion armada, as it ploughed its way sedately across the Channel below. There was just one 6 Group casualty, a 426 Squadron Halifax, which blew up over Norfolk while outbound in the early hours of the 6th, and there were no survivors.

D-Day Night brought a thousand more aircraft into action, including another 6 Group record of 204 Halifaxes and forty-four Lancasters to attack road and railway communications targets in or near towns on the approaches to the beachhead. 6 Group's targets were at Coutances and Conde Sur Noireau, which they attacked from as low as two to four thousand feet. For the second night in a row a Thunderbird aircraft was involved in an incident, this time being struck by bombs from above. This time, however, there was a happy ending as the crew baled out over the Devon coast. The following night brought attacks on four railway targets by over three hundred Halifaxes and Lancasters, while elements of 1, 5 and 8 Groups went for a six-way road junction in the Forêt de Cerisy between Bayeux and St-Lo. 6 Group was assigned to a road/rail junction at Achères and railway yards at Versailles. During the course of the operation a 408 Squadron Lancaster crashed in a wooded area killing its eight-man crew, and they lay undisturbed until the bomb load went off in November 1945, six months after the war ended. Another eight-man crew was lost in a 420 Squadron Halifax. A 426 Squadron Halifax was coned by searchlights and hit by flak, and P/O Mann threw the aircraft into a steep dive in order to escape. Once back on an even keel it was discovered that four members of the crew had baled out. Only the two gunners remained, and they assisted their pilot in bringing the aircraft back home. 427 Squadron's LV987 failed to return after crashing in France, but all on board survived. W/O Foster and four of his crew managed to evade capture, but the remaining two men fell into enemy hands. 431 and 432 Squadrons each posted missing one crew.

The assault on enemy railway communications continued on the 8/9th at five locations, one of which was the 6 Group objective at Mayenne. Ten Lancasters and seventy Halifaxes took part in the operation to prevent German reinforcements from moving up to the beachhead, and bombing took place from between three and seven thousand feet. 426 Squadron's incident-packed month continued with the tragedy of LW598, which suffered an engine fire while in the Linton circuit and lost height, eventually side-slipping into houses in the town of Newton-on-Ouse. The mid-upper gunner, Sgt Neil, pulled his seriously injured pilot, P/O Craig, out of the wreckage, but there were no other survivors.

The Thunderbirds' commanding officer, W/C Hamber, returned to claim a BF109 as a probable. The following night was devoted to attacks on four airfields situated south of the beachhead, which might be used by the enemy to bring up reinforcements. All were successfully dealt with by elements of 1, 4, 6 and 8 Groups, the Canadians dispatching twenty-four Lancasters and seventy-six Halifaxes to le Mans, which some bombed from as low as one thousand feet.

Four railway objectives occupied over four hundred aircraft on the 10/11th, 6 Group going for the locomotive sheds at Versailles with ten 419 Squadron Lancasters and one hundred Halifaxes. A Snowy Owl Halifax failed to return with an eight-man crew, only two of whom survived to ultimately evade capture. A 429 Squadron Halifax also went down, this time with six evaders, while just the pilot made the ultimate sacrifice. In contrast all eight men died in the wreckage of a 434 Squadron aircraft.

Since early in the month Lancasters had been arriving at Middleton St George, and they would soon bring an end to 428 Squadron's relative isolation from main force activities. It must have been a great relief to the crews to relinquish the unpopular Merlin-powered Halifax, particularly as most other units had done so months earlier in favour of the Mk III. 428 Squadron had actually begun to convert to the new type back in January, but the process was cancelled, when it was decided to re-equip the squadron with Canadian-built Lancasters. For a time the squadron would operate both Halifaxes and Lancasters until crew conversion was completed. A training accident on the 11/12th involving JN953 bestowed upon it the dubious honour of being the last Mk II Halifax to be written off by a main force squadron. Engine failure forced F/O Martin to force-land in Yorkshire, and he and his crew were able to walk away.

A new campaign beginning on the night of the 12/13th would be prosecuted right through to the end of the war. With Germany now firmly on the back foot a concerted effort was to be made by both Bomber Command and the American 8th Air Force against its synthetic oil industry. Three hundred Lancasters and Mosquitos of 1, 3 and 8 Groups carried out a stunningly accurate attack on the Nordstern refinery at Gelsenkirchen, hitting it with fifteen hundred bombs, and halting all production for a number of weeks. This deprived the German war effort of a thousand tons of vital aviation fuel for each day of the stoppage. While this was in progress, over six hundred aircraft drawn from 4, 5, 6 and 8 Groups bombed six communications targets leading to the Normandy front. 6 Group contributed thirty-two Lancasters and sixty Halifaxes to an effective and destructive attack at Cambrai, but night fighters got amongst the bombers, bringing down nine of the Canucks. Three 408 Squadron Lancasters containing experienced crews, including that of a flight commander, fell victim, and just two men out of twenty-three lived to tell the tale. It was also a bad if heroic night for 419 Squadron, which likewise posted missing three of its crews. KB726 was intercepted by a JU88 before reaching the target, and its cannon fire put both port engines out of action, set fire to the wing, and ignited hydraulic fluid in the rear fuselage. F/O De Breyne ordered his crew to bale out, and he and four others did so safely. Before leaving the stricken aircraft, W/O Mynarski, the mid-upper gunner, realised that the rear gunner was trapped in his turret, the doors of which had become jammed, and made his way through the flames to attack them with an axe. Surrounded by flames which set his clothing alight, the gallant Mynarski vainly persisted with his attempts to free his colleague, F/O Brophy, but was eventually waved away, and having done all he could, he too exited the Lancaster, his clothing and parachute pack trailing fire. Miraculously, Brophy survived the impact unhurt, and along with his pilot and two others, evaded capture, but sadly, Mynarski succumbed to his terrible burns while in the hands of members of the French Resistance who had observed his descent. In October 1946, he was posthumously award the Victoria Cross, the only 6 Group man to be so honoured.

While these events were being played out, KB714 was falling to the guns of a night fighter over Belgium, with no survivors from the crew of F/O Wilson, and flak accounted for KB731, the only two survivors from F/O Lacey's crew ultimately evading capture. 426 Squadron's S/L McRobie and crew were in NA510, which was shot down by a night fighter over the Pas-de-Calais. The pilot and one other lost their lives, two men fell into enemy hands, but four managed to evade a similar fate. 432 Squadron posted missing two crews from this operation.

Meanwhile, eighty-nine 6 Group Halifaxes were targeting railway yards at Arras, and undergoing a similarly torrid time. Three 427 Squadron aircraft crashed in the Pas de Calais, among them LW165, which failed to survive an encounter with a night fighter, and F/O Proudfoot died with his crew. Four men died in the wreckage of LV995, but F/O Fulton and two of his crew managed to save themselves and evade capture. F/O Pearson and four of his crew were killed in LW135, while one man evaded and the other became a PoW. 434 Squadron was engaged at the same target and was also taking a beating from a fierce night fighter response. If it had been hoped and expected that Mk III Halifax would bring an end to the squadron's prohibitive losses of the past, there would be disappointment. This night brought three failures to return, one of which was LW173, the aircraft containing the commanding officer and his crew. W/C Bartlett and all but one of those on board were killed when they were shot down by a night fighter over the Pas de Calais. MZ293 crashed near Dunkerque without survivors from the crew of P/O Tandy, but all but the pilot, P/O Wood, survived the loss of LW713, four of them to evade capture. P/O Hawley and crew were attacked by a JU88, and both starboard engines caught fire, although the flames were extinguished. The rear gunner shot the assailant down, and a safe landing was ultimately carried out at West Raynham on two engines. W/C Watkins took over command of the squadron later on the 13th.

The first daylight operations by Bomber Command since the departure of 2 Group a year earlier were conducted against Le Havre on the evening of the 14th. The port was home to E-Boats and other fast, light naval craft, which posed a threat to Allied shipping serving the beachhead. The two-phase operation was opened by a 617 Squadron attack on the concrete pens with Tallboys, closely followed by a predominantly 1 Group force. 3 Group completed the assault at dusk, and few if any marine craft escaped the carnage unscathed. As this was in progress, elements of 4, 5 and 8 Groups were concentrating their efforts against enemy troop and transport positions at Aunay-sur-Odon and Evrecy. A third operation saw 6 Group contribute thirty-seven Lancasters and 155 Halifaxes to a joint effort with elements of 4 and 8 Groups against railway installations at Cambrai and St Pol. This was 428 Squadron's maiden Lancaster operation, and all returned safely, while 424 and 433 Squadrons each posted missing a crew, the former surviving intact and the latter all killed. The evening of the 15th was devoted to the bombing of Boulogne in a repeat of the previous night's operation against Le Havre, and this operation, by elements of 1, 4, 5, 6 and 8 Groups, was equally effective, although the town itself suffered its worst experience of the war. 6 Group provided thirty-two Lancasters and 130 Halifaxes, of which a single 425 Squadron Halifax was lost.

A second new campaign opened on the night of the 16/17th, this one against flying bomb launching and storage sites. Some 101 Halifaxes from 6 Group joined elements of 1, 4, 5 and 8 Groups to make up an overall force of four hundred aircraft to attack four targets in the Pas-de-Calais. Meanwhile on this night a second force from 1, 4, 6 and 8 Groups continued the oil offensive at Sterkrade/Holten, but failed to inflict more than slight damage in the face of complete cloud cover. Thirty-seven Lancasters and sixty-three Halifaxes represented 6 Group on a night that would be remembered for all the wrong reasons. Among the many missing aircraft were two Lancasters from 419 Squadron, KB728 falling to a night fighter over Holland with no survivors from the crew of F/O Morrison, and KB734 also crashed onto Dutch soil killing F/L Smith and four of his crew, while one man was captured and another evaded the same fate. The crew of 1st Lt Hartshorn of the USAAF almost became another statistic after they were attacked by a night fighter and were then hit by flak. The astrodome disappeared, and there were holes in the windscreen, fuselage and bomb doors, while the wireless operator sustained injuries as shrapnel invaded his compartment. An ME410 became the next unwelcome visitor, but the rear gunner sent it packing with a port engine on fire and the Lancaster eventually made it home to a safe landing. The night became a total disaster for Croft, where eight empty dispersals provided grim testimony of the fortunes of both squadrons, each of which had lost four aircraft and crews. It would be learned later, that thirty-four men had made the ultimate sacrifice, eighteen survived as PoWs and four managed to retain their freedom. 426 and 432 Squadrons each posted missing one crew to complete an unhappy night for the Group.

Railways were the principal objectives on the 17/18th, but twelve Lancasters and ninety Halifaxes from 6 Group acted as the main force for an attack on a constructional site at Oisement/Neuville-au-Bois in the Abbeville area. Thirty-nine Lancasters and sixty-six Halifaxes from 6 Group went to a similar site at St Martin L'Hortier by daylight on the 21st, while eighty-four Halifaxes from 424, 427, 429, 431, 433 and 434 Squadrons joined in at Oisemont, although not all participants bombed because of complete cloud cover. Later that night 5 Group embarked on its first involvement in the current oil campaign, when sending one force to the oil refinery at Wesseling, on the west bank of the Rhine south of Cologne, and another to Scholven/Buer near Gelsenkirchen. Those bound for the former were picked up by night fighters as they made their way across the frontier region of Holland and Belgium, and a bitter battle ensued. By the time the badly mauled survivors reached home, thirty-seven Lancasters had fallen victim to the defences, mostly to night fighters. Four 5 Group squadrons, 44, 49, 57 and 619, had each lost six aircraft, although one of the 57 Squadron crews was plucked from the sea off Yarmouth without injury. From this point on daylight operations were to become increasingly common as the summer progressed, while night operations continued unabated. The target for some 6 Group squadrons on the 23/24th was a V-1 site at Bientques, one of four flying bomb sites assigned to forces from 3, 4, 6 and 8 Groups. 6 Group put up thirty-nine Lancasters and sixty-five Halifaxes, and all returned safely. On the following day three more sites were hit, 6 Group contributing ninety-nine Halifaxes to the one at Bonnetot. On the 24/25th 408, 419 and 428 Squadrons contributed thirty-eight Lancasters and 420, 425, 426 and 432 Squadrons sixty-five Halifaxes to an operation against a V-1 launching site at Bameries, and again there were no losses. In total 101 Halifaxes from the other 6 Group squadrons were in action later on the 25th to hit a site at Gorenflos, and the bombing was accurate in clear conditions. There were six aiming points for more than seven hundred aircraft on the 27/28th, when 6 Group put up forty-one Lancasters and 169 Halifaxes, whose crews were briefed to attack a site at Wizernes and another in the Forêt de Eawy. All operations were declared successful, and there were no losses among 6 Group aircraft until they arrived home. 425 Squadron's MZ683 landed at Tholthorpe on three engines and swung into LW680, which was loaded with bombs, and MZ618, which had also just returned. All three aircraft caught fire, and a major rescue effort ensued by air and ground crew to pull their comrades to safety amidst explosions and flames. Miraculously, there were no fatalities, but the base commander, Air Commodore Ross, lost a hand when a 500-pounder went off as he battled with others to save a rear gunner.

While some 6 Group squadrons were now stood down for the month, operations continued for others. The railway yards at Metz provided the target for a hundred Halifaxes from 6 Group on the 28/29th, while Blainville was the objective for 4 Group. Both targets were hit, but a total of eighteen Halifaxes was shot down, along with one Lancaster from each operation. 424 Squadron lost two aircraft, with one crew surviving intact and the other crew all killed. It was the final operation of a busy month for 426 Squadron, and it resulted in two missing aircraft, although many of the occupants would manage to escape the clutches of the enemy. LW198 was shot down over France by a night fighter killing just one member of the crew, while F/O Gerard and five others went on the run and were soon in friendly hands. NP683 suffered a similar fate at the hands of a night fighter, and although all of its occupants survived initially on the run, the navigator and mid-upper gunner ultimately fell into enemy hands, and their deaths were recorded on the 22nd of August. Two other crew members were also captured, but F/L Logan and the remaining two managed to retain their freedom. These were the first Mk VII Halifaxes to be lost by Bomber Command. 427 Squadron's LV938 was brought down by flak over France killing one of the crew, while W/O King and four others were taken into captivity and one man was apprehended by the enemy. On a night when an unusually high proportion of crewmen survived being shot down, one entire 429 Squadron crew did likewise, but only one got out alive from 432 Squadron's missing Halifax. It had been a busy month for the whole Command, and it ended with a raid on a road junction at Villers-Bocage on the evening of the 30th. It provided access for a German counter attack at a weak point in the Anglo-American lines, but after accurate bombing by the 3 and 4 Group main force crews, who were brought down by the Master Bomber to four thousand feet, the planned German attack was scrubbed.

June, July and August were to be Bomber Command's most hectic months of the year, as the side-by-side campaigns against communications, oil and flying bomb sites all demanded attention. To this was about to be added tactical support for the ground forces as they broke out of the beachhead into Normandy, but the main emphasis during the first two weeks of July was unquestionably on flying bomb sites. Some 6 Group Halifax squadrons, 420, 425, 426, 431, 432 and 434, opened their July account on the afternoon of the 1st at Biennais, one of three sites to be targeted. Bombing had to be conducted on Oboe sky markers in the face of almost complete cloud cover, and results could not be assessed. Following a two-night rest the same squadrons returned to Biennais with ninety-nine aircraft by daylight on the 4th, and W/C Burgess had a tyre blow on his 426 Squadron chariot on landing at Linton-on-Ouse on return. Officially on the strength of 433 Squadron, it is likely that he was gaining operational experience with 426 Squadron before assuming command on the 11th. That night of the 4/5th thirty-eight Lancasters and sixty-four Halifaxes of the other 6 Group units carried out their first operation of the new month, when joining in on an attack on the railway yards at Villeneuve-St-Georges. It was a night of fierce night fighter activity, and many crews came home with combat reports. Of the eleven missing Lancasters, three were from 419 Squadron, and a fourth was a 35 Squadron aircraft containing the previously mentioned S/L Alec Cranswick, who had served with the Moosemen in January 1943. He had recently embarked on his fourth tour of operations and at the time of his death had more than one hundred operations to his name. All three 419 Squadron aircraft came down in France, KB718 and KB727 after encounters with night fighters, and all survived from the crews of F/O Frame and F/O Stevenson, both pilots and three others from the former evading capture. KB723 was brought down by flak, and F/O Steepe and two of his crew also evaded capture, while one didn't and three were killed. Three 427 Squadron crews were among those coming back with reports of encounters with night fighters, all of which were hit by return fire. LW166 didn't make it back, however, having crashed in France killing F/O Moss and his flight engineer, while two men evaded capture and three fell into enemy hands. 433 Squadron posted missing three crews, and later learned that seven of the survivors were in enemy hands, and five others had evaded capture. 424 and 428 Squadrons each registered one missing aircraft.

420, 425, 426, 431, 432 and 434 Squadrons returned to Biennais with ninety-nine Halifaxes on the night of the 5/6th, and all returned safely after a successful operation in clear conditions. There should have been one hundred aircraft, but 431 Squadron's MZ657 veered off the runway during take-off, crashed and exploded. Although all of the crew survived the accident, the bomb-aimer later succumbed to his injuries. While this operation was in progress six 428 Squadron Halifaxes conducted mining operations, and these were the final sorties by the older versions in 6 Group service. Operations on the 6th involved over five hundred aircraft attacking five V-1 storage sites, four of which were clear of cloud. One 6 Group target was at Siracourt, to which went thirty-one Lancasters and fifty-nine Halifaxes. One 424 Squadron aircraft was shot down by flak, and the crew was killed. A second target for the Canucks was at Coquereaux, which was attended by twelve Lancasters and forty-eight Halifaxes without loss. The first major operation in support of the ground forces was mounted on the evening of the 7th by 467 aircraft drawn from 1, 4, 6 and 8 Groups. The target was the northern rim of Caen, behind a series of fortified villages from where enemy units were facing British and Canadian forces. W/C Daniels of 35 Squadron acted as Master Bomber, and the attack was accurate, if ultimately counter-productive, as few enemy troops were killed and eventual passage through the town was rendered difficult by rubble-blocked streets. Twenty-seven Lancasters and sixty-one Halifaxes from 6 Group took part, and all returned without major incident. Briefings took place at 3, 4, 6 and 8 Group stations on the 9th for six flying bomb sites, for which over two hundred aircraft from 4, 6 and 8 Groups were to be involved. The 6 Group targets were a storage dump at Thiverny, and launching sites at Mont Candon and Ardouval, but the month's persistent cloud cover led to a lack of concentration at some of the aiming points. 6 Group committed eight Lancaster and ninety-two Halifaxes to the operations, and again all returned safely. Almost two hundred Halifaxes from 4 and 6 Groups attacked four sites during the course of the 12th, beginning with twenty-seven Lancasters and sixty-five Halifaxes returning to Thiverny. Later, eight 428 Squadron Lancasters and ninety-one 6 Group Halifaxes were assigned to aiming points at Bremont and Acquet, and there were no losses. A similar target at Anderbelck occupied fifty Halifaxes from 424, 427, 429 and 433 Squadrons on the 14/15th, and all came home safely. This was the first operation presided over by 427 Squadron's new commanding officer, W/C Cribb, who had been promoted from flight commander to replace W/C Turnbull on the 13th. The hectic month's operation continued on the following evening when twenty-seven Lancasters and sixty-four Halifaxes of 6 Group participated in attacks on a V-1 storage site at Nucourt and a launching site at Bois des Jardines.

6 Group returned to the fray in the early hours of the 18th with forty-two Lancasters and 155 Halifaxes to help provide tactical support for the British Second Army. The ground forces were about to launch Operation *Goodwood*, an armoured attack on enemy positions around Caen, and over nine hundred aircraft were to deliver a major assault on five fortified villages. American bombers also participated, but RAF aircraft carried

5,000 of the 6,800 tons of bombs delivered onto the aiming points. The operations were a stunning success, and in the absence of enemy fighters, only six aircraft were lost to flak. One of these was 427 Squadron's LV985, which failed to return from Mondeville having crashed in France killing P/O Kelly and his crew. A 429 Squadron Halifax was hit by bombs from above, and the pilot and three others escaped by parachute before the inevitable crash. A 432 Squadron aircraft fell victim to flak, and all but a wounded crew member were able to escape. Later in the day twenty-eight Halifaxes from 431 and 434 Squadrons attacked railway yards at Vaires, and two Iroquois aircraft failed to return. One contained the eight-man crew of a flight commander, S/L Bull, and there were no survivors, and just the pilot escaped with his life from the other Halifax. That night brought much further activity, including an attack by elements of 1, 6 and 8 Groups on the oil refinery at Wesseling near Cologne. Forty-two Lancasters and 111 Halifaxes from 6 Group took part in what developed into a highly effective operation for the loss of a single 425 Squadron Halifax. All thirteen 6 Group squadrons contributed to attacks on V-1 sites at L'Hey, Anderbelck, Ferme du Forestal and Ferme du Grand Bois in the Pas-de-Calais on the 20th, and there were no losses among the forty-one Lancasters and 157 Halifaxes.

There had been no major operations against a German city target since Dortmund in May, while the Normandy landings and consolidation of the Allied foothold had been the overriding considerations. Now, on the night of the 23/24th, Harris launched an attack on Kiel by over six hundred aircraft, all but 110 of them Lancasters. The force appeared suddenly and with complete surprise from behind a Mandrel RCM screen laid on by 100 Group, and inflicted heavy damage on the town and the port area, where all of the U-Boat yards were hit. 6 Group provided forty-two Lancasters from its three operators of the type, and the only major incident involved DS692 of 408 Squadron. A wing leading edge opened up shortly after take-off, preventing the aircraft from gaining speed and altitude. A successful crash-landing was carried out at Marston Moor, and the crew was able to walk away before fire consumed the wreckage. While the Kiel operation was in progress, another took place against oil storage facilities at Donges with one hundred 6 Group Halifaxes in attendance. Bombing was accurate, and much damage was inflicted upon the installations and a ship was sunk in the harbour. This was followed on the 24/25th by the first of three major raids on Stuttgart over a five-night period, involving a force of over six hundred aircraft. Stuttgart had always proved a difficult target to hit because of its location in a series of valleys, although extensive damage had been inflicted upon it during the three raid series in February and March. The central districts became heavily damaged on this night for the loss of twenty-one aircraft. 6 Group dispatched forty Lancasters, and just one failed to return. 419 Squadron's KB719 crashed in France, possibly having been hit by a rocket, and F/S Phillis and one of his crew evaded capture, while another became a PoW and four others were killed. It was during this operation that F/O Clothier and his crew logged 408 Squadron's 3,000th sortie of the war while flying in LL722. Meanwhile, a hundred 6 Group Halifaxes from all but 431 and 434 Squadrons attacked two flying bomb sites at L'Hey and Ferfay. Poor weather intervened, however, and the Master Bomber sent most of the crews home with their bomb loads intact. One 420 Squadron Halifax went down in the Channel, and all eight men were lost.

In total 550 aircraft set out to return to Stuttgart on the following night, including a contingent from 6 Group of thirty-seven Lancasters and 140 Halifaxes. They delivered what would prove to be the most devastating of the three attacks. Among the missing aircraft was MZ858, which was brought down by flak over Germany. On board was the commanding officer of 431 Squadron, W/C Dow, who survived with four of his crew to become PoWs. Also missing were two 432 Squadron aircraft, including NP687, which was hit by flak over the target and had to be abandoned over France by W/C MacDonald and five of his crew, all of whom evaded capture. One man was killed after apparently going down with the aircraft. A 427 Squadron Halifax was severely damaged by flak, and the crew baled out successfully over Normandy to land in Allied territory. 429 Squadron was the other 6 Group unit to post missing a crew. W/C MacDonald would return to 432 Squadron in September. Meanwhile, S/L Lowe was promoted from his flight commander post to succeed him as commanding officer, and W/C Mitchell was installed as the new boss of 431 Squadron on the 27th. During the course of July 408 and 432 Squadrons began to receive Mk VII Halifaxes, and the former's B Flight was completely converted by the end of the month. These aircraft, with a few Mk IIIs thrown in, would see both squadrons through to the end of the bombing war. For the time being, however, 408 Squadron would operate Halifaxes and Lancasters alongside each other.

While all this activity was ongoing 415 Squadron became the latest and, indeed, the last squadron to join the ranks of 6 Group, which it did on the 26th. It had by then spent two years in Coastal Command since its formation. W/C McNeill had been appointed as the squadron's commanding officer on the 12th of July, having served with 426 Squadron during the previous year, but a tragic flying accident a few weeks later would prematurely end his tenure, and, sadly, his life. Having already operated Halifaxes in Coastal Command the squadron was quickly able to begin bombing operations on the type, and having moved in to East Moor, a station it would share with 432 Squadron, it prepared itself for the fray.

An all-Lancaster force from 1, 3, 5 and 8 Groups returned to Stuttgart on the 28/29th, while forty-six Lancasters and 186 Halifaxes from 6 Group joined elements from 1 and 8 Groups to target Hamburg. The latter operation heralded the arrival of 415 Squadron on the operational scene, and it would prove to be an eventful debut. MZ686 lost an engine on take-off at East Moor and crashed, but P/O Andrews and his seven crew mates walked away with only slight injuries. The night soon degenerated into a disaster for the Command, as night fighters intercepted the Stuttgart-bound bomber stream over France in bright moonlight, and others caught the Hamburg force on the way home, with the result that thirty-nine and twenty-two aircraft respectively were brought down. 415 Squadron's P/O Little reported being attacked four times by a single engine enemy aircraft without sustaining damage to MZ690, and P/O Forbes survived the attention of three more in NA582. Three other crews also had stories to relate about encounters with night fighters, including one in a Halifax borrowed from 432 Squadron, but they likewise came through their experiences unscathed. However, 415 Squadron did have to post missing the nine-man crew of F/O Stein. The pilot and all but one of those on board LW595 were killed in the crash in Germany, while the sole survivor was taken into captivity. 408 Squadron's contribution included six Halifaxes on their first operation, and one of them was among the four 'Goose' aircraft missing. It was one of the paradoxes of the period, that the Group could operate for days without a single loss, and then suddenly, suffer a hammer-blow to redress the balance. 424 Squadron lost its commanding officer, W/C Blane, who was killed with one other of his crew, and 425 Squadron had two aircraft go missing without trace, one with nine men on board and the other with eight. 426 and 434 Squadrons also posted missing two crews, 420, 427, 428, 432 and 433 Squadrons one each, but it was 431 Squadron that sustained the night's heaviest casualties with five lost aircraft, from which twenty-eight men were killed and seven survived in captivity. In the early morning of the 30th, almost seven hundred aircraft took off to attack six German positions facing predominantly American ground forces in the Villers Bocage – Caumont area. Ninety-nine 6 Group Halifaxes took part at Amaye-sur-Suelles, some bombing from as low as fifteen hundred feet, and this time there were no losses. The month ended for the Group with a raid by seventy-six Halifaxes on a V-1 launching site at Forêt du Croc on the night of the 31st, and this scattered attack cost a single 429 Squadron aircraft. It had been a hectic but generally rewarding month for the Command, but it had also been expensive, and many squadrons had sustained heavy casualties.

The first week of August was dominated by the campaign against flying bomb sites, and over 750 aircraft were involved in daylight operations on the 1st. 6 Group dispatched thirty-seven Lancasters and 103 Halifaxes to targets at L'Hey, Acquet and Ferme du Forestal, but only one 6 Group aircraft bombed before the Master Bomber called a halt to proceedings in the face of complete cloud cover. The Canadians remained on the ground on the 2nd, when almost four hundred aircraft launched effective attacks on one launching and three supply sites. 6 Group was now at peak strength, and this enabled it to put up a record fifty-one Lancasters and 210 Halifaxes on the 3rd for attacks on V-1 storage sites at Forêt de Nieppe and Bois de Cassan. More than eleven hundred aircraft were active at these and others at Trossy-St-Maxim and L'Isle Adam, and the operations were deemed successful in clear weather conditions. The success was made even sweeter for 6 Group when all of its aircraft returned home. The 427 Squadron crew of F/O Murphy had a lucky escape after falling bombs left a hole in the starboard wing and another through the fuselage behind the mid-upper turret, but they got back otherwise in one piece. A 6 Group main force of forty-two Lancasters and 159 Halifaxes went back to the Bois de Cassan and Trossy-St-Maximin sites on the 4th, delivering effective attacks in clear conditions, and a modest four aircraft were lost from the 291 dispatched. 424 and 434 Squadrons each posted missing one crew, and a 433 Squadron Halifax had its rudder controls shot off by flak. The crew got home by manipulating the rudders manually from the rear of the aircraft, but with no hope of a controlled landing F/O Simpson and his crew baled out over the airfield and all landed safely. On the 5th more than seven hundred aircraft pounded the storage sites in the Forêt de Nieppe and at St-Leu-d'Esserent. 6 Group was assigned to the latter with fifty-two Lancasters and 172 Halifaxes, and a single 425 Squadron Halifax containing flight commander S/L Philbin and his crew, was the only failure to return from a successful operation. Only the pilot and one other survived after they were brought down by flak, and the former evaded capture.

From mid evening on the 7th aircraft began taking off to attack five aiming points ahead of Allied ground forces in the Normandy battle area. 6 Group put up what amounted to a maximum effort comprising forty Lancasters and 182 Halifaxes as part of a force of over a thousand heavy bombers, but because of the close proximity of Allied troops the attacks were carefully controlled by the Master Bombers, and only two thirds of the aircraft actually bombed. The sole 6 Group failure to return was KB755, a 419 Squadron Lancaster, which crashed in France with no survivors from the crew of F/O Walker.

The Group was up again on the 8th with forty-three Lancasters and 148 Halifaxes for a raid on fuel and oil storage facilities in the Forêt de Chantilly, which were left burning. A 429 Squadron Halifax was seen to be on fire while outbound, and was descending through five thousand feet when it exploded, and only the navigator survived. This was the day on which W/C Hull became 428 Squadron's new commanding officer, having previously served as a flight commander with 420 Squadron.

The 9th saw thirty-seven Lancasters and ninety-one Halifaxes from 6 Group contribute to raids on six V-1 sites, including one at Le Neuville, from which 427 Squadron's MZ363 failed to return, and news eventually came through that F/L Wyse and his crew had lost their lives. That night nine Lancasters and 104 Halifaxes of 6 Group attacked launching and storage sites in the Forêt de Nieppe, and all returned without incident.

The busy schedule continued on the evening of the 10/11th with attacks on two oil storage depots at Bordeaux and La Pallice. While 5 Group attended to the former, 6 Group sent thirty-seven Lancasters and 101 Halifaxes to the latter, and a successful operation ensued without loss. A similar target in the Forêt de Mont Richard occupied nine Lancasters and ninety-four Halifaxes of 6 Group, and although no aircraft were brought down, the Halifax of 420 Squadron's commanding officer, W/C McKenna, was hit by flak before the target was reached and his navigator was killed.

The night of the 12/13th was to be particularly busy, with over eleven hundred sorties being launched on various major and minor operations. One of them involved 380 crews of the main force being briefed for a raid on Brunswick, in which no Pathfinder aircraft were to take part. The intention was to gauge the ability of crews to locate and bomb an urban target purely on the strength of H2s. Meanwhile, almost three hundred aircraft would split the defences by attacking the Opel motor works at Rüsselsheim in southern Germany, 144 others were to bomb German troops and a road junction at Falaise, and a small raid would take place against flying bomb targets. In addition, numerous other sweeps, mining and support activity would keep the enemy night fighter controller on his toes, and make it more difficult to decide upon a response. 6 Group participated at Brunswick with twenty-one Lancasters and forty-eight Halifaxes, at Falaise with twelve Lancasters and thirty-six Halifaxes, and at the V-1 sites at La Breteque and Le Neuville with forty Halifaxes. Generally, apart from the Falaise operation, the night's huge effort was not rewarded with great success. At Brunswick the bombing was scattered across the town and up to twenty miles distant, thus demonstrating that Pathfinders remained a necessity. Even so, their presence at the attack on the Opel works did not prevent much of the bombing from being wasted on open country, and the damage inflicted on the factory was insufficient to cause a loss of production. Twenty-seven and twenty aircraft respectively were lost, however, and this was a high price to pay for the poor return. 427 Squadron's LV821 failed to make it home from the Brunswick raid, having crashed in the North Sea and taking with it the crew of F/L Cronyn. Three other crews reported encounters with enemy night fighters, and two of them each claimed an ME210 as destroyed. Happily the squadron would not lose another crew for almost two months. 424, 428, 429 and 434 Squadrons each had one crew fail to return from Brunswick, but there were no losses for the Group from the other operations. Ten Lions of 427 Squadron carried out the only 6 Group operation on the night of the 13/14th, when mining off La Rochelle.

The time was now fast approaching when Harris could claim that he had discharged his obligation to SHAEF, and could turn his attention once more upon industrial Germany almost to the exclusion of all else. However, tactical support for the ground forces was still required, and the afternoon of the 14th was devoted to large-scale operations in the Falaise area under Operation *Tractable*. Eight hundred aircraft were involved in the bombing of seven aiming points ahead of the Third Canadian Division, each controlled by a Master Bomber and deputy. 6 Group was involved with fifty-nine Lancasters and 159 Halifaxes, and most of the bombing was accurate, although some fell amongst Canadian troops in a quarry, killing thirteen men and injuring over fifty. Recriminations abounded thereafter over who was to blame, and some commanding officers were carpeted after their crews bombed too early. It seems, though, to have been a genuine accident brought about as much by events on the ground as in the air, and while conducting ground support operations.

In preparation for his new night offensive against Germany Harris launched a thousand aircraft on the morning of the 15th to attack nine night fighter airfields in Holland and Belgium. Among those attended to by 6 Group's thirty-seven Lancasters and 177 Halifaxes were Brussels, Melsbroek and Soesterberg, and the impression was of successful operations for the loss of a single 428 Squadron Lancaster. 408 Squadron went to Melsbroek and Brussels, and this was the final operation for its Mk II Lancasters, which were to go on to an even more testing time in the hands of trainee crews, mostly at 1668 Conversion Unit. The new Hercules-powered Halifax was a completely different animal from its ancestor, and many crews preferred it to the Lancaster, because of its more accessible escape hatches in an emergency. Its performance was also a match for the Lancaster, but nothing could compete with the latter's capacity to lift an enormous tonnage of bombs, and carry them to wherever they were required. The 15th was also the day on which W/C Roy began his second term as commanding officer of 424 Squadron in place of W/C Blane, having previously occupied the position between April and October 1943.

Now was the time for a gentle start to a new offensive against Germany, which, once in full swing, would continue without let-up or mercy until there was nothing significant left to bomb. On the night of the 16/17th over eight hundred aircraft set out for northern Germany, 348 of them containing crews briefed to attack the port of Kiel, among them a contingent of 144 Halifaxes from 6 Group. When the Halifaxes peeled off for their target the Lancasters, including twenty-seven from 6 Group, carried on eastwards to the Baltic port of Stettin, where a highly accurate raid ensued, in which over fifteen hundred houses and twenty-nine industrial premises were destroyed, and five ships were sunk in the harbour for the modest loss of five Lancasters. Among these was one from 428 Squadron. The attack on Kiel was moderately successful, and caused severe damage to the docks area and shipyards, but many bomb loads also fell outside of the town. A 420 Squadron aircraft went down in the North Sea, and one man was picked up alive after two days in a dinghy to become a PoW. A 431

Squadron Halifax suffered a similar end, and all on board were lost. There was better news for a 434 Squadron crew, whose aircraft was holed by flak on the run-up to the target. They leaked fuel all the way home, and finally ran out twenty-eight miles off Scarborough, where they ditched and were picked up safely. Meanwhile, a mining operation took place in Kiel Bay under cover of the main affair, and this cost 6 Group three 433 Squadron Halifaxes, from which just two men survived in captivity.

Between 21.00 and 22.00 hours on the 18th almost three hundred aircraft set out for Bremen, the objective for countless raids over the preceding years, including the last of the thousand bomber raids in June 1942. The force on this night was not particularly large, and included thirty-five Lancasters and sixty-five Halifaxes from 6 Group. The bomb tonnage delivered was only half that used in any one of the *Gomorrah* raids on Hamburg, but the damage it inflicted was extreme. Over 8,500 houses and apartment blocks were gutted by fire in central and north-western districts, the port area was devastated, and eighteen ships were sunk. It was impossible to list the number of industrial and commercial buildings reduced to ruins, or precisely how many people had been killed, but the latter figure certainly exceeded a thousand. This notable success was gained for the loss of just one 428 Squadron Lancaster. A simultaneous operation was mounted against the synthetic oil refinery at Sterkrade by a predominantly 4 Group force of over two hundred aircraft. 6 Group, meanwhile, sent 102 Halifaxes to support an attack on railway yards at Connantre, and seven 427 Squadron aircraft to mine the waters around La Rochelle. The 22nd brought a change of command for 419 Squadron, as W/C Pleasance was posted out at the end of a long tour, and the former A Flight commander, S/L Hagerman, was promoted to Wing Commander to step into his shoes.

There followed a week's lull in main force operations, during which tragedy struck 415 Squadron. W/C McNeill and S/L Wilmot were ferrying a Halifax each from Exeter on the 21st, when they collided and crashed south-west of Selby in Yorkshire. The commanding officer was in NA609 with a crew of five, while his flight commander was in MZ633, a Halifax officially belonging to 432 Squadron, but which may have been transferred to 415 Squadron and was awaiting the completion of paperwork. This also contained six men, and not one survived from either aircraft. W/C Joe Lecomte was immediately posted in from his command of 425 Squadron to take over the reins, and he would occupy the position for two months. W/C Ledoux took command at 425 Squadron, and he would remain in post for the remainder of the war and beyond. The renewed assault on Germany continued on the night of the 25/26th, when a record 1,311 sorties were flown on major and support operations. The main effort was by over four hundred Lancasters of 1, 3, 6 and 8 Groups, whose crews were briefed to attack the Opel motor works at Rüsselsheim, which had escaped a telling blow two weeks earlier. Although the factory was quite severely damaged on this night, production of lorries was barely affected, and fifteen Lancasters were lost. Thirty-four Lancasters from 6 Group took part, among them 419 Squadron's KB775, which struck another aircraft on approach to the target and plunged towards the ground out of control. Suddenly, it broke up, throwing the pilot, F/O Witwer, clear, and he alone of his crew survived. KB708 ran out of fuel and crashed while trying to land at Boscombe Down in foggy conditions, and F/O Milner and three of his crew were tragically killed, while the remainder sustained injuries. Meanwhile, 5 Group was failing to deliver an effective attack on Darmstadt, and the bulk of 6 Group, amounting to 182 Halifaxes, was contributing to a 4, 6 and 8 Group raid on coastal batteries at Brest. A 431 Squadron Halifax ran out of fuel at home while trying to divert, and the crew baled out safely. On the following night Kiel received its second heavy raid in less than two weeks, this time at the hands of around 350 Lancasters of 1, 3 and 8 Groups. Smoke screens created difficulties for the marker force, but heavy and widespread damage was inflicted upon the town's central and surrounding districts, and strong winds fanned the fires.

On the 27th the Command launched its first major daylight raid over Germany since August 1941. The target was the Rhein-Preussen synthetic oil refinery at Meerbeck near Homberg, and the force of 220 Halifaxes and thirteen Lancasters from 4 and 8 Groups was escorted on the outward flight by nine squadrons of Spitfires. The attack was delivered through partial cloud cover on Mosquito-borne Oboe markers, backed up by Pathfinder heavies. Some accurate bombing was claimed, but the operation was generally inconclusive. Seven squadrons of Spitfires covered the withdrawal, and no aircraft were lost. 6 Group was also active during the day dispatching thirty-two Lancasters and 176 Halifaxes as part of a force sent against the V-3 super gun site at Mimoyecques. 419 Squadron's KB724 lost two engines shortly after take-off, and had to be crash-landed in a crop field by W/O McDonald, and he and his crew were able to walk away. W/C Bryson became the new commanding officer of 427 Squadron on the 28th, the day on which the final operations took place against the flying bomb menace. He had previously served as a flight commander with Leeming neighbours 429 Squadron. Twelve sites were attacked by small numbers of aircraft employing the Oboe leader system, and seventy-two 6 Group Halifaxes were assigned to eight sites at L'Hey, Anderbelck, Oeuf en Ternois, Bois St Remy, Ferfay, Fresnoy, Ferme du Forestal and Ferme du Grand Bois, where the crews encountered flak over the target. Within a few days of these operations the Pas-de-Calais was in Allied hands. W/C Watkins relinquished command of 434 Squadron on the 29th, and handed over the reins to W/C Blackburn. Stettin hosted its second heavy raid of the month on the 29/30th, when four hundred aircraft again inflicted heavy damage on the port city, with particular emphasis on areas not previously hit. Over fifteen hundred houses were destroyed along with thirty-two industrial premises, a two thousand-ton ship was sunk, and more than a thousand people lost their lives. 6 Group put up thirty-six Lancasters, and one from 428 Squadron failed to return. The Group closed its August account when sending 165 Halifaxes to participate in an attack on a coastal battery at Ile de Cezembre near St Malo on the 31st. A 433 Squadron aircraft was seen to stall and crash into the sea without survivors.

As the Allied ground forces advanced, the need for port facilities became pressing to maintain a steady supply line. Much of September would be devoted to the liberation of the major French ports still in enemy hands, principally Le Havre, Boulogne and Calais, and in preparation for this six enemy airfields in southern Holland were bombed by daylight on the 3rd. 6 Group sent 105 Halifaxes to Volkel, and the bombing fell squarely onto the target. Tragedy struck a 426 Squadron crew early on, when LW206 entered a spin at 14,000 feet over Cambridgeshire. Five of the crew managed to leave the aircraft, three of them landing safely. Sadly, the flight engineer slipped out of his harness and fell to his death, and the mid-upper gunner's parachute caught on the tail wheel, causing him to be dragged down to earth. The Halifax crashed on Duxford airfield, killing him and the pilot, P/O Lamb, along with the rear gunner, neither of whom had been able to get out in time. Five minutes after impact the wreckage exploded, killing a number of US servicemen. At forty years of age the flight engineer, Sgt Robinson, was among the oldest airmen to give his life in the service of Bomber Command.

The assault on Le Havre began on the 5th, when over three hundred aircraft from 1, 3 and 8 Groups attacked enemy strong points around the port. While a similar operation was conducted on the following day, 138 mostly Halifaxes from 6 Group joined others from 8 Group to carry out the final raid of the war on Emden, a target that had been left in peace for more than two years. 1, 3 and 8 Groups returned to Le Havre in bad weather on the 8th, and only a third of the three hundred-strong force released their bombs, doing so more in hope than expectation. Another operation was mounted against Le Havre on the 9th involving 105 Halifaxes from 6 Group, but the continuing poor weather caused the Master Bomber to send the force home without bombing. On the way home a fire broke out between the port engines on 426 Squadron's NP681, and as it flew over Oxfordshire the wing burned through. Most of the crew were able to get out, but F/O Wilding, the pilot, and one other died in the ensuing crash. Almost a thousand aircraft returned on the following day to pound eight enemy strong points, 6 Group contributing forty Lancasters and 166 Halifaxes without loss.

Two hundred aircraft concluded the series on the 11th, this time with a 6 Squadron contingent of fifty-five Halifaxes from 424, 427 and 433 Squadrons in attendance, but twenty-five of these crews were sent home by the Master Bomber with their bombs still aboard. The German garrison surrendered to British forces a few hours later. Also by daylight on the 11th other elements of the Command raided synthetic oil plants at Castrop-Rauxel, Kamen and Gelsenkirchen, each force operating under the umbrella of a strong fighter escort. Ninety Halifaxes from 6 Group partic-ipated at the first-mentioned without loss, but 408 Squadron's NP710 crashed on landing at Linton-on-Ouse after returning early with a failed engine. P/O Smith and five of his crew died at the scene along with a man on the ground, while one of the survivors succumbed shortly afterwards to his injuries.

Similar targets were attacked at Dortmund, Scholven-Buer and Wanne-Eickel on the 12th, the two latter in the face of an effective smoke screen and flak defence. 122 Halifaxes from 6 Group took part, and four 426 Squadron Halifaxes were hit by flak on the run-up. One of them, NP741, failed to survive, but all of the crew got out, although the pilot, F/O Buck, succumbed to his injuries in a German hospital later that day. 429 Squadron sat out the daylight operations, but contributed to a mining operation in Oslo Fjord that night in company with 427 Squadron. MZ864 was hit by flak in the target area, which put both outer engines out of action, and caused one of the propellers to fly off. F/O Kingsland put the Halifax down on the water, and the crew took to the dinghy to await rescue.

Also on the night of the 12/13th a two-pronged attack was mounted against southern Germany. In total 378 Lancasters of 1, 3 and 8 Groups returned to Frankfurt for the first time since the devastating raids in March, while a predominantly 5 Group force of two hundred Lancasters targeted Stuttgart. The former resulted in severe damage to the city's western districts, at a time when a large part of its fire brigade was absent helping to quell the fires at nearby Darmstadt, which had suffered the ordeal of a firestorm at the hands of 5 Group on the previous night. For Frankfurt this would prove to be the last raid of the war by RAF heavy bombers. It was a similar story of destruction at Stuttgart, where the north and west-central districts were ravaged by a firestorm, and over eleven hundred people were killed, all for the modest loss of four Lancasters. A 6 Group main force of one hundred Halifaxes carried out a daylight raid on Osnabrück on the 13th, while seven 429 Squadron crews set off from Leeming to search the North Sea for their colleagues, F/O Kingsland and crew. F/L Morris spotted the dinghy, dropped a Lindholme boat, and then circled the area until a launch arrived to pick the men up.

An intended raid on Wilhelmshaven involving thirty Lancasters and forty-one Halifaxes of 6 Group by daylight on the 14th was recalled, because the fighter escort was unable to take off in the weather conditions. The night of the 15/16th brought a typical raid on Kiel, with much damage within the town, but a large wastage of bombs outside. 6 Group contributed twenty-eight Lancasters and 172 Halifaxes to the force, and just two of them failed to return. A 432 Squadron Halifax was lost with all hands, and another from 420 Squadron had to be ditched. NA629 suffered a complete hydraulics failure on the way home, which caused the wheels, flaps and bomb doors to flop down. The drag proved too much, and the Halifax gradually sank towards the North Sea, where a ditching ultimately took place some seventy miles out from the English coast. F/L Motherwell and his seven crew mates gained the relative safety of their dinghy, and settled down to see what fate had in store. On the following afternoon two 420 squadron aircraft and another from 425 Squadron departed Tholthorpe to carry out a search. They crossed the coast at Flamborough Head, and shortly before 17.30 hours, two and a quarter hours after take-off, they spotted the dinghy, and a Lindholme boat was dropped. Some time later a Walrus arrived to pick the crew up after fourteen hours afloat.

The ill-fated Operation *Market Garden*, the 'Bridge Too Far' Montgomery-inspired assault on the Rhine bridges, began on the morning of the 17th in the wake of attacks on enemy airfields and gun positions by elements of 1, 3 and 8 Groups during the night. By breakfast time the first of over seven hundred aircraft had taken off to begin the liberation of Boulogne. 6 Group's contribution to the operation amounted to thirty-six Lancasters and 173 Halifaxes, not all of which reached the target area. 424 Squadron's LW117 was soon out of the equation, after swinging on take-off and crashing through a hedge on the airfield boundary. Fortunately F/O King of the USAAF and his crew were able to walk away from the scene. F/L Arbuckle's Halifax was hit by flak during the outward flight, and the bomb-aimer, F/O Morgan, was fatally wounded. The pilot aborted the sortie and returned home without further incident. 429 Squadron played its part in the operation, during which MZ900 sustained flak damage. Both starboard engines were knocked out and a fire broke out, but fortunately, F/O Lanin and crew in MZ303 watched as the Halifax was abandoned by F/O Prentice and crew, who landed in calm waters off the French coast. The latter crew took a fix, met up with a Walrus and two Spitfires at the English coast, and returned with them to the scene. Two of F/O Prentice's crew were together in the water, while the remaining five were aboard their dinghy, but all were rescued some time later.

A total of three thousand tons of bombs was delivered onto enemy positions around the port, and shortly afterwards Allied ground forces began their advance. Within a week Boulogne was returned to Allied hands. Access to the much needed Belgian port of Antwerp was blocked by heavy gun emplacements on the island of Walcheren at the mouth of the Scheldt, and the first of a number of operations was mounted against them by 6 and 8 Groups on the 18th. Bad weather forced the attempt to be abandoned before any bombing took place, and a second attempt on the 19th was recalled. While burning off fuel in preparation for landing, 434 Squadron's MZ908 shed its starboard-outer propeller. It flew off with such force, that it took off the starboard-inner propeller as well, and a decision was taken to bale the crew out. The pilot, P/O Lees, stayed with the aircraft intending to land at Milfield, but control was lost south of Berwick, and he was killed in the ensuing crash. During the previous night Bremerhaven had wilted under its first heavy raid of the war at the hands of a 5 Group force of two hundred Lancasters. Accurate low level marking by the Mosquito element led to the destruction of over 2,600 buildings, as the central and port areas in particular were razed by fire.

The first operations in the campaign to liberate Calais took place on the 20th and involved over six hundred aircraft, including a contingent of twenty-six Lancasters and eighty-one Halifaxes from 6 Group. They bombed German positions accurately in clear visibility, but further attacks would be required before the port was surrendered. It was not until the 23rd that conditions were right for another go at Domburg, and 1 and 6 Groups provided the main force for what was an accurate attack on the battery. The main fare that night was an attack on Neuss in the Ruhr by over five hundred aircraft drawn from 1, 3, 4 and 8 Groups, while 5 Group operated elsewhere. Over eight hundred aircraft departed their stations either side of 19.00 hours for their respective targets, and the bombing of Neuss, close by Düsseldorf, was concluded successfully for the loss of seven aircraft.

Later on the 24th operations continued against enemy positions around Calais, but were hampered by low cloud, and a third of the force was unable to bomb. 6 Group sent thirty-one Halifaxes from 427 and 429 Squadrons, and these were among the ones coming below the two thousand feet cloud base to release their loads, and in so doing expose themselves to the lethal light flak. Eight aircraft were brought down, including 429 Squadron's LW136, which was hit shortly after bombing. The Halifax sustained damage to all of its engines, both turrets and flying surfaces and controls, so F/O Clarke headed for Allied-held territory, where the navigator and bomb-aimer baled out. The remaining crew members stayed on board because of the diminishing altitude, and the pilot carried out a crash-landing near Quer Camp, where the aircraft was consumed by fire. Sadly, the bomb-aimer succumbed to injuries sustained as a result of his baling out.

It was a similar story over Calais on the 25th, and only a third of more than eight hundred aircraft were able to bomb through breaks in the cloud. This day brought a big effort from 6 Group of forty Lancasters and 210 Halifaxes, all of which returned safely. Conditions improved on the 26th, when 6 Group contributed thirty-one Lancasters and 133 Halifaxes to a force of over seven hundred aircraft, which concentrated their bombing on three aiming points near Calais and four gun emplacements at Cap Gris Nez. After a month at the helm of 427 Squadron W/C Bryson stepped down, and was replaced by W/C Ganderton, who had worked his way up through the Lions' ranks, and would now remain in post until the end of hostilities.

The 27th brought yet another tilt at German positions around Calais by 1, 3, 4 and 8 Groups, along with attacks on oil refineries at Bottrop and Sterkrade by 6 and 8 Groups. 6 Group put up a maximum effort of forty-four Lancasters and 239 Halifaxes, and despite a spirited flak defence, all of them returned. 432 Squadron crews were briefed for Bottrop, and on arrival over the target they were met by a fierce flak barrage. NP692 was hit immediately after bombing, and the pilot, F/L Woodward, was severely wounded. The Halifax entered a steep dive, which was arrested when the navigator, F/O Hay, took over the controls, and he flew the aircraft home while his colleagues attended to their pilot. The crew intended to bale out over England, but the pilot's parachute was found to be torn, and this reduced their options somewhat. It was decided to attempt a landing at Woodbridge, and another Halifax came up to meet them and talk F/O Hay down. The touch-down was heavy, and the Halifax bounced, causing the undercarriage to collapse. The crew scrambled clear before a fire took hold, and F/L Woodward was rushed away for medical attention. Sadly, he died later that morning, while F/O Hay was awarded the DSO for his actions.

The last assault on Calais took place on the 28th, and six gun batteries at Cap Gris Nez were again bombed. 6 Group contributed thirty-eight Lancasters and 214 Halifaxes to the various operations, although many, including all from 424 and 427 Squadrons, were sent home by the Master Bomber with their bombs still aboard. Shortly afterwards Canadian ground forces moved in and took the surrender of the enemy garrison. Having evaded capture following his failure to return from Stuttgart in late July, W/C MacDonald resumed his command of 432 Squadron on the 29th.

The 30th brought further operations against the oil installations at Sterkrade and Bottrop, for which 6 Group put up 107 Halifaxes from 408, 415, 420, 425, 426 and 432 Squadrons. Briefed for the former 426 Squadron's LW197 was brought down by flak in Germany, and F/O Frederickson died with four of his crew, while the two survivors fell into enemy hands.

October was to be characterised by an unprecedented concentration of bombing on German cities, and a second Ruhr campaign would begin at the end of the first week. Ports were still a pressing priority, however, as the need for supplies increased to keep the Allied advance mobile, and Bomber Command was to play its part in weakening enemy resistance. The efforts to neutralise the batteries on Walcheren had proved ineffective, and it was decided instead to breach the sea walls, and thereby to inundate the gun positions, and also create difficult terrain for the defenders when the land offensive began. During daylight on the 3rd eight waves of thirty Lancasters each attacked the sea defences at Westkapelle, and the fifth wave created a breach, which was widened by those following. 617 Squadron aircraft were on hand with Tallboys, but in the event they were not needed.

Many 6 Group squadrons opened their October account on the 4th with a daylight raid on the port of Bergen in Norway. The closure to the enemy of the Biscay ports had resulted in a concentration of U-Boots at that location, and the majority of the main force of thirty-nine Lancasters and eighty-nine Halifaxes was assigned to the concrete pens, which were in the process of being enlarged, while a smaller element was to bomb individual vessels. The operation was successful, but collateral damage in the town caused the deaths of sixty children in a school basement. 419 Squadron's KB745 crashed near Barwick in Scotland on return, and F/O Duncan was killed with his entire crew. 427 Squadron's first operation for almost a week involved a few crews joining forces with some from 429 Squadron to lay mines in Oslo Fjord that night. MZ756 disappeared without trace with the very experienced crew of flight commander, S/L Moseley-Williams.

The night of the 5/6th was devoted to the first raid on Saarbrücken for two years, which involved over five hundred aircraft from 1, 3 and 8 Groups. The raid was of the saturation variety, and almost six thousand houses were destroyed for the loss of just three Lancasters. This high return-low loss outcome would be repeated throughout the month and on to the end of the war, with only isolated occasions on which the defences gained the upper hand. Ten crews from 433 Squadron spent that night mining in the Heligoland area, and all delivered their stores without intervention from the enemy. Shortly after turning for home, however, F/O Watson's Halifax was raked from stem to stern by a night fighter, killing the American rear gunner, P/O Zareikin, and severely damaging the tailplane. The damage to control surfaces prevented violent evasive action, and it was only possible to dive straight ahead. The mid-upper gunner, P/O Cochrane, another American, had to wait for an opportune moment before being able to bring his guns to bear, but the over-confident enemy pilot eventually presented his aircraft as a close-range target. Hits were observed on the cockpit, starboard wing and engine, and the JU88 was seen to flip over and dive straight for the sea with its undercarriage deployed. After the crew's safe return, which involved a landing at the emergency strip at Carnaby, P/O Cochrane was awarded an immediate DFC, and was credited with a 'probable'.

During the afternoon of the 6th over three hundred aircraft took off to raid the oil refineries at Sterkrade and Scholven-Buer. The operations were carried out in clear conditions, and the predominantly 4 Group crews produced good bombing on accurate Pathfinder marking. The new Ruhr offensive opened at Dortmund that night, when over five hundred aircraft from 3, 6 and 8 Groups pounded the city, causing extensive damage to housing, industry and communications for the loss of five of their number. This proved to be 6 Group's mightiest effort of the entire war, amounting to forty-five Lancasters and 248 Halifaxes, of which just two failed to return. 426 Squadron's NP739 was a victim of flak, but F/L Scott survived with three others, and all became PoWs. LW129 from 433 Squadron was also hit by flak at twenty thousand feet while approaching the target, and lost both port engines. With the target only five minutes away, F/O Valentine elected to press on and bomb, with the intention of reaching Allied territory on the way home before the wounded Halifax ran out of height. Flak continued to take chunks out of the aircraft until the bombs were delivered onto the target from 7,500 feet, and then course was set to the west with the ground getting closer all the time. At five thousand feet the aircraft stalled, was briefly recovered at five hundred feet, but ultimately crashed into a factory in Duisburg. Four members of the crew were killed at their crash positions, including yet another 'Porcupine' American, but the pilot, navigator and bomb-aimer all survived with injuries, and ultimately made a full recovery. F/O Kelly's aircraft from the same squadron was damaged by an incendiary bomb dropped from above, which took away the nose and seriously injured the bomb-aimer, F/S Nixon. Nixon remained at his post to deliver the bomb load, while the resulting wind tunnel effect from the gaping hole stripped the interior of the aircraft of all materials not secured, including all of the navigator's charts and equipment. Using only a small pilot's chart the navigator, F/O Burnett, continued to guide the aircraft home, while rendering assistance to the bomb-aimer, and for his devotion to duty he was awarded the DFC, while Nixon received the DFM. Among the pilots on duty with 427 Squadron at this time was W/C Ball, who was attached to gain operational experience before assuming command of 415 Squadron at the end of the month.

Following the failure of Operation *Market Garden* the Allied right flank had become exposed to a possible danger from enemy forces approaching through the frontier towns of Cleves and Emmerich. On the afternoon of the 7th both towns were left extensively damaged by forces of over three hundred aircraft. 1, 4, 6 and 8 Groups delivered a scattered and ineffective raid on Bochum on the 9/10th, for which the Canadian effort amounted to thirty Lancasters and 179 Halifaxes. 424 Squadron had to post missing yet another commanding officer, after MZ802 failed to return, although W/C Roy and all but one of his crew survived to be marched off into captivity. The sole Lancaster loss was 419 Squadron's KB754, which was caught by a night fighter when leaving the target and exploded, throwing clear just one survivor from the crew of P/O Cohen. A 432 Squadron Halifax was seen to be struck by bombs from above, but F/O Diamond and his crew all floated to earth under their canopies and were soon in enemy hands. Until the appointment of a successor at 424 Squadron, flight commander S/L Loudoun stepped into the breach. W/C Avant relinquished command of 429 Squadron, and was replaced on the 10th by W/C Bolduc, who had previously served the Bisons as a flight commander. On the 12th ninety-six 6 Group Halifaxes raided the oil refinery at Wanne-Eickel, but the marking and bombing were not accurate on this occasion, and the refinery escaped damage, although a nearby chemicals works was destroyed.

There were no major operations on the night of the 12th or on the following night, as Harris marshalled his forces for a spectacular twenty-four hours on the 14th. This was the day selected to launch Operation *Hurricane*, a demonstration to the enemy of the overwhelming superiority of the Allied air forces ranged against it. It was also the day on which 408 Squadron welcomed W/C Easton as its new commanding officer on promotion from flight commander, but his stay would be brief. Hours before his arrival, in fact at around first light, over one thousand aircraft took off for Duisburg, arriving overhead shortly after breakfast time to deliver something like 4,400 tons of high explosives and incendiaries under the protection of a large fighter escort. 6 Group's contribution was forty Lancasters and 218 Halifaxes, whose crews found that to be over the Ruhr in daylight was still a dangerous practice, and the flak defences claimed fourteen aircraft before being overwhelmed. Of the thirteen Lancasters and one Halifax that failed to return, KB800 was from 419 Squadron, and this aircraft blew up over the target after being hit by flak, throwing clear the pilot, F/O Roy, and he alone of his crew survived. 428 Squadron's KB780 was lost with all hands, while the Halifax came from 425 Squadron, and the pilot and three others survived as PoWs. 429 Squadron's MZ453 was hit by flak and had to be abandoned over Allied territory near Brussels. That night similar numbers returned to Duisburg to press home the point about superiority, 6 Group managing this time to put up thirty-nine Lancasters and 200 Halifaxes. One 425 Squadron aircraft crashed in Allied territory with the loss of two crew members, a 434 Squadron Halifax crashed shortly after take-off with an engine fire, and another from 415 Squadron came down short of the runway on return. Thus 2,018 aircraft had been dispatched against the city in around eighteen hours, and something like nine thousand tons of bombs had been dropped for the loss of twenty-one aircraft. It is remarkable, that this enormous effort was achieved without the inclusion of any 5 Group aircraft. They were consequently available for other duties, and took advantage of the night-time activity over the Ruhr to finally devastate Brunswick, which had escaped relatively lightly during four previous attacks in 1944.

On the night of the 15/16th over five hundred aircraft took part in the last heavy raid of the war on Wilhelmshaven, and 6 Group provided a contingent of fifteen Lancasters and 119 Halifaxes for the occasion. 408, 431, and 432 Squadrons each had an aircraft fail to return, and a 424 Squadron Halifax was lost on a gardening sortie to the Kattegat. Four nights later, after a rest for the heavy squadrons, elements of 1, 3, 6 and 8 Groups carried out a two-phase assault on Stuttgart, with four and a half hours between waves. The bombing was not concentrated, but severe damage was never the less inflicted upon central and eastern districts, and an important Bosch factory was hit. 6 Group's contribution was forty-two Lancasters, all of which returned without major incident. After almost a week off 427 Squadron sent ten aircraft to mine the Kattegat, and nine landed away as weather conditions at home continued to be inhospitable. Earlier in the day the newly promoted W/C Marshall had vacated his post as a flight commander with 433 Squadron, and become installed as 424 Squadron's new commanding officer. The largest Bomber Command force of the war, amounting to 1,055 aircraft, took off between 16.00 and 17.00 hours on the 23rd to deliver Operation *Hurricane*'s message to Essen. 6 Group weighed in with forty-three Lancasters and 229 Halifaxes, many of whose crews reported flying through icing conditions to reach the target. In view of the destruction already inflicted upon the city, and the likelihood that there was little left to burn, the bulk of the 4,500 tons of bombs was high explosive, which the Canadians delivered from between 18,000 and 21,000 feet. Six hundred buildings were destroyed, while a further eight hundred sustained serious damage in a city that had already surrendered its status as a major centre of war production. 419 Squadron's S/L McGuffin and crew failed to return in KB776, and there were no survivors, and a 429 Squadron Halifax went missing without trace. This was the day on which W/C McKenna relinquished command of 420 Squadron to be replaced by W/C Edwards, who had been serving as a flight commander with 428 Squadron. Only minor operations took place on the following night, and then, on the afternoon of the 25th the Hurricane force returned to Essen with over seven hundred aircraft. This number included forty-six Lancasters from 419 and 428 Squadrons, and they contributed to the destruction of a further eleven hundred buildings. The Krupp complex was among the industrial concerns badly damaged, and parts of it would remain out of action for the remainder of the war. Most of the city's surviving industry had been dispersed to other parts of Germany by this point, but its location within easy reach of Germany's western frontier would ensure further attention from Bomber Command, particularly as the ground action approached close to the end. A single 428 Squadron aircraft was the Group's only casualty from this operation. While this activity was in progress over Essen, 6 Group also supported a raid on the Meerbeck oil plant at Homberg with 198 of its Halifaxes. The target could not be seen through the complete cloud cover, and this prevented any assessment of the outcome. During the course of the month Mk X Lancasters had been arriving at Croft, and 431 Squadron lost its first example on this day, when KB813 crashed in Bedfordshire during a training flight, and P/O Wrigley's crew perished.

Cologne's turn to face the Hurricane force came first in the late afternoon of the 28th at the hands of over seven hundred aircraft, of which thirty-six Lancasters and 195 Halifaxes were provided by 6 Group. More than 2,200 apartment blocks were destroyed in districts north-east and south-west of the city centre, and much damage was inflicted upon power, railway and dockland installations. 419 Squadron's KB712 fell victim to the defences and crashed in Germany, killing F/L Nelligan and his crew. The assault on Walcheren had been ongoing throughout the month, and 5 Group carried out the final attacks on the 30th. The ground forces arrived on the following day to clear enemy resistance, and after a week of heavy fighting the island was taken. Even so, it would be a further three weeks before the approaches to Antwerp had been sufficiently cleared of mines to allow access for shipping. Later on the 30th nine hundred aircraft returned to Cologne and dropped four thousand tons of mostly high explosive bombs onto what remained of the city, causing massive damage. 6 Group put up forty Lancasters and 202 Halifaxes for its last outing of the month, and apart from a few incidents on landing, all returned safely. At 415 Squadron W/C Lecomte handed over the reins of command to W/C Ball on the 31st. It will be recalled that he had been with 427 Squadron to gain operational experience, and he would now see the Swordfish through to the end of the war and beyond.

November began with 6 Group operating as the main force against Oberhausen on the night of the 1/2nd with forty-seven Lancasters and 202 Halifaxes. It was a scattered attack delivered through cloud, and other Ruhr towns probably felt the effects. On the way home, an FW190 seriously damaged 419 Squadron's KB767, wounding two members of the crew, and starting a fire in the navigator's position. The port inner stopped immediately, and the starboard inner followed suit shortly after the Belgian coast was crossed. A temporary loss of control almost sent the Lancaster spinning into the sea, but F/O Cox rescued the situation, and eventually pulled off a crash-landing at Manston, having completed the flight without navigation instruments, intercom and hydraulics, and with an aircraft that was riddled with holes and boasted two burst tyres. In recognition of their fortitude, three DFCs and a DFM were immediately awarded to the pilot, navigator, wireless operator and rear gunner. 427 Squadron's F/O Tegerdine and F/L Sherlock returned to report being attacked by a total of three jet fighters between them, all of which had burst into flames after being hit by return fire, and two were claimed as probables. This operation brought 431 Squadron's debut on Lancasters, but an unhappy start to its career on the type saw KB817 crash in Holland, as a result of which F/O Connor and one of his crew were killed, and the remaining five fell into enemy hands. 426 Squadron lost two Halifaxes, while 424, 425 and 434 Squadrons lost one each.

The Hurricane force went to Düsseldorf on the evening of the 2nd with almost a thousand aircraft, and they pounded the northern half of the city, leaving over five thousand houses destroyed or seriously damaged. 6 Group provided forty-two Lancasters and 180 Halifaxes, and a number of squadrons underwent a testing time. 415 Squadron's MZ882 was attacked

by a JU88 immediately after bombing, and the rear turret became uninhabitable as fire took hold. The hydraulics system was also damaged,
causing the flaps and bomb doors to drop down. The crew of F/O Forbes
managed to put the fire out, and on landing at Woodbridge claimed their
assailant as destroyed, but the Halifax was declared damaged beyond
repair. The return of two other 415 Squadron Halifaxes was awaited in
vain, and these were the first to go missing since the squadron's maiden
operation against Hamburg back in July. F/O Knobovitch and five of his
crew lost their lives in MZ603, and the two survivors were taken into
captivity. There were no survivors at all from the eight-man crew captained
by F/O Regimbal, after NA583 crashed close to the Belgian/German
frontier. On a positive note, these would prove to be the squadron's final
losses of the year. 424 Squadron's MZ822 was hit by flak on the way home,
which damaged the port tailplane and started a fire behind the port-outer
engine's bulkhead. Now back over Allied territory F/O King gave the order
to bale out, and all of his crew complied, only one of them sustaining an
injury on landing. The fire then died down, and F/O King was able to carry
out a forced landing in a field, and most of the crew was back home within
a week. Less fortunate were their colleagues, P/O Bonar and crew in
LW131, which also failed to make it home. The pilot and three others died
in the wreckage, while the remaining three survived to fall into enemy
hands. 426 Squadron's W/C Burgess returned early after the failure of his
electrical system, and three others failed to return altogether, although two
of these were soon accounted for. NP686 had been attacked and damaged
by fighters, and crash-landed in Belgium without injury to F/O Brodie and
his crew. NP696 was hit by flak over the target, and P/O Hamilton crash-
landed the Halifax at Brussels, again without injury to the crew. LW199
became another victim of the flak defences over the city and crashed, killing
three of the occupants, while F/L Boddington and three others parachuted
into captivity. As events were to prove, this was the final heavy raid of the
war on this much-bombed city.

Bochum was the target for over seven hundred aircraft from 1, 4, 6 and
8 Groups on the 4/5th, of which forty-one Lancasters and 173 Halifaxes
were Canadian. Here too damage was immense, amounting to more than
four thousand buildings destroyed or severely afflicted, with almost a
thousand people killed. German night fighters made contact with the
bomber stream, and twenty-eight aircraft, most of them Halifaxes, were
shot down. 426 Squadron's unhappy start to the month continued with the
failure to return of two more aircraft. NP775 was lost over enemy territory,
but the entire crew of F/O Jones escaped with their lives to become PoWs.
NP800 was set on fire by a night fighter and was abandoned by most of the
crew to crash east of Aachen. Two men died in the wreckage, while two
others managed to evade capture. F/O Elder, his mid-upper gunner and the
severely wounded flight engineer were taken prisoner, but Sgt Newberry

died in hospital in Siegen on the 9th. The crew of NP768 returned home to report an encounter with a jet fighter, which was hit by the Halifax's return fire. 424 and 425 Squadrons each posted missing a crew, as did 433 Squadron, but a total of thirteen men survived from these as PoWs. Gelsenkirchen became the next Ruhr town to face a heavy Bomber Command assault, its ordeal coming during daylight on the 6th. The Nordstern synthetic oil refinery was the aiming point, and over five hundred aircraft bombed in its general area, while almost two hundred others attacked the town. 6 Group put up forty Lancasters and 176 Halifaxes, and other than a Halifax each from 408 and 432 Squadrons, which produced twelve captive survivors between them, all returned home. This was the first operation presided over by 433 Squadron's new commanding officer, W/C Tambling, who arrived from his flight commander post at 408 Squadron. He succeeded W/C Lewington, who, at the end of his second tour on the 5th, was posted to Dishforth as station commander. An attempt by an all-Lancaster main force to bomb the oil refinery at Wanne-Eickel on the 9th was thwarted by heavy cloud, which extended up to 21,000 feet. The Master Bomber ordered the more than two hundred crews to bomb any built-up area, but the town of Wanne-Eickel reported very little damage. Twelve aircraft from 427 and 433 Squadrons continued the mining offensive in Oslo Fjord on the 11/12th.

The lull in operations for all but the now largely independent 3 Group took the Command through to the 16th, when a massive assault on the three small Rhineland towns of Heinsberg, Jülich and Düren was launched. They lay in an arc from north to east respectively of Aachen, and the attacks were to help an American advance towards enemy lines between Aachen and the Rhine, by cutting communications to the front. In total 1,188 Bomber Command aircraft were committed to the destruction of the towns, 1 and 5 Groups forming the largest force of almost five hundred aircraft with Pathfinder support to attack Düren. The assault took place in mid afternoon in good bombing conditions, and over three thousand people were killed as the built-up area was levelled. Jülich was assigned to over four hundred Halifaxes and Lancasters of 4, 6 and 8 Groups, for which the Canadian contribution amounted to forty-five Lancasters and 159 Halifaxes, while 3 Group dealt with Heinsberg, and both towns were also left severely damaged. On the 18th over 450 aircraft from 4, 6 and 8 Groups delivered a scattered attack on Münster. 6 Group sent forty-four Lancasters and 140 Halifaxes, of which one of the latter from 408 Squadron was abandoned by its crew over Belgium on the way back, and they were back home within a matter of days. Later that evening a 1 Group raid was mounted against the oil refinery at Wanne-Eickel. Some additional damage was caused, and a nearby colliery was put out of action.

1, 6 and 8 Groups raided the oil refinery at Castrop-Rauxel on the 21/22nd, and it is believed, that the plant was put out of action for the remainder of the war. 6 Group contributed fifty-five Lancasters and 175 Halifaxes, of which four failed to return. Two of them were from 433 Squadron, and they represented the first multiple loss for the Porcupine unit since mid August. Both Halifaxes were hit during the final approach to the target, one by a night fighter and the other by the intense flak barrage, which greeted the crews as they flew down the avenue of search-lights to the aiming point. F/O Bond and his crew had reached somewhere around the mid-point of their tour when embarking on this trip, and they had just begun their run-up to bomb when MZ284 came under attack from an unseen night fighter. The mid-upper gunner, F/S Allan, was mortally wounded during the engagement, and died within minutes, by which time the Halifax was on fire from the fuselage to the port outer engine. The flames could not be extinguished, and the crew was forced to bale out, although the bomb-aimer and wireless operator lost their lives, presumably having failed to leave the aircraft. The others landed safely, and were taken into captivity until being liberated shortly before the end of hostilities. According to an article in the *Roundel* magazine, the rear gunner, F/S Slack, was drowned in the River Elbe on the 9th of May 1945, while attempting to rescue a German soldier, who had got into difficulties. The second 433 Squadron casualty was NP949, which contained the experi-enced crew of F/O Guy. This was hit by flak a couple of minutes short of the aiming point, and the resulting fires in the rest position and the star-board outer engine could not be quelled. The bomb load was jettisoned in the target area before F/O Guy ordered the crew to bale out. The mid-upper gunner alone had managed to comply before the Halifax was torn apart by an explosion, which flung the pilot, bomb-aimer and rear gunner into space. All four men arrived safely on the ground to be taken prisoner, but their three colleagues were killed.

W/C Phalen replaced W/C Edwards as commanding officer of 420 Squadron on the 24th after the latter had completed just a month at the helm. The general decrease in operational activity during November allowed most of the heavy squadrons to enjoy a rest period over the ensuing few days, but 427 Squadron joined forces with 424, 429 and 433 Squadrons on the night of the 24/25th, to send a total of thirteen aircraft mining in the Kattegat. On the way home 427 Squadron's MZ304 crashed just off the east coast of Scotland, killing F/L Hardy and his crew. On the 26th W/C Easton was posted out of 408 Squadron to be replaced by W/C 'Freddie' Sharp, who was posted in on promotion from 433 Squadron and would be the Goose's last wartime commander. He presided over his first operation on the following night, a modestly effective attack on Neuss by 1, 6 and 8 Groups. The target on the 27/28th was Neuss, where the eastern districts received most of the bombs causing moderate damage. 6 Group's fifty-three Lancasters and 173 Halifaxes all returned, most of them safely, although poor weather conditions at home forced many to land away from their stations. On the last night of the month 6 Group provided a contingent of fifty-two Lancasters and 172 Halifaxes to join 1, 4 and 8 Groups to attack Duisburg, where, despite complete cloud cover, over five hundred houses were destroyed. 429 Squadron's MZ288 was lost without trace with the crew of F/O Bell, and MZ314 collided in the air over Belgium with NR193 of 578 Squadron from Burn. P/O Clarke and his crew were killed, along with those on board the 4 Group Halifax.

December began for 6 Group with a heavy raid on Hagen in the Ruhr on the 2/3rd when almost five hundred aircraft from 1, 4, 6 and 8 Groups pounded central, eastern and southern districts, leaving over sixteen hundred houses and ninety industrial buildings destroyed or seriously damaged. Of 6 Group's contribution of forty-eight Lancasters and 131 Halifaxes just two failed to return. 428 Squadron's KB766 became uncontrollable after icing up at the French coast, and F/O Laturner ordered his crew to bale out before carrying out a crash-landing near Beauvais. He and four others came through unscathed, but two members of the crew were killed. A 433 Squadron Halifax also went down over France, and just one man survived after receiving treatment in a French hospital.

Two nights later 1, 6 and 8 Groups delivered a heavy raid on Karlsruhe, which turned into another crushing blow on a German city target. 6 Group put up forty-six Lancasters and 144 Halifaxes, all of which returned safely. This operation was carried out simultaneously with the 5 Group destruction of the unimportant and hitherto unmolested town of Heilbronn, where seven thousand people died under the bombs.

Almost five hundred aircraft from 1, 4, 6 and 8 Groups targeted Soest on the 5/6th, a town just north of the by now famous Möhne Dam. Forty-two Lancasters and 152 Halifaxes from 6 Group took part, and the first casualty occurred as the Canadians flew south over Warwickshire. 428 Squadron's KB768 collided with Halifax LW200 of 426 Squadron an hour after take-off, and both aircraft crashed near Rugby without survivors from the crew of F/L Shewfelt in the former and F/O Carter in the latter. 426 Squadron's LW204 was shot down by flak, and F/L Chipman and all but one of his crew survived to be taken prisoner. A 434 Squadron Halifax was also lost without survivors. The northern districts were hardest hit, where the railway installations were situated, and a thousand houses were destroyed.

A busy night on the 6/7th saw three major operations and many of a minor nature, which in total involved over thirteen hundred sorties. 1, 3 and 8 Groups raided the oil refinery at Leuna near Merseburg in eastern Germany, while a predominantly 4, 6 and 8 Group assault took place at Osnabrück and 5 Group attacked Giessen. 6 Group launched fifty-nine Lancasters and 140 Halifaxes, of which one Lancaster and three Halifaxes failed to return, the former from 419 Squadron and the others from 424, 429 and 432 Squadrons. 426 Squadron's NP740 was attacked by an ME163 rocket-propelled fighter, which was seen to explode after return fire from the Halifax struck home. LW209 was attacked by two ME163s, and S/L Stinson and crew claimed both as destroyed as they too exploded.

While 434 Squadron now enjoyed eleven days off the order of battle to undertake Lancaster conversion training, the last heavy night raid on Essen was delivered by over five hundred aircraft on the 12/13th. The Krupp complex was in the centre of the bombing pattern, and nearly seven hundred houses were also destroyed.

A three hundred strong Lancaster heavy force drawn from 1, 6 and 8 Groups targeted two IG Farben chemicals factories at Ludwigshafen and nearby Oppau on the 15/16th, and caused serious damage at both sites. 6 Group's contribution amounted to fifty-one Lancasters, and all returned safely.

The ancient city of Ulm was earmarked for its first and only raid of the war on the evening of the 17th. Unlike Freiburg and Heilbronn, however, it did contain targets of industrial significance, principally two large lorry factories. In total 317 Lancasters from 1 and 8 Groups provided the battering ram, and in twenty-five horrific minutes over fourteen hundred tons of bombs rained down, laying waste to 80% of the city's built-up area. Fortunately, an evacuation of women and children had taken place earlier in the day, but even so, seven hundred people lost their lives. A simultaneous operation by over five hundred aircraft from 4, 6 and 8 Groups on Duisburg brought forty-two Lancasters and 188 Halifaxes from the Canadian squadrons to action, and this too was a highly destructive raid. 425 Squadron's MZ538 crashed within minutes of taking off in the hands of F/O Desmarais, and all eight men died in the wreckage. 426 Squadron's LW209 was brought down by flak, but F/O Layman survived with four of his crew as guests of the *Reich*. Two 432 Squadron aircraft went missing, NP699, from which the pilot, F/O Krakovsky, was the sole survivor after possibly colliding in mid-air with a 10 Squadron Halifax over Belgium, and NP701, which crashed in France killing all but the pilot, F/O McKinnon, and one other. A 434 Squadron Halifax was the Group's other casualty from this operation.

On the 21/22nd 6 Group sent forty-one Lancasters and four Halifaxes to join elements of 4 and 8 Groups to attack the Nippes railway yards at Cologne, but poor weather conditions rendered the operation ineffective. The Canadian Halifaxes were from 434 Squadron, which was operating the type for the final time. Also on this night 424, 427, 429 and 433 Squadrons went mining in Oslo Fjord. Christmas Eve brought a daylight operation against Lohausen airfield at Düsseldorf involving fifty-three Lancasters and ninety-eight Halifaxes from 6 Group. This was 434 Squadron's first Lancaster operation, and all returned home without major incident from a concentrated and effective attack. A 408 Squadron Halifax and a 419 Squadron Lancaster were less fortunate and failed to return. The latter,

KB715, was hit by flak, which tore out an engine and set fire to two others. F/O Cowtan and his crew successfully abandoned the Lancaster to its fate, but the bomb-aimer, F/O Hale, was shot and killed by German troops immediately on landing, while the others were taken into captivity. That night 424, 427, 429 and 433 Squadrons sent a dozen Halifaxes mining in Oslo Fjord.

The final wartime Christmas Day was celebrated peacefully on the stations, but the Boxing Day festivities were curtailed for some crews from each Group when the Command called for attacks on troop positions around St Vith following the German break-out in the Ardennes on the 16th. It fell to sixty-four 6 Group crews from 424, 427, 429 and 433 Squadrons to have their festivities interrupted, and all returned safely.

6 Group carried out an inconclusive raid on the railway yards at Opladen during the early hours of the 28th, which 427 Squadron's F/O Bell and his crew missed after MZ291 blew a tyre on take-off, and hit an abandoned house on the edge of the airfield. The crew had scrambled clear by the time the Halifax caught fire and exploded. 419 and 428 Squadrons each had a Lancaster brought down over Germany without survivors.

The usual suspects went mining in Oslo Fjord with sixteen Halifaxes on the night of the 28/29th, and a 429 Squadron aircraft failed to return. There was a mid-afternoon take-off for forty-eight 6 Group Lancaster crews on the 29th, as they joined up with elements of 1 and 8 Groups to form a force of more than three hundred aircraft bound for the Ruhr. The target was the oil refinery at Scholven-Buer, where around three hundred high explosive bombs found the mark. Over three thousand others landed in the town and its environs, causing damage to property and two collieries. Of four missing aircraft two were from 419 Squadron, both suffering remarkably similar ends with identical consequences for the crews involved. KB753 was a victim of flak and exploded, throwing the rear gunner clear, he alone of P/O Adam's crew surviving. KB765 was likewise hit by flak, but was finished off by a night fighter and also exploded, catapulting its rear gunner into the night sky to be the sole survivor of F/O McVicar's crew. Meanwhile, 149 Halifaxes from 6 Group formed the main force for an ineffective attack on the railway yards at Troisdorf.

Forty-nine Lancasters and 151 Halifaxs from 6 Group took part in an operation on the evening of the 30th, when over 450 aircraft attacked the Kalk-Nord railway yards at Cologne. The size of the 4 and 6 Group main force suggested that this was an area raid on that part of the city containing the yards. Cloud made precision difficult, but the yards were severely damaged, along with two adjacent passenger stations. Two ammunition trains are reported to have blown up, and road communications were also disrupted. 427 Squadron's W/C Ganderton lost his port-inner engine while outbound, but pressed on to bomb the target and return safely, despite an encounter with an ME410. Part of New Year's Eve was spent by some crews from 424, 427, 429 and 433 Squadrons crews over Oslo Fjord, where they were to deliver another batch of mines. 427 Squadron's NR257 was attacked by a JU88, which F/O Brittain's gunners shot down into the sea.

All things considered, it had been a had been a better year for the Group. The 'chop' tag had been cast off, and the Canadians were beginning to earn for themselves a fine reputation for professionalism and efficiency. This was not, however, a time for complacency, as the German Ardennes offensive had demonstrated when taking the Allies completely by surprise. Now that it had faltered, however, it was clear that the coming year would bring victory, although much remained to be done before the tenacious and courageous enemy forces finally laid down their arms. Some squadrons would sail through the final four months of the bombing war with barely a scratch, while others would sustain heavy casualties.

1945

Over on the continent the New Year started with a bang, as the *Luftwaffe* launched its ill-conceived and ultimately ill-fated Operation *Bodenplatte* at first light on New Year's Morning. The intention to destroy Allied aircraft on the ground at the recently liberated airfields in France, Holland and Belgium was only modestly achieved, and at an unacceptably high price. The entire day fighter strength was committed to low level bombing and strafing attacks into the teeth of the airfield flak defences, and the survivors then had to run the gauntlet of Allied fighters to make their escape. Around 250 aircraft failed to get home, with approximately 150 of their pilots being killed, wounded or taken prisoner, and this was a setback from which the *Luftwaffe* would never recover. The operation also produced some very jittery American anti-aircraft gunners, who, for the remainder of the day and night, fired at anything that flew, and a number of Bomber Command aircraft fell victim to 'friendly fire' incidents. The major priorities for the Command in these final months of the bombing war were the continued dislocation of Germany's railway network, and the assault on her oil production. Both had been ongoing for a long time, but the offensives would now gain momentum. Any city with a functioning railway or an oil-related production site was to be area bombed, and the familiar names of the past would continue to feature. W/C Hull relinquished command of the Ghosts on this day, and was succeeded by W/C Gall, who would remain in post to the end of hostilities and beyond.

W/C Burgess bade farewell to 426 Squadron at the end of his tour in command on the 2nd, and W/C Carling-Kelly took over the reins. Two major operations were mounted on the night of the 2/3rd, the larger an all-Lancaster assault on Nuremberg involving over five hundred aircraft from 1, 3, 6 and 8 Groups, the Canadians putting up forty-nine aircraft. For almost the first time at this target an accurate and concentrated attack was delivered, in which over 4,600 houses, most of them apartment blocks, were destroyed, along with two thousand medieval houses and four hundred industrial buildings. More than eighteen hundred people lost their lives on the ground, and in return the defenders claimed five Bomber Command aircraft. A famous Lancaster came to grief on return, after faulty hydraulics caused 419 Squadron's KB700 *Ruhr Express*, the first Canadian-built Lancaster to enter service, to land badly, and end up in a heap beyond the runway, where it burst into flames. F/L Warner and crew managed to scramble away before the aircraft was consumed by the fire, but it was a sad way for the old girl to finish her forty-ninth operation, particularly as she was due to be retired at fifty, and flown back to Canada. Ludwigshafen was also heavily bombed on this night by a force of almost four hundred aircraft, which included 156 Halifaxes from 6 Group, and two of the synthetic oil-producing I G Farben chemicals works were severely damaged, as were a number of railway installations. For A Flight of 433 Squadron this was to be the month's only operation, as it was now stood down to convert to Lancasters. This left B Flight to carry on the war against Germany with its Halifaxes. Fellow Skipton residents 424 Squadron did not take part, and by now had already begun the process of converting to Lancasters, the first examples of which arrived on station on the 4th.

The last large-scale area raid of the war on Hanover, and the first against the city since October 1943, was undertaken by six hundred aircraft from 1, 4, 6 and 8 Groups on the night of the 5/6th. 6 Group's contribution amounted to fifty-seven Lancasters and 133 Halifaxes, which participated in a successful attack, which left almost five hundred apartment blocks in ruins. It was an eventful and expensive night for the Canadians, which left a number of squadrons with empty dispersals next morning. 408 Squadron posted missing its first crew of the year, that of F/L Scheelar in NR209, which crashed in Germany, and the pilot was killed along with three others of his crew, while the survivors all fell into enemy hands. 415 Squadron's excellent casualty record was dented by MZ476 crashing in Germany two and a half hours after take-off, killing three of the crew. F/O McFadden and three others survived to be taken prisoner, although the navigator, F/O Connor, was lucky to escape with his life after passing through the arc of a propeller and losing his left leg. He was later repatriated. 419 Squadron's KB722 fell foul of a gunner in another Lancaster while outbound, and P/O Mallen was forced to set course for Brussels, before eventually crash-landing at St Quentin with only minor injuries among the crew. 420 Squadron's MZ471 was shot down by a night fighter over Germany, and F/L Brand was killed along with two of his crew. Three other members of the crew were taken into captivity, as was the rear gunner, F/S Noble, after initially evading capture despite being seriously injured. He eventually succumbed to those injuries on the 20th of January while in captivity. 425 Squadron was the hardest-hit amongst 6 Group's participants with three failures to return. MZ860 was shot down in the target area killing two of the crew, while F/S Cauely and four others found themselves in enemy hands. NP999 and NR178 also crashed in Germany, and both pilots, F/O Brimicombe from the former and F/O Sequin from the latter, survived with five and four members of their crews respectively, and they too were taken prisoner. 427 Squadron's NR257 was shot down by flak over Germany, and S/L Crew was killed with three others, while the remaining three men were taken prisoner. LV964 crashed in Germany, and 429 Squadron's P/O Hay was killed on the thirtieth and final operation of his tour, while his crewmates, who died alongside him, were also close to the end of theirs. Finally, 432 Squadron's NP759 was shot down by flak over Germany, killing F/L Sales and his rear gunner, while the five survivors soon found themselves in enemy hands. NP701 also failed to return with the crew of W/C Stephenson, who were all taken prisoner. It must be assumed, that W/C Stephenson was being groomed to take over the squadron on the departure of W/C MacDonald, who was approaching the end of his tour.

Fifty-seven Lancasters and 132 Halifaxes of 6 Group joined forces with elements of 1, 4 and 8 Groups to pound Hanau and its railway yards on the 6/7th, as elements of 1 and 3 Groups did likewise at Neuss. 427 Squadron's LW130 was fired upon by another Halifax, which left holes in a wing and the nose, and the bomb-aimer was wounded. This crew was more fortunate than that of 415 Squadron's MZ456, which collided with a 10 Squadron Halifax over Germany. Both aircraft plunged to the ground before anyone was able to escape, and F/O Belcher died with his crew. A 431 Squadron Lancaster also failed to return, and all on board were killed.

On the 7/8th, elements from all but 4 Group carried out the final heavy raid of the war on Münich, and returning crews claimed a successful attack. 6 Group put up a modest thirty Lancasters, and all returned safely. On the 10th W/C Eric Mitchell relinquished command of 431 Squadron to be replaced by W/C Davenport on the 14th.

There was little activity for the heavy squadrons after Münich until the 13th, but 424, 427, 429 and 433 Squadrons sent a total of sixteen Halifaxes on a mining expedition to Flensburg on the 12/13th, from which two 424 and one 429 Squadron aircraft failed to return. Two operations were mounted on the 13th against the railway yards at Saarbrücken, firstly by 3 Group, and later by 4, 6 and 8 Groups. 6 Group supported the latter with 130 Halifaxes, and there were no losses, although 415 Squadron's F/O Falconer and crew experienced a testing time. A problem developed with the hydraulics system during the outward flight, and this meant that the undercarriage could not be retracted. They pressed on to the target, which they bombed from 14,500 feet, well below the rest of the stream, and managed to make it back to Manston for a safe landing with dwindling fuel

F/O J Egan and F/S J Stogryn of 415 (Swordfish) Squadron relax with a mug of tea and a cigarette.

415 Squadron commanding officer, W/C F W Ball (right) shakes hands with F/L R J McGill.

P/O James Cavanah and
F/O Hal Stephens of 415
Squadron.

F/S J H Taylor of 415
Squadron at debriefing.

F/O W F Brown of 415 Squadron with air and ground crew at East Moor.

F/L Bill Brown of 415 Squadron in front of his MkIII Halifax at East Moor.

415 Squadron's F/O J S McGuire apparently reading tea leaves during debriefing.

F/O A J Walker and F/S Stogryn of 415 Squadron.

419 (Moose) Squadron official photograph at Middleton-St-George during the Lancaster era post Feb 1944.

The 419 Squadron Moose emblem painted on a MkX Lancaster. The squadron was named in honour of W/C "Moose" Fulton, the unit's first commanding officer, who was killed on operations in a Wellington in 1942 when the squadron operated within 3 Group.

A/C LETTER	A/C NUMBER	NUMBER	RANK	NAME	NO. OF SORTIES	DUTY
LANCASTERS						
A	KB706	J7905	FL	JD Virtue	7 2/3	P N
		J24921	FO	JR Johnson		AB
		R157135	Sgt	Dodds VF		WO
		R107620	WO1	Britts AJ		FE
		1582850	Sgt	Gilbert PN		UG
			Sgt	Turner LG		RG
		R15?/.54	Sgt	Stoyko MS		
B	KB701	J85360	PO	CEG Patterson	12 2/3	P
		R158761	WO2	Bailey WA		N
		R219897	FS	Derbyshire LE		AB
		1507140	FS	Jones O		WO
		1709160	Sgt	Wood REN		FE
		R196076	Sgt	Chawanski AP		UG
		R159331	FS	Beckett AC		RG
C	KB711	J85395	PO	JC McNary	11 1/6	P
		J21188	FO	FH Love		N
		R145370	FS	Long RC		AB
		R109823	WO1	Chartrand JLE		WO
		1604133	Sgt	Hill AG		FE
		R188126	Sgt	Wilson JJ		UG
		R163568	Sgt	Sangster DSM		RG
D	KB716	J22142	FL	AJ Byford	18½	P
		J21355	FO	RV Daly		N
		R114756	FS	Prentice FW		AB
		1249334	Sgt	Tenny R		WO
		1845031	Sgt	Holder AL		FE
		R188973	Sgt	Fraser NC		UG
		1834457	FS	Darnley L		RG
L	KB712	R110454	FS	Hartford GP	6 5/6	P
		J24552	FO	ND Johnston		N
		R155149	Sgt	Foster BW		AB
		J27953	FO	J Knox		WO
		1384674	Sgt	Butler R		FE
		R216214	Sgt	Piotrowsky P		UG
		R172132	Sgt	Toit, SOV		RG
T	KB719	R128369	WO2	Johnson IW	8 5/6	P
		R93589	WO2	Sachs LMT		N
		R160198	FS	Rodman BT		AB
		R97352	WO1	Wade LA		WO
		R16??4	Sgt	Shuman A		FE
		R191910	Sgt	Morris J		UG
		R176776	Sgt	Rogers HW		RG
V	KB728	C1395	WC	WP Pleasance	16½	P
		J21910	FO	LA Rotstein		N
		J28895	FO	MJ Bernardi		AB
		1213524	FS	Emsley RM		WO
		C19702	PO	MD McGill		FE
		R193140	Sgt	Tagg JF		UG
		R159397	FS	Ihde EH		RG
X	KB713	R128415	WO2	Krantz WT	6 2/3	P
		J20924	FO	JR Forris		N
		R159001	FS	Scott AM		AB
		1349734	Sgt	Thompson TR		WO
		1590804	Sgt	Pollard M		FE
		CAN7674	Sgt	Keeler W		UG
		2209079	Sgt	Dye SO		RG

Order of Battle for the night of the 27/28th of April 1944, when the railway yards at Montzen were the target. At the time 419 Squadron was in the process of converting from MkII Halifaxes to the Canadian-built MkX Lancaster, and dispatched both types on this night. This was the maiden operation for the MkX.

A ceremony at Fulton Field, Kamloops, Canada, where many bomber crewmen were trained.

Another view of the 419 Squadron Lancaster element before the Montzen operation on the 27th of April 1944.

A 419 Squadron Halifax MKII, a type that the Moosemen were happy to exchange for Lancasters between February and May 1944.

Out with the old and in with the new. 419 Squadron's new "Chariots of Fire", the Canadian built Lancaster X.

A motivational poster exhorting 419 Squadron to match 425 (Allouette) Squadron's zeal for war bonds.

Bombing up a 419 Squadron Halifax.

419 Squadron Lancs in line astern before the Montzen operation 27th April 1944.

Home sweet home. A motley collection of nissen huts at Skipton-on-Swale provide living accommodation for the crews of 424 (Tiger) and 433 (Porcupine) Squadrons.

Inside the luxurious accommodation at Skipton. Airmen froze in the winter and baked in the summer.

F/L Close and crew of 420 (Snowy Owl) Squadron, which flew Halifaxes throughout its operational career with 6 Group.

Another 420 Squadron crew in full flying kit prior to boarding their Halifax.

A fine example of Canadian nose art on a MkIII Halifax. The Hercules powered MkIII and VII Halifaxes represented a major improvement on the Merlin powered earlier variants. Although the type could never match the Lancaster's bomb-carrying capacity, its performance in other respects was comparable.

A 427 (Lion) Squadron Lancaster at Leeming near war's end. 427 took delivery of Mk 1 and III Lancasters in March 1945 and carried out sixteen bombing and seven mining operations without loss. Standing in front of the port-inner is the crew of F/L Gardiner, who is 4th from the left. The others from the left are S/L F D Smith, F/L EC Stewart, F/O H E Thornicroft, F/O H H McDaniel and F/L E E Morgan.

The diminutive S/L Frank Guillevin, a 431 (Iroqois) Squadron flight commander, seen line-shooting to impress Flt Officer Peggy Tyndale at Croft on the 13th of September 1944 following a raid on Osnabrück. Looking on are F/Ls Borland and MacLeod and the squadron crest.

A typical autumnal day at a rainy Croft as crews file out of the crew room and head for the transports waiting to take them to dispersals. The impending operation is believed to be against coastal guns at Cap Gris Nez on the 28th of September. The weather in the target area was equally bleak, and the Master Bomber sent many crews home with their bombs still aboard.

An earlier incarnation of the 431 Squadron crest at Croft when S/L Guillevin, (5th from left) was still a flight lieutenant. Standing in the centre is the Squadron commanding officer, W/C Eric Mitchell. Far left is flight commander S/L W Vanexan DFC.

When the Canadians arrived at Croft it was a mud patch. This photo, taken on the 27th of April 1945, after the bombing war was over, shows 431 Squadron's last wartime commanding officer, W/C McKinnon, (far left), with other squadron members in a neatly manicured section of garden.

A 434 (Bluenose) Squadron Halifax is christened on behalf of the Rotary Club of Canada at Croft on the 14th of December 1944. Commanding officer W/C A P Blackburn (2nd from left) looks on.

reserves. On the following night the Group participated in an attack on railway yards at Grevenbroich with 136 Halifaxes, all of which returned, but 415 Squadron's NA611 swung out of control on take-off in the hands of F/S Sirtonski, and ended up in a wood on the edge of the airfield. Fortunately, injuries to the occupants were restricted to cuts and bruises. Meanwhile the synthetic oil plant at Leuna was being severely damaged in a two-phase assault by fifty-three 6 Group Lancasters in company with others of the type from 1, 5 and 8 Groups. Two 419 Squadron aircraft failed to return, as did one from 431 Squadron, which collided with a BF109 fighter in the target area.

On the 16/17th, elements of 1, 6 and 8 Groups joined forces to attack the Braunkohle-Benzin synthetic oil plant at Zeitz near Leipzig, part of which sustained heavy damage for the loss of ten Lancasters. 6 Group contributed fifty-one Lancasters, of which just one failed to return, the first to be lost by 434 Squadron since converting. The Halifax force, meanwhile, was pounding the city of Magdeburg in an operation claimed by the Command to be highly destructive. In total 127 Halifaxes from 6 Group were involved, and it became an expensive night that cost seven aircraft. Hardest-hit was 420 Squadron with four missing aircraft from which thirteen men survived as PoWs. This operation proved to be the swansong for 433 Squadron's association with the Halifax as its B Flight undertook the final sorties without loss.

The weather during the second half of the month was generally appalling, but it did not interrupt A Flight's progress towards operational status on the Lancaster, and it would be declared ready to return to the fray on the 29th. B Flight was now stood down for three weeks to learn the ways of the Lancaster. Minor operations held sway from then until 280 Lancasters of 1, 3 and 8 Groups attacked a benzol plant at Duisburg on the 22/23rd. The target was identified in the moonlight and severely damaged, as was a nearby steelworks belonging to the Thyssen concern. W/C Hagerman was posted out of 419 Squadron on the 26th, to be replaced as commanding officer by W/C Ferguson, who had previously served as a flight commander with 428 Squadron, and he would see the Moosemen through to the end of hostilities. W/C MacDonald departed 432 Squadron on the 29th at the conclusion of his tour, and was succeeded temporarily by flight commander S/L Minhinnick. 420 Squadron also had a new commanding officer from the 28th after, S/L McCarthy was promoted from flight commander on the 28th to replace W/C Phalen.

The only other significant raid before the end of the month came on the night of the 28/29th against railway yards and an aero-engine factory on the northern edge and surrounds of Stuttgart. Six hundred aircraft took part, including fifty-five Lancasters and 124 Halifaxes of 6 Group, but cloud cover led to a scattered and inconclusive outcome. 426 Squadron's NP768 fell victim to a night fighter over Germany, and W/C Carling-Kelly and three of his crew parachuted into the arms of their captors, while both gunners and the navigator perished in the wreckage. S/L Black was posted over from 419 Squadron on promotion to Wing Commander to step into the breach later on the 29th, and he would see the squadron through to the end of hostilities and beyond. 424 Squadron contributed a contingent for what would be the Tigers' final outing on Halifaxes. LW164 swung out of control during take-off, and its bomb load went up after the undercarriage collapsed. The rear gunner was thrown clear of the burning wreckage and was seriously injured, but W/C Williams and the remainder of the crew were killed. W/C Williams was beginning a second tour of operations, and although he may have been preparing to assume command of 424 Squadron, it is more likely that he was being groomed to take over one of the other 6 Group units. 408 Squadron posted missing two crews, and 428 Squadron lost a flight commander.

The weather was not helpful during the first week of February either, as large areas of Germany were concealed by cloud. 433 Squadron Lancasters went to war for the first time on the night of the 1/2nd, when contributing to a force of 382 Lancasters from 1, 6 and 8 Groups bound for the southern city of Ludwigshafen. The total of fifty-nine Lancasters from 6 Group also included a contingent from 424 Squadron on its maiden outing on the type. Cloud cover forced the use of sky markers, but most of the bombs fell within the city, destroying or seriously damaging nine hundred houses, and causing chaos within the railway yards. Six aircraft failed to return, and 433 Squadron sustained its first Lancaster casualty, after NG460 was hit by flak over the target. The damage was not terminal, and the A Flight commander, S/L Stinson DFC, was able to bring the Lancaster home to within miles of a safe landing. Once over Yorkshire, however, and while flying through cloud at three thousand feet, turbulence caused control to be lost, and the aircraft crashed a few miles south of Skipton-on-Swale with five of the crew still on board. Only the bomb-aimer and a gunner had managed to bale out at two thousand feet to survive. It was a tragic loss of an experienced crew, who were all into the final third of their first tour, while S/L Stinson was on the sixth operation of his second. 424 Squadron's NG451 was attacked four times by JU88s, and a cannon shell passed through the nose, but F/O Mitchell brought it home to a safe landing. Meanwhile, eighty-six 6 Group Halifaxes took part in a simultaneous raid on Mainz, and came through without casualty.

Three heavy raids were mounted on the following night, 109 Halifaxes from 6 Group supporting one at Wanne-Eickel, but the three hundred aircraft failed to find the oil refinery with their bombs through cloud. An hour after taking-off, engine vibration forced 408 Squadron's F/O Baird and his crew to abandon NP757 to its fate over Lincolnshire, and all arrived safely on the ground. 426 Squadron's NP819 was severely damaged by flak, presumably over the target, and F/O Talocka decided to land at Manston.

He aborted his first approach, and then caught the slipstream of the aircraft ahead, which caused the Halifax to flip over and dive in from six hundred feet. Only the wireless operator survived. The Group's single failure to return was a 432 Squadron aircraft. A simultaneous operation against Wiesbaden occupied sixty-five Canadian Lancasters, and despite cloud cover serious damage was inflicted. 419 Squadron's KB750 became the Moosemen's first failure to return of the month, and just one man survived from the crew of P/O Martin when the Lancaster was shot down by flak over Germany on the way home. 428 Squadron's KB725 turned back after its port-outer engine failed, and both inner engines then became troublesome. F/L Gadkin attempted a landing at Sandy Tees airfield with the crew at crash positions, but both gunners lost their lives, while the pilot and flight engineer sustained injuries, the latter serious. KB792 exploded over the target, and the rear gunner somehow managed to escape with his life, but F/L Berry and the rest of his crew perished.

An ineffective raid on a coking plant at Osterfeld on the 4/5th involved one hundred 6 Group Halifaxes, and there were no losses. Seventy-one of the Group's Lancasters went to Bonn, meanwhile, and contributed to a scattered attack. 419 Squadron's KB787 was not among those returning after colliding with 433 Squadron's PA219 over Belgium on the outward journey. F/L Barlow and his crew were killed, along with F/L Mara and his seven colleagues on board the Porcupine aircraft.

In preparation for an advance into Germany by the British XXX Corps in the Reichswald region the Command was ordered to bomb the frontier towns of Goch and Cleves, which formed part of the enemy defences. On the night of the 7/8th 4, 6 and 8 Groups attacked the former, and 1 and 8 Groups the latter, leaving both heavily damaged. Not all of 6 Group's sixty-nine Lancasters and 131 Halifaxes bombed after smoke and dust compelled the Master Bomber to call a halt to proceedings. Only five of the 427 Squadron crews bombed, and two of its crews, those of F/Ls Brittain and Storms each claimed an ME163 destroyed after the rocket propelled fighters were seen to burst into flames.

On the following night 475 Lancasters from 1, 5 and 8 Groups took off for Pölitz near Stettin to attack the oil refinery, and they put an end to all further wartime production. In contrast, a simultaneous raid on the refinery at Wanne-Eickel by ninety-six Halifaxes from 6 Group along with others from 4 Group failed to find the mark, and little damage resulted. It was actually in the early hours of the 9th when the crews got away, and 426 Squadron's NP682's starboard-outer engine burst into flames during the climb out. The Halifax began to lose height immediately, and crash-landed near Wetherby before the bombs could be jettisoned. Soon afterwards the aircraft was torn apart by an explosion, and only the pilot, F/O Wadleigh, and one other survived, albeit with injuries. Flak brought down a 415 Squadron Halifax over Dunkerque, and a 425 Squadron aircraft was abandoned over Belgium because of an engine fire. Thereafter, the Group had four nights off until returning to the fray on a night that would unjustly define for many post-war commentators the character of Bomber Command's war.

The night of the 13/14th brought the first of the Churchill-inspired heavy raids on Germany's eastern cities under Operation *Thunderclap*. The target was the beautiful and historic city of Dresden, which had not been attacked by the Command before, but was now to face a two-phase assault opened by 5 Group employing its low level marking method. A layer of cloud stretched across the target area, and this interfered to an extent with the precision of this part of the raid, in which 244 Lancasters delivered more than eight hundred tons of bombs. Fires gained a hold, however, and they acted as a beacon to the 529 Lancasters of 1, 3, 6 and 8 Groups following three hours behind. By the time of their arrival the skies had cleared, and a further eighteen hundred tons of bombs rained down onto the hapless city. The result was a firestorm of gigantic proportions, certainly equalling that at Hamburg eighteen months earlier, and there was no escape for the population, massively swelled by an influx of refugees from the eastern front. A figure of 35,000 fatalities has been settled upon, although some commentators believe the figure to be substantially higher. 6 Group's contribution to the operation was sixty-seven Lancasters, all of which returned home.

A second operation on this night took the Halifax brigade to Böhlen to attack the Braunkohle-Benzin oil plant. Conditions were very poor, and the bombing was consequently scattered and inconclusive, but at least losses amounted to just one Halifax, which did not come from 6 Group's contingent of 115. The following night was devoted largely to Chemnitz, but heavy cloud helped to spare the city from a fate similar to that of Dresden, and much of the bombing found open country. 6 Group put up fifty-two Lancasters and sixty-six Halifaxes, and the first casualty occurred early on. 420 Squadron's NA179 suffered the failure of its starboard-outer engine shortly after take-off, and F/O Anderson had no choice but to abort the sortie. While making the final approach to land the Halifax stalled and spun in from six hundred feet a mile from the runway, killing all but the mid-upper gunner, who sustained injuries. 427 Squadron's MZ422 crashed in Germany killing F/O Roy and three of his crew, who were undertaking their maiden operation, and the three survivors began a short spell as guests of the *Reich*. 432 and 434 Squadrons each posted missing one Lancaster and crew. Also on this night ten Lancasters from 424 and 433 Squadrons and ten Halifaxes from 427 and 429 Squadrons were sent mining in the Kadet Channel. 427 Squadron's MZ355 failed to return, and although both gunners lost their lives, S/L Brittain and four others survived in enemy hands. 429 Squadron's MZ865 strayed into Swedish airspace, and the entire crew died when the Halifax was brought down by flak. A 424 Squadron Lancaster was also lost without trace.

On the following night 427 and 429 Squadrons sent six Halifaxes mining in Oslo Fjord, and this time all returned. A series of raids on the Rhine town of Wesel, which stood in the way of the Allied advance, began on the 16th, and by its conclusion in March there would be little of it left standing. 420 Squadron took part in an attack there on the 17th, but only one of its crews bombed before the Master Bomber called a halt. Many crews landed away on return, and in the course of a ferry flight back to base on the following day, NR126 flew into a hill in Northumberland, killing F/O Stock and all but one of his crew.

Among the operations during the remainder of the month were the last raids of the war on some familiar names. Dortmund experienced its final night raid on the 20/21st at the hands of five hundred aircraft, including eighty-two Lancasters from 6 Group, but it still had one major daylight ordeal to undergo in March. The bombing on this night was accurate and much fresh damage was inflicted. 419 Squadron's KB804 was brought down by flak, and 431 Squadron's KB809 was also missing. 424 Squadron's ME456 was hit by flak on approach to the aiming point, and was then attacked by a night fighter, which caused both starboard engines and the hydraulics system to fail. Five of the crew baled out over No Man's Land, three of them coming down in Allied territory, while the two others drifted over onto the enemy side of the lines and were captured. F/S Cozens remained with the aircraft, possibly because the flight engineer was wounded, and he pulled off a remarkable forced landing for which he was awarded the DFM. The flight engineer, Sgt Kubin, did not survive, and he has no known grave. The Group's Halifax contingent of 112 aircraft, meanwhile, was engaged in an operation against an oil refinery at Monheim. 427 Squadron's NP942 failed to return, but F/L Murphy and four of his crew survived in enemy hands, while two others lost their lives. A 432 Squadron aircraft was also lost along with the pilot and two of his crew. An area attack on Worms followed twenty-four hours later, which left almost 40% of the town in ruins, but six of the Group's 102 Halifaxes failed to return. Two 408 Squadron crews were posted missing, and it was later established that one had been killed to a man, while the other escaped intact to become PoWs. A 427 Squadron aircraft was lost with six of its crew, only the pilot of NR288, P/O Wilson, surviving, and he was taken into captivity. On a happier note, this was the last 427 Squadron crew to be lost during the long-running conflict. Three Lion crews returned with reports of encounters with night fighters, those of F/O Kaye and F/L Towne claiming their attackers as destroyed. It was 432 Squadron that sustained the heaviest casualties on this night after three of its aircraft failed to return. Also on this night Duisburg wilted under its last pounding of the war, and more of its buildings were reduced to rubble. 6 Group contributed eighty-two Lancasters, and all returned safely.

A daylight raid on the 23rd by 118 Halifaxes of 6 Group along with a 4 Group contingent delivered three hundred high explosive bombs onto the Krupp works at Essen, while that night, thirty-seven 6 Group Lancasters joined others from 1 and 8 Groups to carry out the only area bombing raid of the war on Pforzheim. In twenty-two horrific minutes an absolute catastrophe was visited upon the town and its inhabitants, as a large part of the built-up area was engulfed in flames, and seventeen thousand people lost their lives, the third highest death toll at a German urban target.

Some 110 Halifaxes from 6 Group took part in a raid at Kamen in the Ruhr on the 24th, where an oil refinery was the objective. A 415 Squadron aircraft became the only loss after it exploded over the target killing all on board. A number of 6 Group crews were sent mining over the ensuing few nights, and while gardening in Oslo Fjord on the 25/26th a 429 Squadron crew went missing without trace in MZ452, a Halifax borrowed for the night from 427 Squadron. Mainz provided the objective for eighty-five Lancasters and 102 Halifaxes from 6 Group on the 27th. 429 Squadron again borrowed from fellow Leeming residents 427 Squadron, but RG347 crashed on take-off before exploding and killing all but one of the occupants. The city was bombed through complete cloud cover on sky markers, but it was a devastatingly accurate assault, which destroyed over 5,600 buildings and killed more than eleven hundred people. At East Moor S/L Minhinnick stepped aside on the 28th to make way for 432 Squadron's new commanding officer, W/C France, who would remain in post until disbandment.

Mannheim's long and unhappy association with Bomber Command came to an end on the afternoon of the 1st of March, although its final ordeal was unobserved by the 1, 6 and 8 Group crews above the cloud cover. Seventy Lancasters and ninety Halifaxes of 6 Group were called into action for this first operation of what would prove to be a surprisingly busy month, considering the enemy's hopeless situation, and all returned safely. On the following morning two forces set out to bomb Cologne for the last time, the first numbering seven hundred aircraft. This number included eighty-four Lancasters and ninety-eight Halifaxes from 6 Group, which helped add massively to the damage already inflicted on the shattered city. The remaining inhabitants were spared further misery when the second attack by 3 Group had to be abandoned after only fifteen aircraft had bombed, when a fault developed with the G-H blind bombing device station in England. It hardly mattered, and the city fell to American forces four days later. One 408 Squadron Halifax was shot down by flak, and five of the crew survived to fall into enemy hands. 427 Squadron became less active at the start of the month, the main reason for which was the arrival of Lancasters at Leeming on the 2nd, onto which the crews would convert over the succeeding eight days. 429 Squadron would do likewise a couple of weeks hence. One further Halifax operation was mounted by the Lions, when a number of crews were sent mining in the Kattegat on the night of the 2/3rd.

Having escaped serious damage on the night after Dresden, Chemnitz eventually succumbed to Operation *Thunderclap* in a raid by over seven hundred aircraft on the evening of the 5th. 6 Group contributed eighty-four Lancasters and eighty-six Halifaxes, many of which experienced difficulties in the form of icing conditions within minutes of taking off. As a result many crashes occurred, and it became a black night for the Canadians. Twenty minutes after leaving Tholthorpe 420 Squadron's NA184 crashed in Yorkshire near Dishforth airfield, killing F/O Clark and three of his crew and injuring the others. Thirty minutes later NA190 went into the ground south-west of Tadcaster, and only the mid-upper gunner from P/O Sollie's crew had time to take to his parachute and save himself. NP959 then crashed in Germany, and the eight-man crew captained by F/L Glover survived to fall into enemy hands, although one of the gunners succumbed to his injuries within hours of being admitted to a German hospital. The conditions caused higher than expected fuel consumption, and a number of crews were watching their fuel gauges on the way home and had to put down before reaching Tholthorpe. P/O Menary decided to land at Juvincourt in France, but as he let down through cloud NR144 clipped a pole on high ground and crash-landed, slightly injuring two crew members. It was twenty-two minutes after leaving Tholthorpe that 425 Squadron's MZ454 crashed in Yorkshire after icing up, and F/O Lowe died with three of his crew. For P/O Anderson and five of his crew the end came just eleven minutes after take-off, when MZ845 collided with a 426 Squadron Halifax, and only the wireless operator had time to bale out. PN173 was then brought down over Germany, and F/O Desbiens died with two of his crew, while the four survivors would spend a relatively short time as guests of the *Reich*. The 426 Squadron aircraft mentioned above was PN228, which had been airborne for only ten minutes, and this tragic collision cost the lives of flight commander S/L Garrett and his crew. Twenty minutes seemed to be the critical juncture, because it was after being aloft for this length of time that 426 Squadron's LW210 broke up in the air through icing up, and crashed in York. F/L Emerson and four of his crew were killed, and five people lost their lives on the ground, while a further eighteen were injured after one of the Halifax's engines landed in a school kitchen. NP793 also crashed in Yorkshire as a result of icing just fifteen minutes after take-off, and F/O Watts and his crew all died. If these events weren't bad enough, NP799 was dispatched by a night fighter over Germany, and only one man survived as a PoW from the crew of F/L Kirkpatrick.

In addition to these multiple tragedies for a number of squadrons there were individual losses for others. A 415 Squadron Halifax failed to return, but the crew all survived in enemy hands, and a 419 Squadron Lancaster crashed short of the runway after returning early, and the crew were all killed. 424 Squadron posted missing one crew, and a 428 Squadron Lancaster crashed in the Ardennes while returning at low level. A 429 Squadron Halifax ran out of fuel and crashed near Gillingham in Kent, killing all on board, and this was the final casualty for the Bisons on the type. A 431 Squadron Lancaster failed to return, and a bad night was capped off when 432 Squadron's RG475 was shot down by friendly fire from a battery on the Essex coast at Walton-on-Naze. The captain of the Halifax was flight commander S/L Hayes, and among his seven crew colleagues was F/L Clothier, who was flying as second pilot having just begun his third tour of operations after remustering from gunner to pilot. As far as the target city was concerned, parts of its central and southern districts became engulfed in flames, and a number of important war industry factories were put out of action.

The town of Dessau had to wait until this penultimate month of the bombing war to receive its one and only heavy raid, and this took place at the hands of over five hundred aircraft from 1, 3, 6 and 8 Groups on the 7/8th. 6 Group put up eighty-one Lancasters for the attack, which was almost certainly aimed at the railway installations, but it turned into another devastating area raid. It was not a good night for 424 Squadron, which had to post missing two of its crews. Only the pilot, F/O Lighthall, escaped with his life from NG346, suggesting, perhaps, that the Lancaster exploded in mid-air throwing him clear, his body protected from the blast by the armour-plated backrest of his seat. The crew of F/O Foley was operating together for the first time, and the rear gunner was the sole survivor after NG457 crashed in the Ruhr. A 419 Squadron Lancaster also failed to return. Ninety-nine Halifaxes of 6 Group joined others from 4 Group on this night to direct their effort at Hemmingstedt, where the intended target, the Deutsche Erdölwerke refinery, was missed by at least two miles. A 408 Squadron aircraft was dispatched by a night fighter, and another from 425 Squadron went missing without trace. The following night was devoted to Hamburg and Kassel, the former attacked by a predominantly Halifax main force, including ninety-three from 6 Group, which had the shipyards as a specific objective. These were assembling the new Type XXI U-Boats, which could remain submerged for extended periods, and would have been a serious threat had they been available to the *Kriegsmarine* earlier. In the event, Hamburg lay beneath a layer of cloud, and the bombing was not concentrated. A single 415 Squadron aircraft failed to return, but the crew survived to spend a brief period as guests of the *Reich*.

A new record was set in the late morning of the 11th, when 1,079 aircraft took off for the final raid of the war on Essen. 6 Group contributed 102 Lancasters and eighty-four Halifaxes to what was the largest force ever sent to a single target. They delivered another punishing assault on this ravaged city at the end of an almost personal battle spanning a little under five years. Even so, it had only been during the last two years, since the introduction of Oboe, that the bomber had prevailed. Many gallant crews had fallen during the various campaigns, but Essen now lay totally ruined, having lost seven thousand of its inhabitants to air raids. This operation signalled the return to action of 427 Squadron, now as a Lancaster unit, and all of its participating crews returned. 431 and 434 Squadrons each posted missing one crew, the former's KB853 crashing in the target area with the crew of W/C Davenport on board, and all were killed. S/L Smith assumed temporary command of the squadron pending the arrival of a new permanent commanding officer.

The record set on the 11th was short-lived, and was surpassed a little over twenty-four hours later, when 1,108 aircraft departed their stations in the early afternoon of the 12th to deliver the final raid of the war on Dortmund, an operation that effectively finished it as a functioning city. 6 Group put up ninety-nine Lancasters and ninety-three Halifaxes, all of which returned safely. A mining operation in the Kattegat cost a 433 Squadron Lancaster on the night of the 12/13th. The Group's Lancaster squadrons rested on the 13/14th, while 101 Halifaxes joined their 4 Group counterparts in the bombing of Wuppertal-Barmen without loss. Zweibrücken was another new name on a target TABLE, and this town was attacked by a 6 Group main force comprising ninety-eight Lancasters and an equal number of Halifaxes on the evening of the 14th. The intention to block the through-passage of all enemy troops and equipment was achieved, and, in fact, every public building and 80% of the houses were flattened. A 424 Squadron Lancaster crashed near Dishforth with faulty controls on return, but there were no major injuries.

Benzol plants at Bottrop and Castrop-Rauxel occupied seventy Halifaxes from 6 Group and a contingent from 4 Group on the 15th, during which three 429 Squadron Halifaxes sustained minor flak hits. In the event all returned safely from what proved to be 429 Squadron's final operation before completing conversion to the Lancaster. That night ninety-nine Lancasters and forty-three Halifaxes from 6 Group joined others from 4 Group for what became a destructive attack on Hagen. It was a night of clear conditions, which assisted the defenders in fighting back, and 419 Squadron sustained two losses. A night fighter accounted for KB814 over the Rhine, and F/S Parrish and three of his crew were killed, while three others parachuted over enemy territory, and ultimately evaded capture. F/L McLaughlin and three of his crew survived the demise at the hands of a night fighter of KB870 over Allied held ground, albeit with injuries, but the remaining three men lost their lives. There were single losses also to 425, 428, 431, 432 and 434 Squadrons, and a total of thirty-one 6 Group men lost their lives.

On the 16/17th almost three hundred Lancasters and Mosquitos of 1 and 8 Groups carried out the final raid of the war on Nuremberg, the city that had been the target on the Command's blackest night a year earlier. A punishing blow was delivered, but the night fighter response was fierce, and twenty-four 1 Group Lancasters were shot down. As this operation was in progress, two hundred 5 Group Lancasters attacked the historic and minimally industrial city of Würzburg in central-southern Germany. In seventeen minutes of carnage, over eleven hundred tons of bombs were dropped with great accuracy, destroying 89% of the built-up area and killing between four and five thousand people. In the light of this and other similar catastrophes visited upon the German homeland at a time of imminent defeat, it is possible to comprehend, if not to condone, the murderous attitudes of a small minority of German officials, who took their vengeance upon downed Allied airmen. 424, 427 and 433 Squadrons were in action on this night, providing twelve aircraft between them for mining duties around Heligoland.

431 Squadron welcomed W/C McKinnon as its new commanding officer on the 18th, and he would remain at the helm until after the end of hostilities. He had served previously with 419 Squadron.

Two nights later Witten was area-bombed by three hundred aircraft from 4, 6 and 8 Groups, of which the Canadian contribution amounted to eighty-three Halifaxes. Clear conditions allowed the attackers to inflict severe damage on the town, and around 60% of its built-up area was reduced to rubble. After two nights off the Tholthorpe squadrons, 420 and 425 Squadrons were back on the order of battle for this operation, and both registered casualties. 425 Squadron's MZ495 was abandoned by P/O Racicot and his crew over Germany, and all but one arrived safely on the ground to become PoWs. The exception was the flight engineer, who died instantly on landing, and the precise circumstances of his death are uncertain. MZ482 was in collision with a Mosquito of 100 Group's 515 Squadron over Belgium, and both aircraft plunged to the ground. P/O Temple's rear gunner was thrown clear, and he alone from the two crews survived. Finally, NP939 lost an engine on the way home, and P/O Giguere carried out a forced-landing in Buckinghamshire, in which the wireless operator sustained injuries. 420 Squadron's MZ910 failed to return, and it was later established that F/O Keeper and all but one of his crew had survived and were in enemy hands.

Oil refineries at Böhlen and Hemmingstedt were put out of action on the 20/21st, the latter by Lancasters of 1, 6 and 8 Groups of which 110 were Canadian. 419 Squadron's KB786 was shot down by a night fighter, and just one man survived in captivity. On the afternoon of the 21st ninety 6 Group Halifaxes joined others from 4 Group to attack the railway yards at Rheine near Münster, and severe damage was caused. On the following afternoon two hundred 1, 6 and 8 Group Lancasters attacked the railway yards at Hildesheim, and in the process reduced 70% of the town to ruins, destroying over 3,300 apartment blocks and killing more than sixteen hundred people. Eighty 6 Group Lancasters took part, and two failed to return. 428 Squadron's KB777 was observed to be homebound at below five thousand feet with its port-inner engine feathered and streaming flames. The stricken aircraft was subsequently partially abandoned, but F/L Hadley and two of his crew lost their lives, while the four survivors were taken prisoner. 431 Squadron's KB808 was seen to blow up over the target with the eight-man crew of F/L Duggan on board, and there were no survivors. This was a particularly tragic loss of a crew undertaking their final sortie before being screened. Meanwhile, one hundred 6 Group Halifaxes provided the main force for an attack on the town of Dorsten, a railway and canal centre on the northern approaches to the Ruhr, which also contained a *Luftwaffe* fuel dump. A successful operation was concluded without loss. This was followed up two days later with a devastating raid on nearby Gladbeck, for which 6 Group again provided one hundred Halifaxes without loss. 1 and 6 Groups provided the main force for a simultaneous assault on the Mathias Stinnes oil plant at Bottrop, for which the Canadians put up seventy-five Lancasters. All returned, but a 433 Squadron aircraft lost both inner engines, and the crew had to extinguish fires within the fuselage before a landing was carried out safely in Belgium.

Münster was the objective for ninety-nine 6 Group Halifaxes along with a contingent from 4 Group on the 25th, when smoke prevented an assessment of the results. 408 and 415 Squadrons each lost an aircraft to flak, and just three men survived of the fourteen on board. 426 Squadron's NP818 swung off the runway during take-off and ended up in a ditch, but F/O Alward and his crew had scrambled clear by the time the bomb load went up, wrecking NP684 in the process. NP811 was brought down by flak over Germany on the way to the target, but F/O Levis and all but the bomb-aimer survived to spend a short time in captivity. Meanwhile, one hundred Lancasters of 6 Group joined others from 1 Group to pay another visit to Hanover, and all returned, although a 431 Squadron aircraft crash-landed at Manston on return after sustaining serious flak damage over the target.

W/C Marshall was posted out of 424 Squadron on the 26th, to be replaced for the final weeks of the war by W/C Norris, who had previously served with the squadron, but was now posted in from 408 Squadron, where he had been a flight commander. On the 27th Paderborn was virtually erased from the map in a fifteen-minute assault by an all-Lancaster heavy force, and on the 31st an attempt to hit the Blohm & Voss U-Boat yards at Hamburg resulted in further destruction within the city. 6 Group put up a hundred Lancasters and an equal number of Halifaxes for this operation, which was 429 Squadron's first as a Lancaster unit. It became a baptism of fire for the Canadians, who were assigned to the final wave of the attack, as enemy day fighters responded vigorously to the violation of their airspace. Five Bison crews reported being attacked by ME262 jet fighters, one of which was claimed as a probable. NG345 also encountered a ME262 in the target area, and failed to survive the exchange of fire. The pilot, F/O Jones, and his bomb-aimer managed to take to their parachutes, but the remains of the rest of the crew were found amongst the wreckage. This was one of eleven aircraft to be lost from the raid, and it would be the last time that the Command's losses reached double figures. It also proved to be the final occasion on which 429 Squadron would have the sad duty of posting missing one of its own. In addition, ME262s certainly accounted for a Halifax each from 408 and 415 Squadrons, two Lancasters from 419 and another from 434 Squadron, which was apparently hit by rockets. Other aircraft to fail to return were a 425 Squadron Halifax, in which the pilot was the sole fatality, and a 431 Squadron Lancaster, from which the pilot was the sole survivor.

April, the final month of the bombing war, began for 6 Group on the night of the 4/5th with operations against the Rhenania oil refinery at Harburg, situated on a branch of the Elbe south of Hamburg, and a similar target at Leuna in eastern Germany. Ninety of the Group's Halifaxes went to northern Germany, and while the operation was outstandingly successful, it cost two Pathfinder Lancasters and NP712 of 408 Squadron. The port-outer engine failed over the target, and then the others followed suit on the way home, forcing P/O Brown to order his crew out. Although three crew members landed in the sea, all survived and were taken into captivity. Meanwhile, ninety-three of the Group's Lancasters went east, and whilst all returned safely to home airspace, 424 Squadron's RF150 flew into a hill near High Wycombe in Buckinghamshire in poor visibility, and F/O Watson and crew were killed. W/C Mulvihill became 434 Squadron's final commanding officer on the 8th, on a posting from his flight commander post with 427 Squadron, and that night Hamburg hosted its last major raid of the war, when over four hundred aircraft from 4, 6 and 8 Groups went for the shipyards. 6 Group contributed one hundred Lancasters and ninety Halifaxes, and 408 Squadron's NP769 crashed in Germany with just one survivor from the crew of F/O Jensen. A 419 Squadron Lancaster lost an engine outbound, but the pilot pressed on to the target and bombed as briefed. On the way home the other starboard engine burst into flames, forcing F/O Cram and crew to abandon ship, which they did safely over Allied territory. The Americans had attacked the same area earlier in the day, and it was impossible to distinguish the damage between the two operations. During the course of the 9th W/C Evans was appointed as the final wartime commanding officer of 429 Squadron. The following night was devoted to a 1, 3 and 8 Group Lancaster assault on Kiel, where almost six hundred aircraft damaged all three shipyards, capsized the *Admiral Scheer* pocket battleship, and hit the *Admiral Hipper* and the *Emden*. Under cover of the main raid twenty aircraft from 424, 427, 429 and 433 Squadrons slipped in to lay mines in Kiel Bay.

Railway yards at Leipzig occupied a mixed force of 110 Lancasters and ninety Halifaxes from 6 Group on the 10th, when a successful operation was marred by the loss of a 415 Squadron Halifax and a 433 Squadron Lancaster, both with all hands. The latter was seen to be hit by flak and an engine was feathered, before a small explosion flipped the aircraft onto its back to spiral to earth. 3 and 6 Groups joined forces on the 13/14th to provide the main force for an attack on Kiel's U-Boat yards. 6 Group's contribution was 105 Lancasters and 104 Halifaxes, of which a Lancaster each from 419 and 428 Squadrons failed to return. An FW190 attacked 427 Squadron's RA539, and was seen to go down in flames after being hit by return fire. 424, 427, 429 and 433 Squadrons also carried out mining sorties in Kiel Bay while the main operation was in progress. The last area-bombing raid of the war was directed at Potsdam on the 14/15th, and this was the first incursion by RAF heavy bombers into the Berlin defence zone since March 1944. The attack, which did not involve 6 Group, was accurate, although some of the bombing spilled over into Berlin itself. Two nights later 122 Lancasters from 6 Group provided the main force for an attack on the railway yards at Schwandorf in south-eastern Germany, where extensive damage resulted. At the same time nineteen Halifaxes from 408 and 426 Squadrons bombed the airfield at Gablingen without loss.

On the 18th almost a thousand aircraft presented themselves over the island of Heligoland, and left behind them a cratered moonscape. 111 Halifaxes took part from 6 Group, and one each from 408 and 420 Squadrons failed to return. The latter was seen to crash into the sea during the outward flight, and there were no survivors. Twenty Lancasters from 424, 427, 429 and 433 Squadrons went mining for the last time on the night of the 21/22nd, when the Kattegat was the garden, and all returned safely.

The heavy-bombing war ended for some squadrons at Bremen on the 22nd, on what proved to be the Command's penultimate day of operations. The south-eastern suburbs of the city were targeted ahead of the British XXX Corps assault, which was to follow two days later. Although over seven hundred aircraft were present, the Master Bomber called a halt after less than two hundred had bombed, when the target disappeared beneath smoke, dust and cloud. All one hundred Canadian Halifaxes returned safely with their bombs still aboard.

It was all over for 420 Squadron by the time W/C Gray was appointed as its final wartime commanding officer on the 24th, and he would remain in post until September. During the course of April the squadron started receiving Mk X Lancasters, but conversion to the type had not been completed in time for operations to be carried out on the type.

The long-awaited final day of heavy bomber operations dawned on the 25th to the sound of over 350 Lancasters of 1, 5 and 8 Group taking off for the SS barracks at Hitler's Eagle's Nest retreat at Berchtesgaden in the Bavarian mountains. It was almost a symbolic operation and the bombing appeared to be accurate. Later that afternoon elements of 4, 6 and 8 Groups attacked heavy gun positions on the island of Wangerooge in the German Frisians. They were barring the approaches to the German ports, but little damage was done to them in their concrete housings. This proved to be a tragic final main force operation, in which one hundred Lancasters and ninety-two Halifaxes from 6 Group participated. During the outward flight and on final approach to the target, one aircraft hit the slipstream of another, and lurched into a third, and a further four aircraft were lost to similar and unrelated collisions in the target area. The first mentioned incident involved NP796 of 408 Squadron and NP820 of 426 Squadron, fellow residents of Linton-on-Ouse, and each crashed into the sea with no survivors. Two 431 Squadron Lancasters, KB831 and KB822, also made contact and crashed with total loss of life, bringing the Group's death toll to twenty-eight. That night 5 Group carried out a raid on an oil refinery at Tonsberg in Norway, and then, for all but 100 Group and the 8 Group Mosquito contingent, it was all over.

After an uncertain start in 1943, 6 Group gained confidence, and by the middle of 1944 had become a highly efficient and effective component of Bomber Command. Some of its squadrons suffered disproportionately high casualties for periods, but the quality of leadership at squadron level saw the Group achieve a magnificent record of service by war's end. 6 Group's contribution to victory stands for all time as a monument to the skill, dedication and courage of a magnificent people, who have always stood shoulder to shoulder with Britain during times of crisis. Almost ten thousand Canadians lost their lives in the service of Bomber Command between September 1939 and May 1945, and this figure is second only to the number of British dead. May their deeds on behalf of this country and freedom never be forgotten.

CHAPTER TWO

Quick Reference

AIR OFFICERS COMMANDING

Air Vice Marshal	G E Brookes	25.10.42 to 28.02.44
Air Vice Marshal	C M McEwin	29.02.44

OPERATIONAL STATIONS

Croft	Dalton	East Moor
Leeming	Linton-on-Ouse	Middleton St George
Skipton-on-Swale	Tholthorpe	Topcliffe

AIRCRAFT TYPES

Wellington	Halifax	Lancaster

QUICK REFERENCE AIRCRAFT/SQUADRON

405 (Vancouver) Squadron

Halifax II	First received	23.04.42
	First operation Cologne	30/31.05.42

408 (Goose) Squadron

Halifax II/V	First received		11.10.42
	First operation	Mining	9/10.01.43
Lancaster II	First received		12.08.43
	First operation	Stuttgart	7/8.10.43
	Last operation	Brussels & Melsbroek	15.08.44
Halifax III/VII	First operation	Hamburg	28/29.07.44

415 (Swordfish) Squadron

Halifax III/VII	First operation	Hamburg	28/29.07.44

419 (Moose) Squadron

Halifax II	First received		11.42
	First operation	Mining	09/10.01.43
	Last operation	Montzen	27/28.04.44
Lancaster X	First received		03.44
	First operation	Montzen	27/28.04.44

420 (Snowy Owl) Squadron

Wellington	Last operation	Duisburg	26/27.04.43
Halifax	First received		11.43
	First operation	Berlin	15/16.02.44

424 (Tiger) Squadron

Wellington	First received	BJ658	
	First operation	Lorient	15/16.01.43
	Last operation	Mannheim	16/17.04.43
	Last disposed of		01.44
Halifax III	First received		12.43
	First operation	Berlin	15/16.02.44
	Last operation	Stuttgart	28/29.01.45
Lancaster	First received		01.45
	First operation	Ludwigshafen	1/2.02.45

425 (Alouette) Squadron

Wellington	First operation	Aachen	5/6.10.42
	Last operation	Duisburg	26/27.04.43
	Last disposed of		12.43
Halifax III	First received		12.43
	First operation	Leipzig	19/20.02.44

426 (Thunderbird) Squadron

Wellington	First operation	Lorient	14/15.01.43
	Last offensive op.	Düsseldorf	11/12.06.43
	Last operation	Sea search	14.06.43
Lancaster II	First received		06.43
	First operation	Peenemünde	17/18.08.43
	Last operation	St Ghislain	1/2.05.44
Halifax III	First received		04.44
	First operation	Sea search	19.04.44
	First offensive op.	St Valery en Caux	7/8.05.44

427 (Lion) Squadron

Wellington	Last operation	Mining	28/29.4.43
	Last disposed of		04.05.43
Halifax V	First received		05.43
	First operation	Wuppertal	29/30.05.43
	Last operation	Berlin	28/29.01.44
Halifax III	First operation	Berlin	15/16.02.44
	Last operation	Mining	02/03.03.45
Lancaster I/III	First received		02.03.45
	First operation	Essen	11.03.45

428 (Ghost) Squadron

Wellington	Last operation	Düsseldorf	11/12.06.43
	Last disposed of		06.43
Halifax II/V	First received		06.43
	First operation	Le Creusot	19/20.06.43
	Last operation	Mining	05/06.07.44
Lancaster X	First received		06.44
	First operation	St Pol/Cambrai	14/15.06.44

429 (Bison) Squadron

Wellington	Last operation	Mining	3/4.08.43
	Last disposed of		08.43
Halifax II/V	First received		08.43
	First operation	Montluçon	15/16.09.43
	Last operation	Le Mans	13/14.03.44
Halifax III	First operation	Stuttgart	15/16.03.44
	Last operation	Castrop-Rauxel	15.03.45
Lancaster	First received		03.45
	First operation	Hamburg	31.03.45

431 (Iroquois) Squadron

Wellington	Last operation	Mining	12/13.07.43
Halifax II/V	First received		07.43
	First operation	Mining	2/3.10.43
	Last operation	Amiens	16/17.03.44
Halifax III	First received		03.44
	First operation	Noisy-le-Sec	18/19.04.44
	Last operation	Cologne	30.10.44
Lancaster X	First received		10.44
	First operation	Oberhausen	1/2.11.44

432 (Leaside) Squadron

Wellington	First received		2.05.43
	First operation	Dortmund	23/24.05.43
	Last operation	Mining	22/23.10.43
Lancaster II	First received		25.10.43
	First operation	Sea search	19.11.43
	First offensive op.	Berlin	26/27.11.43
	Last operation	Berlin	30/31.01.44
Halifax III/VII	First received		02.44
	First operation	Sea search	16.02.44
	First offensive op.	Schweinfurt	24/25.02.44

433 (Porcupine) Squadron

Halifax III	First received	HX268	3.11.43
	First operation	Mining	2/3.01.44
	Last operation	Magdeburg	16/17.01.45
Lancaster I/III	First received		01.45
	First operation	Ludwigshafen	1/2.02.45

434 (Bluenose) Squadron

Halifax V	First received		06.43
	First operation	Milan	12/13.08.43
	Last operation	Boulogne-sur-Mer	11/12.05.44
Halifax III	First received		05.44
	First operation	Trouville	24/25.05.44
	Last operation	Nippes/Cologne	21/22.12.44
Lancaster X	First received		12.44
	First operation	Lohausen	24.12.44

GROUP STRENGTH

As of 1st January 1943

Operational Squadrons
408, 419, 420, 424, 425, 426, 427, 428

As of April 1945

Operational Squadrons
408, 415, 419, 420, 424, 425, 426, 427, 428, 429, 431, 432, 433, 434

Quick Reference Station/Squadron

Croft	408, 427, 431, 434
Dalton	420, 428
Dishforth	425, 426
East Moor	415, 429, 432
Leeming	405, 408, 427, 429
Linton-on-Ouse	408, 426
Middleton St George	419, 420, 428

Skipton on Swale	424, 432, 433
Tholthorpe	420, 425, 431, 434
Topcliffe	405, 424

Quick Reference Station/Squadron Dates

Croft	408	09.12.41 to 13.09.42
	427	07.11.42 to 04.05.43
	431	10.12.43 to 06.06.45
	434	11.12.43 to 09.06.45
Dalton	428	07.11.42 to 01.06.43
	420	06.11.43 to 11.12.43
Dishforth	425	25.06.42 to 15.05.43
	426	15.10.42 to 17.06.43
	425	06.11.43 to 09.12.43
East Moor	429	07.11.42. to 12.08.43
	432	19.09.43. to 15.05.45
	415	26.07.44 to 15.05.45
Leeming	408	17.09.42 to 27.08.43
	405	06.03.43 to 19.04.43
	427	05.05.43 to 29.08.45
	429	13.08.43 to 29.08.45
Linton-on-Ouse	426	18.06.43 to 24.05.45
	408	27.08.43 to 13.06.45
Middleton St George	420	14.10.42 to 15.05.43
	419	09.11.42 to 01.06.45
	428	01.06.43 to 31.05.45
Skipton on Swale	432	01.05.43 to 18.09.43
	433	25.09.43. to 30.08.45
	424	16.11.43 to 29.08.45
Tholthorpe	431	15.07.43. to 09.12.43
	434	13.06.43 to 10.12.43
	425	10.12.43 to 12.06.45
	420	12.12.43 to 11.06.45
Topcliffe	424	15.10.42 to 07.04.43
	405	01.03.43 to 06.03.43

6 Group Sorties and Losses

Aircraft	Sorties	Losses
Wellington	3,287	127 (3.9%)
Halifax	28,126	508 (1.8%)
Lancaster	8,171	149 (1.8%)
Total	39,584	784 (2.0%)

Quick Reference Records

6 Group

Most overall operations	427 (Lion) Squadron (270)
Most bombing raids	419 (Moose) Squadron (232)
Highest aircraft operational losses	419 (Moose) Squadron (105)
Highest % losses	405 (Vancouver) Squadron (7.3%)
Most sorties	419 (Moose) Squadron (3,645)

CHAPTER THREE

The Squadrons

405 (VANCOUVER) SQUADRON

Motto: Ducimus (We lead)   Code LQ

405 Squadron was the first Canadian unit to form in Bomber Command, and this it did on the 23rd of April 1941 on the 4 Group station at Driffield in Yorkshire. It became the second squadron in the Command to fully equip with the Merlin-powered Wellington II, and operated these until they were replaced with Halifaxes in April 1942. In Late October the squadron departed Bomber Command for a five-month tour of duty with Coastal Command. In February 1943, shortly before the completion of this maritime interlude, the squadron was officially adopted by the city of Vancouver, and would proudly carry its name into battle for the remainder of the war. It was in March 1943 that the squadron joined 6 Group, but just six weeks later it became the only Canadian unit to join the Pathfinder Force, which it served with distinction until war's end. Lancasters began to replace the Halifaxes in August 1943, and just as the war was ending it re-equipped again with the Canadian-built Mk X. Among its commanding officers was W/C Johnny Fauquier, who served two terms at the helm, and saw out the last four months of the bombing war as the commanding officer of 617 Squadron, better known as the Dambusters.

STATIONS

Topcliffe   01.03.43 to 06.03.43
Leeming   06.03.43 to 19.04.43

COMMANDING OFFICERS

Wing Commander A C P Clayton DFC   19.11.42 to 19.04.43

AIRCRAFT

Halifax II   04.42 to 09.43

OPERATIONAL RECORD

Halifaxes

Operations	Sorties	Aircraft Losses	% Losses
13	55	47	3

Category of Operations
Bombing
13

TABLE OF STATISTICS

Out of 15 squadrons in 6 Group

Lowest number of overall operations, sorties and aircraft operational losses in 6 Group.

Out of 15 Halifax squadrons in 6 Group

Lowest number of Halifax overall operations, sorties and operational losses in 6 Group.

AIRCRAFT HISTORIES

W7803 LQ-B	FTR Stuttgart 11/12.3.43.
W7810	To 1659 CU.
W7853	To 1659 CU.
W7885	From 35 Sqn. Returned to 35 Sqn.
BB210	To 1659 CU.
BB212 LQ-P/U	FTR Stuttgart 11/12.3.43.
BB250 LQ-E	FTR Stuttgart 11/12.3.43.
BB334	From 138 Sqn. Returned to 138 Sqn.
BB367	From NTU. To 1669 CU.
BB369	From NTU. To 1664 CU.

BB372	To 35 Sqn.
BB373	To 78 Sqn.
BB374	To 1658 CU.
DT507	To 1659 CU.
DT515	To 76 Sqn.
DT551	To 1659 CU.
DT553	To 1659 CU.
DT560	To 1666 CU.
DT565	To 1659 CU.
DT573	To 1659 CU.
DT695	To 1652 CU.
DT699 LQ-G	FTR from mining sortie 6/7.4.43.
DT704 LQ-H	FTR Kiel 4/5.4.43.
DT723 LQ-F	FTR Essen 3/4.4.43.
DT741 LQ-P	FTR Essen 30.4/1.5.43.
DT745 LQ-V	FTR Stuttgart 11/12.3.43.
DT772	To 408 Sqn.
DT802	To 1659 CU.
DT808 LQ-V	From 102 Sqn. FTR Essen 3/4.4.43.
HR723	To 35 Sqn.
HR796	From NTU. To 1667CU.
HR797 LQ-A	FTR Düsseldorf 11/12.6.43.
HR800	From NTU. To 1666 CU.
HR804	To 35 Sqn.
HR805	To 10 Sqn.
HR806 LQ-D	Crashed almost immediately after take-off from Gransden Lodge when bound for Düsseldorf 25.5.43.
HR807 LQ-G	FTR Essen 27/28.5.43.
HR808	Crashed on landing at Gransden Lodge while training 18.6.43.
HR809	Crashed on landing at Gransden Lodge while training 2.9.43.
HR810 LQ-X	FTR Mannheim 5/6.9.43.
HR811	To 35 Sqn.
HR813 LQ-H	FTR Cologne 3/4.7.43.
HR816 LQ-C	FTR Wuppertal 24/25.6.43.
HR817 LQ-C	FTR Peenemünde 17/18.8.43.
HR832	Crashed in Norfolk during training flight 16.6.43.
HR833	To 35 Sqn.
JB797	To 1658 CU.
JB798	To 78 Sqn.
JB875	To 78 Sqn.

JB893	Struck JB906 at Leeming 4.4.43. Repaired. To 408 Sqn.
JB896 LQ-C	FTR Dortmund 23/24.5.43.
JB897 LQ-T	Crash-landed on approach to Wyton on return from Dortmund 5.5.43.
JB899	To 10 Sqn.
JB904 LQ-E	FTR Dortmund 4/5.5.43.
JB905 LQ-G	To 1658 CU.
JB906	Struck by JB893 at Leeming 4.4.43 and damaged beyond repair.
JB907	To 78 Sqn.
JB914	Crashed on landing at Leeming during training 13.4.43.
JB916	To 1659 CU.
JB917	To 419 Sqn.
JB919	To 77 Sqn.
JB920 LQ-F	FTR Duisburg 26/27.4.43.
JB957 LQ-A	Crash-landed in Huntingdonshire on return from Dortmund 5.5.43.
JB963	To 77 Sqn.
JB966 LQ-D	FTR Bochum 13/14.5.43.

408 (GOOSE) SQUADRON

Motto: For Freedom   Code EQ

408 Squadron was formed in 5 Group in June 1941 as the second Canadian unit in Bomber Command. The squadron operated Hampdens throughout its time in the east Midlands, but did manage just one sortie in a Manchester before transferring to 4 Group in September 1942. There the squadron operated Halifaxes, and retained these after becoming a founder member of 6 Group on the 1st of January 1943. In August 1943 the squadron took on the Hercules-powered Mk II Lancasters, but within a year these were succeeded by the similarly powered Halifax III and VII, with which the squadron saw out the war having served throughout with distinction.

STATIONS

Leeming	17.09.42 to 27.08.43
Linton-on-Ouse	27.08.43 to 13.06.45

COMMANDING OFFICERS

Wing Commander W D S Ferris DFC	01.09.42 to 26.10.43
Wing Commander A C Mair DFC	28.10.43 to 26.11.43
Wing Commander D S Jacobs DFC	27.11.43 to 22.05.44
Wing Commander A R McLernon DFC	24.05.44 to 14.10.44
Wing Commander J F Easton DFC	14.10.44 to 26.11.44
Wing Commander F R Sharp DFC	26.11.44 to 05.09.45

AIRCRAFT

Halifax II/V	12.42 to 08.43
Lancaster II	08.43 to 08.44
Halifax III	07.44 to 02.45
Halifax VII	07.44 to 05.45

OPERATIONAL RECORD

Operations	Sorties	Aircraft Losses	% Losses
198	2,679	61	2.3

All bombing.

Halifaxes

Operations	Sorties	Aircraft Losses	% Losses
98	1,469	20	1.4

All bombing.

Lancasters

Operations	Sorties	Aircraft Losses	% Losses
100	1,210	41	3.4

All bombing.

TABLE OF STATISTICS

Out of 59 Lancaster squadrons

43rd highest number of Lancaster overall operations in Bomber Command.
45th highest number of Lancaster sorties in Bomber Command.
33rd highest number of Lancaster operational losses in Bomber Command.

Out of 32 Halifax squadrons

14th highest number of Halifax overall operations in Bomber Command.
19th highest number of Halifax sorties in Bomber Command.
11th equal (with 434 Sqn) highest number of Halifax operational losses in Bomber Command.

Out of 15 squadrons in 6 Group

2nd equal (with 419 Sqn) highest number of overall operations in 6 Group.
4th highest number of sorties in 6 Group.
2nd highest number of aircraft operational losses in 6 Group.

Out of 11 Lancaster squadrons in 6 Group

3rd highest number of Lancaster overall operations in 6 Group.
3rd highest number of Lancaster sorties in 6 Group.
Highest number of Lancaster operational losses in 6 Group.

Out of 15 Halifax squadrons in 6 Group

4th highest number of Halifax overall operations in 6 Group.
8th highest number of Halifax sorties in 6 Group.
3rd equal (with 434 Sqn) highest number of Halifax operational losses in 6 Group.

Halifax II	From October 1942 to August 1943.
L9524	From 1659 CU. Conversion Flt only. Became ground instruction machine.
L9532	From 102 Sqn. Conversion Flt only. To 1659 CU.
R9363	From 405 CF. Conversion Flt only. to 1659 CU.
R9382	From 76 CF. Conversion Flt only. To 1659 CU.
BB311 EQ-L	FTR Stuttgart 14/15.4.43.
BB332 EQ-H	FTR Berlin 27/28.3.43.
BB336 EQ-O	FTR Kiel 4/5.4.43.
BB343 EQ-X	FTR Pilsen 16/17.4.43.
BB375 EQ-T	FTR Krefeld 21/22.6.43.
DG231	To 1663 CU.
DG233	To 1659 CU and back. To 518 Sqn.
DG234	To 1659 CU.
DG235	To 1659 CU and back. To Rolls-Royce.
DG236	To 1663 CU.
DG237	To 518 Sqn.
DG239	To 1659 CU.
DG240	To 518 Sqn.

DG241	To 1668 CU.
DG242	SOC 28.4.45.
DG243	To 1668 CU.
DG246	To 1663 CU.
DG247	To 1664 CU.
DG248	To 1663 CU.
DG249	To Rotol.
DG253	To 138 Sqn.
DG227	To 1663 CU.
DT546	From 10 Sqn. To 1659 CU.
DT673 EQ-G/A	Crash-landed at Leeming on return from Essen 4.4.43.
DT674 EQ-A	FTR Essen 27/28.5.43.
DT675	To 1656 CU.
DT676	To 1659 CU.
DT677	To 1659 CU.
DT678 EQ-C	Crash-landed in Nottinghamshire on return from Lorient 23.1.43.
DT679 EQ-Q	FTR Berlin 29/30.3.43.
DT680 EQ-D	FTR Hamburg 3/4.2.43.
DT682 EQ-F	Crashed in Nottinghamshire soon after take-off during transit 2.2.43.
DT749 EQ-O	FTR Hamburg 27/28.7.43.
DT750 EQ-U	Crashed in Yorkshire on return from Cologne 14.2.43.
DT752 EQ-W	FTR Pilsen 16/17.4.43.
DT769 EQ-J	FTR Aachen 13/14.7.43.
DT772 EQ-F/E	From 405 Sqn. FTR Krefeld 21/22.6.43.
DT781 EQ-D	To 1668 CU.
DT790 EQ-S	Crashed near Leeming on return from Essen 13.3.43.
DT797 EQ-H	FTR Berlin 1/2.3.43.
HR654 EQ-R	FTR Berlin 29/30.3.43.
HR655 EQ-S	FTR Lorient 7/8.2.43.
HR656 EQ-T	FTR Stuttgart 11/12.3.43.
HR657	To 78 Sqn.
HR658 EQ-V	FTR Dortmund 4/5.5.43.
HR659	To 78 Sqn.
HR662 EQ-H	FTR Lorient 29/30.1.43.
HR664	To 78 Sqn.
HR713 EQ-F	FTR Essen 3/4.4.43.
JB790 EQ-V	FTR Bochum 12/13.6.43.
JB796 EQ-C	FTR Cologne 3/4.7.43.
JB841 EQ-K	FTR Dortmund 23/24.5.43.

JB854 EQ-D	FTR Pilsen 16/17.4.43.
JB858 EQ-S	FTR Gelsenkirchen 25/26.6.43.
JB866 EQ-T	FTR Essen 3/4.4.43.
JB893	From 405 Sqn. To 429 Sqn.
JB898 EQ-Q	FTR Dortmund 4/5.5.43.
JB909 EQ-G	FTR Stuttgart 14/15.4.43.
JB913 EQ-F	FTR Cologne 3/4.7.43.
JB922 EQ-H	FTR Gelsenkirchen 9/10.7.43.
JB925 EQ-R	FTR Pilsen 16/17.4.43.
JB931 EQ-O	FTR Bochum 13/14.5.43.
JB959 EQ-L	Crashed on take-off from Leeming when bound for Gelsenkirchen 9.7.43.
JB967	To 429 Sqn.
JB968	To 429 Sqn.
JB969 EQ-D	To 429 Sqn.
JB971	To 429 Sqn.
JB972 EQ-Q	FTR Düsseldorf 11/12.6.43.
JD107 EQ-Y	FTR Le Creusot 19/20.6.43.
JD164	To 429 Sqn.
JD174 EQ-A	Abandoned near Leeming following early return from Aachen 14.7.43.
JD209 EQ-B	FTR Krefeld 21/22.6.43.
JD216 EQ-P	FTR Gelsenkirchen 9/10.7.43.
JD268	To 429 Sqn.
JD271	To 429 Sqn.
JD274	To 429 Sqn.
JD275	To 429 Sqn.
JD278	To 429 Sqn.
JD317	To 429 Sqn.
JD318	To 429 Sqn.
JD323	To 429 Sqn.
JD326	To 429 Sqn.
JD327	To 429 Sqn.
JD332	To 429 Sqn.
JD333	To 429 Sqn.
JD361	To 429 Sqn.
JD363	To 429 Sqn.
JD365 EQ-J	FTR Remscheid 30/31.7.43.
JD372	To 429 Sqn.
JD374	To 429 Sqn.
JD384	To 429 Sqn.
JD386	To 429 Sqn.
JD411	To 429 Sqn.
JD412	To 102 Sqn.

JD419	To 1659 CU.

Lancaster II   From August 1943 to July 1944.

DS601	From 1679 CU. To 1668 CU.
DS614 EQ-U	From 115 Sqn via 1678 and 1668 CUs.
DS621 EQ-O	From 426 Sqn via 1666 CU. Force-landed in Yorkshire while training 2.7.44.
DS626	From 426 Sqn. To 1668 CU.
DS631 EQ-D/I	From 115 Sqn via 1668 CU. To 1668 CU.
DS632 EQ-I/O	
DS634 EQ-A	From 426 Sqn. FTR Hamburg 28/29.7.44.
DS651 EQ-I/Q	From 426 Sqn via 1679CU.
DS656	From 426 Sqn. Crashed on take-off at Linton-on-Ouse while training 10.6.44.
DS657 EQ-L	From 426 Sqn via 1679 CU. To 1668 CU.
DS688 EQ-R	From 426 Sqn via 1679 CU & 1666 CU. FTR Cambrai 12/13.6.44.
DS692 EQ-S	From 426 Sqn. Crashed on landing at Marston Moor following early return from Kiel 23/24.7.44.
DS704 EQ-W	FTR Frankfurt 20/21.12.43.
DS705 EQ-K	Crashed on approach to Dalton while training 23.7.43.
DS707 EQ-C/D/M	From 426 Sqn. To 1668 CU.
DS708 EQ-A	From 426 Sqn. To Short Bros.
DS709 EQ-K/P	From 426 Sqn. FTR Berlin 27/28.1.44.
DS710 EQ-H/A	From 426 Sqn. FTR Berlin 27/28.1.44.
DS712 EQ-G	Crash-landed near Lincoln on return from Berlin 27.11.43.
DS718 EQ-R	From 426 Sqn. FTR Berlin 29/30.12.43.
DS719 EQ-U	From 426 Sqn. FTR Essen 26/27.4.44.
DS723 EQ-B/D	FTR Berlin 26/27.11.43.
DS724 EQ-C/X	Abandoned soon after take-off when bound for Stuttgart 7.10.43.
DS725 EQ-B	To 115 Sqn.
DS726 EQ-E/T/Y	From 426 Sqn. FTR Cambrai 12/13.6.44.
DS727 EQ-A/O/X	From 426 Sqn. To 1668 CU.
DS729 EQ-D/H	From 426 Sqn. SOC 29.3.45.
DS730 EQ-K/V	To 1679 CU & 1666 CU and back. To 1668 CU.
DS731 EQ-U/O	FTR Schweinfurt 24/25.2.44.
DS732 EQ-F	Crash-landed in Yorkshire during fighter affiliation exercise 7.9.43.
DS737 EQ-C	Crashed in Yorkshire on return from Berlin 16.12.43.
DS739	To 432 Sqn via 1679 CU.

DS758 EQ-H	FTR Frankfurt 20/21.12.43.
DS759 EQ-A	From 426 Sqn. FTR Dortmund 22/23.5.44.
DS761 EQ-J/S/V	From 115 Sqn. To 46 MU.
DS763 EQ-E	From 426 Sqn. To 1668 CU.
DS767 EQ-Q	FTR Brunswick 14/15.1.44.
DS768 EQ-J	Written off in landing accident in Worcestershire on return from Coutances 6/7.6.44.
DS769 EQ-J	To 115 Sqn.
DS770 EQ-F	To 426 Sqn.
DS771	To 426 Sqn.
DS772 EQ-T	To 426 Sqn and back. FTR Cambrai 12/13.6.44.
DS774 EQ-F	FTR Düsseldorf 3/4.11.43.
DS775	To 426 Sqn.
DS776	To 426 Sqn.
DS778 EQ-U	FTR Kassel 22/23.10.43.
DS788 EQ-C	From 432 Sqn. FTR Leipzig 19/20.2.44.
DS790 EQ-B	FTR Magdeburg 21/22.1.44.
DS791 EQ-F	FTR Augsburg 25/26.2.44.
DS797 EQ-H/M	FTR Frankfurt 22/23.3.44.
DS830 EQ-H/W	From 426 Sqn. To 1668 CU.
DS838 EQ-A/I	From 426 Sqn. To 1668 CU.
DS841 EQ-Q/X	From 426 Sqn. To 1668 CU.
DS844 EQ-X	From 432 Sqn. FTR Schweinfurt 24/25.2.44.
DS845 EQ-V/T	Flew 11 Berlin operations. FTR Augsburg 25/26.2.44.
DS846	To 426 Sqn.
DS848 EQ-D/X	From 426 Sqn. To 1668 CU.
DS849 EQ-X	FTR Berlin 27/28.1.44.
LL617 EQ-F/P	From 426 Sqn. To 1668 CU.
LL621 EQ-Y	From 426 Sqn. To 1668 CU.
LL623 EQ-J/U	FTR Berlin 23/24.11.43.
LL631 EQ-G	FTR Berlin 2/3.1.44.
LL632 EQ-G	From 432 Sqn. FTR Leipzig 19/20.2.44.
LL633 EQ-L	FTR Nuremberg 30/31.3.44.
LL634 EQ-F	From 426 Sqn. To 1668 CU 8.44.
LL636 EQ-G	Destroyed on the ground at Bottesford 6.1.45.
LL637 EQ-P	From 432 Sqn. FTR Stuttgart 15/16.3.44.
LL642 EQ-B	To 1668 CU.
LL643 EQ-Q	FTR Acheres 7/8.6.44.
LL675 EQ-K/M/T	From 426 Sqn. Crashed in Leicestershire while training 11.7.44.
LL676 EQ-E	FTR Berlin 16/17.12.43.
LL687 EQ-M/H	From 115 Sqn via 426 Sqn. FTR Hamburg 28/29.7.44.

LL699 EQ-C   FTR Brunswick 14/15.1.44.
LL700 EQ-J/R/X   From 426 Sqn. To 1668 CU.
LL717 EQ-F/W   FTR Frankfurt 22/23.3.44.
LL718 EQ-E   From 432 Sqn. FTR Stuttgart 15/16.3.44.
LL719 EQ-V   From 432 Sqn. FTR Leipzig 19/20.2.44.
LL720 EQ-R   FTR Leipzig 19/20.2.44.
LL722 EQ-N   To 1668 CU.
LL723 EQ-H   From 432 Sqn. FTR Dortmund 22/23.5.44.
LL724   From 432 Sqn. FTR Magdeburg 21/22.1.44.
LL725 EQ-Z/C   From 432 Sqn. FTR Hamburg 28/29.7.44.

Halifax III–VII   From July 1944 to May 1945.
LK201   From 426 Sqn.
LW207   From 426 Sqn.
MZ421   From 434 Sqn. To 425 Sqn.
MZ435   From 434 Sqn. Returned to 434 Sqn.
MZ495   From 434 Sqn. To 425 Sqn.
MZ904   From 427 Sqn. To 431 Sqn.
MZ907   From 429 Sqn. To 434 Sqn.
MZ908   From 429 Sqn. To 434 Sqn.
NP685   From 426 Sqn.
NP710 EQ-S   From 432 Sqn. Crashed on landing at Linton-on-
                    Ouse following early return from Castrop-Rauxel
                    11.9.44.
NP711 EQ-O   From 426 Sqn. FTR Worms 21/22.2.45.
NP712 EQ-R/N   From 432 Sqn. FTR Harburg 4/5.4.45.
NP713 EQ-X   From 426 Sqn. Crashed on landing at East Moor
                    on return from Forêt de Chantilly 7/8.8.44.
NP714 EQ-V   From 426 Sqn.
NP716 EQ-P   From 432 Sqn. FTR Hamburg 28/29.7.44.
NP717 EQ-W   From 426 Sqn.
NP718 EQ-Z/B   From 432 Sqn. FTR Hemmingstedt 7/8.3.45.
NP737   From 624 Sqn.
NP740   From 426 Sqn.
NP742 EQ-U
NP743 EQ-K   FTR Stuttgart 28/29.1.45.
NP744 EQ-X   FTR Düsseldorf 2/3.11.44.
NP745 EQ-H   Abandoned over Cumberland while training
                    17.10.44.
NP746 EQ-E   FTR Stuttgart 28/29.1.45.
NP747 EQ-N
NP749 EQ-Y
NP750 EQ-F   FTR Bochum 4/5.11.44.
NP751 EQ-L

NP754	To 415 Sqn.
NP756 EQ-T	
NP757 EQ-B	Abandoned over Lincolnshire while bound for Wanne-Eickel 2.2.45.
NP761 EQ-A	FTR Gelsenkirchen 6.11.44.
NP768	To 426 Sqn.
NP769 EQ-D	FTR Hamburg 8/9.4.45.
NP770 EQ-G	FTR Münster 18.11.44.
NP771 EQ-S	To 426 Sqn.
NP772	
NP773 EQ-M	FTR Wilhelmshaven 15/16.10.44.
NP775	To 426 Sqn.
NP776 EQ-R	FTR Heligoland 18.4.45.
NP777	
NP780 EQ-N	
NP781 EQ-U	FTR Düsseldorf airfield (Lohausen) 24.12.44.
NP796 EQ-M	Collided with NP820 (426 Sqn) and FTR Wangerooge 25.4.45.
NP798 EQ-J	Caught fire and blew up at Linton-on-Ouse while being prepared for operations 14.1.45.
NP804 EQ-K	From 432 Sqn. FTR Münster 25.3.45.
NP806 EQ-Q	FTR Hamburg 31.3.45.
NP807	From 432 Sqn.
NP809	
NP810 EQ-H	From 426 Sqn. FTR Castrop-Rauxel 21/22.11.44.
NP811	From 426 Sqn. Returned to 426 Sqn.
NP813	From 426 Sqn.
NP814	From 426 Sqn.
NP819	To 426 Sqn.
NP820	To 426 Sqn.
NR116	From 426 Sqn. To 425 Sqn.
NR124	From 434 Sqn. To 415 Sqn.
NR126	From 434 Sqn. To 420 Sqn.
NR199	From 434 Sqn. To 420 Sqn and back. To 415 Sqn.
NR209 EQ-A	From 425 Sqn. To 425 Sqn and back. FTR Hanover 5/6.1.45.
PN208	To 432 Sqn.
PN223	
PN225	
PN227	From 426 Sqn.
PN230 EQ-V	
PN232	
PN234	
PN240	To 415 Sqn.

RG450	To 432 Sqn.
RG453 EQ-Z	From 426 Sqn.
RG472 EQ-T	FTR Cologne 2.3.45.
RG473	
RG474	
RG477 EQ-N	FTR Worms 21/22.2.45.

Heaviest Single Loss

16/17.04.43	Pilsen. 4 Halifaxes FTR.
19/20.02.44	Leipzig. 4 Lancasters FTR.
28/29.07.44	Hamburg. 3 Lancasters & 1 Halifax FTR.

415 (SWORDFISH) SQUADRON

Motto: Ad Metam (To the mark)   Code 6U

415 Squadron joined 6 Group towards the end of July 1944 after two years' service with Coastal Command. It was the last of fifteen squadrons to join the Group, and spent its entire Bomber Command service at East Moor operating Halifaxes.

STATIONS

East Moor   26.07.44 to 15.05.45

COMMANDING OFFICERS

Wing Commander J G McNeill DFC	12.07.44 to 21.08.44
Wing Commander J H L Lecomte DFC	22.08.44 to 30.10.44
Wing Commander F W Ball	31.10.44 to 15.05.45

AIRCRAFT

Halifax III	07.44 to 15.05.45
Halifax VII	02.45 to 15.05.45

OPERATIONAL RECORD

Operations	Sorties	Aircraft Losses	% Losses
104	1526	13	0.9
All bombing.			

TABLE OF STATISTICS

Out of 32 Halifax squadrons

28th highest number of Halifax overall operations in Bomber Command.
23rd highest number of Halifax sorties in Bomber Command.
28th equal (with 462 Sqn) highest number of Halifax operational losses in Bomber Command.

Out of 15 squadrons in 6 Group

14th highest number of overall operations in 6 Group.
14th highest number of sorties in 6 Group.
14th highest number of aircraft operational losses in 5 Group.

Out of 15 Halifax squadrons in 6 Group

13th highest number of Halifax overall operations in 6 Group.
11th highest number of Halifax sorties in 6 Group.
14th highest number of Halifax operational losses in 6 Group.

AIRCRAFT HISTORIES

Halifax	From July 1944.
HX343	From 466 Sqn. To 10 Sqn.
LK755	From 426 Sqn. To 1666 CU.
CU.LK765	From 432 Sqn. To 1666 CU.
LK766 6U-V/Q	From 432 Sqn. To 187 Sqn.
LL593	To 1665 CU.
LV860	From 10 Sqn. To 429 Sqn.
LV941	From 425 Sqn. Damaged beyond repair during an operation to Heligoland 18.4.45.
LW122	From 433 Sqn. To 420 Sqn.
LW552	From 432 Sqn. To 1664 CU.
LW595 6U-Q	From 432 Sqn. FTR Hamburg 28/29.7.44.
LW686 6U-H	From 432 Sqn. Crashed on landing at East Moor on return from Caen 8.8.44.
MZ356	From 424 Sqn. To 158 Sqn.
MZ416	From 431 Sqn. To 187 Sqn.
MZ456 6U-P	From 431 Sqn. FTR Hanau 6/7.1.45.
MZ474	From 429 Sqn.
MZ476 6U-Y	FTR Hanover 5/6.1.45.
MZ483 6U-M	

MZ586 6U-Y/A	From 432 Sqn. To 187 Sqn.
MZ590	From 432 Sqn. To 1659 CU.
MZ603 6U-E	From 426 Sqn. FTR Düsseldorf 2/3.11.44.
MZ633	From 432 Sqn.
MZ686 6U-U	From 432 Sqn. Crashed on take-off from East Moor when bound for Hamburg 28.7.44.
MZ690 6U-X	From 426 Sqn. To 1666 CU.
MZ814	From 427 Sqn.
MZ861	From 431 Sqn. To 187 Sqn.
MZ882 6U-C	From 431 Sqn. Declared damaged beyond repair on return from Düsseldorf 2.11.44.
MZ907 6U-P	From 431 Sqn. FTR Münster 25.3.45.
MZ922 6U-C	From 431 Sqn. FTR Hamburg 31.3.45.
MZ946	To 187 Sqn.
MZ947 6U-C	To 1665 CU.
MZ949 6U-G	To 187 Sqn.
NA124	To 1665 CU.
NA181 6U-D	To 429 Sqn.
NA185 6U-B	FTR Leipzig 10.4.45.
NA186 6U-U	FTR Hamburg 8/9.3.45.
NA201	To 425 Sqn and back.
NA202	To 426 Sqn and back.
NA204 6U-J	From 426 Sqn. FTR Chemnitz 5/6.3.45.
NA517	From 432 Sqn. To 190 Sqn.
NA582 6U-D	From 420 Sqn. Crashed on approach to East Moor on return from Duisburg 15.10.44.
NA583 6U-F	From 420 Sqn. FTR Düsseldorf 2/3.11.44.
NA587 6U-Q	From 419 Sqn.
NA600 6U-U	To 187 Sqn.
NA607	To 1664 CU.
NA608	To 1664 CU.
NA609	Crashed in Yorkshire on transit flight after collision with MZ633 (415 Sqn) 21.8.44.
NA610	From 420 Sqn.
NA611 6U-T	From 420 Sqn. Crashed on take-off at East Moor when bound for Grevenbroich 14.1.45.
NA612	From 425 Sqn. To 1664 CU.
NP754	From 408 Sqn.
NP935 6U-I	From 433 Sqn. Crash-landed at Woodbridge on return from Wanne-Eickel 12.10.44.
NP936 6U-P	From 424 Sqn. FTR Kamen 24.2.45.
NP938 6U-T	From 424 Sqn. FTR Witten 18/19.3.45.
NP940	From 424 Sqn.
NP961	From 432 Sqn. To 420 Sqn.

NR122	From 431 Sqn.
NR124	From 408 Sqn. To 420 Sqn.
NR140	From 434 Sqn. To 1666 CU.
NR145	From 432 Sqn.
NR146	From 424 Sqn.
NR156 6U-H	
NR172 6U-V	To 420 Sqn.
NR199	From 408 Sqn.
NR206	From 424 Sqn.
NR228	From 424 Sqn.
NR249 6U-J	FTR Wanne-Eickel 8/9.2.45.
NR253 6U-L	FTR Magdeburg 16/17.1.45.
NR256	From 429 Sqn.
NR288	To 427 Sqn.
PN174	
PN236	From 432 Sqn.
PN237	From 432 Sqn. To 1665 CU.
PN240 6U-W	From 408 Sqn. To 1665 CU.
PN367	
RG447 6U-S	From 426 Sqn. To 1665 CU.

419 (MOOSE) SQUADRON

Motto: Moosa Aswayita (Beware of the moose)   Code VR

Formed in December 1941 as the third Canadian unit in Bomber Command 419 Squadron began life operating Wellingtons in 3 Group. Its first commanding officer, W/C John 'Moose' Fulton, became a legend, and after his death on operations his name was officially adopted by the squadron. In August 1942 the squadron was posted to 4 Group, and continued operations on Wellingtons until the arrival of Halifaxes in November. Working up on the new type kept the squadron away from the operational scene until the New Year, by which time it had become a founder member of 6 Group. In March 1944 the squadron began converting to the Canadian-built Lancaster Mk X, and by the end of hostilities it had flown the highest number of Lancaster operations and sorties in 6 Group.

STATIONS

Middleton St George   09.11.42 to 01.06.45

COMMANDING OFFICERS

Wing Commander M M Fleming DSO DFC	08.09.42 to 08.10.43
Wing Commander G A McMurdy	11.10.43 to 23.10.43
Wing Commander W P Pleasance DFC*	25.10.43 to 21.08.44
Wing Commander D C Hagerman DFC*	22.08.44 to 25.01.45
Wing Commander C M E Ferguson	26.01.45 to 06.08.45

AIRCRAFT

Halifax II	11.42 to 04.44
Lancaster X	03.44 to 09.45

OPERATIONAL RECORD

Operations	Sorties	Aircraft Losses	% Losses
266	3,645	105	2.9

Halifax

Operations	Sorties	Aircraft Losses	% Losses
139	1,616	66	4.1

Category of Operations

Bombing	Mining	Other
105	33	1

Lancaster

Operations	Sorties	Aircraft Losses	% Losses
127	2,029	39	1.9

All bombing.

TABLE OF STATISTICS

Out of 32 Halifax squadrons

21st highest number of Halifax overall operations in Bomber Command.
22nd highest number of Halifax sorties in Bomber Command.
9th highest number of Halifax operational losses in Bomber Command.

Out of 59 Lancaster squadrons

38th highest number of Lancaster overall operations in Bomber Command.

37th highest number of Lancaster sorties in Bomber Command.

34th highest number of Lancaster operational losses in Bomber Command.

Out of 15 squadrons in 6 Group

2nd equal (with 408 Sqn) highest number of overall operations in 6 Group.

Highest number of sorties in 6 Group.

Highest number of aircraft operational losses in 6 Group.

Out of 15 Halifax squadrons in 6 Group

10th highest number of Halifax overall operations in 6 Group.

11th highest number of Halifax sorties in 6 Group.

Highest number of Halifax operational losses in 6 Group.

Out of 11 Lancaster squadrons in 6 Group

Highest number of Lancaster overall operations in 6 Group.

Highest number of Lancaster sorties in 6 Group.

2nd highest number of Lancaster operational losses in 6 Group.

AIRCRAFT HISTORIES

Halifax	From November 1942 to April 1944.
W1019	From 405 Sqn. To 1659 CU.
W1235	From 460 Sqn. To 1666 CU.
W1271VR-P	From 10 Sqn. FTR Krefeld 21/22.6.43.
W7817VR-A	From 460 Sqn. FTR Dortmund 4/5.5.43.
W7857VR-O	From 102 Sqn. FTR from mining sortie 9/10.1.43.
W7869	From 10 Sqn. To 1666 CU.
BB283 VR-O	FTR St Nazaire 28/29.3.43.
BB323 VR-R	FTR Aachen 13/14.7.43.
BB327 VR-Q	FTR Duisburg 8/9.4.43.
BB376 VR-S	FTR Bochum 29/30.9.43.
BB384	Crash-landed near Middleton St George on return from Dortmund 24.5.43.
DT500	From 10 Sqn. To 1659 CU.
DT540 VR-C	From 102 Sqn. Crashed on landing at Middleton St George while training 30.11.42.
DT548	From 102 Sqn. To 1659 CU.
DT615 VR-P	FTR from mining sortie 27/28.2.43.

DT616 VR-K	FTR Bochum 12/13.6.43.
DT617 VR-G	FTR Essen 3/4.4.43.
DT619	To 1658 CU.
DT623	Undercarriage collapsed at Middleton St George 30.1.43.
DT629	From 77 Sqn. To 1659 CU.
DT630 VR-T	FTR Hamburg 3/4.2.43.
DT634 VR-E	FTR Berlin 27/28.3.43.
DT639 VR-B	FTR from mining sortie 18/19.2.43.
DT641 VR-R	FTR Berlin 1/2.3.43.
DT646 VR-C	FTR Essen 5/6.3.43.
DT669	To 1668 CU.
DT672 VR-D	FTR Bochum 13/14.5.43.
DT689	To 1666 CU.
DT731 VR-M	From 158 Sqn. FTR Berlin 20/21.1.44.
DT794 VR-Y	FTR Dortmund 4/5.5.43.
DT798 VR-T	FTR Hamburg 2/3.8.43.
HR780	From 158 Sqn. To 1666 CU.
HR910 VR-R	From 405 Sqn. FTR from mining sortie 12/13.2.44.
HR912 VR-F	From 35 Sqn. FTR Vaires 29/30.3.44.
HR925	From 35 Sqn. To 428 Sqn.
HX162 VR-X	FTR Berlin 20/21.1.44.
HX168	From 35 Sqn. To 1659 CU.
HX189 VR-J	FTR Laon 22/23.4.44.
JB791 VR-X	FTR Duisburg 12/13.5.43.
JB793 VR-X	From 77 Sqn. FTR Wuppertal 29/30.5.43.
JB805 VR-B	FTR Wuppertal 29/30.5.43.
JB859	To 1666 CU.
JB860	Crashed while landing at Middleton St George following early return from Berlin 29/30.3.43.
JB861 VR-C	FTR Duisburg 12/13.5.43.
JB862 VR-U	FTR Dortmund 23/24.5.43.
JB900 VR-E	To 1666 CU.
JB912 VR-B	FTR Stettin 20/21.4.43.
JB917	From 405 Sqn. To 1666 CU.
JB923 VR-Q	FTR from mining sortie 28/29.4.43.
JB929 VR-J	To 1659 CU.
JB965 VR-W	Crash-landed at Middleton St George following air-test 22.8.43.
JB967 VR-F	From 429 Sqn via 1659 CU. Crash-landed during final approach to Middleton St George on return from Kassel 3/4.10.43.
JB969	From 429 Sqn. To 1659 CU.
JB971 VR-X	From 429 Sqn. FTR Mannheim 23/24.9.43.

JD113 VR-Z	FTR Bochum 13/14.5.43.
JD114 VR-O/R	To 1666 CU and back. FTR Leipzig 19/20.2.44.
JD143 VR-A	FTR Düsseldorf 11/12.6.43.
JD147 VR-C	FTR Wuppertal 24/25.6.43.
JD158 VR-D	FTR Peenemünde 17/18.8.43.
JD159 VR-Y	FTR Cologne 3/4.7.43.
JD163 VR-N	FTR Peenemünde 17/18.8.43.
JD204 VR-L	FTR Frankfurt 4/5.10.43.
JD210 VR-S	FTR Mannheim/Ludwigshaven 5/6.9.43.
JD212	From 429 Sqn. To 1666 CU.
JD214 VR-U	FTR Wuppertal 24/25.6.43.
JD215 VR-B	FTR Cologne 28/29.6.43.
JD256 VR-A	FTR Essen 25/26.7.43.
JD257 VR-F	FTR Mannheim 9/10.8.43.
JD258 VR-K	FTR Wuppertal 24/25.6.43.
JD270 VR-P	FTR Berlin 31.8/1.9.43.
JD325 VR-X	To 429 Sqn.
JD331 VR-K	FTR Berlin 31.8/1.9.43.
JD372	From 429 Sqn. To 1666 CU.
JD381 VR-R	Damaged beyond repair during operation to Mönchengladbach 30/31.8.43.
JD382 VR-A	FTR Kassel 22/23.10.43.
JD410 VR-V	FTR Mannheim/Ludwigshaven 5/6.9.43.
JD420 VR-T/D	FTR Magdeburg 21/22.1.44.
JD456 VR-B	FTR Berlin 15/16.2.44.
JD457 VR-F	FTR Mannheim 23/24.9.43.
JD458 VR-C	FTR Peenemünde 17/18.8.43.
JD459 VR-Q	Crash-landed at Middleton St George following early return from Le Mans 13.3.44.
JD463 VR-D	FTR Frankfurt 4/5.10.43.
JD464 VR-N	FTR Berlin 31.8/1.9.43.
JD466 VR-E	FTR Magdeburg 21/22.1.44.
JD468 VR-W	Ditched in North Sea on return from mining sortie 22/23.3.44.
JN953	To 428 Sqn.
JN954 VR-R	From 428 Sqn. FTR Montzen 27/28.4.44.
JP111	To 3 OAPU.
JP112 VR-R	Crash-landed at Middleton St George while training 19.12.43.
JP119 VR-O	FTR Berlin 28/29.1.44.
JP125 VR-L	Crash-land at Ford following early return from Aulnoye 25/26.3.44.
JP130	To 428 Sqn.
JP131 VR-S	To 1666 CU.

JP200 VR-G	FTR from mining sortie 25/26.2.44.
JP201 VR-P	To 428 Sqn.
JP202 VR-T	FTR from mining sortie 18/19.4.44.
JP203 VR-M	To 428 Sqn.
JP204 VR-E	To 428 Sqn.
LW231 VR-F	FTR Berlin 22/23.11.43.
LW238	To 1658 CU.
LW239 VR-K	FTR Mannheim 18/19.11.43.
LW240 VR-S	FTR Modane 16/17.9.43.
LW242 VR-N	FTR Stuttgart 26/27.11.43.
LW243	To CRD.
LW279	From 428 Sqn. To 1666 CU.
LW282 VR-Y	FTR Berlin 29/30.12.43.
LW325 VR-H	To 428 Sqn.
LW327 VR-A	From 428 Sqn. FTR Leipzig 19/20.2.44.
LW328 VR-L	FTR Mannheim 18/19.11.43.
NA587	To 1666 CU.

Lancaster	From March 1944.
KB700 VR-Z	From 405 Sqn. Crashed on landing at Middleton St George on return from Nuremberg 2/3.1.45.
KB701 VR-B	Crashed in Yorkshire during night training flight 15/16.5.44.
KB704 VR-Y	Crashed at Middleton St George on return from Gent 10/11.5.44. To 428 Sqn.
KB706 VR-A	FTR Aachen 24/25.5.44.
KB707 VR-W	Crashed on landing at Middleton St George while in transit 19.9.44.
KB708 VR-E	From Rolls-Royce. Crashed while trying to land at Boscombe Down on return from Rüsselsheim 25/26.8.44.
KB710 VR-W	FTR Louvain 12/13.5.44.
KB711 VR-C	FTR St Ghislain 1/2.5.44.
KB712 VR-B/E/L	FTR Cologne 28.10.44.
KB713 VR-X	FTR Louvain 12/13.5.44.
KB714 VR-Y	FTR Cambrai 12/13.6.44.
KB715 VR-T	FTR Lohausen Airfield 24.12.44.
KB716 VR-E/D	Crashed on landing at Middleton St George while training 7.5.44.
KB717 VR-E	FTR Dortmund 22/23.5.44.
KB718 VR-J	FTR Villeneuve-St-Georges 4/5.7.44.
KB719 VR-T	FTR Stuttgart 24/25.7.44.
KB720 VR-P	To 1664 CU.
KB721 VR-B/E	From A&AEE.

KB722 VR-A	Crash-landed at St Quentin after being hit by friendly fire 6.1.45.
KB723 VR-U	FTR Villeneuve-St-Georges 4/5.7.44.
KB724 VR-K	Crashed in Yorkshire when bound for Mimoyecques 27.8.44.
KB726 VR-A	FTR Cambrai 12/13.6.44.
KB727 VR-H	FTR Villeneuve-St-Georges 4/5.7.44.
KB728 VR-V	FTR Sterkrade 16/17.6.44.
KB731 VR-S	FTR Cambrai 12/13.6.44.
KB732 VR-X	
KB733 VR-G	
KB734 VR-F	FTR Sterkrade 16/17.6.44.
KB735 VR-O	Crashed on landing at East Moor on return from Walcheren 18.9.44.
KB736 VR-A/M	To 1660 CU.
KB738 VR-D	FTR Opladen 27/28.12.44.
KB745 VR-V	Crashed in Scotland during the course of an operation to Bergen 4.10.44.
KB746	
KB748 VR-O	
KB750 VR-N	FTR Wiesbaden 2/3.2.45.
KB752 VR-S/V	Abandoned over Allied territory on return from Hamburg 8/9.4.45.
KB753 VR-L	FTR Scholven-Buer 29/30.12.44.
KB754 VR-C	FTR Bochum 9/10.10.44.
KB755 VR-F	FTR Caen 7/8.8.44.
KB761 VR-H	FTR Hamburg 31.3.45.
KB762 VR-J	Damaged in taxying accident at Middleton St George while training 23.4.45.
KB765 VR-M/Q	FTR Scholven-Buer 29/30.12.44.
KB767 VR-U	Crash-landed at Manston on return from Oberhausen 1/2.11.44.
KB769 VR-I	FTR Leuna 14/15.1.45.
KB772 VR-R	
KB774 VR-P	To 431 Sqn.
KB775 VR-Y	FTR Rüsselsheim 25/26.8.44.
KB776 VR-F	FTR Essen 23.10.44.
KB779 VR-B	FTR Osnabrück 6/7.12.44.
KB783 VR-Z	From 428 Sqn.
KB785 VR-Y	Crashed in County Durham while training 24.11.44.
KB786 VR-P	FTR Heide 20/21.3.45.
KB787 VR-M	FTR Bonn 4/5.2.45.
KB788	To 431 Sqn.
KB796	To 431 Sqn.

KB797 VR-K	FTR Dessau 7.3.45.
KB799 VR-W	FTR Leuna 14/15.1.45.
KB800 VR-C	FTR Duisburg 14.10.44.
KB802	To 431 Sqn.
KB804 VR-E	FTR Dortmund 20/21.2.45.
KB807	To 431 Sqn.
KB809	To 431 Sqn.
KB811	To 431 Sqn.
KB814 VR-N	From 434 Sqn. FTR Hagen 15/16.3.45.
KB815	To 431 Sqn.
KB817	To 431 Sqn.
KB824	To 434 Sqn.
KB830	To 434 Sqn.
KB831	To 431 Sqn.
KB832	To 434 Sqn.
KB833	To 434 Sqn.
KB839 VR-D	From 431 Sqn.
KB841	
KB844	To 434 Sqn.
KB845 VR-L	Crashed in Buckinghamshire on return from Chemnitz 5/6.3.45.
KB850	To 434 Sqn.
KB851	From 428 Sqn.
KB854 VR-T	
KB855	To 428 Sqn.
KB857	
KB860	
KB865 VR-E	
KB866 VR-M	FTR Kiel 13/14.4.45.
KB869 VR-Q	FTR Hamburg 31.3.45.
KB870 VR-K	FTR Hagen 15/16.3.45.
KB871	To 431 Sqn.
KB875 VR-Z	
KB878 VR-I	To 428 Sqn.
KB884 VR-K	From 434 Sqn.
KB888	From 428 Sqn. To 431 Sqn.
KB892	
KB896	
KB909	
KB915	From 431 Sqn.
KB921	No operations.
KB999 VR-M	No operations. To 405 Sqn.

Heaviest Single Loss

24/25.06.43.	Wuppertal	3 Halifaxes FTR (One 428 Sqn Crew).
17/18.08.43.	Peenemünde	3 Halifaxes FTR.
31.08/01.09.43.	Berlin	3 Halifaxes FTR.
12/13.06.44.	Cambrai	3 Lancasters FTR.
04/05.07.44.	Villeneuve-St-George	3 Lancasters FTR.

420 (SNOWY OWL) SQUADRON

Motto: Pugnamus Finitum (We fight to the finish)   Code PT

Formed as a 5 Group unit at Waddington on the 19th of December 1941, 420 Squadron went to war for the first time a month later. It operated Hampdens until the end of July 1942, when it was posted to 4 Group and converted to Wellingtons. The squadron became a founder member of 6 Group at the start of 1943, and continued to operate Wellingtons until being posted for a tour of duty in the Middle East. On return to the UK and 6 Group in November 1943 the squadron converted to the Halifax Mk III, and operated the type until war's end.

STATIONS

Middleton-St-George	14.10.42 to 15.05.43
Detached to Middle East	15.05.43 to 06.11.43
Dalton	06.11.43 to 11.12.43
Tholthorpe	12.12.43 to 11.06.45

COMMANDING OFFICERS

Wing Commander D A R Bradshaw	19.12.41 to 11.04.43
Wing Commander D McIntosh	12.04.43 to 07.04.44
Wing Commander G McKenna	08.04.44 to 23.10.44
Wing Commander G Edwards	24.10.44 to 23.11.44
Wing Commander W Phalen	24.11.44 to 27.01.45
Wing Commander F McCarthy	28.01.45 to 23.04.45
Wing Commander R Gray	24.04.45 to 05.09.45

AIRCRAFT

| Wellington III/X | 08.42 to 11.43 |
| Halifax III | 11.43 to 05.45 |

OPERATIONAL RECORD

Operations	Sorties	Aircraft Losses	% Losses
200	2,802	39	1.4

Category of Operations

Bombing	Mining	Other
190	10	0

Wellington

Operations	Sorties	Aircraft Losses	% Losses
40	325	14	4.3

Category of Operations

Bombing	Mining	Other
30	10	0

Halifax

Operations	Sorties	Aircraft Losses	% Losses
160	2,477	25	1.0

All bombing.

TABLE OF STATISTICS

Out of 42 Wellington squadrons

29th highest number of Wellington overall operations in Bomber Command.
32nd highest number of Wellington sorties in Bomber Command.
30th highest number of Wellington operational losses in Bomber Command.

Out of 32 Halifax squadrons

17th highest number of Halifax overall operations in Bomber Command.
13th highest number of Halifax sorties in Bomber Command.
24th highest number of Halifax operational losses in Bomber Command.

Out of 15 squadrons in 6 Group

10th highest number of overall operations in 6 Group.
8th highest number of sorties in 6 Group.
11th highest number of aircraft operational losses in 6 Group.

Out of 8 Wellington squadrons in 6 Group

4th highest number of Wellington overall operations in 6 Group.

7th highest number of Wellington sorties in 6 Group.

5th highest number of Wellington operational losses in 6 Group.

Out of 15 Halifax squadrons in 6 Group

7th highest number of Halifax overall operations in 6 Group.

3rd highest number of Halifax sorties in 6 Group.

12th highest number of Halifax operational losses in 6 Group.

AIRCRAFT HISTORIES

Wellington	From July 1942 to January 1944.
X3335	To 18 OTU.
X3392	From 115 Sqn. To 22 OTU.
X3553	From 425 Sqn. To 427 Sqn.
X3800	To 18 OTU.
X3808 PT-B	FTR Cologne 15/16.10.42.
X3809 PT-O	To 26 OTU.
X3814 PT-P	FTR Bochum 29/30.3.43.
X3926	To 26 OTU.
X3963 PT-D	Crashed in Norfolk on return from Kiel 13/14.10.42.
Z1679 PT-B	FTR Hamburg 9/10.11.42.
Z1724 PT-X/C	Crashed in Yorkshire following structural failure while training 1.3.43.
BJ644	To 1485 Flt.
BJ717	To 26 OTU.
BJ915	To 18 OTU.
BJ917	To 26 OTU.
BJ966 PT-R	FTR from mining sortie 21/22.1.43.
BK235 PT-T	To 1485 Flt.
BK295	To 23 OTU.
BK296 PT-J	FTR from mining sortie 13/14.3.43.
BK297	To 29 OTU.
BK330 PT-K	FTR Lorient 13/14.2.43.
BK331	To 18 OTU.
BK365	To 18 OTU.
BK457	To 26 OTU.
BK468 PT-R	From 427 Sqn. FTR Cologne 26/27.2.43.
DF615 PT-S	FTR Lorient 29/30.1.43.
DF626 PT-Y	To 156 Sqn and back. Crashed at Exeter on return from Lorient 29/30.1.43.

DF636 PT-S	Crashed while trying to land at Leeming on return from Kiel 13/14.10.42.
DF637 PT-F	To 16 OTU.
HE157	To 426 Sqn.
HE160	From 429 Sqn. To 27 OTU.
HE259	SOC 1.10.43.
HE280 PT-V	FTR Essen 5/6.3.43.
HE281	To 426 Sqn.
HE294	To 427 Sqn.
HE329	To 425 Sqn.
HE370	To Middle East.
HE375 PT-H	From 426 Sqn. To 3 OTU.
HE417	To 426 Sqn.
HE421	To Middle East.
HE422 PT-Q	Abandoned over Welsh coast on return from Frankfurt 10/11.4.43.
HE481	To 427 Sqn.
HE514	To 425 Sqn.
HE520	To Middle East.
HE524	To Middle East.
HE550 PT-C	FTR Stuttgart 14/15.4.43.
HE552	To Middle East.
HE555	To 427 Sqn.
HE568	To 425 Sqn.
HE569	To 104 Sqn.
HE630 PT-P	To 427 Sqn.
HE632 PT-R	To 426 Sqn.
HE681	To 427 Sqn.
HE682 PT-T	FTR Mannheim 16/17.4.43.
HE683	To 427 Sqn.
HE690 PT-U	FTR Essen 12/13.3.43.
HE693 PT-P	FTR Duisburg 26/27.4.43.
HE695	To 18 OTU.
HE732	To 427 Sqn.
HE771 ZL-F	On loan from 427 Sqn. Crashed at Croft on return from Duisburg 27.4.43.
HE802	To 429 Sqn.
HE863 PT-G	FTR Stuttgart 14/15.4.43.
HE873	To 427 Sqn.
HE961	To 1 OADU.
HE964	To 311 FTU.
HE965	To Middle East.
HE969	To Middle East.
HE975	To Middle East.

HF458	To Middle East.
HZ356	To Middle East.
HZ372	To 305 Sqn.
HZ414	
HZ468	To 425 Sqn.
HZ572	To Middle East.
LN430	To Middle East.
LN431	To Middle East.
LN434	To Middle East.
MS478	To Middle East.
MS479 PT-F	FTR Duisburg 8/9.4.43.
MS480 PT-X	To 22 OTU.
MS484 PT-V	FTR Bochum 29/30.3.43.
Halifax	From January 1944.
HX346 PT-U	From 620 Sqn. Crash-landed in Yorkshire on return from Castrop-Rauxel 21.11.44.
LK803 PT-H	From 432 Sqn. Crashed soon after take-off from Tholthorpe for fighter affiliation exercise 19.7.44.
LK884	To 431 Sqn.
LL550	Crashed on take-off for ferry flight from Linton-on-Ouse 16.6.44.
LL574	To 1666 CU.
LL575	To 1666 CU.
LL580 PT-U	To 1659 CU.
LL589	To 1666 CU.
LL592	To 1659 CU.
LL605 PT-K	To 1664 CU.
LV860	From 429 Sqn.
LV953	From 424 Sqn. SOC 4.5.45.
LW122	From 415 Sqn. To 425 Sqn.
LW197	To 426 Sqn.
LW198	FTR from Blainville-Sur-L'Eau 28/29.6.44.
LW199	FTR from operations 2.11.44.
LW200	Crashed in Warwickshire after collision with Lancaster KB768 5.12.44.
LW201	To 426 Sqn.
LW202	To 426 Sqn.
LW203	To 426 Sqn.
LW204	To 426 Sqn.
LW205	To 426 Sqn.
LW206	To 426 Sqn.
LW207	To 426 Sqn.
LW208	To 426 Sqn.

LW209	To 426 Sqn.
LW210	To 426 Sqn.
LW366	Crashed in Wales during training 29.2.44.
LW373 PT-W	FTR Berlin 24/25.3.44.
LW377	To 426 Sqn.
LW380 PT-B	To 1666 CU.
LW383	To 578 Sqn.
LW386	
LW388 PT-D	Crashed on landing at Manston on return from Cologne and hit by a Lancaster 30.10.44.
LW389 PT-N	To 434 Sqn.
LW392 PT-S	To 1666 CU.
LW393	To 1666 CU.
LW396 PT-T	Crashed on approach to Tholthorpe on return from Berlin16.2.44.
LW414	To 425 Sqn.
LW416	From 426 Sqn. To 1659 CU.
LW418 PT-E	Damaged beyond repair during an operation to Stuttgart 15/16.3.44.
LW419	
LW420 PT-U	FTR Augsburg 25/26.2.44.
LW421 PT-K	Crash-landed at Linton-on-Ouse on return from Biennais 1.7.44.
LW423	
LW426 PT-Q	FTR Stuttgart 15/16.3.44.
LW427 PT-C	FTR Schweinfurt 24/25.2.44.
LW476 PT-J	FTR Somain 30.4/1.5.44.
LW575	From 427 Sqn. To 1666 CU.
LW590	To 426 Sqn.
LW645	To 1659 CU.
LW674 PT-E	FTR Versailles 10/11.6.44.
LW676 PT-Y	To 1659 CU.
LW683 PT-C	To 76 Sqn.
LW692 PT-V	FTR Lens 20/21.4.44.
MZ375 PT-X	From 431 Sqn. Damaged beyond repair while stationary at Tholthorpe 10.2.45.
MZ378	From 431 Sqn. To 425 Sqn.
MZ423	From 427 Sqn.
MZ435 PT-M	From 426 Sqn.
MZ471 PT-V	FTR Hanover 5/6.1.45.
MZ473	To 425 Sqn.
MZ502 PT-U	FTR Bourg Leopold 27/28.5.44.
MZ503 PT-L	FTR Karlsruhe 24/25.4.44.
MZ505 PT-X	To 1659 CU.

MZ540 PT-H	To 1664 CU.
MZ569	To 297 Sqn.
MZ587	To 1666 CU.
MZ594 PT-W	Damaged beyond repair during operation to Anderbelck 28.8.44.
MZ595 PT-M	To 1666 CU.
MZ596	FTR from night cross-country exercise 3/4.5.44.
MZ625 PT-Q	To 1659 CU.
MZ626	To 434 Sqn.
MZ645 PT-N	From 426 Sqn. FTR Hamburg 28/29.7.44.
MZ687 PT-L	FTR Kiel 16/17.8.44.
MZ713 PT-U	From 425 Sqn. FTR Ferfay 24/25.7.44.
MZ747	From 426 Sqn. To 1666 CU.
MZ910 PT-Q	From 433 Sqn. FTR Witten 18/19.3.45.
MZ951	To 187 Sqn.
MZ952 PT-I	To 1664 CU.
MZ953	To 187 Sqn.
NA169	
NA178	From 429 Sqn.
NA179 PT-B	From 429 Sqn. Crashed on approach to Tholthorpe following early return from Chemnitz 14.2.45.
NA183 PT-M	FTR Magdeburg 16/17.1.45.
NA184 PT-W	Crashed near Dishforth when bound for Chemnitz 5.3.45.
NA188 PT-E	FTR Magdeburg 16/17.1.45.
NA190 PT-U	Crashed in Yorkshire when bound for Chemnitz 5.3.45.
NA192 PT-Q	FTR Magdeburg 16/17.1.45.
NA505 PT-J	From 425 Sqn. FTR Acheres 7/8.6.44.
NA509 PT-V	From 102 Sqn. Crashed on landing at Wellesbourne on return from Essen 23.10.44.
NA528 PT-G	Crashed on landing at White Waltham on return from Amaye-sur-Seulles 30.7.44.
NA579 PT-J	To 1664 CU.
NA580 PT-K	From 425 Sqn. Crashed on landing at Tangmere on return from la Hoque 8.8.44.
NA582	To 415 Sqn.
NA583	To 415 Sqn.
NA610	To 415 Sqn.
NA611	To 415 Sqn.
NA629 PT-W	Ditched in the North Sea on return from Kiel 16.9.44.
NA630 PT-N	To 1664 CU.

NA631 PT-Z	To 187 Sqn.
NA632 PT-E	To 1664 CU.
NP681	To 426 Sqn.
NP682	To 426 Sqn.
NP683	To 426 Sqn.
NP686	FTR Hamburg 28/29.7.44.
NP939	From 434 Sqn. To 425 Sqn.
NP946 PT-L	From 429 Sqn. FTR Heligoland 18.4.45.
NP951 PT-Y	From 424 Sqn.
NP959 PT-N	From 434 Sqn. FTR Chemnitz 5/6.3.45.
NP961	From 415 Sqn.
NR117	From 433 Sqn.
NR123 PT-F	From 431 Sqn. Crashed on landing at Carnaby on return from training flight 10.3.45.
NR124	From 415 Sqn.
NR126 PT-X	From 408 Sqn. Crashed in Northumberland during ferry flight 18.2.45.
NR135	From 433 Sqn. To 425 Sqn.
NR138 PT-T	From 431 Sqn.
NR139	From 431 Sqn.
NR141	From 431 Sqn.
NR144 PT-H	Crash-landed in Yorkshire on return from Chemnitz 6.3.45.
NR171 PT-P	From 427 Sqn.
NR172 PT-Y	From 415 Sqn. FTR Hagen with 425 Sqn crew 15/16.3.45.
NR199	From 408 Sqn. Returned to 408 Sqn.
NR205 PT-L	From 424 Sqn. FTR Magdeburg 16/17.1.45.
NR207	
NR208 PT-D	
NR227 PT-V	From 424 Sqn. To 425 Sqn.
NR230	From 429 Sqn.
NR258	From 424 Sqn.
NR290 PT-K	
RG347	To 427 Sqn.

424 (TIGER) SQUADRON

Motto: Castigandos Castigamus (We chastise those who deserve to be chastised)   Code QB

Formed in mid October 1942 as a 4 Group Wellington unit, 424 Squadron conducted no operations until its posting as a founder member to 6 Group on New Year's Day 1943. In early May it was posted to the Middle East for a temporary tour of duty, and returned to the UK and 6 Group in November 1943. Halifax Mk IIIs arrived in the following month and conversion was completed during January 1944. Halifaxes remained on charge for the next twelve months as the squadron played its part in the Command's campaigns. Conversion to the Lancaster took place during January 1945, and the type saw the squadron through to the end of hostilities.

STATIONS

Topcliffe	15.10.42 to 07.04.43
Leeming	08.04.43 to 02.05.43
Detached to Middle East	03.05.43 to 05.11.43
Skipton-on-Swale	06.11.43 to 29.08.45

COMMANDING OFFICERS

Wing Commander H M Carscallen	15.10.42 to 16.04.43
Wing Commander G S Roy	17.04.43 to 02.10.43
Wing Commander A N Martin	18.12.43 to 21.01.44
Wing Commander J D Blane	27.01.44 to 28.07.44
Wing Commander G S Roy	15.08.44 to 09.10.44
Squadron Leader N Loudoun (Temp)	10.10.44 to 18.10.44
Wing Commander C Marshall	19.10.44 to 26.03.45
Wing Commander R Norris	27.03.45 to 30.09.45

AIRCRAFT

Wellington III/X	10.42 to 01.44
Halifax III	12.43 to 01.45
Lancaster I/III	01.45 to 09.45

OPERATIONAL RECORD

Operations	Sorties	Aircraft Losses	% Losses
235	2,531	37	1.4

Category of Operations

Bombing	Mining
176	59

Wellingtons

Operations	Sorties	Aircraft Losses	% Losses
37	332	5	1.5

Category of Operations

Bombing	Mining
24	13

Halifaxes

Operations	Sorties	Aircraft Losses	% Losses
156	1,811	23	1.3

Category of Operations

Bombing	Mining
123	33

Lancasters

Operations	Sorties	Aircraft Losses	% Losses
42	388	5	1.3

Category of Operations

Bombing	Mining
29	13

TABLE OF STATISTICS

(Heavy squadrons)

Out of 59 Lancaster squadrons

53rd highest number of Lancaster overall operations in Bomber Command.
55th highest number of Lancaster sorties in Bomber Command.
53rd highest number of Lancaster operational losses in Bomber Command.

Out of 32 Halifax squadrons

18th highest number of Halifax overall operations in Bomber Command.
21st highest number of Halifax sorties in Bomber Command.
23rd highest number of Halifax operational losses in Bomber Command.

Out of 42 Wellington squadrons

39th equal (with 427 Sqn) highest number of overall Wellington operations in Bomber Command.

37th highest number of Wellington sorties in Bomber Command.

40th highest number of Wellington operational losses in Bomber Command.

Out of 15 squadrons in 6 Group

6th highest number of overall operations in 6 Group.

12th highest number of sorties in 6 Group.

11th highest number of aircraft operational losses in 5 Group.

Out of 11 Lancaster squadrons in 6 Group

6th highest number of Lancaster overall operations in 6 Group.

8th highest number of Lancaster sorties in 6 Group.

7th highest number of Lancaster operational losses in 6 Group.

Out of 15 Halifax squadrons in 6 Group

8th highest number of Halifax overall operations in 6 Group.

10th highest number of Halifax sorties in 6 Group.

11th highest number of Halifax operational losses in 6 Group.

Out of 8 Wellington squadrons in 6 Group

6th highest number of Wellington overall operations in 6 Group.

6th highest number of Wellington sorties in 6 Group.

Lowest number of Wellington operational losses in 6 Group.

AIRCRAFT HISTORIES

Wellington	From October 1942 to January 1944.
X3284	From 57 Sqn. To 426 Sqn.
X3401	To 18 OTU.
X3409	From 466 Sqn. To 82 OTU.
X3426	To 18 OTU.
X3460	From 57 Sqn. To 426 Sqn.
X3789	To 1485 Flt.
X3790	From 466 Sqn. To 26 OTU.
Z1674 QB-G	To 21 OTU.
Z1691 QB-R	To 1485 Flt.
Z1692	From 466 Sqn. To 26 OTU.
BJ658 QB-Q	FTR from mining sortie 6/7.2.43.
BJ712	To 18 OTU.
BJ714 QB-F	FTR Lorient 26/27.1.43.

BK144 QB-V	To 18 OTU.
BK348 QB-J	FTR Essen 12/13.3.43.
BK398 QB-W	To 26 OTU.
BK435 QB-U	From 466 Sqn. FTR from a mining sortie 20/21.2.43.
BK436 QB-P	Abandoned over Wiltshire on return from Lorient 29.1.43.
BK490	To 26 OTU.
BK560	To 12 OTU.
DF613	To 12 OTU.
DF618	From 22 OTU. To 30 OTU.
DF621	To 12 OTU.
DF671	To 18 OTU.
HE159 QB-P	From 427 Sqn. Crashed in Kent when bound for Frankfurt 11.4.43.
HE222	To 427 Sqn.
HE272	To 30 OTU.
HE273	To Middle East.
HE279	To 427 Sqn.
HE367	From 427 Sqn. Crashed on landing at Topcliffe while training 2.4.43.
HE369 QB-P	Crashed on approach to Topcliffe on return from Wilhelmshaven 25.2.43.
HE492	To Middle East.
HE515	To Middle East.
HE523	To 303 FTU.
HE554	To 74 OTU.
HE556	To 74 OTU.
HE589	To 429 Sqn.
HE594	To 305 Sqn.
HE656 QB-L	To 428 Sqn.
HE684	To 429 Sqn.
HE687	To 15 OTU.
HE689	To 305 Sqn.
HE691	To 305 Sqn.
HE692	Crashed while landing at Penrhos during training 2.5.43.
HE694	To 311 FTU.
HE703	To 428 Sqn.
HE705	To 305 Sqn.
HE735	To Middle East.
HE737	To 429 Sqn.
HE738	To 428 Sqn.
HE864 QB-W	To 428 Sqn.

HE898	To 311 OTU.
HE899	To 428 Sqn.
HE929	To Middle East.
HE962	To Middle East.
HE963	To Middle East.
HE966	To 311 FTU.
HE967	To Middle East.
HE968	To Middle East.
HE971	To Middle East.
HE973	To Middle East.
HE974	
HZ272 QB-S	
HZ273 QB-G	From 426 Sqn. FTR Stuttgart 14/15.4.43.
HZ304	To Middle East.
HZ364	
HZ371	To Middle East.
HZ470	To 429 Sqn.
LN402 QB-U	From 192 Sqn. To 20 OTU.
LN433	To Middle East.
LN438	To 429 Sqn.
LN439	To 429 Sqn.
LN441	To Middle East.
MS476	To Middle East.
MS477	To Middle East.
MS481	To 428 Sqn.
MS485	To 432 Sqn.
Halifax	From December 1943 to January 1945.
HX311 QB-A	FTR Berlin 15/16.2.44.
HX313 QB-B	FTR Bourg Leopold 27/28.5.44.
HX314 QB-C	FTR from a mining sortie 10/11.5.44.
HX316	To 1659 CU.
HX318 QB-O	FTR Karlsruhe 24/25.4.44.
HX319	To BCIS.
LV780 QB-M	FTR Düsseldorf 22/23.4.44.
LV879 QB-A	FTR Nuremberg 30/31.3.44.
LV910 QB-Y	FTR Metz 28/29.6.44.
LV944 QB-U	From 431 Sqn. FTR Nuremberg 30/31.3.44.
LV947 QB-S	From 431 Sqn. To 433 Sqn.
LV951 QB-A	From 431 Sqn. FTR Brunswick 12/13.8.44.
LV953	From 431 Sqn. To 420 Sqn.
LV959 QB-R	FTR Bois de Cassan 4.8.44.
LV961 QB-G	FTR Metz 28/29.6.44.
LV962 QB-X	FTR Karlsruhe 24/25.4.44.

LV970 QB-T	FTR Villeneuve-St-Georges 4/5.7.44.
LV988 `	To 427 Sqn.
LV991	To 518 Sqn.
LV997 QB-E	From 431 Sqn. FTR Hamburg 28/29.7.44.
LV998	From 431 Sqn. FTR from a mining sortie 13.1.45.
LW113	From 426 Sqn. To 520 Sqn.
LW117 QB-K	From 426 Sqn. Crashed on take-off from Skipton-on-Swale when bound for Boulogne 17.9.44.
LW119 QB-O	To 187 Sqn.
LW121 QB-X	From 426 Sqn. FTR Cambrai 14/15.6.44.
LW131 QB-J	FTR Düsseldorf 2/3.11.44.
LW157 QB-S	FTR Aachen 24/25.5.44.
LW164 QB-C	Crashed on take-off at Skipton-on-Swale when bound for Stuttgart 28.1.45.
LW169 QB-L	From 434 Sqn. FTR Siracourt 6.7.44.
LW170	From 434 Sqn. To 518 Sqn.
LW194 QB-W	From 433 Sqn. To 51 Sqn.
LW347 QB-X	To 578 Sqn and back. Crashed on landing at Skipton-on-Swale on return from a mining sortie 22.3.44.
LW370	From 433 Sqn. To 429 Sqn.
LW384	To 426 Sqn.
LW385 QB-K	To 431 Sqn.
LW416	To 426 Sqn.
LW432	To 431 Sqn.
LW433	To 434 Sqn.
LW435 QB-R	FTR Berlin 24/25.3.44.
LW436	To 426 Sqn.
LW437 QB-S	To 432 Sqn.
LW438 QB-T	To 346 Sqn.
LW440	To 78 Sqn.
LW444 QB-H	Crashed while trying to land at Skipton-on-Swale during training 22.1.44.
LW460 QB-U	FTR Frankfurt 18/19.3.44.
LW462	To 431 Sqn.
LW552	To 432 Sqn.
MZ304	To 427 Sqn.
MZ356	To 415 Sqn.
MZ376 QB-K	FTR Oberhausen 1/2.11.44.
MZ418	To 415 Sqn.
MZ451 QB-S	To 51 Sqn.
MZ454	To 431 Sqn.
MZ455	To 431 Sqn.
MZ458 QB-G	From 433 Sqn. To 10 Sqn.

MZ754	To 51 Sqn.
MZ802 QB-G	From 431 Sqn. FTR Bochum 9/10.10.44.
MZ805 QB-X	From 431 Sqn. FTR from a mining sortie 12/13.1.45.
MZ807 QB-M	To 433 Sqn.
MZ813 QB-B	To 158 Sqn.
MZ814	To 427 Sqn.
MZ822 QB-F	FTR Düsseldorf 2/3.11.44.
MZ896 QB-Q	FTR Bochum 4/5.11.44.
MZ897	To 51 Sqn.
MZ898	To 187 Sqn.
MZ901 QB-N	FTR from a mining sortie 15/16.10.44.
MZ902	To 102 Sqn.
NP936	To 433 Sqn and back. To 415 Sqn.
NP937	To 433 Sqn.
NP938	To 415 Sqn.
NP940	To 415 Sqn.
NP945 QB-D	FTR Osnabrück 6/7.12.44.
NP947 QB-Y	To 77 Sqn.
NP951	To 420 Sqn.
NP955	To 1652 CU.
NP999	To 431 Sqn.
NR114	To 434 Sqn.
NR115	To 434 Sqn.
NR116	To 426 Sqn.
NR146 QB-N	To 415 Sqn.
NR205	To 420 Sqn.
NR206	To 415 Sqn.
NR210	To 102 Sqn.
NR227	To 420 Sqn.
NR228 QB-Q	To 415 Sqn.
NR256	To 429 Sqn.
NR257	To 427 Sqn.
NR258	To 420 Sqn.
Lancaster	From January 1945.
DS633	To 432 Sqn.
ME456 QB-K	FTR Dortmund 20/21.2.45.
ME458 QB-T	
NG277 QB-G	
NG279 QB-O	
NG280 QB-U	
NG281 QB-X	
NG346 QB-N	FTR Dessau 7/8.3.45.

NG347 QB-P
NG348 QB-Q
NG400 QB-R
NG446 QB-J
NG451 QB-E
NG456 QB-D
NG457 QB-C   FTR Dessau 7/8.3.45.
NG458 QB-H   FTR Chemnitz 5/6.3.45.
NG484 QB-L
NN777 QB-F   Crash-landed near Dishforth on return from Zweibrücken 15.3.45.

NN780 QB-Y
NX587 QB-N
PA286 QB-H
PA324 QB-K
PA326 QB-W
PA328
PB897 QB-B
PB899 QB-A   FTR from a mining sortie 14/15.2.45.
RA504 QB-B/M
RA507 QB-S
RA578
RF128 QB-V
RF148 QB-A
RF150 QB-W   From 433 Sqn. Crashed near High Wycombe on return from Leuna 5.4.45.

RF260

425 (ALOUETTE) SQUADRON

Motto: I shall pluck you   Code KW

425 Squadron was formed in 4 Group in late June 1942 as a French Canadian unit to operate Wellingtons. Operations began in October and continued through the squadron's posting as a founder member to 6 Group on the 1st of January 1943. At the end of April 1943 the squadron was stood down in preparation for a posting to the Middle East. The squadron returned to the UK and 6 Group in November, and the following month began to convert to the Halifax Mk III. Operations began again in February 1944, and continued through to the end of hostilities.

STATIONS

Dishforth	25.06.42 to 15.05.43
Detached Middle East	16.05.43 to 05.11.43
Dishforth	06.11.43 to 09.12.43
Tholthorpe	10.12.43 to 12.06.45

COMMANDING OFFICERS

Wing Commander J W M ST Pierre	25.06.42 to 30.09.43
Wing Commander B D Richer	01.10.43 to 03.04.44
Wing Commander R A McLernon	04.04.44 to 23.05.44
Wing Commander L H Lecomte	24.05.44 to 20.08.44
Wing Commander H C Ledoux	23.08.44 to 10.06.45

AIRCRAFT

Wellington III	25.06.42 to 12.43
Halifax III	01.44 to 05.45

OPERATIONAL RECORD

Operations	Sorties	Aircraft Losses	% Losses
201	2,792	36	1.3

Category of Operations

Bombing	Mining
190	11

Wellington

Operations	Sorties	Aircraft Losses	% Losses
39	347	8	2.3

Category of Operations

Bombing	Mining
28	11

Halifax

Operations	Sorties	Aircraft Losses	% Losses
162	2,445	28	1.1

All bombing.

TABLE OF STATISTICS

Out of 42 Wellington squadrons

30th highest number of Wellington overall operations in Bomber Command.

30th highest number of Wellington sorties in Bomber Command.

37th highest number of Wellington operational losses in Bomber Command.

Out of 32 Halifax squadrons

15th equal (with 433 Sqn) highest number of Halifax overall operations in Bomber Command.

14th highest number of Halifax sorties in Bomber Command.

21st equal (with 433 Sqn) highest number of Halifax operational losses in Bomber Command.

Out of 15 squadrons in 6 Group

9th highest number of overall operations in 6 Group.

9th highest number of sorties in 6 Group.

12th highest number of aircraft operational losses in 6 Group.

Out of 8 Wellington squadrons in 6 Group

5th highest number of Wellington overall operations in 6 Group.

5th highest number of Wellington sorties in 6 Group.

7th highest number of Wellington operational losses in 6 Group.

Out of 15 Halifax squadrons in 6 Group

5th equal (with 433 Sqn) highest number of Halifax overall operations in 6 Group.

4th highest number of Halifax sorties in 6 Group.

9th equal (with 433 Sqn) highest number of Halifax operational losses in 6 Group.

AIRCRAFT HISTORIES

Wellington	From June 1942 to January 1944.
X3361	Crashed soon after take-off from Kingscliffe for ferry flight 1.2.43.
X3364	From 115 Sqn. To 426 Sqn.
X3393	From 115 Sqn. Returned to 115 Sqn.
X3551	To 23 OTU.
X3553 KW-H	From 12 Sqn. To 420 Sqn.

X3648 KW-R	From 101 Sqn. To 18 OTU.
X3763 KW-L	FTR Stuttgart 14/15.4.43.
X3803	To 20 OTU.
X3872 KW-A	To 29 OTU.
X3876	To 12 OTU.
X3943 KW-G	Crashed in Essex on return from Aachen 5/6.10.42.
Z1603 KW-C	To 26 OTU.
Z1729 KW-T	FTR Duisburg 20/21.12.42.
Z1742 KW-C	FTR from mining sortie 6/7.2.43.
BJ605	To 27 OTU.
BJ644 KW-Q	From 1485 Flt. To 27 OTU.
BJ652 KW-E	To 27 OTU.
BJ655	To 156 Sqn via 1483 Flt.
BJ656	To 1483 Flt.
BJ657 KW-G	FTR Mannheim 6/7.12.42.
BJ669	From 156 Sqn. To 26 OTU.
BJ695	Crashed in Yorkshire during fighter affiliation exercise 22.9.42.
BJ699	To RAE.
BJ700	To 1483 Flt.
BJ755	To 429 Sqn.
BJ764	Crashed at Swanton Morley on return from Hamburg 9/10.11.42.
BJ783 KW-F	Force-landed in Yorkshire on return from Kiel 13/14.10.42.
BJ846	Crashed in Yorkshire on return from a mining sortie 11/12.11.42.
BJ892	To 26 OTU.
BJ894 KW-K	Crashed in Essex while training 16.11.42.
BJ918 KW-F	Crashed on take-off from Dishforth when bound for St Nazaire 28.2.43.
BJ958 KW-N	Crashed in Yorkshire soon after take-off from Elsham Wolds on transit flight to Dishforth 23.10.42.
BK153 KW-P	To 23 OTU.
BK308	To 18 OTU.
BK332 KW-O	To 1485 Flt.
BK333	To 17 OTU.
BK334 KW-B	FTR Hamburg 3/4.3.43.
BK337	To 428 Sqn.
BK340 KW-T	FTR Essen 12/13.3.43.
BK344	FTR Hamburg 3/4.3.43.
BK401	To 426 Sqn.
BK465	To 426 Sqn via 16 OTU.

BK496	To 17 OTU.
BK539 KW-S	To 16 OTU.
BK557 KW-S	FTR Hamburg 9/10.11.42.
DF617	To 426 Sqn.
HE260	To Middle East.
HE261	To Middle East.
HE268	From 304 Sqn. To 6 OTU.
HE269	To 311 FTU.
HE324	To 17 OTU.
HE329	From 420 Sqn. To Middle East.
HE423 KW-A	To 429 Sqn.
HE475 KW-E	FTR Mannheim 16/17.4.43.
HE486	To 30 OTU.
HE491 KW-B	FTR from mining sortie 11/12.4.43.
HE500	To 26 OTU.
HE514	From 420 Sqn. To 432 Sqn.
HE516	To 3 ADU.
HE521	To Middle East.
HE522	To Middle East.
HE551	To Middle East.
HE568	From 420 Sqn. To 1 OADU.
HE592 KW-Q	FTR Duisburg 8/9.4.43.
HE595	To 429 Sqn.
HE655	To 166 Sqn.
HE733 KW-S	FTR Stuttgart 14/15.4.43.
HE865	To 429 Sqn.
HE900	To Middle East.
HE901	To 196 Sqn.
HE903	To 3 OTU.
HE930	To Middle East.
HE931	To Middle East.
HE970	To Middle East.
HE976	To Middle East.
HE977	To Middle East.
HE978	To 29 OTU.
HE979	To Middle East.
HZ277	To 199 Sqn.
HZ355	To 429 Sqn.
HZ468	From 420 Sqn.
HZ471	To 429 Sqn.
LN409	To 431 Sqn.
LN436	To Middle East.
LN440	To Middle East.
MS492	To Middle East.

MS493	To 166 Sqn.
MS496	To Middle East.
Halifax	From January 1944.
LK796	To 434 Sqn.
LK798 KW-A	FTR Haine St Pierre 8/9.5.44.
LK810 KW-Y	FTR Le Mans 22/23.5.44.
LL547	From 429 Sqn. To 644 Sqn.
LL576	To 1664 CU.
LL582	To 1659 CU.
LL591	To 1659 CU.
LL594 KW-U	FTR St Leu d'Esserent 5.8.44.
LL595	To 1664 CU.
LL596	To 1664 CU.
LV941	From 429 Sqn. To 415 Sqn.
LW122	From 420 Sqn.
LW375	To 296 Sqn.
LW378 KW-A	Crashed in Yorkshire while training 2.3.44.
LW379 KW-D	FTR Oberhausen 1/2.11.44.
LW381 KW-B	To 1666 CU.
LW387	To 1666 CU.
LW390 KW-J	FTR Stuttgart 20/21.2.44.
LW391 KW-J	FTR Duisburg 14/15.10.44.
LW394 KW-Z	FTR Wanne-Eickel 8/9.2.45.
LW395 KW-O	Crashed in Worcestershire during training 11.2.44.
LW397	SOC 20.6.44.
LW413 KW-Q	Abandoned over Staffordshire on return from Stuttgart 16.3.44.
LW414	From 420 Sqn. To 1659 CU.
LW415	To 429 Sqn.
LW417 KW-G	FTR Frankfurt 22/23.3.44.
LW424	Crashed on landing at Tholthorpe during training 8.2.44.
LW425 KW-V	FTR Berlin 24/25.3.44.
LW428 KW-C	FTR Berlin 24/25.3.44.
LW429 KW-R	FTR Nuremberg 30/31.3.44.
LW431 KW-U	FTR Augsburg 25/26.2.44.
LW467	To 297 Sqn.
LW573	From 76 Sqn. To 1652 CU.
LW590 KW-P	From 426 Sqn. Crashed on take-off from Boulmer for transit flight 4.10.44.
LW591 KW-T	FTR Karlsruhe 24/25.4.44.
LW632	To 21 HGCU.
LW633 KW-O	FTR Düsseldorf 22/23.4.44.

LW672 KW-N	FTR Wesseling 18/19.7.44.
LW680 KW-U	Hit by MZ683 at dispersal at Tholthorpe 28.6.44.
LW693	Crashed in Warwickshire during training 26.3.44.
LW715 KW-Q	FTR Boulogne 15.6.44.
MZ357	From 429 Sqn.
MZ364 KW-N	From 431 Sqn. Crash-landed at Manston on return from Castrop-Rauxel 21.11.44.
MZ378	From 420 Sqn.
MZ417	From 433 Sqn. To 78 Sqn.
MZ418 KW-C	From 424 Sqn. FTR Hamburg 31.3.45.
MZ419 KW-E	
MZ421	From 408 Sqn. To 76 Sqn.
MZ425	From 433 Sqn.
MZ454 KW-S	From 431 Sqn. Crashed in Yorkshire when bound for Chemnitz 5.3.45.
MZ466 KW-P	Crashed in Yorkshire while training 14.1.45.
MZ473	From 420 Sqn.
MZ482 KW-G	FTR Witten 18/19.3.45.
MZ493 KW-H	Crashed while landing at Tholthorpe on return from Troisdorf 29.12.44.
MZ495 KW-R	From 408 Sqn. FTR Witten 18/19.3.45.
MZ525	Crashed near Topcliffe while training 24.4.44.
MZ537	To 431 Sqn.
MZ538 KW-V	Crashed near Tholthorpe soon after take-off for Duisburg 18.12.44.
MZ573 KW-G	FTR Karlsruhe 24/25.4.44.
MZ618	Hit by MZ683 at dispersal at Tholthorpe 28.6.44.
MZ620 KW-T	To 1664 CU.
MZ621 KW-O	Damaged beyond repair during operation to Bochum 4.11.44.
MZ627	Became ground instruction machine.
MZ641 KW-K	FTR Hamburg 28/29.7.44.
MZ672	From 429 Sqn. To 1666 CU.
MZ674	From 432 Sqn. FTR Duisburg 14.10.44.
MZ683 KW-A	From 434 Sqn. Hit LW680 while landing at Croft on return from Forêt de Eawy 28.6.44.
MZ688	To 297 Sqn.
MZ712 KW-S	FTR Hamburg 28/29.7.44.
MZ713	To 420 Sqn.
MZ714	To 187 Sqn.
MZ815 KW-C	From 427 Sqn. FTR Hemmingstedt 7/8.3.45.
MZ831 KW-Z	From 431 Sqn. FTR Bochum 4/5.11.44.

MZ845 KW-W/J	From 433 Sqn. Collided in mid-air with PN228 of 426 Sqn near Linton-on-Ouse when bound for Chemnitz 5.3.45.
MZ860 KW-E	From 431 Sqn. FTR Hanover 5/6.1.45.
MZ950	From 187 Sqn. To 1665 CU.
MZ954 KW-M	To 187 Sqn.
NA180	From 429 Sqn.
NA201	From 415 Sqn. Returned to 415 Sqn.
NA203	
NA204	To 426 Sqn.
NA505	To 420 Sqn.
NA518 KW-I	From 426 Sqn. To 187 Sqn.
NA580	To 420 Sqn.
NA581 KW-U	Crashed in Nottinghamshire while training 8.8.44.
NA612	To 415 Sqn.
NA633	To 1664 CU.
NA634 KW-X	To 1659 CU.
NP937 KW-T	From 433 Sqn.
NP939 KW-V	From 420 Sqn. Crash-landed in Buckinghamshire on return from Witten 19.3.45.
NP941	From 427 Sqn.
NP956	From 427 Sqn.
NP957	From 429 Sqn.
NP999 KW-W	From 431 Sqn. FTR Hanover 5/6.1.45.
NR134	From 426 Sqn.
NR135	From 420 Sqn.
NR136	From 433 Sqn.
NR137	From 433 Sqn.
NR147 KW-L	
NR178 KW-J	FTR Hanover 5/6.1.45.
NR194 KW-J	From 429 Sqn. Crashed while landing at Riccall on return from Münster 25.3.45.
NR196	From 429 Sqn.
NR209	To 408 Sqn and back. To 408 Sqn.
NR227	From 420 Sqn.
NR231	
NR252	
NR271	
NR273	
PN172 KW-G	FTR Hagen 15/16.3.45.
PN173 KW-Q	FTR Chemnitz 5/6.3.45.
RG350	To 426 Sqn.

426 (THUNDERBIRD) SQUADRON

Motto: On wings of fire   Code OW

426 Squadron was formed on the 15th of October 1942 in 4 Group and began to work up on Wellingtons. No operations were carried out by the squadron before its posting as a founder member to 6 Group on New Year's Day 1943. Operations began in mid January and continued with Wellingtons until the arrival of the Lancaster Mk II in June. After conversion training the squadron returned to the operational scene in mid August and took a leading role in the Command's major campaigns over the succeeding eight months. Halifaxes replaced the Lancasters in April 1944, and this was the type operated by the squadron for the remainder of the war.

STATIONS

Dishforth	15.10.42 to 17.06.43
Linton-on-Ouse	18.06.43 to 24.05.45

COMMANDING OFFICERS

Wing Commander S S Blanchard	15.10.42 to 14.02.43
Wing Commander L Crooks DSO DFC	15.02.43 to 17.08.43
Wing Commander C H Swetman DSO DFC	18.08.43 to 04.04.44
Wing Commander E C Hamber DFC	08.04.44 to 10.07.44
Wing Commander C W Burgess DFC	11.07.44 to 02.01.45
Wing Commander F C Carling-Kelly AFC	03.01.45 to 28.01.45
Wing Commander C M Black DFC	29.01.45 to 24.05.45

AIRCRAFT

Wellington III	15.10.42 to 06.43
Lancaster II	06.43 to 05.44
Halifax III	04.44 to 06.45
Halifax VII	06.44 to 06.45

OPERATIONAL RECORD

Operations	Sorties	Aircraft Losses	% Losses
241	3,207	68	2.1

Category of Operations

Bombing	Mining
222	19

Wellingtons

Operations	Sorties	Aircraft Losses	% Losses
52	467	18	3.9

Category of Operations

Bombing	Mining
33	19

Lancasters

Operations	Sorties	Aircraft Losses	% Losses
53	579	28	4.8

All bombing.

Halifaxes

Operations	Sorties	Aircraft Losses	% Losses
136	2,161	22	1.0

All bombing.

TABLE OF STATISTICS

(Heavy squadrons)

Out of 59 Lancaster squadrons

50th highest number of Lancaster overall operations in Bomber Command.
52nd highest number of Lancaster sorties in Bomber Command.
38th highest number of Lancaster operational losses in Bomber Command.

Out of 32 Halifax squadrons

22nd highest number of Halifax overall operations in Bomber Command.
17th highest number of Halifax sorties in Bomber Command.
25th highest number of Halifax operational losses in Bomber Command.

Out of 42 Wellington squadrons

35th highest number of Wellington overall operations in Bomber Command.
32nd highest number of Wellington sorties in Bomber Command.
26th equal (with 304 & 431 Sqns) highest number of Wellington operational losses in Bomber Command.

Out of 15 squadrons in 6 Group
5th highest number of overall operations in 6 Group.
5th highest number of sorties in 6 Group.
5th highest number of aircraft operational losses in 6 Group.

Out of 8 Wellington squadrons in 6 Group
Highest number of Wellington overall operations in 6 Group.
2nd highest number of Wellington sorties in 6 Group.
2nd highest number of Wellington operational losses in 6 Group.

Out of 11 Lancaster squadrons in 6 Group
4th highest number of Lancaster overall operations in 6 Group.
5th highest number of Lancaster sorties in 6 Group.
3rd highest number of Lancaster operational losses in 6 Group.

Out of 15 Halifax squadrons in 6 Group
10th highest number of Halifax overall operations in 6 Group.
6th highest number of Halifax sorties in 6 Group.
13th highest number of Halifax operational losses in 6 Group.

AIRCRAFT HISTORIES

Wellington	From October 1942 to July 1943.
X3284 OW-X	From 424 Sqn. FTR from mining sortie 9/10.3.43.
X3348	From 466 Sqn. To 427 Sqn.
X3364	From 425 Sqn. Crashed on take-off from Dishforth for mining sortie 27.2.43.
X3420 OW-H	From 419 Sqn. FTR Cologne 14/15.2.43.
X3458	From 1418 Flt. To 16 OTU.
X3460	From 424 Sqn. To 17 OTU.
X3461	From 466 Sqn. To 12 OTU.
X3600	From 57 Sqn. To 12 OTU.
X3696 OW-T	From 57 Sqn. FTR Duisburg 26/27.3.43.
X3699	From 419 Sqn. FTR Kiel 4/5.4.43.
Z1599 OW-B/M	From 419 Sqn. FTR Cologne 26/27.2.43.
Z1680 OW-R	From 419 Sqn. FTR from intruder sortie to Oldenburg 30.1.43.
BJ762 OW-O	FTR Bochum 29/30.3.43.
BJ888	To 20 OTU.
BJ919 OW-P	From 419 Sqn. FTR Wilhelmshaven 19/20.2.43.
BK140	To 26 OTU.
BK142 OW-A	To 30 OTU.
BK165 OW-F	From 427 Sqn. FTR Lorient 14/15.1.43.

BK401 OW-M	From 425 Sqn. FTR Essen 5/6.3.43.
BK431	To 29 OTU.
BK440 OW-V	To 26 OTU.
BK452	To 29 OTU.
BK456 OW-C	To 26 OTU.
BK465	From 425 Sqn via 16 OTU. To 29 OTU.
BK471 OW-W	From 466 Sqn. To 18 OTU.
BK505	To 18 OTU.
BK542	To 12 OTU.
DF617	To 425 Sqn.
DF619	To 20 OTU.
DF620	Crash-landed at Topcliffe while training 7.2.43.
HE157 OW-N	From 420 Sqn. FTR Duisburg 12/13.5.43.
HE243 OW-E	FTR Bochum 13/14.5.43.
HE281 OW-D	From 420 Sqn. FTR Dortmund 23/24.5.43.
HE320	To 16 OTU.
HE323	To 1 OADU.
HE375	To 420 Sqn.
HE417	From 420 Sqn. To 82 OTU.
HE431	To 82 OTU.
HE588	To 82 OTU.
HE590 OW-P	FTR Düsseldorf 25/26.5.43.
HE591 OW-R	FTR Mannheim 16/17.4.43.
HE632	From 420 Sqn. To 82 OTU.
HE652	FTR Frankfurt 10/11.4.43.
HE697 OW-M	FTR Bochum 13/14.5.43.
HE739	To 82 OTU.
HE866 OW-A	To 82 OTU.
HE867	Abandoned over Yorkshire on return from Duisburg 27.4.43.
HE868	To 82 OTU.
HE904 OW-C	To 82 OTU.
HE905 OW-V	FTR Duisburg 12/13.5.43.
HE916	To 82 OTU.
HE991	To 429 Sqn.
HE995 OW-R	To 25 OTU.
HF540	To 432 Sqn.
HF572	To 432 Sqn.
HF599	To 432 Sqn.
HZ261 OW-L	FTR Düsseldorf 11/12.6.43.
HZ272	To 427 Sqn.
HZ273	To 424 Sqn.
HZ469	To 432 Sqn.
HZ480	To 432 Sqn.

HZ481	To 432 Sqn.
Lancaster	From June 1943 to April 1944.
DS612 OW-L	From 115 Sqn. To 1678 CU.
DS621 OW-N	From 115 Sqn. To 408 Sqn via 1666 CU.
DS624	From 115 Sqn. To 1679 CU.
DS626	From 115 Sqn. To 408 Sqn.
DS634	From 115 Sqn. To 408 Sqn.
DS649 OW-R	To 1679 CU.
DS650	To 1679 CU.
DS651 OW-A	To 408 Sqn via 1679 CU.
DS656 OW-X	From 115 Sqn. To 408 Sqn.
DS657	From 115 Sqn. To 408 Sqn via 1679 CU.
DS674 OW-M	FTR Peenemünde 17/18.8.43.
DS676 OW-O	FTR Berlin 23/24.8.43.
DS677 OW-W	FTR Berlin 31.8/1.9.43.
DS679 OW-R	FTR Berlin 26/27.11.43.
DS681 OW-V	FTR Peenemünde 17/18.8.43.
DS686 OW-F/D	FTR Berlin 27/28.1.44.
DS688 OW-C	To 408 Sqn via 1679 CU & 1666 CU.
DS689 OW-S	FTR Stuttgart 7/8.10.43.
DS692	To 408 Sqn.
DS707 OW-E/Z	To 408 Sqn.
DS708	To 408 Sqn.
DS709	To 408 Sqn.
DS710	To 408 Sqn.
DS711 OW-B	To 38 MU.
DS713 OW-J/G	FTR Düsseldorf 3/4.11.43.
DS714 OW-L	Crash-landed at Thorney Island on return from Mannheim 24.9.43.
DS716 OW-U	FTR Frankfurt 20/21.12.43.
DS717 OW-T	Borrowed by 408 Sqn. Ditched on return from Hanover 18/19.10.43.
DS718	To 408 Sqn.
DS719	To 408 Sqn.
DS722	To 115 Sqn.
DS726	To 408 Sqn.
DS727	To 408 Sqn.
DS729	To 408 Sqn.
DS733 OW-L	FTR Leipzig 3/4.12.43.
DS740	To 432 Sqn.
DS741 OW-T	FTR Frankfurt 22/23.3.44.
DS757 OW-D	Crashed in North Sea during air-test and sea search 5.3.44.

DS759 OW-K	To 408 Sqn.
DS760 OW-M	FTR Berlin 2/3.1.44.
DS762 OW-V	FTR Berlin 16/17.12.43.
DS763 OW-O	To 408 Sqn.
DS767 OW-P	To 408 Sqn.
DS770 OW-P	From 408 Sqn. FTR Berlin 2/3.12.43.
DS771 OW-P	From 408 Sqn. FTR Stuttgart 15/16.3.44.
DS772	From 408 Sqn. Returned to 408 Sqn.
DS775 OW-W	From 408 Sqn. FTR Berlin 27/28.1.44.
DS776 OW-G/A	From 408 Sqn. FTR Leipzig 19/20.2.44.
DS779 OW-C	Crashed in Yorkshire on return from Berlin 16.12.43.
DS789 OW-A	From 432 Sqn. FTR Essen 26/27.3.44.
DS794 OW-W	From 432 Sqn. FTR Berlin 15/16.2.44.
DS829 OW-J/U	To 432 Sqn and back. FTR Stuttgart 15/16.3.44.
DS830	From 432 Sqn. To 408 Sqn.
DS837 OW-Q	Crashed in Yorkshire on return from Berlin 16.12.43.
DS838 OW-J	To 408 Sqn.
DS840 OW-D/C	FTR Nuremberg 30/31.3.44.
DS841 OW-Q	To 408 Sqn.
DS844	To 432 Sqn.
DS846 OW-X	From 408 Sqn. FTR Berlin 16/17.12.43.
DS848 OW-M	From 432 Sqn. To 408 Sqn.
DS852 OW-P/Q	From 432 Sqn. FTR Nuremberg 30/31.3.44.
LL617	From 432 Sqn. To 408 Sqn.
LL621 OW-N	From 115 Sqn. To 408 Sqn.
LL628 OW-Y	FTR Berlin 20/21.1.44.
LL629 OW-G	Crashed in Yorkshire on return from Berlin 24.11.43.
LL630 OW-D	FTR Frankfurt 20/21.12.43.
LL634 OW-F	To 408 Sqn.
LL647 OW-R	From 432 Sqn. FTR Frankfurt 22/23.3.44.
LL675	To 408 Sqn.
LL687 OW-L	From 408 Sqn. To 115 Sqn.
LL688 OW-R	FTR Berlin 27/28.1.44.
LL700 OW-X	To 408 Sqn.
LL721 OW-U	FTR Berlin 27/28.1.44.
LL723	To 432 Sqn.
Halifax	From April 1944.
LK755	From 432 Sqn. To 415 Sqn.
LK871	To 434 Sqn.
LK878	To 434 Sqn.

LK879 OW-P	FTR Sterkrade/Holten 16/17.6.44.
LK880 OW-C	Undercarriage collapsed on landing at Linton-on-Ouse on return from Le Fevre 1.6.44.
LK883 OW-E	FTR Louvain 12/13.5.44.
LK886	To 434 Sqn.
LK887	To 434 Sqn.
LW113	To 424 Sqn.
LW114	To 427 Sqn.
LW117	To 424 Sqn.
LW121	To 424 Sqn.
LW197 OW-S	From 420 Sqn. FTR Sterkrade 30.9.44.
LW198 OW-V	From 420 Sqn. FTR Metz 28/29.6.44.
LW199 OW-C	From 420 Sqn. FTR Düsseldorf 2/3.11.44.
LW200 OW-N	From 420 Sqn. Collided with 428 Sqn Lancaster over Warwickshire when bound for Soest 5.12.44.
LW201 OW-D	From 420 Sqn. To 408 Sqn.
LW202 OW-P	From 420 Sqn. FTR Hamburg 28/29.7.44.
LW203 OW-F	From 420 Sqn. To 408 Sqn.
LW204 OW-K	From 420 Sqn. FTR Soest 5/6.12.44.
LW205 OW-Y	From 420 Sqn. To 1665 CU.
LW206 OW-Q	From 420 Sqn. Crashed in Cambridgeshire when bound for Volkel 3.9.44.
LW207	From 420 Sqn. To 408 Sqn.
LW208 OW-U	From 420 Sqn. FTR Hamburg 28/29.7.44.
LW209 OW-Y	From 420 Sqn. FTR Duisburg 17/18.12.44.
LW210 OW-Y	From 420 Sqn. Broke up over York when bound for Chemnitz 5.3.45.
LW377 OW-G	From 420 Sqn. Abandoned over Devon coast on return from Coutances 6/7.6.44.
LW382 OW-O	From 420 Sqn. Blew up over Norfolk when bound for Houlgate 6.6.44.
LW384	From 424 Sqn. To 1659 CU.
LW416	From 424 Sqn. To 420 Sqn.
LW436	From 424 Sqn. To 434 Sqn.
LW477	From 640 Sqn.
LW590	From 420 Sqn. To 425 Sqn.
LW598 OW-J	From 432 Sqn. Force-landed in Yorkshire on return from Mayenne 9.6.44.
LW682 OW-M	From 432 Sqn. FTR Louvain 12/13.5.44.
MZ284	To 433 Sqn.
MZ285	To 433 Sqn.
MZ435	From 434 Sqn. To 420 Sqn.
MZ469	FTR Hanover 5/6.1.45.
MZ589	To 431 Sqn.

MZ597	To 431 Sqn.
MZ598 OW-J	FTR Haine St Pierre 8/9.5.44.
MZ600	To 431 Sqn.
MZ602	To 431 Sqn.
MZ603	To 415 Sqn.
MZ645	To 420 Sqn.
MZ650	To 297 Sqn.
MZ682	From 434 Sqn. To 620 Sqn.
MZ690	To 415 Sqn.
MZ747	To 420 Sqn.
NA202 OW-A	From 415 Sqn. Returned to 415 Sqn.
NA204 OW-N	From 425 Sqn. To 415 Sqn.
NA497	From 192 Sqn. To 434 Sqn.
NA510 OW-E	From 434 Sqn. FTR Cambrai 12/13.6.44.
NA518	To 425 Sqn.
NP681 OW-J	From 420 Sqn. Crashed in Oxfordshire on return from Le Havre 9.9.44.
NP682 OW-R	From 420 Sqn. Crash-landed in Yorkshire when bound for Wanne-Eickel 9.2.45.
NP683 OW-M	From 420 Sqn. FTR Metz 28/29.6.44.
NP684	Wrecked by NP818 as it took off for Münster from Linton-on-Ouse 25.3.45.
NP685 OW-L	To 408 Sqn.
NP686 OW-T	From 420 Sqn. FTR Düsseldorf 2/3.11.44.
NP696 OW-M	FTR Düsseldorf 2/3.11.44.
NP700	Abandoned over Yorkshire during training 23.7.44.
NP709 OW-A	FTR Oberhausen 1/2.11.44.
NP711	To 408 Sqn.
NP713	To 408 Sqn.
NP714	To 408 Sqn.
NP717	To 408 Sqn.
NP720	
NP721	To 432 Sqn.
NP737 OW-Z	To 408 Sqn.
NP739 OW-U	FTR Dortmund 6/7.10.44.
NP740 OW-P	To 408 Sqn.
NP741 OW-K	FTR Wanne-Eickel 12.9.44.
NP768 OW-Q	From 408 Sqn. FTR Stuttgart 28/29.1.45.
NP771 OW-J	From 408 Sqn. FTR Oberhausen 1/2.11.44.
NP775 OW-K	From 408 Sqn. FTR Bochum 4/5.11.44.
NP778 OW-A	Crashed while preparing to land at Tholthorpe on return from Sterkrade 21.11.44.
NP779 OW-C	From 432 Sqn.

NP793 OW-H	Crashed in Yorkshire when bound for Chemnitz 5.3.45.
NP794 OW-S	From 297 Sqn.
NP795 OW-T	Crashed on take-off at Linton-on-Ouse when bound for Magdeburg 16.1.45.
NP797	From 432 Sqn.
NP799 OW-J	FTR Chemnitz 5/6.3.45.
NP800 OW-S	FTR Bochum 4/5.11.44.
NP808	
NP810	To 408 Sqn.
NP811 OW-J	To 408 Sqn and back. FTR Münster 25.3.45.
NP813	From 432 Sqn. To 408 Sqn.
NP814 OW-V	To 408 Sqn.
NP815	To 432 Sqn.
NP817	To 432 Sqn.
NP818 OW-M	Crashed on take-off at Linton-on-Ouse when bound for Münster 25.3.45.
NP819 OW-B	From 408 Sqn. Crashed on approach to Manston on return from Wanne-Eickel 3.2.45.
NP820 OW-W	From 408 Sqn. FTR Wangerooge after collision with NP796 (408 Sqn) 25.4.45.
NR116	From 424 Sqn. To 408 Sqn.
NR125	To 466 Sqn.
NR134	From 434 Sqn. To 425 Sqn.
NR144	From 434 Sqn. To 420 Sqn.
PN226 OW-N	Damaged beyond repair during operation to Heligoland 18.4.45.
PN227 OW-Z	To 408 Sqn.
PN228 OW-A	Collided with MZ845 (425 Sqn) over Yorkshire when bound for Chemnitz 5.3.45.
PN231	Undercarriage collapsed during engine run-up at Linton-on-Ouse 3.3.45.
PN238	To 1665 CU.
PN242	To 1665 CU.
RG350 OW-K	From 425 Sqn. FTR Magdeburg 16/17.1.45.
RG447	To 415 Sqn.
RG448	To 432 Sqn.
RG449	To 432 Sqn.
RG452	
RG453	To 408 Sqn.
RG454	To 432 Sqn.
RG456 OW-R	
RG457	
RG458	

Heaviest Single Loss

27/28.1.44 Berlin. 4 Lancasters.

427 (LION) SQUADRON

Motto: Ferte Manus Certe (Strike with a sure hand) Code ZL

Formed on the 7th of November 1942, 427 Squadron began life as a Wellington unit, and was declared operational in remarkably quick time on the 1st of December. It was mid month before the Lions undertook their first operational sorties, but their time with 4 Group was brief, and they were posted as a founder member of 6 Group on the 1st of January 1943. 427 Squadron had the honour of launching 6 Group's operational career on the night of the 3/4th of January, and it remained at the forefront of operations for the remainder of the war. Mk V Halifaxes replaced the ageing Wellingtons in May, and these carried the squadron into battle until the arrival of the Hercules-powered Mk III in February 1944. Lancasters replaced the Halifaxes in March 1945, and the squadron had time to operate a further twenty-three times before hostilities ended. The squadron earned a number of notable records for its wartime service, including the highest number of overall operations and the highest number of Halifax sorties in 6 Group.

STATIONS

Croft	07.11.42 to 04.05.43
Leeming	05.05.43 to 29.08.45

COMMANDING OFFICERS

Wing Commander D H Burnside	07.11.42 to 05.09.43
Wing Commander R S Turnbull	06.09.43 to 13.06.44
Wing Commander C Cribb	14.06.44 to 27.08.44
Wing Commander E Bryson	28.08.44 to 26.09.44
Wing Commander V Ganderton	27.09.44 to 08.05.45

AIRCRAFT

Wellington III/X	11.42 to 05.43
Halifax V/III	05.43 to 03.45
Lancaster I/III	03.45 to 08.45

OPERATIONAL RECORD

Operations	Sorties	Aircraft Losses	% Losses
270 3,	306	68	2.1

Category of Operations

Bombing	Mining
232	38

Operations	Sorties	Aircraft Losses	% Losses
36	267	10	3.7

Wellingtons

Operations	Sorties	Aircraft Losses	% Losses
36	267	10	3.7

Category of Operations

Bombing	Mining
26	10

Halifaxes

Operations	Sorties	Aircraft Losses	% Losses
211	2,800	58	2.1

Category of Operations

Bombing	Mining
190	21

Lancasters

Operations	Sorties	Aircraft Losses	% Losses
23	239	0	0.0

Category of Operations

Bombing	Mining
16	7

TABLE OF STATISTICS

(Heavy squadrons)

Out of 59 Lancaster squadrons

56th highest number of Lancaster overall operations in Bomber Command.

56th highest number of Lancaster sorties in Bomber Command.
Lowest number of Lancaster operational losses in Bomber Command.

Out of 32 Halifax squadrons

9th highest number of Halifax overall operations in Bomber Command.
8th highest number of Halifax sorties in Bomber Command.
10th highest number of Halifax operational losses in Bomber Command.

Out of 42 Wellington squadrons

39th highest number of Wellington overall operations in Bomber Command.
39th highest number of Wellington sorties in Bomber Command.
38th highest number of Wellington operational losses in Bomber Command.

Out of 24 squadrons in 4 Group

Lowest number of overall operations, sorties and losses.

Out of 15 squadrons in 6 Group

Highest number of overall operations in 6 Group.
3rd highest number of sorties in 6 Group.
4th highest number of aircraft operational losses in 6 Group.

Out of 8 Wellington squadrons in 6 Group

7th highest number of overall Wellington operations in 6 Group.
Lowest number of Wellington sorties in 6 Group.
6th highest number of Wellington operational losses in 6 Group.

Out of 15 Halifax squadrons in 6 Group

Highest number of Halifax overall operations in 6 Group.
Highest number of Halifax sorties in 6 Group.
2nd highest number of Halifax operational losses in 6 Group.

Out of 11 Lancaster squadrons in 6 Group

9th highest number of Lancaster overall operations in 6 Group.
9th highest number of Lancaster sorties in 6 Group.
Lowest number of Lancaster operational losses in 6 Group.

AIRCRAFT HISTORIES

Wellington X3348 ZL-Z	From November 1942 to May 1943. From 426 Sqn. Crash-landed in Derbyshire on return from Lorient 26/27.1.43.

X3390 ZL-W	From 419 Sqn. FTR from mining sortie 2/3.3.43.
X3553 ZL-Y	From 420 Sqn. To 29 OTU.
X3562 ZL-H	From 419 Sqn. To 29 OTU.
X3563 ZL-T	From 419 Sqn. Abandoned over Eire on return from St Nazaire 28.2/1.3.43.
X3659	From 419 Sqn. To 1485 Flt.
X3752 ZL-P	From 419 Sqn. To 23 OTU.
X3873 ZL-W/R	From 419 Sqn. FTR from mining sortie 21/22.1.43.
Z1572 ZL-Q	From 419 Sqn. To 16 OTU.
Z1604 ZL-U/P	From 419 Sqn. To 29 OTU.
Z1626 ZL-V/G	From 419 Sqn. To 16 OTU.
Z1676 ZL-S	From 419 Sqn. Crash-landed in Eire on return from Lorient 16/17.2.43.
Z1719 ZL-P/J	To 18 OTU.
BJ604 ZL-A	From 419 Sqn. Crashed on landing at Middleton St George while in transit 8.1.43.
BJ668 ZL-X	From 419 Sqn. FTR Lorient 4/5.2.43.
BJ778 ZL-D	From 419 Sqn. Crashed in Yorkshire on return a from mining sortie 12.2.43.
BJ886 ZL-F	From 419 Sqn. FTR Cologne 26/27.2.43.
BK137 ZL-A	To 12 OTU.
BK143	To 311 FTU.
BK164 ZL-E	To 16 OTU.
BK165	To 426 Sqn.
BK268 ZL-C	From 419 Sqn. Crashed in Rutland on return from Cologne 26/27.2.43.
BK276 ZL-O	From 419 Sqn. Crashed on take-off from Croft while training 15.11.42.
BK337	From 428 Sqn. To 29 OTU.
BK343 ZL-V	From 419 Sqn. FTR St Nazaire 28.2/1.3.43.
BK364 ZL-G	From 419 Sqn. FTR Lorient 15/16.1.43.
BK389 ZL-L	From 419 Sqn. FTR Oldenburg 30.1.43.
BK437 ZL-K	To 29 OTU.
BK438 ZL-R	To 29 OTU.
BK468	To 420 Sqn.
BK558 ZL-Z	To 12 OTU.
HE159	To 424 Sqn.
HE222 ZL-E	From 424 Sqn. To 432 Sqn.
HE278	Crashed almost immediately after take-off from Croft for training flight 14.3.43.
HE279 ZL-S	From 424 Sqn. To 432 Sqn.
HE294	From 420 Sqn. To 432 Sqn.
HE367	To 424 Sqn.

HE425 ZL-W	To 18 OTU.
HE481	From 420 Sqn. To 30 OTU.
HE547 ZL-D	FTR Mannheim 16/17.4.43.
HE553 ZL-J	To 432 Sqn.
HE555	From 420 Sqn. To 432 Sqn.
HE630	From 420 Sqn. To 432 Sqn.
HE637 ZL-G/M	To 432 Sqn.
HE638 ZL-F/N	To 432 Sqn.
HE639	To 3 OTU.
HE653 ZL-C	To 432 Sqn.
HE681 ZL-P	From 420 Sqn. To 18 OTU.
HE683 ZL-U	From 420 Sqn. To 27 OTU.
HE686 ZL-R	To 432 Sqn.
HE688 ZL-V	To 432 Sqn.
HE698 ZL-Q	To 432 Sqn.
HE729 ZL-K	To 432 Sqn.
HE730 ZL-B	To 18 OTU.
HE732	From 420 Sqn. To 432 Sqn.
HE743 ZL-X	Crashed on take-off from Croft for training flight 6.4.43.
HE744 ZL-J	FTR Bochum 29/30.3.43.
HE745 ZL-E	Crashed while trying to land at Twinwood Farm, Bedfordshire, on return from Mannheim 16/17.4.43.
HE771	From 420 Sqn. Force-landed in County Durham with 420 Sqn crew on return from Duisburg 27.4.43.
HE873	From 420 Sqn. To 432 Sqn.
HE906 ZL-H	To 432 Sqn.
HZ264 ZL-L	To 432 Sqn.
HZ272	From 426 Sqn. To 432 Sqn.
HZ313 ZL-Y	To 20 OTU.
LN429	To 432 Sqn.
LN435	To 432 Sqn.
Halifax	From May 1943 to March 1945.
DG363	To 428 Sqn via 1664 CU.
DK135 ZL-B	FTR Wuppertal 24/25.6.43.
DK139 ZL-P	FTR Mülheim 22/23.6.43.
DK140 ZL-Z	Crashed on landing at Leeming while training 16.6.43.
DK141 ZL-C	FTR Mülheim 22/23.6.43.
DK142 ZL-C	FTR Aachen 13/14.7.43.
DK143	To 1664 CU.

DK144 ZL-U	Crashed on take-off from Leeming when bound for Gelsenkirchen 25.6.43.
DK146	To 1664 CU.
DK180 ZL-R	FTR Gelsenkirchen 25/26.6.43.
DK181 ZL-Z	Crash-landed at Woodbridge after early return from Leipzig 4.12.43.
DK182 ZL-E	Crashed in Yorkshire after early return from Kassel 22.10.43.
DK183 ZL-S	FTR Bochum 12/13.6.43.
DK184 ZL-G	FTR Berlin 23/24.8.43.
DK185	To 431 Sqn.
DK186	To 1664 CU.
DK189	Damaged during operations 29.7.43.
DK190 ZL-F	FTR Gelsenkirchen 25/26.6.43.
DK191 ZL-K	FTR Mülheim 22/23.6.43.
DK192	To 1663 CU.
DK225 ZL-J	FTR Mülheim 22/23.6.43.
DK226	To 1664 CU.
DK227 ZL-V	Crashed on landing at Mildenhall on return from Peenemünde 18.8.43.
DK234 ZL-Z	FTR Kassel 22/23.10.43.
DK242	Crash-landed at Leeming while training 29.7.43.
DK243 ZL-F	FTR Peenemünde 17/18.8.43.
DK253 ZL-M	Crashed in Middlesex on return from Montluçon 16.9.43.
DK254	To 301 FTU.
DK255 ZL-B/J	FTR München 6/7.9.43.
DK268	To 1664 CU.
EB148 ZL-S	Crashed in Cambridgeshire on return from Cologne 28/29.6.43.
EB241	To 1664 CU.
EB242 ZL-K	FTR Remscheid 30/31.7.43.
EB243 ZL-H	FTR Berlin 23/24.8.43.
EB246 ZL-S	FTR Berlin 20/21.1.44.
EB247	Abandoned over Hampshire on return from Mannheim 10.8.43.
EB248 ZL-U	To 1666 CU.
EB251 ZL-T	FTR Berlin 31.8/1.9.43.
EB257 ZL-P	To 434 Sqn.
HX279 ZL-Z	FTR Frankfurt 18/19.3.44.
HX339	To 429 Sqn.
LK626	To 431 Sqn.
LK627 ZL-K	FTR Frankfurt 20/21.12.43.
LK628 ZL-N	FTR München 6/7.9.43.

LK629 ZL-F	FTR Mönchengladbach 30/31.8.43.
LK633 ZL-N	FTR Kassel 22/23.10.43.
LK636 ZL-H	FTR Mannheim 5/6.9.43.
LK637 ZL-W	To 1662 CU.
LK643	To 1664 CU.
LK644 ZL-C	FTR Frankfurt 20/21.12.43.
LK656	To 429 Sqn.
LK658	To 431 Sqn.
LK659	To 431 Sqn.
LK663	To 434 Sqn.
LK684	To 429 Sqn.
LK694	To 429 Sqn.
LK700	To 1658 CU.
LK735 ZL-Z	From 429 Sqn. To 1659 CU.
LK746	To 429 Sqn.
LK752 ZL-V	FTR Berlin 24/25.3.44.
LK755	To 432 Sqn.
LK758 ZL-E	Crashed near Leeming during training 7.2.44.
LK759 ZL-Z	FTR Augsburg 25/26.2.44.
LK792	To 434 Sqn.
LK836	Crashed Yorkshire soon after take-off 21.2.44.
LK900 ZL-D	FTR Hanover 8/9.10.43.
LK920 ZL-J	FTR Frankfurt 4/5.10.43.
LK923 ZL-B	FTR Magdeburg 21/22.1.44.
LK953	From 434 Sqn. Returned to 434 Sqn.
LK959 ZL-D	From 428 Sqn. FTR Kassel 22/23.10.43.
LK965	To 429 Sqn.
LK972	To 429 Sqn.
LK974	To 429 Sqn.
LK975	To 429 Sqn.
LK976 ZL-Z	FTR Mannheim 18/19.11.43.
LK989	To 431 Sqn.
LL139 ZL-D	FTR Magdeburg 21/22.1.44.
LL153	To 429 Sqn.
LL167	To 429 Sqn.
LL169 ZL-L	FTR Magdeburg 21/22.1.44.
LL170	To 429 Sqn.
LL171	To 429 Sqn.
LL172	To 429 Sqn.
LL176 ZL-Q	FTR Magdeburg 21/22.1.44.
LL178	To 429 Sqn.
LL191 ZL-N	Crashed while trying to land at Coltishall on return from Berlin 20/21.1.44.
LL194	To 429 Sqn.

LL196	To 429 Sqn.
LL197	To 429 Sqn.
LV789 ZL-U	FTR Noisy-le-Sec 18/19.4.44.
LV821 ZL-N	FTR Brunswick 12/13.8.44.
LV828	Crashed in Northamptonshire during training 1.2.44.
LV829 ZL-G	FTR Leipzig 19/20.2.44.
LV830	To 429 Sqn.
LV831 ZL-P	FTR Bourg Leopold 27/28.5.44.
LV836 ZL-Y	Crashed in Yorkshire soon after take-off for Stuttgart 20/21.2.44.
LV883 ZL-M	FTR Ghent 10/11.4.44.
LV898 ZL-D	FTR Nuremberg 30/31.3.44.
LV902 ZL-T	To 517 Sqn.
LV922 ZL-C	To 1663 CU.
LV923 ZL-W	FTR Nuremberg 30/31.3.44.
LV938 ZL-A	From 433 Sqn. FTR Metz 28/29.6.44.
LV942	To 429 Sqn.
LV945 ZL-F	Damaged beyond repair after accident at Shipdam on return from Neuss 28.11.44.
LV960 ZL-G	Abandoned over Yorkshire on return from Villeneuve-St-Georges 9.4.44.
LV968 ZL-V	FTR Karlsruhe 24/25.4.44.
LV985 ZL-K	FTR Mondeville 18.7.44.
LV986 ZL-V	Damaged beyond repair during operation to Ghent 10/11.5.44.
LV987 ZL-K	FTR Acheres 7/8.6.44.
LV988 ZL-P	From 424 Sqn.
LV994	From 429 Sqn.
LV995 ZL-Y	FTR Arras 12/13.6.44.
LV996	From 429 Sqn. Crashed in Kent on return from Chemnitz 5/6.3.45.
LW114 ZL-S	From 426 Sqn. FTR Boulogne 11/12.5.44.
LW130 ZL-C/L/U	
LW133	Became ground instruction machine 24.3.45.
LW135 ZL-R	FTR Arras 12/13.6.44.
LW161 ZL-V	To 429 Sqn.
LW162 ZL-D	To 429 Sqn.
LW163	From 429 Sqn. To 518 Sqn.
LW165 ZL-M	FTR Arras 12/13.6.44.
LW166 ZL-S	FTR Villeneuve-St-George 4/5.7.44.
LW365 ZL-W	From 429 Sqn. FTR Bourg Leopold 27/28.5.44.
LW370	From 429 Sqn. SOC 10.4.45.
LW548	To 246 Sqn.

LW551 ZL-G	FTR Frankfurt 18/19.3.44.
LW558 ZL-A	FTR Stuttgart 15/16.3.44.
LW559 ZL-F	FTR Stuttgart 15/16.3.44.
LW572	To 431 Sqn.
LW574 ZL-J	FTR Berlin 24/25.3.44.
LW575	To 420 Sqn.
LW576	To 431 Sqn.
LW577 ZL-K	FTR Berlin 24/25.3.44.
LW618 ZL-E	FTR Nuremberg 30/31.3.44.
LW619	To ATTDU.
MZ282	From 429 Sqn. Became ground instruction machine.
MZ285	
MZ288	From 431 Sqn. FTR 30.11.44.
MZ291 ZL-O	From 434 Sqn. Crashed on take-off from Leeming when bound for Opladen 28.12.44.
MZ295	From 434 Sqn. To 429 Sqn.
MZ303	From 429 Sqn.
MZ304 ZL-H/B	From 424 Sqn. FTR from mining sortie 24/25.11.44.
MZ316 ZL-J	FTR Stuttgart 25/26.7.44.
MZ317	To 1663 CU.
MZ318	To 429 Sqn.
MZ355 ZL-W	FTR from mining sortie 14/15.2.45.
MZ357	To 429 Sqn.
MZ363 ZL-Y	FTR Le Neuville 9/10.8.44.
MZ422 ZL-N	FTR Chemnitz 14/15.2.45.
MZ423	To 420 Sqn.
MZ452 ZL-E	FTR from mining sortie with a 429 Sqn crew 25/26.2.45.
MZ755 ZL-R	To 429 Sqn.
MZ756 ZL-E	FTR from mining sortie 4/5.10.44.
MZ757 ZL-Y	FTR Hamburg 28/29.7.44.
MZ814	From 424 Sqn. To 415 Sqn.
MZ819 ZL-S	
MZ823 ZL-A	
MZ866	Destroyed by fire at Leeming during refuelling 28.10.44.
MZ867 ZL-G	Damaged beyond repair on landing at Leeming following early return from Neuss 27.11.44.
MZ903 ZL-Y	Crash-landing at Manston following early return from Cologne 30.10.44.
MZ904	To 408 Sqn.
MZ905	To 433 Sqn.

NP941 ZL-X	To 425 Sqn.
NP942 ZL-Y	From 429 Sqn. FTR Monheim 20/21.2.45.
NP956 ZL-J	To 425 Sqn.
NP957 ZL-L	To 429 Sqn.
NR118	To 434 Sqn.
NR124	To 434 Sqn.
NR126	To 434 Sqn.
NR148	To 429 Sqn.
NR171	To 420 Sqn.
NR194	To 429 Sqn.
NR196	To 429 Sqn.
NR203	To 429 Sqn.
NR230	To 429 Sqn.
NR257 ZL-Y	FTR Hanover 5/6.1.45.
NR288 ZL-F	From 415 Sqn. FTR Worms 21/22.2.45.
RG347 ZL-G/P	From 420 Sqn. Crashed on take-off from Leeming when bound for Mainz with a 429 Sqn crew 27.2.45.

Lancaster	From March 1945.
DV233	To 467 Sqn.
JA675	To 467 Sqn.
JA906	From 467 Sqn. No operations. Returned to 467 Sqn.
ME393 ZL-D	
ME426 ZL-C	
ME498 ZL-K	
ME501 ZL-T	
NX548 ZL-J	
NX549 ZL-U	
NX550 ZL-V	
NX551 ZL-G	
NX552 ZL-S	
NX553 ZL-H	
NX554 ZL-F	
NX555 ZL-R	
PA260 ZL-Q	
PA263 ZL-E	
PA271 ZL-W	
PA323	
RA534 ZL-A	
RA536 ZL-N	
RA537 ZL-P	
RA538 ZL-P	

RA539 ZL-O
RE160 ZL-G
RF257

Heaviest Single Loss

22/23.6.43	Mülheim. 4 Halifaxes.
21/22.1.44	Magdeburg. 4 Halifaxes.

428 (GHOST) SQUADRON

Motto: Usque ad Finem (To the very end)   Code NA

One of three Canadian squadrons formed in Bomber Command on the 7th of November 1942, 428 Squadron began life as a 4 Group Wellington unit, but carried out no operations until after its posting to 6 Group as a founder member on the 1st of January 1943. It was actually early February before the squadron went to war for the first time, but from then onwards it featured constantly on the order of battle. Halifax Mk II and V aircraft replaced the ageing Wellingtons in June 1943, and the squadron soldiered on with this less than ideal type for the next twelve months. Canadian-built Lancaster Mk Xs arrived in June 1944, and these saw the squadron through to war's end.

STATIONS

Dalton	07.11.42 to 01.06.43
Middleton St George	01.06.43 to 31.05.45

COMMANDING OFFICERS

Wing Commander A Earle	07.11.42 to 20.02.43
Wing Commander D W M Smith DFC	21.02.43 to 14.09.43
Wing Commander W R Suggitt DFC	15.09.43 to 30.10.43
Wing Commander D T French DFC	31.10.43 to 08.05.44
Wing Commander W A G McLeish DFC	09.05.44 to 07.08.44
Wing Commander A C Hull DFC	08.08.44 to 01.01.45
Wing Commander M W Gall	02.01.45 to 02.06.45

AIRCRAFT

Wellington III/X	07.11.42 to 06.43
Halifax II/V	06.43 to 06.44
Lancaster X	06.44 to 09.45

OPERATIONAL RECORD

Operations	Sorties	Aircraft Losses	% Losses
268	3,433	67	2.0

Category of Operations

Bombing	Mining
206	62

Wellingtons

Operations	Sorties	Aircraft Losses	% Losses
35	350	17	4.9

Category of Operations

Bombing	Mining
26	9

Halifaxes

Operations	Sorties	Aircraft Losses	% Losses
122	1,406	32	2.3

Category of Operations

Bombing	Mining
69	53

Lancasters

Operations	Sorties	Aircraft Losses	% Losses
111	1,677	18	1.1

All bombing.

TABLE OF STATISTICS

Out of 59 Lancaster squadrons

40th highest number of Lancaster overall operations in Bomber Command.
39th highest number of Lancaster sorties in Bomber Command.
43rd highest number of Lancaster operational losses in Bomber Command.

Out of 32 Halifax squadrons

23rd highest number of Halifax overall operations in Bomber Command.
26th highest number of Halifax sorties in Bomber Command.

20th highest number of Halifax operational losses in Bomber Command.

Out of 42 Wellington squadrons

41st highest number of Wellington overall operations in Bomber Command.
36th highest number of Wellington sorties in Bomber Command.
29th highest number of Wellington operational losses in Bomber Command.

Out of 15 squadrons in 6 Group

12th highest number of overall operations in 6 Group.
2nd highest number of sorties in 6 Group.
6th highest number of aircraft operational losses in 6 Group.

Out of 8 Wellington squadrons in 6 Group

Lowest number of Wellington overall operations in 6 Group.
4th highest number of Wellington sorties in 6 Group.
3rd highest number of Wellington operational losses in 6 Group.

Out of 11 Lancaster squadrons in 6 Group

2nd highest number of Lancaster overall operations in 6 Group.
2nd highest number of Lancaster sorties in 6 Group.
4th highest number of Lancaster operational losses in 6 Group.

Out of 15 Halifax squadrons in 6 Group

12th highest number of Halifax overall operations in 6 Group.
14th highest number of Halifax sorties in 6 Group.
8th highest number of Halifax operational losses in 6 Group.

AIRCRAFT HISTORIES

Wellington	From November 1942 to June 1943.
X3541 NA-N	To 29 OTU.
X3543	To 29 OTU.
X3545	From 466 Sqn. To CGS.
X3546	From 466 Sqn. To CGS.
X3550 NA-J	To 17 OTU.
Z1718	To 18 OTU.
Z1719 NA-P	To 18 OTU.
Z1722	To 17 OTU.
Z1727 NA-K	From 156 Sqn. To 1485 Flt.
BK154	To 16 OTU.
BK155	To 1485 Flt.

BK156	To 18 OTU.
BK337	From 425 Sqn. To 427 Sqn.
BK562	To 30 OTU.
BK563 NA-R	To 29 OTU.
BK564 NA-R	FTR Bochum 29/30.3.43.
DF635 NA-I	From 156 Sqn. FTR Duisburg 8/9.4.43.
DF668	From 156 Sqn. To 16 OTU.
HE158 NA-G	To 21 OTU.
HE173	Crashed soon after take-off from Dishforth for night training exercise 31.1.43.
HE174	To 20 OTU.
HE175 NA-U	FTR Bochum 29/30.3.43.
HE176 NA-F	FTR Stuttgart 14/15.4.43.
HE177 NA-G	Crashed on landing at East Moor on return from mining sortie 22.5.43.
HE239 NA-Y/L	To 20 OTU.
HE282	To 20 OTU.
HE319 NA-Y	FTR Wuppertal 29/30.5.43.
HE321 NA-Z	FTR Duisburg 12/13.5.43.
HE322 NA-J	Crashed on take-off from Middleton St George when bound for Düsseldorf 11.6.43.
HE432 NA-C	FTR Kiel 4/5.4.43.
HE505 NA-X	To 30 OTU.
HE543 NA-D	FTR from mining sortie 28/29.4.43.
HE656 NA-A	From 424 Sqn. FTR Duisburg 12/13.5.43.
HE684	From 429 Sqn. To 432 Sqn.
HE689 NA-X	
HE703	From 424 Sqn. To 27 OTU.
HE727 NA-K	FTR Dortmund 4/5.5.43.
HE728 NA-B	FTR from mining sortie 28/29.4.43.
HE738 NA-L	From 424 Sqn. To 30 OTU.
HE750	To 82 OTU.
HE751	To 20 OTU.
HE864 NA-D	From 424 Sqn. FTR Dortmund 4/5.5.43.
HE873	From 432 Sqn. To 27 OTU.
HE899 NA-B	From 424 Sqn. FTR from mining sortie 21/22.5.43.
HE911	To 432 Sqn.
HE917	To 30 OTU.
HE918	To 432 Sqn.
HE981	To 429 Sqn.
HF495	To 429 Sqn.
HF571	To 432 Sqn.
HF600	To 429 Sqn.

HZ365 NA-U	FTR Duisburg 26/27.4.43.
HZ367	To 20 OTU.
HZ476 NA-A	FTR Düsseldorf 25/26.5.43.
HZ485 NA-G	FTR Essen 27/28.5.43.
JA112	To 82 OTU.
LN424 NA-E	FTR Wuppertal 29/30.5.43.
LN481 NA-N	
MS481 NA-Q	From 424 Sqn. FTR Essen 27/28.5.43.

Halifax — From June 1943 to June 1944.

DG363	From 427 Sqn via 1664CU.
DK196 NA-Z	FTR Münich 6/7.9.43.
DK228 NA-D	FTR Aachen 13/14.7.43.
DK229 NA-W	FTR Gelsenkirchen 9/10.7.43.
DK230 NA-V	FTR Peenemünde 17/18.8.43.
DK233 NA-X	FTR Berlin 31.8/1.9.43.
DK235	To 1659 CU.
DK237 NA-L	FTR Magdeburg 21/22.1.44.
DK238 NA-I	FTR Peenemünde 17/18.8.43.
DK239 NA-Q	FTR Hamburg 29/30.7.43.
DK249 NA-K	FTR Berlin 31.8/1.9.43.
DK252 NA-O	Crash-landed at Ludford Magna on return from Hanover 27/28.9.43.
DK257 NA-Q	FTR Aachen 13/14.7.43.
DK267 NA-H	FTR Berlin 23/24.8.43.
DK270 NA-U	Crashed while landing at Framlingham on return from Hanover 28.9.43.
DK271 NA-Q	FTR Mannheim 23/24.9.43.
EB205	To 431 Sqn.
EB206	To 1664 CU.
EB207 NA-B	FTR Mannheim 23/24.9.43.
EB209 NA-C	FTR Aachen 13/14.7.43.
EB210 NA-E	Damaged beyond repair during operation to Kassel 3/4.10.43.
EB211 NA-F	FTR Peenemünde 17/18.8.43.
EB212 NA-U	FTR Hamburg 2/3.8.43.
EB213 NA-G	FTR Kassel 3/4.10.43.
EB214 NA-S	FTR Kassel 3/4.10.43.
EB215 NA-T	FTR Hanover 27/28.9.43.
EB216 NA-R	FTR Nuremberg 27/28.8.43.
EB252 NA-P	FTR Frankfurt 20/21.12.43.
EB274 NA-H	FTR Hamburg 2/3.8.43.
EB275	To 431 Sqn.
HR802	From 35 Sqn. To 1659 CU.

HR855	From 35 Sqn. To 1666 CU.
HR857	From 35 Sqn. To 1659 CU.
HR916	From 35 Sqn. To 1659 CU.
HR925	From 419 Sqn. To 1666 CU.
HR988	From 405 Sqn. To 1666 CU.
HX147	From 35 Sqn. To 1666 CU.
HX183	
JB968 NA-R	From 429 Sqn. FTR Hanover 27/28.9.43.
JD271 NA-M	From 429 Sqn. FTR Leipzig 19/20.2.44.
JD274	From 429 Sqn. To 1666 CU.
JD278	From 429 Sqn. To 1662 CU.
JD386	From 429 Sqn. Returned to 429 Sqn. From 429 Sqn. To 1666 CU.
JN953	From 419 Sqn. Force-landed in Yorkshire while training 12.6.44.
JN954	From 35 Sqn. To 419 Sqn.
JN955	From 35 Sqn. SOC 22.2.45.
JN966 NA-V	Collided with Lancaster ED417 (103 Sqn) on return from Stuttgart, and crashed near Middleton St George 27.11.43.
JN967 NA-X	To 1662 CU.
JN968 NA-I	To 1664 CU.
JN969	To 1666 CU.
JN971	To 1659 CU.
JN973 NA-U	FTR from mining sortie 17/18.4.44.
JP113 NA-A	Crash-landed at Attlebridge on return from Lens 21.4.44.
JP122	From 35 Sqn. To 1664 CU.
JP124	From 35 Sqn. To 1662 CU.
JP127 NA-T	To 1659 CU.
JP130	From 419 Sqn. To 1664 CU.
JP132	To 1659 CU.
JP191 NA-B	To 1664 CU.
JP192	To 1652 CU.
JP195	
JP197	To 1664 CU.
JP198	To 1664 CU.
JP199 NA-O	Abandoned over Berkshire on return from a mining sortie 21.4.44.
JP201	From 419 Sqn. To 1666 CU.
JP203	From 419 Sqn. To 1664 CU.
JP204	From 419 Sqn. To 1664 CU.
LK635 NA-H	FTR Hanover 22/23.9.43.
LK661	To 429 Sqn.

LK662	To 429 Sqn.
LK680	To 434 Sqn.
LK739 NA-P	From 434 Sqn. FTR Berlin 20/21.1.44.
LK901	To 1662 CU.
LK906 NA-D	FTR Berlin 22/23.11.43.
LK908 NA-I	Damaged beyond repair during operation to Kassel 22/23.10.43.
LK913 NA-N	FTR Montluçon 15/16.9.43.
LK914 NA-K	FTR Hanover 22/23.9.43.
LK915 NA-V	FTR Hanover 27/28.9.43.
LK924	To 429 Sqn.
LK927	To 431 Sqn.
LK928 NA-B	FTR Frankfurt 20/21.12.43.
LK930	To 429 Sqn.
LK931 NA-W	FTR Frankfurt 4/5.10.43.
LK947	To 429 Sqn.
LK950 NA-T	Abandoned over Kent on return from Leverkusen 19.11.43.
LK952	To 431 Sqn.
LK953	To 434 Sqn.
LK954 NA-E	Crashed in Lincolnshire on return from Düsseldorf 3.11.43.
LK956 NA-S	FTR Leverkusen 19/20.11.43.
LK959	To 427 Sqn.
LK969 NA-G	FTR Frankfurt 25/26.11.43.
LL180	From 431 Sqn. Returned to 431Sqn.
LW279	From 429 Sqn. To 419 Sqn.
LW285 NA-Z	From 429 Sqn. FTR from mining sortie 23/24.4.44.
LW323	To 35 Sqn.
LW325	From 419 Sqn. To 1666 CU.
LW326	To 35 Sqn.
LW327	To 419 Sqn.
Lancaster	From June 1944.
KB704 NA-E/X	From 419 Sqn. Crashed while landing at Middleton St George 11.5.44.
KB705 NA-F	From Rolls-Royce. To 1664 CU.
KB709 NA-G	FTR Stettin 29/30.8.44.
KB725 NA-L	Crashed in County Durham after returning early from Wiesbaden 3.2.45.
KB737 NA-R	FTR Essen 25.10.44.
KB739 NA-W	

KB740 NA-V	Crash-landed at Woodbridge on return from Stuttgart 25.7.44.
KB741	To 431 Sqn.
KB742 NA-M	Crashed on landing at Middleton St George on return from Bochum 4.11.44.
KB743 NA-I	FTR Bremen 18/19.8.44.
KB744 NA-J	
KB747 NA-X	
KB749 NA-A	FTR Soesterberg 15.8.44.
KB751 NA-Q	FTR Stettin 16/17.8.44.
KB756 NA-Q	FTR Villeneuve-St-Georges 4/5.7.44.
KB757 NA-C	
KB758 NA-Z	FTR Brunswick 12/13.8.44.
KB759 NA-K	FTR Hamburg 28/29.7.44.
KB760 NA-P	
KB763 NA-S	Crashed in County Durham while training 28.1.45.
KB764 NA-B	
KB766 NA-O	Abandoned over France when bound for Hagen 2.12.44.
KB768 NA-E	Collided with 426 Sqn Halifax LW200 over Warwickshire on return from Soest and crashed 5/6.12.44.
KB770 NA-D	FTR Stuttgart 28/29.1.45.
KB771	
KB773	To 431 Sqn.
KB777 NA-V	FTR Hildesheim 22.3.45.
KB778 NA-Y	Crashed in Belgium on return from Chemnitz 5.3.45.
KB780 NA-T	FTR Duisburg 14.10.44.
KB781 NA-U	
KB782 NA-H	FTR Düsseldorf 2/3.11.44.
KB783	From A&AEE. To 419 Sqn.
KB784 NA-K	FTR Kiel 13/14.4.45.
KB789	To 434 Sqn.
KB791 NA-A/W	
KB792 NA-I	FTR Wiesbaden 2/3.2.45.
KB793 NA-E	Crashed in County Durham while training 13.1.45.
KB794 NA-W	
KB795 NA-Q	Crashed on landing Middleton St George during training 7.4.45.
KB798 NA-G	FTR Opladen 27/28.12.44.
KB801	To 431 Sqn.

KB803	To 431 Sqn.
KB806	To 431 Sqn.
KB808	To 431 Sqn.
KB813	To 431 Sqn.
KB814	To 434 Sqn.
KB816 NA-E	From 434 Sqn. Crashed on landing at Church Broughton 14.4.45.
KB820 NA-N/T/M	
KB822	To 431 Sqn.
KB823	To 431 Sqn.
KB825	To 434 Sqn.
KB826	To 434 Sqn.
KB829	To 434 Sqn.
KB838 NA-O	
KB840	To 434 Sqn.
KB842	To 434 Sqn.
KB843 NA-D	From 434 Sqn.
KB846 NA-I	From 434 Sqn. FTR Hagen 15/16.3.45.
KB848 NA-G	
KB850 NA-O	From 434 Sqn.
KB851	To 419 Sqn.
KB855 NA-F	From 419 Sqn. Crashed on approach to Middleton St George while training 20.2.45.
KB864 NA-S	
KB867 NA-L	
KB876	
KB878	From 419 Sqn.
KB879 NA-Y	Crashed in Staffordshire while training 30.4.45.
KB882 NA-R	
KB888	To 419 Sqn.
KB889	
KB891 NA-F	
KB895	To 434 Sqn.
KB898	
KB899 NA-V	
KB900	To 431 Sqn.
KB908	From 431 Sqn.
KB910	
KB920 NA-K	From 434 Sqn.

429 (BISON) SQUADRON

Motto: Fortunae Nihil (Nothing to chance)   Code AL

One of three Canadian squadrons formed in 4 Group on the 7th of November 1942, 429 Squadron was not posted with its fellow Canadian units as founder members of 6 Group on New Year's Day 1943, but remained with 4 Group. Its first operation was a sea search on the 21st of January 1943, and its maiden offensive sorties were launched later that night to lay mines. The posting to 6 Group eventually came on the 1st of April, and the squadron took its place on the order of battle with its now ageing Wellingtons. A move to Leeming in mid August signalled the end of Wellington operations, and the squadron returned to the fray a month later as a Halifax unit. The much improved Hercules-powered variant arrived on squadron charge in January 1944, and this enabled the Bisons to play a full part in operations for the remainder of the war. Canadian-built Lancasters replaced the Halifaxes in March 1945, and the squadron managed just thirteen operations on these before the end.

STATIONS

East Moor	07.11.42 to 12.08.43
Leeming	13.08.43 to 29.08.45

COMMANDING OFFICERS

Wing Commander J A P Owen	07.11.42 to 31.05.43
Wing Commander J L Savard DFC	01.06.43 to 22.06.43
Wing Commander J A Piddington	28.06.43 to 27.07.43
Wing Commander J D Patterson DFC	30.07.43 to 02.03.44
Wing Commander A F Avant AFC	01.05.44 to 10.10.44
Wing Commander R L Bolduc	10.10.44 to 09.04.45
Wing Commander E Evans	09.04.45 to 31.05.45

AIRCRAFT

Wellington X	07.11.42 to 09.43
Halifax II/V	09.43 to 01.44
Halifax III	03.44 to 03.45
Lancaster X	03.45 to 05.46

OPERATIONAL RECORD

Operations	Sorties	Aircraft Losses	% Losses
248	3,017	71	2.3

Category of Operations

Bombing	Mining
211	37

Wellingtons

Operations	Sorties	Aircraft Losses	% Losses
46	384	21	5.5

Category of Operations

Bombing	Mining
31	15

Halifaxes

Operations	Sorties	Aircraft Losses	% Losses
189	2,519	49	1.9

Category of Operations

Bombing	Mining
172	17

Lancasters

Operations	Sorties	Aircraft Losses	% Losses
13	114	1	0.9

Category of Operations

Bombing	Mining
8	5

TABLE OF STATISTICS

Out of 59 Lancaster squadrons

58th highest number of Lancaster overall operations in Bomber Command.
58th highest number of Lancaster sorties in Bomber Command.
58th equal (with 138 Sqn) highest number of Lancaster operational losses in Bomber Command.

Out of 32 Halifax squadrons

10th highest number of Halifax overall operations in Bomber Command.
10th highest number of Halifax sorties in Bomber Command.
13th highest number of Halifax operational losses in Bomber Command.

Out of 42 Wellington squadrons

28th highest number of Wellington overall operations in Bomber Command.

25th highest number of Wellington sorties in Bomber Command.

20th highest number of Wellington operational losses in Bomber Command.

Out of 15 squadrons in 6 Group

4th highest number of overall operations in 6 Group.

7th highest number of sorties in 6 Group.

3rd highest number of aircraft operational losses in 6 Group.

Out of 8 Wellington squadrons in 6 Group

3rd highest number of overall Wellington operations in 6 Group.

3rd highest number of Wellington sorties in 6 Group.

Highest number of Wellington operational losses in 6 Group.

Out of 15 Halifax squadrons in 6 Group

2nd highest number of Halifax overall operations in 6 Group.

2nd highest number of Halifax sorties in 6 Group.

Highest number of Halifax operational losses in 6 Group.

Out of 11 Lancaster squadrons in 6 Group

Lowest number of Lancaster overall operations in 6 Group.

Lowest number of Lancaster sorties in 6 Group.

10th highest number of Lancaster operational losses in 6 Group.

AIRCRAFT HISTORIES

Wellington	From November 1942 to September 1943.
X3357	From 196 Sqn. To 18 OTU.
X3399	To 26 OTU.
X3480	From 75 Sqn. To 419 Sqn.
X3704	From 196 Sqn. To 23 OTU.
Z1670	From 196 Sqn. Crashed in Yorkshire during air-test 3.4.43.
Z1696	To 18 OTU.
BJ715	From 196 Sqn. To 30 OTU.
BJ755 AL-Z	From 425 Sqn. Crashed soon after take-off from East Moor when bound for Essen 5.3.43.
BJ798	From 466 Sqn. Crashed on landing at Henley while training 24.2.43.
BJ799	To 30 OTU.
BJ908	From 466 Sqn. To 23 OTU.

BJ920 AL-E	FTR Bochum 29/30.3.43.
BK146	To 30 OTU.
BK162 AL-B	FTR Mannheim 16/17.4.43.
BK163 AL-H	FTR Lorient 26/27.1.43.
BK429 AL-Q	FTR from mining sortie 9/10.3.43.
BK430	From 196 Sqn. To 20 OTU.
BK432 AL-S	FTR from mining sortie 21/22.1.43.
BK499	From 196 Sqn. To 86 OTU.
BK540 AL-C	FTR Bochum 29/30.3.43.
DF624	From 156 Sqn. Abandoned over Yorkshire during training 21.12.42.
DF625	From 466 Sqn. To 26 OTU.
HE160 AL-R	To 420 Sqn.
HE161	To 196 Sqn.
HE162	To 196 Sqn.
HE163	To 196 Sqn.
HE164	To 466 Sqn.
HE165	To 196 Sqn.
HE166	To 196 Sqn.
HE167	To 196 Sqn.
HE168	To 196 Sqn.
HE169	To 196 Sqn.
HE170	To 196 Sqn.
HE171	To 196 Sqn.
HE172	To 17 OTU.
HE350	To 1485 Flt.
HE365	To 1485 Flt.
HE382 AL-Y	FTR Duisburg 26/27.4.43.
HE414 AL-H	Crash-landed at Exeter on return from a mining sortie 21.4.43.
HE423 AL-O	FTR Duisburg 12/13.5.43.
HE429	To 27 OTU.
HE430	To 20 OTU.
HE572 AL-K	To 432 Sqn.
HE589 AL-V	From 424 Sqn. To 83 OTU.
HE593 AL-Z	FTR Düsseldorf 11/12.6.43.
HE595	From 425 Sqn. To 21 OTU.
HE635	To 83 OTU.
HE636 AL-Q	FTR Frankfurt 10/11.4.43.
HE684	From 424 Sqn. To 428 Sqn.
HE737 AL-B	From 424 Sqn. FTR Duisburg 26/27.4.43.
HE801	To 20 OTU.
HE803 AL-W	FTR Essen 25/26.7.43.
HE820	To 432 Sqn.

HE821	To 27 OTU.
HE823	To 23 OTU.
HE824	To 23 OTU.
HE865 AL-A	From 425 Sqn. To 20 OTU.
HE912	To 11 OTU.
HE913 AL-L	FTR Duisburg 12/13.5.43.
HE914	To 30 OTU.
HE915	To 17 OTU.
HE981 AL-T	From 428 Sqn. FTR Krefeld 21/22.6.43.
HE991	From 426 Sqn. To 83 OTU.
HE992	To 82 OTU.
HE993	To 18 OTU.
HF457 AL-H	FTR Mülheim 22/23.6.43.
HF495	From 428 Sqn. To 28 OTU.
HF514	To 82 OTU.
HF515	To 1485 Flt.
HF541	To 1485 Flt.
HF542 AL-O	FTR Düsseldorf 11/12.6.43.
HF600	From 428 Sqn. To 17 OTU.
HZ260 AL-K	FTR from mining sortie 2/3.3.43.
HZ303	Crashed in Yorkshire during an air-test 14.4.43.
HZ312 AL-F	FTR Mülheim 22/23.6.43.
HZ354	To 20 OTU.
HZ355 AL-G	From 425 Sqn. FTR Düsseldorf 11/12.6.43.
HZ363	To 27 OTU.
HZ470	From 424 Sqn. To 83 OTU.
HZ471 AL-M	From 425 Sqn. FTR Wuppertal 29/30.5.43.
HZ473	To 311 FTU.
HZ482	To 26 OTU.
HZ517 AL-M	FTR Krefeld 21/22.6.43.
HZ519 AL-L	FTR Krefeld 21/22.6.43.
HZ520 AL-Z	FTR Krefeld 21/22.6.43.
HZ521 AL-W	FTR Wuppertal 24/25.6.43.
JA111	To 16 OTU.
JA113	To 26 OTU.
JA114 AL-A	FTR Hamburg 27/28.7.43.
JA115	To 17 OTU.
LN281 AL-V	To 14 OTU.
LN296 AL-P	FTR Cologne 3/4.7.43.
LN438	From 424 Sqn. Crashed on landing at East Moor while training 4.5.43.
LN439 AL-N	From 424 Sqn. FTR Bochum 13/14.5.43.
LN444	To 17 OTU.
LN447	To 17 OTU.

LN448	To 18 OTU.
LN449	To 27 OTU.
MS474	To 17 OTU.
MS487 AL-B/C	FTR Duisburg 26/27.3.43.
MS488	To 196 Sqn.
MS489	To 431 Sqn.
Halifax	From September 1943 to March 1945.
HX339 AL-D	From 427 Sqn. SOC 30.9.44.
HX352 AL-L	From 433 Sqn. FTR Aachen 24/25.5.44.
JB893	From 408 Sqn. To 1659 CU.
JB967	From 408 Sqn. To 419 Sqn via 1659 CU.
JB968	From 408 Sqn. To 433 Sqn.
JB969	From 408 Sqn. To 419 Sqn.
JB971	From 408 Sqn. To 419 Sqn.
JD164 AL-K	From 408 Sqn. Ditched off south coast on return from Stuttgart 26/27.11.43.
JD212	From A&AEE. To 419 Sqn.
JD268	From 408 Sqn. To 1659 CU.
JD271	From 408 Sqn. To 428 Sqn.
JD274	From 408 Sqn. To 428 Sqn.
JD275 AL-T	From 408 Sqn. FTR Mannheim 18/19.11.43.
JD278	From 408 Sqn. To 428 Sqn.
JD317	From 408 Sqn. To 1659 CU.
JD318 AL-F	From 408 Sqn. FTR Berlin 29/30.12.43.
JD323 AL-S	From 408 Sqn. FTR Hanover 8/9.10.43.
JD325 AL-F	From 419 Sqn. FTR Frankfurt 25/26.11.43.
JD326 AL-P	From 408 Sqn. FTR Düsseldorf 3/4.11.43.
JD327 AL-F	From 408 Sqn. Abandoned over Sussex on return from Frankfurt 5.10.43.
JD332 AL-U	From 408 Sqn. FTR Kassel 22/23.10.43.
JD333 AL-W	From 408 Sqn. Crash-landed soon after take-off for Stuttgart 26.11.43.
JD361 AL-Y	From 408 Sqn. FTR Leipzig 3/4.12.43.
JD363 AL-J	From 408 Sqn. FTR Kassel 22/23.10.43.
JD371	From 77 Sqn. Returned to 77 Sqn.
JD372	From 408 Sqn. To 419 Sqn.
JD374 AL-M	From 408 Sqn. FTR Leipzig 3/4.12.43.
JD384	From 408 Sqn. To 1666 CU.
JD386	From 408 Sqn. To 428 Sqn and back. To 428 Sqn.
JD411 AL-A	From 408 Sqn. FTR Frankfurt 25/26.11.43.
LK656	From 427 Sqn. To 434 Sqn.
LK661	From 428 Sqn. To 1664 CU.
LK662 AL-Q	From 428 Sqn. FTR Leipzig 19/20.2.44.

LK684	From 427 Sqn. To 1666 CU.
LK694	From 427 Sqn. To 434 Sqn.
LK697 AL-D	From 434 Sqn. FTR Berlin 28/29.1.44.
LK734 AL-C	From 431 Sqn. Force-landed near Leeming while training 2.1.44.
LK735	From 431 Sqn. To 427 Sqn.
LK746 AL-K	From 427 Sqn. FTR Berlin 28/29.1.44.
LK799	To 434 Sqn.
LK800 AL-N	FTR Nuremberg 30/31.3.44.
LK801	To 434 Sqn.
LK802 AL-F	FTR Düsseldorf 22/23.4.44.
LK803	To 432 Sqn.
LK804 AL-Q	Ditched in Channel on return from Nuremberg 31.3.44.
LK805 AL-H	FTR Berlin 24/25.3.44.
LK806	
LK924	From 428 Sqn. To 434 Sqn.
LK930	From 428 Sqn. To 1664 CU.
LK947	From 428 Sqn. To 434 Sqn.
LK965	From 427 Sqn. To 434 Sqn.
LK972	From 427 Sqn. To 431 Sqn.
LK974 AL-Z	From 427 Sqn. FTR Leipzig 19/20.2.44.
LK975	From 427 Sqn. To 434 Sqn.
LK993 AL-J	From 431 Sqn. FTR Leipzig 19/20.2.44.
LK995 AL-C	From 434 Sqn. FTR Frankfurt 25/26.11.43.
LL153	From 427 Sqn. To 431 Sqn.
LL167	From 427 Sqn. To 434 Sqn.
LL168	From 427 Sqn. To 434 Sqn.
LL170	From 427 Sqn. To 431 Sqn.
LL171 AL-U	From 427 Sqn. To 434 Sqn.
LL172	From 427 Sqn. To 431 Sqn.
LL178	From 427 Sqn. To 434 Sqn.
LL194	From 427 Sqn. To 77 Sqn.
LL196	From 427 Sqn. Crashed on take-off from Leeming while training 1.2.44.
LL197 AL-L	From 427 Sqn. FTR Berlin 20/21.1.44.
LL283	To 1664 CU.
LL286	To 1659 CU.
LL547	From 432 Sqn. To 425 Sqn.
LV830 AL-Q	From 427 Sqn. To 187 Sqn.
LV860	From 415 Sqn. To 420 Sqn.
LV866	From 10 Sqn. To 520 Sqn.
LV913 AL-N	Crashed on take-off from Leeming for air-test 13.7.44.

LV914 AL-V	FTR Berlin 24/25.3.44.
LV941 AL-V	From 433 Sqn. To 425 Sqn.
LV942 AL-Q	From 427 Sqn.
LV950 AL-C	FTR Coquereaux 31.7/1.8.44.
LV963 AL-V	FTR Düsseldorf 22/23.4.44.
LV964 AL-T	FTR Hanover 5/6.1.45.
LV965 AL-J	Crashed on landing at Old Buckenham (USAAF) on return from Bochum 9.10.44.
LV967	From 433 Sqn. To 1664 CU.
LV969	To 520 Sqn.
LV973 AL-X	FTR Versailles 10/11.6.44.
LV989 AL-R	Crashed in Yorkshire when bound for Le Mans 23.5.44.
LV993	To 1664 CU.
LV996 AL-K	From 427 Sqn. Crashed in Kent on return from Chemnitz 5.3.45.
LW122 AL-F	From 415 Sqn. To 425 Sqn.
LW124 AL-N	FTR Aachen 24/25.5.44.
LW127 AL-F	FTR Mondville 18.7.44.
LW128	Abandoned over Oxfordshire on return from Acheres 8.6.44.
LW132 AL-H	FTR Chantilly 7/8.8.44.
LW136 AL-Z	FTR Calais 24.9.44.
LW137 AL-K	FTR Aachen 24/25.5.44.
LW139 AL-P	Crashed in Yorkshire while training 23.2.45.
LW161	To 1665 CU.
LW162	To 187 Sqn.
LW163	To 427 Sqn.
LW279	To 428 Sqn.
LW285	To 428 Sqn.
LW365	To 427 Sqn.
LW370	From 424 Sqn. To 427 Sqn.
LW412	To 431 Sqn.
LW415 AL-K	From 425 Sqn. FTR St Ghislain 1/2.5.44.
LW684	To 434 Sqn.
LW685 AL-C	Ditched in the North Sea off Scotland during training 10.3.44.
LW688 AL-J	FTR Berlin 24/25.3.44.
LW689	To 51 Sqn.
LW690 AL-T	FTR Stuttgart 15/16.3.44.
LW691	To 296 Sqn.
LW694	To 620 Sqn.
LW713	To 434 Sqn.
LW714	To 434 Sqn.

MZ282	From 431 Sqn. To 427 Sqn.
MZ285 AL-U	From 433 Sqn. To 427 Sqn.
MZ288 AL-O	From 431 Sqn. FTR Duisburg 30.11/1.12.44.
MZ295 AL-Y	From 427 Sqn. FTR Bourg Leopold 27/28.5.44.
MZ302 AL-E	FTR Metz 28/29.6.44.
MZ303 AL-R	To 427 Sqn.
MZ314 AL-W	FTR Duisburg 30.11/1.12.44.
MZ318 AL-C/F	From 427 Sqn. SOC 10.4.45.
MZ357 AL-N	From 427 Sqn. To 425 Sqn.
MZ362 AL-Y	FTR Stuttgart 25/26.7.44.
MZ377 AL-D	FTR Castrop-Rauxel 21/22.11.44.
MZ424 AL-Z	Destroyed on the ground when 207 Sqn Lancaster PD290 blew up at Spilsby 1.11.44.
MZ427 AL-E	FTR Magdeburg 16/17.1.45.
MZ435	To 434 Sqn.
MZ447	To 434 Sqn.
MZ453 AL-J	FTR Duisburg 14.10.44.
MZ463 AL-J	FTR Osnabrück 6/7.12.44.
MZ474 AL-B	To 415 Sqn.
MZ478	
MZ493	To 425 Sqn.
MZ672 AL-B	From 432 Sqn. To 425 Sqn.
MZ755	From 427 Sqn.
MZ824 AL-G	Damaged beyond repair when 207 Sqn Lancaster PD290 blew up at Spilsby 1.11.44.
MZ825 AL-E	FTR Brunswick 12/13.8.44.
MZ864 AL-B	FTR from mining sortie 12/13.9.44.
MZ865 AL-V	FTR from mining sortie 14/15.2.45.
MZ872 AL-Z	From 433 Sqn.
MZ880 AL-H	Damaged beyond repair when 207 Sqn Lancaster PD290 blew up at Spilsby 1.11.44.
MZ900 AL-K	FTR Boulogne 17.9.44.
MZ906 AL-H	FTR Essen 23.10.44.
MZ907	To 408 Sqn.
MZ908	To 408 Sqn.
NA178	To 420 Sqn.
NA179	To 420 Sqn.
NA180	To 425 Sqn.
NA181	To 158 Sqn.
NA201 AL-W	From 415 Sqn. To 415 Sqn.
NP942	To 427 Sqn.
NP943	To 111 OTU.
NP946	To 420 Sqn.
NP952	To EANS.

NP954 AL-T	Damaged beyond repair when 207 Sqn Lancaster PD290 blew up at Spilsby 1.11.44.
NP957	From 427 Sqn. To 425 Sqn.
NR148	From 427 Sqn.
NR173 AL-D	FTR from mining sortie 12/13.1.45.
NR194 AL-X	From 427 Sqn. To 425 Sqn.
NR196 AL-A	From 427 Sqn. To 425 Sqn.
NR197 AL-Z	FTR from mining sortie 28/29.12.44.
NR203 AL-P	From 427 Sqn. Abandoned over Yorkshire while training 21.11.44
NR230 AL-H	From 427 Sqn. To 420 Sqn.
NR256	From 424 Sqn. To 415 Sqn.
PN367 AL-J	To 415 Sqn.
Lancaster	From March 1945.
ME426 AL-C	
ME534 AL-O	
ME536 AL-Q	
ME537 AL-N	
ME538 AL-E	
ME539 AL-A	
ME540 AL-P	
ME543 AL-B	
ND967 AL-O	From 460 Sqn.
NG343 AL-J	
NG344 AL-U	
NG345 AL-V	FTR Hamburg 31.3.45.
NG967 AL-L	
NN701 AL-T	
NX581 AL-W	
PA225 AL-G/H	
PA226 AL-H	
PA272 AL-C	
PA273 AL-R	
PA274 AL-F	
PD209 AL-H/K	From 207 Sqn.
PD324	From 514 Sqn.
RA571 AL-D	
RE153 AL-V	
RE155 AL-X/Y	
RF207 AL-S	
RF252 AL-G	
RF253 AL-W	
RF257 AL-W	
RF259 AL-H	

431 (IROQUOIS) SQUADRON

Motto: Warriors of the Air   Code SE

431 Squadron was formed in 4 Group on 11th of November 1942, and was, in fact the eleventh Canadian bomber squadron to join Bomber Command's ranks. It was equipped with Mk X Wellingtons, but did not begin operations until early March 1943. In mid July the squadron was posted to 6 Group and began to re-equip with Halifaxes. Operations resumed in early October, but the vulnerability of the Mk II and V Halifaxes saw them withdrawn from operations over Germany following the Leipzig catastrophe in February 1944. 431 Squadron contributed to mining operations and interdiction raids until conversion to the Hercules-powered Mk III Halifax was complete in April 1944. From that point the squadron returned to the forefront of operations, ultimately re-equipping with Canadian-built Lancaster Xs in October 1944, and this type saw it through the remainder of the war.

STATIONS

Burn	11.11.42 to 14.07.43
Tholthorpe	15.07.43 to 09.12.43
Croft	10.12.43 to 06.06.45

COMMANDING OFFICERS

Wing Commander J Coverdale	01.12.42 to 22.06.43
Wing Commander W D M Newson	26.06.43 to 10.05.44
Wing Commander H R Dow	14.05.44 to 25.07.44
Wing Commander E M Mitchell	27.07.44 to 10.01.45
Wing Commander R F Davenport	14.01.45 to 11.03.45
Wing Commander W McKinnon	18.03.45 to 15.06.45

AIRCRAFT

Wellington X	11.42 to 07.43
Halifax V/III	07.43 to 10.44
Lancaster X	10.44 to 06.45

OPERATIONAL RECORD

Operations	Sorties	Aircraft Losses	% Losses
168	2,257	57	2.5

Category of Operations

Bombing	Mining
162	6

Halifaxes

Operations	Sorties	Aircraft Losses	% Losses
117	1,461	46	3.1

Category of Operations

Bombing	Mining
111	6

Lancasters

Operations	Sorties	Aircraft Losses	% Losses
51	796	11	1.4

All bombing.

TABLE OF STATISTICS

Out of 59 Lancaster squadrons
51st highest number of Lancaster overall operations in Bomber Command.
50th highest number of Lancaster sorties in Bomber Command.
49th highest number of Lancaster operational losses in Bomber Command.

Out of 32 Halifax squadrons
25th highest number of Halifax overall operations in Bomber Command.
24th highest number of Halifax sorties in Bomber Command.
14th highest number of Halifax operational losses in Bomber Command.

Out of 42 Wellington squadrons
36th highest number of Wellington overall operations in Bomber Command.
38th highest number of Wellington sorties in Bomber Command.
26th highest number of Wellington operational losses in Bomber Command.

Out of 24 squadrons in 4 Group
18th highest number of overall operations in 4 Group.
19th highest number of sorties in 4 Group.
14th highest number of aircraft operational losses in 4 Group.

Out of 12 Wellington squadrons in 4 Group
2nd highest number of overall Wellington operations in 4 Group.
5th highest number of Wellington sorties in 4 Group.
6th highest number of Wellington operational losses in 4 Group.

Out of 15 squadrons in 6 Group
14th highest number of overall operations in 6 Group.
14th highest number of sorties in 6 Group.
9th highest number of aircraft operational losses in 6 Group.

Out of 15 Halifax squadrons in 6 Group
12th highest number of Halifax overall operations in 6 Group.
13th highest number of Halifax sorties in 6 Group.
5th highest number of Halifax operational losses in 6 Group.

Out of 11 Lancaster squadrons in 6 Group
5th highest number of Lancaster overall operations in 6 Group.
4th highest number of Lancaster sorties in 6 Group.
5th highest number of Lancaster operational losses in 6 Group.

AIRCRAFT HISTORIES

Wellington	From November 1942 to July 1943.
HE182 SE-A	FTR Bochum 29/30.3.43.
HE183 SE-J	FTR Bochum 13/14.5.43.
HE184 SE-M	FTR Düsseldorf 11/12.6.43.
HE197	To 17 OTU.
HE198 SE-D	To 17 OTU.
HE199	To 82 OTU.
HE200 SE-P	FTR from mining sortie 21/22.5.43.
HE201 SE-T	To 82 OTU.
HE202 SE-Z	FTR from mining sortie 7/8.3.43.
HE203 SE-B	FTR Wuppertal 29/30.5.43.
HE204	To 17 OTU.
HE205 SE-X	To 18 OTU.
HE213 SE-F	FTR Frankfurt 10/11.4.43.
HE265	To 82 OTU.
HE374 SE-X	FTR Stuttgart 14/15.4.43.
HE379 SE-H	FTR Mannheim 16/17.4.43.
HE392 SE-L	From 196 Sqn. FTR Düsseldorf 11/12.6.43.
HE394 SE-V	From 196 Sqn. FTR Mülheim 22/23.6.43.
HE396	To 6 OTU.
HE440 SE-Y	FTR Duisburg 12/13.5.43.

HE443 SE-O	FTR Cologne 28/29.6.43.
HE476 SE-Z	Crash-landed in Yorkshire on return from Duisburg 27.4.43.
HE502	To 17 OTU.
HE503 SE-S	FTR Duisburg 26/27.3.43.
HE518	From 30 OTU. Returned to 30 OTU.
HE748	To 82 OTU.
HE983	To 18 OTU.
HE990 SE-Z	FTR Düsseldorf 25/26.5.43.
HF518 SE-J	FTR Krefeld 21/22.6.43.
HF543 SE-P	Damaged beyond repair in collision with Halifax DK192 (427 Sqn) on the ground at Oulton on return from Düsseldorf 12.6.43.
HF603	To 166 Sqn.
HF604	To 15 OTU.
HZ357 SE-S	FTR Stuttgart 14/15.4.43.
HZ484	To 466 Sqn.
LN282	To 82 OTU.
LN283	To 82 OTU.
LN284 SE-Q	FTR Cologne 3/4.7.43.
LN290	To 82 OTU.
LN291	To 82 OTU.
LN295	To 27 OTU.
LN403	To 17 OTU.
LN405	To 17 OTU.
LN409	From 425 Sqn. To 17 OTU.
MS475	To 27 OTU.
MS489	From 429 Sqn. To 17 OTU.
Halifax	From July 1943 to October 1944.
DG296	From 1664 CU. To 1664 CU.
DK185	From 427 Sqn. To 1664 CU.
DK236	From 76 Sqn. To 44 MU.
DK246	From 192 Sqn. To 1664 CU.
DK264 SE-C	Crashed while trying to land at Tholthorpe during training 7.11.43.
DK265 SE-C	FTR Hanover 8/9.10.43.
EB137 SE-N	From 1664 CU. FTR Leipzig 3/4.12.43.
EB205	From 428 Sqn. To 1664 CU.
EB275 SE-M	From 428 Sqn. To 1659 CU.
HX346 SE-R	From 158 Sqn. To 420 Sqn.
LK626	From 427 Sqn. Force-landed in North Wales during training 22.2.44.
LK632 SE-M	FTR Mannheim 18/19.11.43.

LK639 SE-E	FTR Kassel 22/23.10.43.
LK640 SE-Q	FTR Mannheim 18/19.11.43.
LK649	From 434 Sqn. Returned to 434 Sqn.
LK657 SE-K	FTR Hanover 8/9.10.43.
LK658 SE-V	From 427 Sqn. To 1667 CU.
LK659 SE-A	From 427 Sqn. FTR Berlin 29/30.12.43.
LK680 SE-R	From 434 Sqn. FTR Magdeburg 21/22.1.44.
LK685 SE-C	From 434 Sqn. FTR Leipzig 3/4.12.43.
LK698 SE-W	From 434 Sqn. Crashed in County Durham while training 5.1.44.
LK701 SE-L	FTR Berlin 29/30.12.43.
LK705 SE-X	FTR from mining sortie 25/26.2.44.
LK708 SE-Y	To 434 Sqn.
LK734	To 429 Sqn.
LK735 SE-O	To 429 Sqn.
LK828 SE-S	To 1659 CU.
LK833 SE-R	FTR Hamburg 28/29.7.44.
LK837 SE-L	FTR Sterkrade/Holten 16/17.6.44.
LK842 SE-N	FTR Montzen 27/28.4.44.
LK845 SE-J	From 51 Sqn. FTR Hamburg 28/29.7.44.
LK868 SE-O	From 432 Sqn. To 171 Sqn.
LK884 SE-X	From 420 Sqn. FTR Haine St Pierre 8/9.5.44.
LK895	Crash-landed at Tholthorpe while training 8.9.43.
LK896 SE-B	To 1664 CU.
LK897	Crashed while landing at Tholthorpe during training 8.10.43.
LK898 SE-O	To 434 Sqn and back. FTR Leipzig 3/4.12.43.
LK905 SE-D	FTR Leipzig 19/20.2.44.
LK918 SE-F	From 434 Sqn. Crashed on landing at Dishforth on return from Berlin 29.1.44.
LK925 SE-R	FTR Kassel 3/4.10.43.
LK927 SE-H	From 428 Sqn. To 1659 CU.
LK952 SE-K	From 428 Sqn. To 1659 CU.
LK963 SE-H	FTR Berlin 28/29.1.44.
LK964 SE-T	FTR Leipzig 19/20.2.44.
LK967 SE-J	FTR Frankfurt 25/26.11.43.
LK968 SE-P	FTR Leipzig 3/4.12.43.
LK972	From 429 Sqn. To 1664 CU.
LK973 SE-E	FTR Frankfurt 25/26.11.43.
LK975 SE-N	From 429 Sqn. To 1667 CU.
LK989 SE-Z	From 427 Sqn. To 1659 CU.
LK991 SE-U	To 1667 CU.
LK993	To 429 Sqn.
LL142 SE-E	From 434 Sqn. To 1659 CU.

LL150 SE-N	Abandoned over Lincolnshire coast on return from Berlin 30/31.1.44.
LL151 SE-P	To 1664 CU.
LL152 SE-U	Destroyed on landing at Croft on return from Amiens 15.3.44.
LL153 SE-X	From 429 Sqn. To 1667 CU.
LL168	From 434 Sqn. To 1659 CU.
LL170	From 429 Sqn. To 434 Sqn.
LL172 SE-B	From 429 Sqn. To 1659 CU.
LL173 SE-C	
LL174 SE-O/Z	To 1664 CU.
LL175 SE-A/G	To 1664 CU.
LL177	To 434 Sqn.
LL179	To 434 Sqn.
LL180	To 428 Sqn and back. To 434 Sqn.
LL181 SE-Q	FTR Berlin 28/29.1.44.
LL225	To 434 Sqn.
LL230	To 1667 CU.
LL231 SE-J	To 1667 CU.
LL232 SE-R	To 434 Sqn.
LL233 SE-Y	To 434 Sqn.
LL245	To 1664 CU.
LL258 SE-W	FTR Montzen with 434 Sqn crew 27/28.4.44.
LL597	To 102 Sqn.
LV944	To 424 Sqn.
LV947	To 424 Sqn.
LV951	To 424 Sqn.
LV953	To 424 Sqn.
LV997	To 424 Sqn.
LV998	To 424 Sqn.
LW385 SE-M	To 190 Sqn.
LW412 SE-F	From 429 Sqn. To 432 Sqn.
LW432 SE-P	From 424 Sqn. Hit by MZ685 (431 Sqn) at Croft while parked 17.7.44.
LW462 SE-B	From 424 Sqn. To 297 Sqn.
LW572 SE-Q	From 427 Sqn. FTR Vaires 18.7.44.
LW576 SE-F	From 427 Sqn. To 432 Sqn and back. To AFEE.
LW614	To 432 Sqn.
MZ282	To 429 Sqn.
MZ288	To 427 Sqn.
MZ364 SE-M	To 425 Sqn.
MZ372 SE-Y	FTR Kiel 16/17.8.44.
MZ375 SE-U	To 420 Sqn.
MZ378 SE-H	To 420 Sqn.

MZ405 SE-C	To 158 Sqn via 434 Sqn on loan.
MZ416	To 415 Sqn.
MZ434 SE-O	FTR Wilhelmshaven 15/16.10.44.
MZ454 SE-X	From 424 Sqn. To 425 Sqn.
MZ455	From 424 Sqn. To 171 Sqn.
MZ456	To 415 Sqn.
MZ509 SE-C	Crashed on take-off from USAAF Membury for transit flight 26.8.44.
MZ514 SE-P	FTR Düsseldorf 22/23.4.44.
MZ517 SE-D	To 432 Sqn.
MZ520 SE-O	FTR Sterkrade/Holten 16/17.6.44.
MZ521 SE-T	FTR Haine St Pierre 8/9.5.44.
MZ522 SE-U	FTR Montzen 27/28.4.44.
MZ526	To 76 Sqn.
MZ529 SE-E	FTR Montzen 27/28.4.44.
MZ536 SE-F	From 432 Sqn. FTR Montzen 27/28.4.44.
MZ537 SE-L/H	From 425 Sqn. FTR Sterkrade/Holten 16/17.6.44.
MZ589 SE-H	From 426 Sqn. FTR Hamburg 28/29.7.44.
MZ597 SE-B	From 426 Sqn. FTR Hamburg 28/29.7.44.
MZ600 SE-N	From 426 Sqn. To 1659 CU.
MZ602 SE-U	From 426 Sqn. FTR Versailles 7/8.6.44.
MZ628 SE-Y	FTR Vaires 18.7.44.
MZ629 SE-B	FTR Leuven 12/13.5.44.
MZ637 SE-E	To 297 Sqn.
MZ655 SE-T	To 1659 CU.
MZ656 SE-X	From 432 Sqn. To 1659 CU.
MZ657 SE-K	Crashed on take-off from Croft when bound for V-weapon site at Biennais 6.7.44.
MZ658 SE-E	Abandoned over Northumberland on return from Brest 26.8.44.
MZ681 SE-V	From 434 Sqn. To 1659 CU.
MZ685 SE-A	Collided with parked Halifax LW432 (431 Sqn) on take-off from Croft while training 17.7.44.
MZ802	To 424 Sqn.
MZ805	To 424 Sqn.
MZ831 SE-K	To 425 Sqn.
MZ853 SE-L	From 434 Sqn. Crashed on landing at Croft on return from Acquet 1.8.44.
MZ858 SE-Y	FTR Stuttgart 25/26.7.44.
MZ859 SE-A	FTR Hamburg 28/29.7.44.
MZ860 SE-P	To 425 Sqn.
MZ861 SE-Q	To 415 Sqn.
MZ881	To 434 Sqn.
MZ882 SE-B	To 415 Sqn.

MZ904	From 408 Sqn. To EANS.
MZ907	From 434 Sqn. To 415 Sqn.
MZ920 SE-C	To 434 Sqn.
MZ922	From 434 Sqn. To 415 Sqn.
NA494	From 192 Sqn. To 434 Sqn.
NA498 SE-G	To 1659 CU.
NA499 SE-W	To 1659 CU.
NA514 SE-B	FTR Sterkrade/Holten 16/17.6.44.
NA516	To 432 Sqn.
NA517	To 432 Sqn.
NA550 SE-U	From 432 Sqn. To 434 Sqn.
NP959	To 434 Sqn.
NP999	From 424 Sqn. To 425 Sqn.
NR121 SE-B	From 433 Sqn. To 434 Sqn.
NR122 SE-Y	From 433 Sqn. To 415 Sqn.
NR123	From 433 Sqn. To 420 Sqn.
NR138	To 420 Sqn.
NR139	To 420 Sqn.
NR141	From 434 Sqn. To 420 Sqn.
Lancaster	From October 1944.
KB741 SE-Y	From 428 Sqn. To 434 Sqn.
KB773 SE-A	From 428 Sqn.
KB774 SE-D	From 419 Sqn.
KB788 SE-C	From 419 Sqn. Damaged beyond repair during operation to Duisburg 30.11/1.12.44.
KB796 SE-A	From 419 Sqn.
KB801 SE-S	From 419 Sqn.
KB802 SE-V	From 419 Sqn.
KB803 SE-N	From 428 Sqn. Crash-landed in Yorkshire while training 26.1.45.
KB806 SE-X	From 428 Sqn. FTR Merseburg 14/15.1.45.
KB807 SE-B	From 419 Sqn.
KB808 SE-Y	From 428 Sqn. FTR Hildesheim 22.3.45.
KB809 SE-Q	From 419 Sqn. FTR Dortmund 20/21.2.45.
KB810 SE-H	
KB811 SE-T	
KB812 SE-F	
KB813 SE-S	Crashed in Bedfordshire while training 25.10.44.
KB815 SE-K	From 419 Sqn. FTR Hagen 15/16.3.45.
KB816	To 434 Sqn.
KB817 SE-P	From 419 Sqn. FTR Oberhausen 1/2.11.44.
KB818 SE-G	Crashed while landing at Ford on return from Goch 7/8.2.45.

KB819 SE-J	
KB821 SE-P	FTR Hanau 6/7.1.45.
KB822 SE-W	From 428 Sqn. FTR Wangerooge following collision with KB831 (431 Sqn) 25.4.45.
KB823 SE-E	From 428 Sqn.
KB827 SE-M	
KB831 SE-E	From 419 Sqn. FTR Wangerooge following collision with KB822 (431 Sqn) 25.4.45.
KB835	To 434 Sqn.
KB836	To 434 Sqn.
KB837 SE-X	
KB839	To 419 Sqn.
KB847 SE-S	
KB849	To 434 Sqn.
KB852	To 434 Sqn.
KB853 SE-A	From 434 Sqn. FTR Essen 11.3.45.
KB856 SE-K	
KB858 SE-G	FTR Chemnitz 5/6.3.45.
KB859 SE-U	FTR Hamburg 31.3.45.
KB861 SE-Q	
KB868 SE-E	
KB871	From 419 Sqn.
KB872 SE-N	
KB874 SE-C	From TRE. Crash-landed at Manston on return from Hanover 25.3.45.
KB885	To 434 Sqn.
KB886	
KB888 SE-O	From 419 Sqn.
KB893	To 434 Sqn.
KB900 SE-C	From 428 Sqn.
KB908	To 428 Sqn.
KB915	To 419 Sqn.
KB922	
KB946	
ME534	

Heaviest Single Loss

28/29.7.44	Hamburg. 5 Halifaxes.

432 (LEASIDE) SQUADRON

Motto: Saeviter ad Lucem (Ferociously towards the light)   Code QO

432 Squadron was formed in 6 Group on the 1st of May 1943, and was initially equipped with Wellingtons. A little over three weeks later the squadron went to war for the first time, and continued to carry out bombing and mining operations, actually taking part in the final bombing operation by Bomber Command Wellingtons. Conversion to Mk II Lancasters took place in October, and operations resumed in November in time to participate in all but the first few rounds of the winter campaign, when Berlin was the main objective. Hercules-powered Halifaxes began to arrive at the start of February 1944, and these would see the squadron through to the end of the war.

STATIONS

Skipton-on-Swale	01.05.43 to 18.09.43
East Moor	19.09.43 to 15.05.45

COMMANDING OFFICERS

Wing Commander H W Kerby	01.05.43 to 29.07.43
Wing Commander W A McKay	30.07.43 to 30.05.44
Wing Commander J F K MacDonald	31.05.44 to 25.07.44
Wing Commander A D R Lowe	26.07.44 to 28.09.44
Wing Commander J F K MacDonald	29.09.44 to 27.01.45
Squadron Leader S H Minhinnick	29.01.45 to 27.02.45
Wing Commander K A France	28.02.45 to 15.05.45

AIRCRAFT

Wellington X	01.05.43 to 10.43
Lancaster II	25.10.43 to 02.44
Halifax III	02.44 to 07.44
Halifax VII	06.44 to 15.05.45

OPERATIONAL RECORD

Operations	Sorties	Aircraft Losses	% Losses
230	3,100	65	2.1

Category of Operations

Bombing	Mining
201	29

Wellingtons

Operations	Sorties	Aircraft Losses	% Losses
47	494	16	3.2

Category of Operations

Bombing	Mining
18	29

Lancasters

Operations	Sorties	Aircraft Losses	% Losses
16	190	8	4.2

All bombing.

Halifaxes

Operations	Sorties	Aircraft Losses	% Losses
167	2,416	41	1.7

All bombing.

TABLE OF STATISTICS

Out of 59 Lancaster squadrons

57th highest number of Lancaster overall operations in Bomber Command.

57th highest number of Lancaster sorties in Bomber Command.

50th equal (with 186 Sqn) highest number of Lancaster operational losses in Bomber Command.

Out of 32 Halifax squadrons

13th highest number of Halifax overall operations in Bomber Command.

16th highest number of Halifax sorties in Bomber Command.

16th highest number of Halifax operational losses in Bomber Command.

Out of 42 Wellington squadrons

37th highest number of Wellington overall operations in Bomber Command.

29th highest number of Wellington sorties in Bomber Command.

30th equal (with 420 Sqn) highest number of Wellington operational losses in Bomber Command.

Out of 15 squadrons in 6 Group
7th highest number of overall operations in 6 Group.
6th highest number of sorties in 6 Group.
7th highest number of aircraft operational losses in 6 Group.

Out of 8 Wellington squadrons in 6 Group
3rd highest number of Wellington overall operations in 6 Group.
Highest number of Wellington sorties in 6 Group.
5th highest number of Wellington operational losses in 6 Group.

Out of 11 Lancaster squadrons in 6 Group
10th highest number of Lancaster overall operations in 6 Group.
10th highest number of Lancaster sorties in 6 Group.
6th highest number of Lancaster operational losses in 6 Group.

Out of 15 Halifax squadrons in 6 Group
3rd highest number of Halifax overall operations in 6 Group.
5th highest number of Halifax sorties in 6 Group.
7th highest number of Halifax operational losses in 6 Group.

AIRCRAFT HISTORIES

Wellington	From May 1943 to October 1943.
HE222	From 427 Sqn. To 30 OTU.
HE279	From 427 Sqn. To 18 OTU.
HE294 QO-P	From 427 Sqn. FTR Essen 27/28.5.43.
HE348 QO-P	FTR from mining sortie 12/13.8.43.
HE352	To 12 OTU.
HE353 QO-R	FTR Aachen 13/14.7.43.
HE514 QO-K	From 425 Sqn. Ditched off Norfolk coast on return from Essen 25/26.7.43.
HE553 QO-S	From 427 Sqn. Crashed in Yorkshire on return from Wuppertal 29/30.5.43.
HE555	From 427 Sqn. To 17 OTU.
HE572	From 429 Sqn. To 26 OTU.
HE630 QO-B	From 427 Sqn. Crashed in Kent on return from Cologne 3/4.7.43.
HE637	From 427 Sqn. To 20 OTU.
HE638	From 427 Sqn. To 26 OTU.
HE653	From 427 Sqn. To 27 OTU.
HE684	From 428 Sqn. To 20 OTU.
HE686	From 427 Sqn. To 17 OTU.
HE688 QO-V	From 427 Sqn. To 17 OTU.

HE698	From 427 Sqn. To 27 OTU.
HE729 QO-U	From 427 Sqn. FTR Düsseldorf 11/12.6.43.
HE732	From 427 Sqn. To 30 OTU.
HE800	To 18 OTU.
HE817 QO-K	FTR Hanover 27/28.9.43.
HE818	To 18 OTU.
HE820	From 429 Sqn. To 15 OTU.
HE825	To 23 OTU.
HE873	From 427 Sqn. To 428 Sqn.
HE906 QO-H	From 427 Sqn. FTR Hamburg 2/3.8.43.
HE911	From 428 Sqn. To 83 OTU.
HE918	From 428 Sqn. To 82 OTU.
HF456	To 12 OTU.
HF493 QO-C	Abandoned over Kent on return from Cologne 3/4.7.43.
HF494	Crash-landed in Yorkshire during training 19.7.43.
HF540 QO-G	From 426 Sqn. Crashed on landing at Skipton-on-Swale while training 12.8.43.
HF546	
HF567	
HF568 QO-Y	FTR from a mining sortie 26/27.6.43.
HF571	From 428 Sqn. To 26 OTU.
HF572 QO-J	From 426 Sqn. FTR Wuppertal 24/25.6.43.
HF599	From 426 Sqn. To 14 OTU.
HF638	From 22 OTU. To 26 OTU.
HZ264	From 427 Sqn. To 17 OTU.
HZ272	From 427 Sqn. To 82 OTU.
HZ469	From 426 Sqn. To 82 OTU.
HZ480	From 426 Sqn. To 18 OTU.
HZ481 QO-W	From 426 Sqn. FTR Cologne 3/4.7.43.
HZ483	To 84 OTU.
HZ484	From 300 Sqn. To 84 OTU.
HZ518 QO-A	From 466 Sqn. FTR Wuppertal 24/25.6.43.
JA118 QO-G	FTR Mönchengladbach 30/31.8.43.
JA119	Broke up over Yorkshire during an air-test 16.7.43.
JA128	To 16 OTU.
JA451	To 300 Sqn.
LN236	To 12 OTU.
LN240	To 18 OTU.
LN241	To 23 OTU.
LN285 QO-K	FTR Cologne 3/4.7.43.
LN294 QO-E	FTR Hamburg 29/30.7.43.
LN394	To 14 OTU.

LN395 QO-R	Crashed while trying to land at Skipton-on-Swale while training 19.8.43.
LN429	From 427 Sqn. To 83 OTU.
LN435 QO-J	From 427 Sqn. FTR Wuppertal 29/30.5.43.
LN451 QO-W	FTR Hanover 8/9.10.43.
LN452	To 29 OTU.
LN454	To 84 OTU.
LN457	From 1585 Flt. To 1690 Flt.
LN546	To 23 OTU.
LN547 QO-G	FTR Hanover 22/23.9.43.
LN554 QO-P	Ditched in North Sea on return from Hanover 22/23.9.43.
LN589	To 29 OTU.
LN706	To 20 OTU.
LN708	To 26 OTU.
MS482	From 40 Sqn. To 20 OTU.
MS485 QO-T	From 424 Sqn. Destroyed by fire at Skipton-on-Swale 15.6.43.
Lancaster	From October 1943 to February 1944.
DS633	From 424 Sqn. To 115 Sqn via 1678 CU.
DS739 QO-Y	From 408 Sqn. FTR Berlin 2/3.1.44.
DS740 QO-Z	From 426 Sqn. FTR Brunswick 14/15.1.44.
DS757 QO-D	From 426 Sqn. Returned to 426 Sqn.
DS788 QO-E	To 408 Sqn.
DS789 QO-V	To 426 Sqn.
DS792 QO-U	Stored at 46 MU.
DS794 QO-W	To 426 Sqn.
DS829 QO-A	From 426 Sqn. Returned to 426 Sqn.
DS830 QO-S	To 426 Sqn.
DS831 QO-N	FTR Berlin 16/17.12.43.
DS832 QO-K	Abandoned over Yorkshire on return from Berlin 16/17.12.43.
DS839	To 1679 CU.
DS843 QO-O	FTR Magdeburg 21/22.1.44.
DS844 QO-H	From 426 Sqn. To 408 Sqn.
DS847	Abandoned over Lincolnshire after engine fire during training 16.11.43.
DS848 QO-R	To 426 Sqn.
DS850 QO-M	FTR Brunswick 14/15.1.44.
DS851 QO-D	Crashed on landing at Skipton-on-Swale on return from Berlin2/3.12.43.
DS852 QO-C	To 426 Sqn.
LL617 QO-J	To 426 Sqn.

LL618 QO-F	FTR Berlin 2/3.12.43.
LL632 QO-G	To 408 Sqn.
LL636 QO-B	To 408 Sqn.
LL637 QO-Z	To 408 Sqn.
LL638 QO-M	FTR Berlin 27/28.1.44.
LL647 QO-D	To 426 Sqn.
LL686 QO-F	Crashed on approach to East Moor while training 2.2.44.
LL718 QO-K	To 408 Sqn.
LL719 QO-U	To 408 Sqn.
LL723 QO-H	From 426 Sqn. To 408 Sqn.
LL724 QO-N	FTR Magdeburg 21/22.1.44.
LL725 QO-O	To 408 Sqn.

Halifax	From February 1944.
LK754 QO-Z	To 76 Sqn.
LK755	From 427 Sqn. To 426 Sqn.
LK761	Crashed in Yorkshire while training 15.2.44.
LK764	To 434 Sqn.
LK765	To 415 Sqn.
LK766	To 415 Sqn.
LK779 QO-W	From 429 Sqn. FTR Frankfurt 22/23.3.44.
LK807 QO-J	FTR Montzen 27/28.4.44.
LK811 QO-N	FTR Bourg Leopold 27/28.5.44.
LK868	To 431 Sqn.
LV547	To 429 Sqn.
LW412	From 431 Sqn. To 1666 CU.
LW437	From 424 Sqn. To 434 Sqn.
LW552	From 424 Sqn. To 415 Sqn.
LW576	From 431 Sqn. To 431 Sqn.
LW582 QO-N	FTR Acheres 7/8.6.44.
LW583 QO-L	FTR Haine St Pierre 8/9.5.44.
LW584 QO-Y	FTR Frankfurt 22/23.3.44.
LW592 QO-A	FTR Montzen 27/28.4.44.
LW593 QO-O	FTR Berlin 24/25.3.44.
LW594 QO-G	FTR Haine St Pierre 8/9.5.44.
LW595	To 415 Sqn.
LW596 QO-D	To 434 Sqn.
LW597 QO-C	FTR Augsburg 25/26.2.44.
LW598	Crashed in Yorkshire 9.6.44.
LW614 QO-S	From 431 Sqn. Crashed in Yorkshire while training 12.4.44.
LW615 QO-U	Crashed on landing at East Moor during training 7.5.44.

LW616 QO-R	FTR Cambrai 12/13.6.44.
LW617	To 158 Sqn.
LW643 QO-E	FTR Noisy-le-Sec 18/19.4.44.
LW682 QO-C	
LW686	To 415 Sqn.
LW687 QO-Z	FTR Nuremberg 30/31.3.44.
MZ504 QO-C	FTR Nuremberg 30/31.3.44.
MZ506 QO-X	FTR Le Mans 22/23.5.44.
MZ536	To 431 Sqn.
MZ585	To 1659 CU.
MZ586	To 415 Sqn.
MZ588 QO-W	FTR Montzen 27/28.4.44.
MZ590	To 415 Sqn.
MZ591 QO-K	FTR Metz 28/29.6.44.
MZ601 QO-A	FTR Cambrai 12/13.6.44.
MZ632	To 1665 CU.
MZ633 QO-B	To 415 Sqn.
MZ653	
MZ654	To 1666 CU.
MZ656	To 431 Sqn.
MZ660	To 1666 CU.
MZ672	To 429 Sqn.
MZ674	To 425 Sqn.
MZ686	To 415 Sqn.
NA500 QO-G	FTR Boulogne 11/12.5.44.
NA516 QO-A	From 431 Sqn. To 434 Sqn and back. FTR Sterkrade/Holten 16/17.6.44.
NA517	From 431 Sqn. To 415 Sqn.
NA527	To 1665 CU.
NA550	To 434 Sqn.
NP687 QO-A	FTR Stuttgart 25/26.7.44.
NP688 QO-X	FTR Stuttgart 25/26.7.44.
NP689 QO-M	FTR Hagen 15/16.3.45.
NP690 QO-G	Crashed on take-off from East Moor when bound for Bremen 18.8.44.
NP691 QO-V	Damaged by night fighter during operation to Grevenbroich 14/15.1.45, and damaged beyond economical repair.
NP692 QO-D	Crash-landed at Woodbridge on return from Bottrop 27.9.44.
NP693 QO-K	
NP694 QO-R	
NP695 QO-K	FTR Osnabrück 6/7.12.44.
NP697 QO-F	

NP698 QO-X/U
NP699 QO-O   FTR Duisburg 17/18.12.44.
NP701 QO-G   FTR Duisburg 17/18.12.44.
NP702 QO-B   FTR Hamburg 28/29.7.44.
NP703 QO-H
NP704 QO-L   Wanne-Eickel 2/3.2.45.
NP705 QO-Y
NP706 QO-J   FTR Caen 18.7.44.
NP707
NP708 QO-E
NP710   To 408 Sqn.
NP712   To 408 Sqn.
NP716   To 408 Sqn.
NP718   To 408 Sqn.
NP719 QO-N   FTR Kiel 15/16.9.44.
NP721 QO-X   From 426 Sqn. Crashed on take-off from East
                   Moor when bound for Soest 5.12.44.
NP722 QO-N   Crashed on landing at Manston on return from
                   Essen 23.10.44.
NP723 QO-D   FTR Wilhelmshaven 15/16.10.44.
NP736
NP738 QO-J   Crashed on approach to Woodbridge on return
                   from Wanne-Eickel 12.10.44.
NP755
NP759 QO-C   FTR Hanover 5/6.1.45.
NP774
NP778   To 426 Sqn.
NP779   To 426 Sqn.
NP797 QO-N   To 426 Sqn.
NP801 QO-N   FTR Bochum 9/10.10.44.
NP802 QO-S
NP803 QO-I   FTR Worms 21/22.2.45.
NP804   To 408 Sqn.
NP805 QO-J   Crashed on take-off for air-test at East Moor
                   16.4.45.
NP807   To 408 Sqn.
NP808   To 426 Sqn.
NP812
NP813   To 426 Sqn.
NP815 QO-A   From 426 Sqn. FTR Gelsenkirchen 6.11.44.
NP817 QO-D   From 426 Sqn. FTR Hanover 5/6.1.45.
NP961   From 434 Sqn. To 415 Sqn.
NP968   To 466 Sqn.
NP971   To 466 Sqn.

NR145	From 434 Sqn. To 415 Sqn.
PN208	From 408 Sqn.
PN224	
PN233	
PN235 QO-S	Crashed on take-off for air-test at East Moor 16.4.45.
PN236	To 415 Sqn.
PN237	To 415 Sqn.
PN241 QO-I	To 1665 CU
RG448	From 426 Sqn.
RG449 QO-S	From 426 Sqn. FTR Chemnitz 14/15.2.45.
RG450 QO-Q	From 408 Sqn.
RG451 QO-D	FTR Worms 21/22.2.45.
RG454	From 426 Sqn.
RG455 QO-X	FTR Monheim 20/21.2.45.
RG475 QO-L	Shot down by British AA on Essex coast during operation to Chemnitz 5/6.3.45.
RG476 QO-T	FTR Worms 21/22.2.45.
RG478	
RG479	

433 (PORCUPINE) SQUADRON

Motto: Qui s'y frotte, s'y pique (Who opposes it gets hurt)   Code BM

433 Squadron was formed on the 25th of September 1943 as the last Canadian unit to be formed in 6 Group. It took some time for the squadron to work up, and initially trained in borrowed Wellingtons. The first Halifax Mk III arrived on the 3rd of November, and thus 433 Squadron became the second in the Command to equip with the improved, Hercules-powered variant. Operations began with four mining sorties on the night of the 2nd/3rd of January 1944. During the course of January 1945 a gradual conversion to Lancasters took place, and these saw the squadron through to war's end.

STATIONS

Skipton-on-Swale	25.09.43 to 30.08.45

COMMANDING OFFICERS

Wing Commander C B Sinton DFC	09.11.43 to 30.05.44
Wing Commander A J Lewington	31.05.44 to 05.11.44

Wing Commander G A Tambling   06.11.44 to 01.08.45

AIRCRAFT

Halifax III   11.43 to 01.45
Lancaster I/III   01.45 to 10.45

OPERATIONAL RECORD

Operations	Sorties	Aircraft Losses	% Losses
204	2,316	31	1.3

Category of Operations

Bombing	Mining
151	53

Halifax

Operations	Sorties	Aircraft Losses	% Losses
162	1,926	28	1.5

Category of Operations

Bombing	Mining
123	39

Lancaster

Operations	Sorties	Aircraft losses	% Losses
42	390	3	0.8

Category of Operations

Bombing	Mining
28	14

4 Halifaxes and 1 Lancaster were lost in crashes in the UK.

TABLE OF STATISTICS

Out of 30 Halifax squadrons

(Excluding 100 Group)

15th equal (with 425 Sqn) highest number of overall Halifax operations in Bomber Command.
20th highest number of Halifax sorties in Bomber Command.
21st highest number of Halifax operational losses in Bomber Command.

Out of 59 Lancaster squadrons

53rd highest number of Lancaster operations in Bomber Command.
54th highest number of Lancaster sorties in Bomber Command.
56th highest number of Lancaster operational losses in Bomber Command.

Out of 15 squadrons in 6 Group

8th highest number of overall operations in 6 Group.
13th highest number of sorties in 6 Group.
13th highest number of aircraft operational losses in 6 Group.

Out of 15 Halifax squadrons in 6 Group

4th equal (with 425 Sqn) highest number of Halifax operations in 6 Group.
8th highest number of Halifax sorties in 8 Group.
8th equal (with 425 Sqn) highest number of Halifax operational losses in 6 Group.

Out of 11 Lancaster squadrons in 6 Group

6th equal (with 424 Sqn) highest number of Lancaster operations in 6 Group.
7th highest number of Lancaster sorties in 6 Group.
9th highest number of Lancaster operational losses in 6 Group.

AIRCRAFT HISTORIES

Halifax	From November 1943 to January 1945.
HX230 BM-P	FTR Leipzig 19/20.2.44.
HX245	Crashed on take-off from Skipton-on-Swale while training 19.12.43.
HX265 BM-D	Ditched off north-east coast on return from Berlin 29.1.44.
HX268 BM-A	To 1659 CU.
HX269 BM-J	FTR Schweinfurt 24/25.2.44.
HX272 BM-N	FTR Nuremberg 30/31.3.44.
HX275 BM-S	Abandoned on return from Bois de Cassan 4.8.44.
HX277	Destroyed on the ground at Skipton-on-Swale when HX245 crashed 19.12.43.
HX280 BM-O	To 1659 CU.
HX281 BM-H	Abandoned over Yorkshire on return from Berlin 29.1.44.
HX282 BM-K	FTR Frankfurt 18/19.3.44.
HX283 BM-R	FTR Magdeburg 21/22.1.44.
HX284 BM-B	FTR Berlin 24/25.3.44.
HX285 BM-E	Crashed in Yorkshire on return from Berlin 29.1.44.

HX287 BM-U	FTR Noisy-le-Sec 18/19.4.44.
HX288 BM-F	Crashed on landing at Skipton-on-Swale on return from Düsseldorf 22/23.4.44.
HX289 BM-T	Ditched in North Sea on return from Magdeburg 22.1.44.
HX290 BM-V	To 1659 CU.
HX291 BM-W	FTR Düsseldorf 22/23.4.44.
HX292 BM-G	To 1659 CU.
HX352	To 429 Sqn.
HX353 BM-X	FTR Villeneuve-St-Georges 4/5.7.44.
LV797 BM-L	FTR Berlin 30/31.1.44.
LV839	To 517 Sqn.
LV840 BM-E	FTR Düsseldorf 22/23.4.44.
LV841 BM-H	FTR Berlin 24/25.3.44.
LV842 BM-D	To 517 Sqn.
LV871 BM-M	FTR Schweinfurt 24/25.2.44.
LV911 BM-I	Crashed on take-off from Skipton-on-Swale when bound for Stuttgart 25.7.44.
LV935	To 1659 CU.
LV938	To 427 Sqn.
LV941	To 429 Sqn.
LV947	From 424 Sqn. To 76 Sqn.
LV966 BM-P	FTR Cambrai 14/15.6.44.
LV967 BM-B	To 429 Sqn.
LV971 BM-N	FTR from Noisy-le-Sec 19.4.44.
LV972	To 1666 CU.
LV990 BM-J	FTR Düsseldorf 22/23.4.44.
LV992	To 518 Sqn.
LW115 BM-U	Broke-up over the Isle of Man during training 14.7.44.
LW120 BM-E	FTR Villeneuve-St-Georges 4/5.7.44.
LW122	To 415 Sqn.
LW123 BM-W	FTR Villeneuve-St-Georges 4/5.7.44.
LW129 BM-G	FTR Dortmund 6/7.10.44.
LW194	To 424 Sqn.
LW361 BM-R	To 1659 CU.
LW368 BM-L	To 1659 CU.
LW370	To 424 Sqn.
LW374	
MZ284 BM-T	From 426 Sqn. FTR Castrop-Rauxel 21/22.11.44.
MZ285 BM-H	From 426 Sqn. To 429 Sqn.
MZ417	To 425 Sqn.
MZ419	To 425 Sqn.
MZ425 BM-L	To 425 Sqn.

MZ458	To 424 Sqn.
MZ464	To 10 Sqn.
MZ807 BM-C	From 434 Sqn. FTR Hagen 2/3.12.44.
MZ808 BM-P	From 434 Sqn. FTR from mining sortie 17.8.44.
MZ815	To 425 Sqn.
MZ816 BM-W	FTR Hamburg 28/29.7.44.
MZ818	To 158 Sqn.
MZ828 BM-H	Crashed in Yorkshire while training 5.8.44.
MZ845	To 425 Sqn.
MZ857 BM-N	To 187 Sqn.
MZ863 BM-I	FTR from mining sortie 17.8.44.
MZ869	
MZ872 BM-Q	To 429 Sqn.
MZ879 BM-O	FTR Ile de Cezembre 31.8.44.
MZ883 BM-S	
MZ895	Destroyed by fire during refuelling at Skipton-on-Swale 8.8.44.
MZ899 BM-D	FTR from mining sortie 17.8.44.
MZ905 BM-J	From 427 Sqn. To 76 Sqn.
MZ909 BM-H	To 347 Sqn.
MZ910	To 420 Sqn.
NP935	To 415 Sqn.
NP936 BM-O	From 424 Sqn. Returned to 424 Sqn.
NP937	From 424 Sqn. To 425 Sqn.
NP944 BM-M	To EANS.
NP948	To EANS.
NP949 BM-R	FTR Castrop-Rauxel 21/22.11.44.
NP992 BM-F	FTR Bochum 4/5.11.44.
NR117	To 420 Sqn.
NR120 BM-A	To 77 Sqn.
NR121	To 431 Sqn.
NR122	To 431 Sqn.
NR123	To 431 Sqn.
NR135	To 420 Sqn.
NR136 BM-R	To 425 Sqn.
NR137 BM-G	To 425 Sqn.
PN229	
Lancaster	From January 1945.
ME375 BM-D	
ME457 BM-U	
NF930	From 50 Sqn.
NG232 BM-H	
NG233 BM-E	FTR from mining sortie 12/13.3.45.

NG441 BM-L	
NG459 BM-K	
NG460 BM-A	Abandoned over Yorkshire on return from Ludwigshafen 1/2.2.45.
NG493	
NG496 BM-N	
NG498 BM-T	
NN779 BM-J	
PA219 BM-W/M	FTR Bonn 4/5.2.45.
PA327	
PB893 BM-G	
PB903 BM-F	FTR Leipzig 10.4.45.
PB908 BM-C	
RA505 BM-K	
RA506 BM-O	
RA509 BM-P	
RA511 BM-Q	
RA512 BM-S	
RA513 BM-Y	
RF149	BM-A
RF150	To 424 Sqn.
SW273 BM-U/V	

434 (BLUENOSE) SQUADRON

Motto: In Excelsis Vincimus   Codes IP WL

434 Squadron came into existence on the 13th of June 1943 as the last but one unit to be formed in 6 Group. The squadron was initially equipped with Merlin-powered Mk V Halifaxes. The first operation was mounted in mid August 1943 against Milan, and thereafter the squadron remained at the forefront of 6 Group's efforts until the Mk II and V Halifaxes were withdrawn from operations over Germany following the Leipzig disaster in February 1944. In May the squadron converted to the improved Hercules-powered Mk III variant, and these remained on charge until the arrival of Lancasters in December 1944.

STATIONS

Tholthorpe	13.06.43 to 10.12.43
Croft	11.12.43 to 09.06.45

COMMANDING OFFICERS

Wing Commander C E Harris   15.06.43 to 06.02.44
Wing Commander C S Bartlett   07.02.44 to 12.06.44
Wing Commander F H Watkins   13.06.44 to 29.08.44
Wing Commander A L Blackburn 30.08.44 to 07.04.45
Wing Commander J C Mulvihill   08.04.45 to 05.09.45

AIRCRAFT

Halifax V/III   06.43 to 12.44
Lancaster I/X   12.44 to 09.45

OPERATIONAL RECORD

Operations	Sorties	Aircraft Losses	% Losses
193	2,597	58	2.2

Category of Operations

Bombing	Mining
173	17

Halifaxes

Operations	Sorties	Aircraft Losses	% Losses
152	2,038	53	2.6

Category of Operations

Bombing	Mining
135	17

Lancasters

Operations	Sorties	Aircraft Losses	% Losses
41	559	5	0.9

All bombing.

TABLE OF STATISTICS

Out of 59 Lancaster squadrons

55th highest number of Lancaster overall operations in Bomber Command.
53rd highest number of Lancaster sorties in Bomber Command.

53rd equal (with 424 Sqn) highest number of Lancaster operational losses in Bomber Command.

Out of 32 Halifax squadrons
20th highest number of Halifax overall operations in Bomber Command.
18th highest number of Halifax sorties in Bomber Command.
11th equal (with 408 Sqn) highest number of Halifax operational losses in Bomber Command.

Out of 15 squadrons in 6 Group
14th highest number of overall operations in 6 Group.
11th highest number of sorties in 6 Group.
12th highest number of aircraft operational losses in 6 Group.

Out of 15 Halifax squadrons in 6 Group
9th highest number of Halifax overall operations in 6 Group.
7th highest number of Halifax sorties in 6 Group.
3rd equal (with 408 Sqn) highest number of Halifax operational losses in 6 Group.

Out of 11 Lancaster squadrons in 6 Group
8th highest number of Lancaster overall operations in 6 Group.
6th highest number of Lancaster sorties in 6 Group.
7th equal (with 424 Sqn) highest number of Lancaster operational losses in 6 Group.

AIRCRAFT HISTORIES

Halifax	From June 1943 to December 1944.
DG361	To 1664 CU.
DG385	To 1664 CU.
DK248	To 1664 CU.
DK250 IP-W	FTR Frankfurt 4/5.10.43.
DK251 IP-F	FTR München 6/7.9.43.
DK258 IP-X	FTR Nuremberg 27/28.8.43.
DK259 IP-L	FTR Bochum 29/30.9.43.
DK260 IP-M	FTR Peenemünde 17/18.8.43.
DK261 IP-V	FTR Berlin 23/24.8.43.
DK262 IP-R	FTR München 6/7.9.43.
EB217 IP-A	FTR Kassel 22/23.10.43.
EB218 IP-N	FTR Kassel 22/23.10.43.
EB219	To 1667 CU.
EB220 WL-B	To 1664 CU.

EB254 IP-D	FTR Leverkusen 19/20.11.43.
EB255 IP-P	FTR Leverkusen 22/23.8.43.
EB256 WL-S	Crashed in Yorkshire on return from Berlin 29.1.44.
EB257 WL-E	FTR Düsseldorf 3/4.11.43.
EB258 IP-T	FTR Peenemünde 17/18.8.43.
EB276 IP-G	FTR Peenemünde 17/18.8.43.
LK634 IP-T	FTR Bochum 29/30.9.43.
LK638 IP-V	FTR Kassel 3/4.10.43.
LK647 IP-C	FTR Hanover 8/9.10.43.
LK648 IP-F	FTR Hanover 27/28.9.43.
LK649 WL-X	To 431 Sqn and back. FTR Berlin 28/29.1.44.
LK656 WL-C	From 429 Sqn. Abandoned over Yorkshire on return from Berlin 21.1.44.
LK663 IP-F	From 427 Sqn. FTR Kassel 22/23.10.43.
LK666 IP-T	FTR Kassel 22/23.10.43.
LK680	From 428 Sqn. To 431 Sqn.
LK682 WL-R	To 1 FU.
LK683 IP-V	FTR Leipzig 3/4.12.43.
LK685	To 431 Sqn.
LK686 IP-L	FTR Frankfurt 20/21.12.43.
LK693 IP-A	FTR Mannheim 18/19.11.43.
LK694 WL-N	From 429 Sqn. To 1664 CU.
LK696 WL-K/F	Crashed on landing at Croft on return from Amiens 15.3.44.
LK697	To 429 Sqn.
LK698	To 431 Sqn.
LK699 WL-Z	FTR Magdeburg 21/22:1.44.
LK702 IP-E	FTR Berlin 22/23.11.43.
LK703 WL-W	To 1664 CU.
LK708	From 431 Sqn. To 1659 CU.
LK709	To 77 Sqn.
LK739	To 428 Sqn.
LK740 WL-V	FTR Berlin 28/29.1.44.
LK764 WL-V/Z	From 432 Sqn. To 1659 CU.
LK792 WL-N	From 427 Sqn. FTR Sterkrade/Holten 16/17.6.44.
LK796 WL-S	From 425 Sqn. Ditched in North Sea on return from Kiel 16.8.44.
LK799 WL-E	From 429 Sqn. Crashed on take-off at Croft when bound for La Hoque 7.8.44.
LK801 WL-D	From 429 Sqn. FTR Sterkrade/Holten 16/17.6.44.
LK871 WL-K	From 426 Sqn. To 1659 CU.
LK878 WL-N	From 426 Sqn. To 1659 CU.
LK886 WL-D	From 426 Sqn. To 1659 CU.

LK887	From 426 Sqn.
LK893 IP-U	FTR Mannheim 18/19.11.43.
LK894 WL-K	FTR Mönchengladbach 30/31.8.43.
LK898	From 431 Sqn. Returned to 431 Sqn.
LK907 WL-M	Crash-landed after bird strike during an air-test 25.2.44.
LK909 IP-G	FTR Hanover 22/23.9.43.
LK916 WL-P	FTR Berlin 28/29.1.44.
LK917 IP-X	FTR Hanover 27/28.9.43.
LK918	To 431 Sqn.
LK919 WL-K	FTR Hanover 27/28.9.43.
LK924	From 429 Sqn. To 1664 CU.
LK945 WL-O	FTR Leipzig 19/20.2.44.
LK947	From 429 Sqn. To 1659 CU.
LK953 WL-C	From 428 Sqn. To 427 Sqn and back. FTR Berlin 22/23.11.43.
LK965 WL-O	From 429 Sqn. To 1659 CU.
LK970 IP-N	FTR Frankfurt 20/21.12.43.
LK971 WL-Y	FTR Berlin 15/16.2.44.
LK975	From 429 Sqn. To 1667 CU.
LK990 IP-X	FTR Leverkusen 19/20.11.43.
LK992 WL-G	To 1664 CU.
LK995	To 429 Sqn.
LL113 WL-J	To 1659 CU.
LL134 WL-U	FTR Berlin 28/29.1.44.
LL135 WL-R	FTR Berlin 20/21.1.44.
LL136 WL-E	To 1659 CU.
LL137 WL-D	To 1664 CU.
LL141 WL-H	FTR Berlin 20/21.1.44.
LL142	To 431 Sqn.
LL167 WL-M	From 429 Sqn. To 1659 CU.
LL168 WL-S	From 429 Sqn. To 431 Sqn.
LL170 WL-X	From 431 Sqn. To 1659 CU.
LL171 WL-T	From 429 Sqn. To 1659 CU.
LL177 WL-A	From 431 Sqn. To 1664 CU.
LL178 WL-R	From 429 Sqn. Crashed in Yorkshire on return from a mining sortie to Heligoland 18.3.44.
LL179 WL-K	From 431 Sqn. FTR Berlin 20/21.1.44.
LL180	From 431 Sqn. To 1667 CU.
LL225 WL-L	From 431 Sqn. Crash-landed at Friston on return from Aulnoye 26.3.44.
LL232	From 431 Sqn. To 1659 CU.
LL233	From 431 Sqn. To 1659 CU.
LL240 WL-C	To 1664 CU.

LL241 WL-H	To 1659 CU.
LL243 WL-U	FTR Montzen 27/28.4.44.
LL247 WL-Q	To 1659 CU.
LL255 WL-V	FTR Leipzig 19/20.2.44.
LL257 WL-Z	FTR Leipzig 19/20.2.44.
LL258 WL-W	From 431 Sqn. FTR Montzen 27/28.4.44.
LL283 WL-Z	To 1664 CU.
LL285 WL-K	To 1659 CU.
LL286 WL-V	To 1664 CU.
LL288 WL-P	To 1659 CU.
LW169	To 424 Sqn.
LW170	To 424 Sqn.
LW171 WL-M	To 520 Sqn.
LW173 WL-K	FTR Arras 12/13.6.44.
LW174 WL-G/R	To 192 Sqn.
LW175 WL-Q	FTR Brunswick 12/13.8.44.
LW176 WL-J	Written off at Croft when struck by LK799 taking off for La Hoque 7.8.44.
LW385	From 431 Sqn. To 190 Sqn.
LW389 WL-F	From 420 Sqn.
LW433 WL-W	From 424 Sqn. FTR Sterkrade/Holten 16/17.6.44.
LW436 WL-Y	From 426 Sqn. FTR Bois de Cassan 4.8.44.
LW437 WL-Y	From 432 Sqn. FTR Hamburg 28/29.7.44.
LW596 WL-Z	From 432 Sqn. FTR Hamburg 28/29.7.44.
LW684 WL-O	From 429 Sqn. FTR Versailles/Matelot 10/11.6.44.
LW689 WL-A	From 51 Sqn. To 1659 CU.
LW713 WL-P	From 429 Sqn. FTR Arras 12/13.6.44.
LW714 WL-H	From 429 Sqn. To 1659 CU.
MZ291	To 427 Sqn.
MZ293 WL-S	FTR Arras 12/13.6.44.
MZ295	To 427 Sqn.
MZ297 WL-Z	FTR Sterkrade/Holten 16/17.6.44.
MZ358 WL-R	To 192 Sqn.
MZ405 WL-C/F	From 431 Sqn. To 158 Sqn.
MZ420 WL-F	Abandoned over Yorkshire on return from Cologne 28.10.44.
MZ421 WL-A	To 408 Sqn.
MZ435 WL-D	From 429 Sqn. To 408 Sqn and back. To 426 Sqn.
MZ447 WL-B	From 429 Sqn. To 462 Sqn.
MZ495	To 408 Sqn.
MZ626 WL-T	From 420 Sqn. Crashed near Croft while training 30.8.44.
MZ681	To 431 Sqn.
MZ682	To 426 Sqn.

MZ683	To 425 Sqn.
MZ716 WL-V	To 1659 CU.
MZ749 WL-P/W	To 1659 CU.
MZ807	To 433 Sqn.
MZ808	To 433 Sqn.
MZ846 WL-O/T/W	To 158 Sqn.
MZ852 WL-P	To 192 Sqn.
MZ853	Crashed on landing at Croft 1.8.44.
MZ876 WL-Y	To BCIS.
MZ878 WL-E	To 1659 CU.
MZ881	From 431 Sqn. To 158 Sqn.
MZ907	From 408 Sqn. To 431 Sqn.
MZ908 WL-O	From 408 Sqn. Crashed in Northumberland on return from Walcheren 19.9.44.
MZ913 WL-J	To 462 Sqn.
MZ920 WL-C	From 431 Sqn. Crashed in Warwickshire on return from Duisburg 14.10.44.
MZ921 WL-Q	To 158 Sqn.
MZ922	To 431 Sqn.
NA494 WL-B	From 431 Sqn. To 1659 CU.
NA497 WL-C	From 426 Sqn. To 1659 CU.
NA510	To 426 Sqn.
NA516	From 432 Sqn. Returned to 432 Sqn.
NA528	Blew up on landing at White Waltham on return from Normandy 30.7.44.
NA550	From 432 Sqn.
NA552 WL-U	From 432 Sqn. To 1659 CU.
NP939 WL-W	To 420 Sqn.
NP959 WL-S	From 431 Sqn. To 420 Sqn.
NP961 WL-N	To 432 Sqn.
NR114 WL-U	From 424 Sqn. FTR Oberhausen 1/2.11.44.
NR115 WL-K	From 424 Sqn. To 1664 CU.
NR116 WL-H	To 426 Sqn.
NR118 WL-S/U	From 427 Sqn. FTR Duisburg 17/18.12.44.
NR121 WL-G/Y	From 431 Sqn. To 76 Sqn.
NR124 WL-W	From 427 Sqn. To 408 Sqn.
NR126 WL-T	From 427 Sqn. To 408 Sqn.
NR134 WL-Z	To 426 Sqn.
NR140 WL-C	To 415 Sqn.
NR141	To 431 Sqn.
NR143 WL-M	FTR Soest 5/6.12.44.
NR144 WL-V	To 426 Sqn.
NR145 WL-L	To 432 Sqn.
NR199	To 408 Sqn.

Lancaster	From December 1944.
KB741 SE-C	On loan from 431 Sqn. FTR Chemnitz 14/15.2.45.
KB789 WL-V	From 428 Sqn.
KB814 WL-S	From 428 Sqn. To 419 Sqn.
KB816 WL-G	From 431 Sqn. To 428 Sqn.
KB824 WL-E	From 419 Sqn.
KB825 WL-A	From 428 Sqn.
KB826 WL-K	From 428 Sqn.
KB829 WL-C	From 428 Sqn.
KB830 WL-D	From 419 Sqn.
KB832 WL-F	From 419 Sqn. Crashed on take-off at Croft 22.3.45.
KB833 WL-B	From 419 Sqn.
KB834 WL-Y	FTR Essen 11.3.45.
KB835 WL-J	From 431 Sqn. FTR Hagen 15/16.3.45.
KB836 WL-H	From 431 Sqn.
KB840 WL-N	From 428 Sqn.
KB842 WL-L	From 428 Sqn. FTR Chemnitz 5/6.3.45.
KB843 WL-Q	To 428 Sqn.
KB844 WL-W	From 419 Sqn.
KB846 WL-P	To 428 Sqn.
KB849 WL-T	From 431 Sqn.
KB850 WL-O	From 419 Sqn. FTR Zeitz 16/17.1.45.
KB852 WL-R	From 431 Sqn.
KB853	To 431 Sqn.
KB862 WL-M/J	
KB863 WL-P	
KB873 WL-G	
KB880 WL-L	
KB881	
KB882	To 428 Sqn.
KB883 WL-S	
KB884	To 419 Sqn.
KB885 WL-Q	From 431 Sqn.
KB890 WL-X	
KB893	From 431 Sqn.
KB895 WL-O	From 428 Sqn.
KB902	
KB911 WL-U	FTR Hamburg 31.3.45.
KB914	
KB920	No operations. To 428 Sqn.
NG343 WL-U	
NG344 WL-Z	
NG345 WL-Q	

NG497 WL-P
PA225 WL-O
PA226 WL-X

Heaviest Single Loss

28/29.1.44   Berlin. 5 Halifaxes. 4 FTR. 1 crashed on return.

Abbreviations

A&AEE	Aeroplane and Armaments Experimental Establishment
AA	Anti-Aircraft fire
AACU	Anti-Aircraft Cooperation Unit
AAS	Air Armament School
AASF	Advance Air Striking Force
AAU	Aircraft Assembly Unit
ACM	Air Chief Marshal
ACSEA	Air Command South-East Asia
AFDU	Air Fighting Development Unit
AFEE	Airborne Forces Experimental Unit
AFTDU	Airborne Forces Tactical Development Unit
AGS	Air Gunners' School
AMDP	Air Members for Development and Production
AOC	Air Officer Commanding
AOS	Air Observers' School
ASRTU	Air-Sea Rescue Training Unit
ATTDU	Air Transport Tactical Development Unit
AVM	Air Vice-Marshal
BAT	Beam Approach Training
BCBS	Bomber Command Bombing School
BCDU	Bomber Command Development Unit
BCFU	Bomber Command Film Unit
BCIS	Bomber Command Instructors' School
BDU	Bombing Development Unit
BSTU	Bomber Support Training Unit
CF	Conversion Flight
CFS	Central Flying School
CGS	Central Gunnery School
C-in-C	Commander in Chief
CNS	Central Navigation School
CO	Commanding Officer
CRD	Controller of Research and Development
CU	Conversion Unit

DGRD	Director General for Research and Development
EAAS	Empire Air Armament School
EANS	Empire Air Navigation School
ECDU	Electronic Countermeasures Development Unit
ECFS	Empire Central Flying School
ETPS	Empire Test Pilots' School
F/L	Flight Lieutenant
Flt	Flight
F/O	Flying Officer
FPP	Ferry Pilots' School
F/S	Flight Sergeant
FTR	Failed to Return
FTU	Ferry Training Unit
G/C	Group Captain
Gp	Group
HCU	Heavy Conversion Unit
HGCU	Heavy Glider Conversion Unit
LFS	Lancaster Finishing School
MAC	Mediterranean Air Command
MTU	Mosquito Training Unit
MU	Maintenance Unit
NTU	Navigation Training Unit
OADU	Overseas Aircraft Delivery Unit
OAPU	Overseas Aircraft Preparation Unit
OTU	Operational Training Unit
P/O	Pilot Officer
PTS	Parachute Training School
RAE	Royal Aircraft Establishment
SGR	School of General Reconnaissance
Sgt	Sergeant
SHAEF	Supreme Headquarters Allied Expeditionary Force
SIU	Signals Intelligence Unit
S/L	Squadron Leader
SOC	Struck off Charge
SOE	Special Operations Executive
Sqn	Squadron
TF	Training Flight
TFU	Telecommunications Flying Unit
W/C	Wing Commander
Wg	Wing
WIDU	Wireless Intelligence Development Unit
W/O	Warrant Officer

Bibliography

Air War Over France. Robert Jackson. Ian Allan
Als Deutschlands Dämme Brachen. Helmut Euler. Motor Buch Verlag
At First Sight. Alan B Webb
Avenging in the Shadows. Ron James. Abington Books
Avro Lancaster. The definitive record. Harry Holmes. Airlife
Avro Manchester. Robert Kirby. Midland Counties Publications
Battle-Axe Blenheims. Stuart R Scott. Budding Books
Battle Under the Moon. Jack Currie. Air Data
Beam Bombers. Michael Cumming. Sutton Publishing
Beware of the Dog at War. John Ward
Black Swan. Sid Finn. Newton
Bomber Command. Max Hastings. Pan
Bomber Command War Diaries. Martin Middlebrook/Chris Everett. Viking
Bomber Group at War. Chaz Bowyer. Book Club Associates
Bomber Harris. Dudley Saward. Cassel
Bomber Harris. Charles Messenger. Arms and Armour Press
Bomber Intelligence. W E Jones. Midland Counties Publications
Bomber Squadron at War. Andrew Brookes. Ian Allan
Bomber Squadrons at War. Geoff D Copeman. Sutton Publishing
Bombers Over Berlin. Alan W Cooper. Patrick Stephens Ltd
Bombing Colours 1937–1973. Michael J F Bowyer. Patrick Stephens Ltd
Confounding the Reich. Martin W Bowman/Tom Cushing. Pen & Sword Aviation
De Havilland Mosquito Crash Log. David J Smith. Midland Counties Publications
Despite the Elements. 115 Squadron History. Private
Diary of RAF Pocklington. M Usherwood. Compaid Graphics
Each Tenacious. A G Edgerley. Square One Publications
Feuersturm über Hamburg. Hans Brunswig. Motor Buch Verlag
Forever Strong. Norman Franks. Random Century
From Hull, Hell and Halifax. Chris Blanchett. Midland Counties Publications

Gordon's Tour with Shiney 10. J Gordon Shirt. Compaid Graphics

Great Raids. Vols 1 and 2. Air Commodore John Searby DSO DFC. Nutshell Press

Halifax at War. Brian J Rapier. Ian Allan

Hamish. The story of a Pathfinder. Group Captain T G Mahaddie. Ian Allan

Heavenly Days. Group Captain James Pelly-Fry DSO. Crecy Books

In Brave Company. W R Chorley. P A Chorley*Joe. The Autobiography of a Trenchard Brat*. Wing Commander J Northrop DSO DFC AFC. Square One Publications

Lancaster at War. Vols 1,2,3. Mike Garbett/Brian Goulding. Ian Allan

Lancaster. The Story of a Famous Bomber. Bruce Robertson. Harleyford Publications Ltd

Lancaster to Berlin. Walter Thompson DFC*. Goodall Publications

Low Attack. John de L Wooldridge. Crecy

Massacre Over the Marne. Oliver Clutton-Brock. Patrick Stephens Ltd

Master Airman. Alan Bramson. Airlife

Melbourne Ten. Brian J Rapier. Air Museum Publications (York) Ltd

Mission Completed. Sir Basil Embry. Four Square Books

Mosquito. C Martin Sharp & Michael J F Bowyer. Crecy

Night Fighter. C F Rawnsley/Robert Wright. Collins

Night Flyer. Squadron Leader Lewis Brandon DSO DFC. Goodall Publications

Night Intruder. Jeremy Howard-Williams. Purnell Book Services

No Moon Tonight. Don Charlwood. Goodall Publications

On The Wings Of The Morning. RAF Bottesford 1941–45. Vincent Holyoak. Privately published

On Wings of War. A history of 166 Squadron. Jim Wright. 166 Squadron Association

Only Owls and Bloody Fools Fly at Night. Group Captain Tom Sawyer DFC. Goodall Publications

Pathfinder. AVM D C T Bennett. Goodall Publications

Pathfinder Force. Gordon Musgrove. MacDonald and Janes

Reap the Whirlwind. Dunmore and Carter. Crecy

Royal Air Force Aircraft Serial Numbers. All Volumes. Air-Britain

Royal Air Force Bomber Command Losses. Vols 1,2,3,4,5,6. W R Chorley. Midland Counties Publications

Silksheen. Geoff D Copeman. Midland Counties Publications

Snaith Days. K S Ford. Compaid Graphics

Start im Morgengrauen. Werner Girbig. Motor Buch Verlag

Stirling Wings. Jonathon Falconer. Alan Sutton Publications

Strike Hard. A bomber airfield at war. John B Hilling. Alan Sutton Publishing

Sweeping the Skies. David Gunby. Pentland Press

The Avro Lancaster. Francis K Mason. Aston Publications

The Berlin Raids. Martin Middlebrook. Viking Press

The Dambusters Raid. John Sweetman. Arms and Armour Press

The Halifax File. Air-Britain

The Hampden File. Harry Moyle. Air-Britain

The Handley Page Halifax. K A Merrick. Aston Press

The Hornets' Nest. History of 100 Squadron RAF 1917–1994. Arthur White. Square One Publications

The Lancaster File. J J Halley. Air-Britain

The Other Battle. Peter Hinchliffe. Airlife

The Pendulum and the Scythe. Ken Marshall. Air Research Publications

The Starkey Sacrifice. Michael Cumming. Sutton Publishing Ltd

The Stirling Bomber. Michael J F Bowyer. Faber

The Stirling File. Bryce Gomersall. Air-Britain

The Wellington Bomber. Chaz Bowyer. William Kimber

The Whitley File. R N Roberts. Air-Britain

The Squadrons of the Royal Air Force. James J Halley. Air-Britain

They Led the Way. Michael P Wadsworth. Highgate

To See the Dawn Breaking. W R Chorley. Compaid Graphics

Valiant Wings. Norman Franks. Crecy

Wellington. The Geodetic Giant. Martin Bowman. Airlife

White Rose Base. Brian J Rapier. Aero Litho Company (Lincoln) Ltd

Wings of Night. Alexander Hamilton. Crecy

2 Group RAF. A Complete History. Michael J F Bowyer. Crecy

101 Squadron. Special Operations. Richard Alexander

207 Squadron RAF Langar 1942–43. Barry Goodwin/Raymond Glynne-Owen. Quacks Books

408 Squadron History. The Hangar Bookshelf. Canada

The 6 Group Bomber Command website. Richard Koval.

Other Titles by Chris Ward

Dambusters, The Definitive History. Red Kite 2003

3 Group Bomber Command. Pen & Sword 2008

5 Group Bomber Command. Pen & Sword 2007

Dambuster Crash Sites. Pen & Sword. 2008

Dambusters. The Forging of a Legend. Pen & Sword 2009

Images of War. 617 Dambuster Squadron at War. Pen & Sword 2009